LESSONS IN

DEPRAVITY

Sex education and the sexual revolution

ES Williams

Belmont House Publishing

London

i

Lessons in Depravity is published by Belmont House Publishing

First published September 2003

ISBN 0 9529939 5 3

Published by Belmont House Publishing
36 The Crescent
Belmont
SUTTON
Surrey SM2 6BJ

A Catalogue record for this book is available from the British Library.

Printed by The Cromwell Press.

Other titles in print by ES Williams include:
> *The Great Divorce Controversy*

The booklets: *Cohabitation or Marriage?* (co-author Declan Flanagan)
Sex education, sexual immorality and the Bible
The King of Glory

Contents

Foreword   vi

Chapter 1. Initiatives to reduce teenage pregnancies   1
Teenage Pregnancy Report (1999)   4
Sex and Relationship Education Guidance (2000)   6
Contraceptives and the 'morning-after' pill for children   7
The age of sexual consent   8

Chapter 2. The amoral ideology of sex education   12
Sex education guidance for schools   13
Values clarification   14
Self-esteem   16
Sex education literature   18

Chapter 3. Sexual morality in Victorian England   31
England in the eighteenth century   32
The Evangelical Revival   34
Victorian modesty   44
Marriage and the family   46

Chapter 4. The early sexual revolutionaries   51
Robert Owen – father of British socialism   51
Francis Place and Thomas Malthus   52
Richard Carlile – author of the first sex manual   53
George Drysdale – advocate of 'free love'   54
John Stuart Mill – philosophy of utilitarianism   54
The trial of Annie Besant – birth control propagandist   55
Friedrich Nietzsche – the original immoralist   56
The sexual philosophy of Sigmund Freud   58

Chapter 5. New men, new women and a new morality   64
Edward Carpenter   65
Havelock Ellis   66
Herbert George Wells   67
Lytton Strachey   68
Bloomsbury Set   70
Roots of the sexual revolution   71

Chapter 6. Beginnings of sex education   74
Influence of Marie Stopes   74
Education Act of 1944   79
Alfred Kinsey – the fraudulent researcher of sexual behaviour   80
Kinsey and the sexual revolution   90

Chapter 7. The permissive 1960s   **94**
    Ideology of Margaret Sanger and the IPPF   94
    Ideology of Wilhelm Reich   98
    Situation ethics   101
    BBC – the shop window of the sexual revolution   103
    Brook Advisory Centres established   105
    SIECUS established in USA   106
    NHS Family Planning Act – 1967   109
    Abortion Act – 1967   111
    A decade of progress for the FPA   112

Chapter 8. Sex education into the 1970s   **117**
    Sex education on television   118
    The booklet *Sex Education: The Erroneous Zone*   124
    The remarkable trial of Dr Robert Browne   127
    The prosecution of Colin Knapman   129
    Longford Report on pornography   131

Chapter 9. House of Lords debates sex education   **135**
    Unplanned Pregnancy Report of the RCOG   137
    Argument for free contraceptives on NHS   138
    House of Lords debate – 1973   139

Chapter 10. Free contraceptives for children on the NHS   **147**
    Policy of free contraceptives for children criticised   148
    FPA develops its role in sex education   151
    Chapter 11. A 'libellous attack' on the FPA   156
    House of Lords debate – 1976   157

Chapter 12. The FPA sets targets   **168**
    The book *Make it Happy*   174

Chapter 13. Sheer pornography   **182**
    Dr Adrian Rogers takes a stand   183
    John Stokes denounces the FPA and Brook in Parliament   186

Chapter 14. The Gillick Saga   **192**
    High Court case   194
    Appeal of the agony aunts   200
    Judgement of the Appeal Court   202
    Appeal to the Law Lords   206

Chapter 15. AIDS moves on to the political agenda   **215**
    The AIDS threat   218
    Local Authorities promote homosexuality   219
    Section 28   223
    Sex Education Forum   224

Chapter 16. 'Safer sex' campaign   **231**
    Encouraging parents to talk about sex   234
    Sex education receives a bad press   236
    Sex education – the propaganda arm of the sexual revolution   240

Chapter 17. Explicit education in the light of sexual purity   **243**
    Talking about sex   243
    Explicit sexual images   247
    Biblical teaching on sexual purity   248
    The virtue of modesty   250
    The virtue of chivalry   258
    Embarrassment   260
    Contrasting the sexual revolutionaries with the Victorians   262

Chapter 18. Sex education, marriage and the family   **265**
    The biblical view of human sexuality   266
    Sex education and marriage   270
    Sex education and the family   275

Chapter 19. The 'Christian' version of sex education   **278**
    Christian views on sex education   280
    CARE's approach to sex education   281
    The case against CARE   290
    Christian Institute   291
    The failure of Christian sex education   292

Chapter 20. A great moral evil   **294**
    The demoralisation of sexual behaviour   295
    Propaganda of sex education   298
    The false presuppositions of sex education   300
    Parental responsibility   307
    A great moral evil   309

Appendix. Statistics of the sex education era   **312**
    Sexual behaviour   313
    Contraception usage among young women   315
    Emergency contraception   315
    Abortion   316
    Sexually transmitted disease   317
    Marriage and cohabitation   318
    Births outside marriage   319
    A profile of child abuse   320

Index   **321**

Foreword

There are few areas in the current education debate that arouse stronger emotions than the teaching of sex education. The past five decades have seen the emergence of an industry devoted to providing 'good quality sex and relationships education' as 'an entitlement for all children and young people' – to use the words of the Sex Education Forum, which claims to be 'the national authority' on the subject. Introduced into the school curriculum ostensibly to address the problem of high teenage pregnancy rates, it has been far from an unqualified success. Yet although sex education and easy access to contraceptive advice and supplies have failed to deliver, the present Government's teenage pregnancy strategy is doggedly pre-scribing more of the same—except now the message is being promoted more vigorously, beginning with children in primary schools.

While the initial fears of some concerned parents have been eased by reassuring sounding terms such as 'positive values' and 'moral framework', those who have delved beneath the surface have invariably discovered an approach that is neither positive nor moral. As Dr Ted Williams demonstrates in this book, sex education in our schools is largely based on the premise of moral relativism. Children are no longer taught what is right and wrong, but are rather encouraged to decide for themselves what is right and wrong for them. Sexual activity is presented as a normal part of growing up; every effort is made to overcome natural inhibitions; respon-sibility is reduced to contraceptive usage; sexual intimacy is divorced from love and marriage; tolerance is upheld as the cardinal virtue; and any attempt to introduce a moral dimension is portrayed as 'unhelpful' and dismissed as 'preaching'.

Dr Williams has investigated the historical roots which have given rise to the current situation in which the boundaries of acceptable behaviour for young people have been pushed further and further back under the guise of sex education. He has done so more thoroughly and comprehensively than I was able to achieve in my own research which was published in 1985 under the title *Sex & Social Engineering*. We are all placed in his debt.

He identifies the chief architects of the sexual revolution and shows how their commitment to removing moral constraints has been advanced by sex education. Marriage has long been recognised as the main obstacle to a sexually free society, and parents the chief conveyors of traditional morality to their children. This was clearly expressed by a teacher at a sex education symposium as long ago as 1972 when he said to the assembly: 'We must get into schools otherwise children will simply follow the mores of their parents.' It is therefore no surprise that the heirs of the original sexual revolutionaries find little room for marriage in their sex education programmes and have laboured to undermine parents by promoting the 'rights' of children to obtain contraceptive advice and supplies without either their parents' knowledge or consent.

Although some may not share Dr Williams' religious perspective, it is refreshing to read an author who is prepared to speak clearly in the moral arena. Nobody reading *Lessons in Depravity* can be in any doubt about the moral message of the book. He makes a powerful case for abandoning the all-too-predictable approach of the Government's teenage pregnancy strategy. The need to embrace a far more radical policy is overwhelming. This must be based on resurrecting the virtues of modesty, chastity, fidelity, responsibility, self-restraint and a renewed commitment to marriage and the family. I wholeheartedly commend this book in the hope that it will enlighten parents, embolden teachers, encourage church leaders and challenge politicians and policy makers to find the courage to face up to the real consequences of the received wisdom on sex education in schools.

Valerie Riches

Founder President
Family Education Trust
April 2003

Dedicated to my friend **Jack Proom**,
whose spiritual wisdom and practical advice played a key role
in the writing of this book.

Chapter 1

Initiatives to reduce teenage pregnancies

The Social Exclusion Unit's report on teenage pregnancy;

the Government's guidance to schools on sex education

The UK has the highest rate of teenage pregnancies in Western Europe. The Prime Minister, in his foreword to *Teenage Pregnancy* – a report of the Government's Social Exclusion Unit – writes: 'It is not a record in which we can take any pride. Every year some 90 thousand teenagers in England become pregnant. They include nearly 8 thousand who are under 16... As a country we can't afford to continue to ignore this shameful record. Few societies find it easy to talk honestly about teenagers, sex and parenthood. It can seem easier to sweep such uncomfortable issues under the carpet. But the consequences of doing this can be seen all round us in shattered lives and blighted futures.'[1] The Prime Minister does not believe that young people should have sex before they are 16. 'I have strong views on this. But I also know that no matter how much we might disapprove, some do.'[2] He continues: 'It shows how we can and must improve education on relationships and sex for teenagers. We must give teenagers the confidence and the information so they don't feel compelled to have sex. No one should become pregnant or contract a sexually transmitted infection because of ignorance.'[3]

Because the Government believes that the answer to unintended teenage pregnancies lies in more easy access to condoms and emergency contraception, the Department of Health has just announced a plan which encourages secondary schools to give pupils free condoms and contraceptive pills. The chief executive of the Family Planning Association, Anne Weyman, welcomed the Government's acceptance of the recommendation that 'health services' should be provided on site in schools. She said, 'The rate of teenage pregnancy in this country is too high and action to bring it down is essential. Measures such as this are eminently sensible.'[4]

Another initiative to reduce teenage pregnancies is a condom card scheme which allows children as young as 13 to collect condoms free of charge and without their parents' knowledge from drop-in community centres. To receive their condom card a boy or girl fills in a registration form and then presents the card to collect a pack of 15 condoms. Each child is entitled to an unlimited supply, although clinic staff try to monitor the number of condoms being handed out. A 16-year-old boy expressed his delight with the scheme in a national newspaper: 'No one can stop young people having sex whether they are teachers, the police or parents. It's a fact of life.' Equally enthusiastic about the scheme, known as Sexual Health Outreach with Teenagers, was the teenage pregnancy co-ordinator for Sunderland Health Authority. 'We have seen girls as young as 12 getting pregnant and if you are trying to tackle that then you need to start in schools at an early stage. What we are trying to do is to send health professionals into schools to train teachers so each school will have a teacher trained in family planning or a family planning nurse. There is no need legally to inform parents if a young person asks for contraception. It can be given without parental consent. However, we encourage young people in such situations to talk to their parents.'[5]

The board game, *Contraception*, which has been developed in line with the Government's sex education guidelines, is another enterprise for teaching children about contraceptives. The aim of the game, which retails at £50, is to encourage children to talk to each other about 'safer sex' in a relaxed, enjoyable group setting.[6] Children throw dice to move their counters, shaped like condoms or packets of pills, around the board. Players come into contact with various contraceptive and sexual health services, condom machines and family planning clinics. They are directed to make assertive statements to strengthen their ability to express their own needs and decline unwanted pressure. Peer education is a feature of the game. During their progress around the board they are presented with a 'question' card which offers two options—the choice might be between using a condom demonstrator to teach the group how to unroll a condom, or answering a question about sex. Two examples of the type of statements presented for discussion by the 'safe' cards are: 'You do not have a partner tonight but are going to a party and you feel safer carrying a condom'[7] and, 'Your partner does not seem to enjoy sex. You show him/her lots of affection and start to talk about sex in your relationship.'[8]

The pupils of Crompton House Church of England school in Oldham are apparently enthusiastic about the game. According to a 13-year-old boy, sex is on a lot of teenagers' minds and the game was a good way of finding out about contraception and 'safe sex'. 'If you're a quiet person, it may be hard to talk about sex. This game provides a way of talking about it without embarrassment.' The head teacher, David Bowes, said the game had proved highly accessible for teenagers, many of whom would make a decision about sex sooner than teachers would wish. What he liked was that the children were in control. They were the decision-makers.[9] He went on, 'There is nothing salacious or unpleasant about this game – I can see it forming a part of our sex education classes in future.'[10]

The programme, *Adding Power and Understanding to Sex Education*, commonly known as *A Pause*, has been developed by Exeter University and is backed by the Departments of Health and Education. The aim of *A Pause*, which is now running in about 150 secondary schools around England, is to help 'young people in their decision to delay intercourse until a time when they are less likely to regret it, assisting them to negotiate stages of intimacy, appropriate contraception and access to services'.[11] According to the programme director, John Rees, it was about getting 14 and 15-year-olds to think about stages of intimacy that did not involve penetrative sex, with its risks of pregnancy and infection.[12] He added: 'It's about saying to them. "You can hold hands, you can kiss and cuddle", it may even get as far as something like oral sex or even mutual masturbation.'[13] Teachers involved with *A Pause* are trained to handle frequently asked questions, such as a 14-year-old girl asking: 'What does semen taste like?' Or a 15-year-old boy: 'How do gay men have sex, and is it possible for a man and woman to do it the same way?'[14] The underlying aim is to encourage school pupils to think about oral and anal sex and mutual masturbation as alternatives to sexual intercourse. The theory is that if children can be taught the pleasures of non-penetrative sex they will be less likely to indulge in vaginal sex, thereby reducing the rates of teenage pregnancy.

Another Government scheme piloted the provision of emergency contraception in supermarkets. In March 2002, two Tesco stores in north Somerset announced that any girl under the age of 20 would be able to pick up the 'morning-after' pill at the pharmacy counter, although she would be subjected to a detailed interview. Vicky O'Loughlin commented on behalf of North Somerset Primary Care Group, 'Some people, even in Weston, do have sex. What this is about is offering services that they can access, as sometimes it is difficult to go to their GP.'[15] After objections from customers and a number of pro-life organisations, Tesco announced that it had decided not to dispense emergency contraception to under-age girls from in-store pharmacies. A month later Sainsbury's announced that five stores in areas with high teenage pregnancy rates had entered into partnership with local health authorities to make emergency contraception available free of charge to teenagers, including girls under 16. A Department of Health spokeswoman said, 'We strongly support the involvement of Sainsbury's, working in partnership with the local NHS, to improve young women's access to free emergency contraception.'[16]

Yet another initiative allows school nurses to give under-16s emergency contraception without the knowledge of their parents. The manager of East Kent Community NHS Trust, an area with a high rate of teenage pregnancies, explained, 'It covers any age group, but nurses have to run through several issues with the girls and check that they know what they are doing.' Acknowledging that nurses faced difficult situations when very young girls asked for emergency contraception, she said, 'We would obviously have to look at child protection issues. The parents will not be told unless we believe the child is at risk in some way and the parents need to be informed.'[17]

Clearly, a key aim of the Government's teenage sexual health strategy is to ensure that children have easy access to contraceptives and, in case of a slip-up, access to emergency contraception. So sexually active children are reassured that the Government is doing all it can to help them avoid unintended pregnancies—they know that if they forget to take their contraceptive pills regularly or have a condom 'accident', the 'morning-after' pill is available from supermarkets and school nurses. And because contraceptive services for children are confidential, they don't have the worry that their parents might find out.

Teenage Pregnancy Report (1999)

The report of the Government's Social Exclusion Unit, *Teenage Pregnancy*, provides a national plan to halve the number of teenage pregnancies within the decade. It offers three reasons for the high rate of unintended pregnancies. The first is low expectations among teenagers. 'One reason why the UK has such high teenage pregnancy rates is that there are more young people who see no prospect of a job and fear they will end up on benefit one way or the other.'[18] The report shows that poverty is a key risk factor for teenage pregnancy. The risk of becoming a teenage mother is almost ten times higher for girls whose families are in social class V (unskilled manual), than those in social class I (professional). Other risk factors are: children of a teenage mother, children in care or leaving care, children with educational problems, and teenagers of 16 and 17 who are not in education, training or work.[19]

A second reason advanced for the high teenage pregnancy rate is ignorance. We are told that 'young people lack accurate knowledge about contraception, sexually transmitted diseases, what to expect in relationships and what it means to be a parent'.[20] The premise that underlies this assertion is that sexual activity is the norm for teenagers. It follows that those who lack 'accurate knowledge about contraception' are at high risk of a teenage pregnancy, while those who have 'accurate knowledge' are able to protect themselves. And so sex education, which provides children with 'accurate knowledge', helps to prevent teenage pregnancies.

A third reason given for teenage pregnancies is mixed messages. 'As one teen-ager put it to the Unit, it sometimes seems as if sex is compulsory but contraception is illegal. One part of the adult world bombards teenagers with sexually explicit messages and an implicit message that sexual activity is the norm. Another part, including many parents and most public institutions, is at best embarrassed and at worst silent, hoping that if sex isn't talked about, it won't happen. The net result is not less sex, but less protected sex.'[21] The Social Exclusion Unit is creating an impression of ignorant, confused children who are having lots of unprotected sex. The inference is that it would be a good thing if more of these children could be persuaded to use contraception. What is disingenuous about this analysis is that it takes no account of the dramatic increase in contraceptive usage among teenagers that has occurred during the last decade (see figure 1, page 8).

The conclusion of the *Teenage Pregnancy* report is that the factors mentioned above 'point to a single fault line in past attempts to tackle this problem: neglect. Governments and society have neglected the issue because it can easily drift

4

into moralising and is difficult for anyone to solve on their own.'[22] According to the assessment of the Social Exclusion Unit the past three decades of sex education have amounted to *neglect*. And worse, there has been a drift into the most serious error of all—moralising. So young people have not only been neglected, but have also been threatened by the moralisers. The Government's action plan makes it plain: 'Preaching is rarely effective. Whether the Government likes it or not, young people decide what they're going to do about sex and contraception. Keeping them in the dark or preaching at them makes it *less* likely they'll make the right decision.'[23] Here the Government is asserting that there is no point in teaching moral standards, for young people are apparently impervious to the restraints imposed by biblical morality and simply make up their own minds how they should conduct their sexual lives. Moreover, not only is moral teaching of no value, it may even be counterproductive in that it antagonises young people, making it *less* likely that they will make the right decision.

Another problem identified by the *Teenage Pregnancy* report is that the parents are not talking to their children about sex. 'During the Unit's consultation, parents repeatedly said that they felt embarrassed and ill-equipped to broach this subject with their children, and this was made worse for many by knowing little about what was taught at school.'[24] The claim is that most parents are not receiving advice on how to address issues of sex and sexual health with their children. The picture that emerges is of growing numbers of young teenagers drifting into sexual relationships because of weaknesses in the sex education they receive from school and their parents. In order to overcome this problem the Department of Health plans to commission a national campaign to help parents talk to their children about sex.[25]

Having dismissed the moral dimension, the Social Exclusion Unit goes on to inform us how the Government plans to achieve its goal of reducing teenage pregnancies. The action plan includes a national campaign involving Government, media and others 'to improve understanding and change behaviour'. The campaign 'will target young people and parents with the facts about teenage pregnancy and parenthood, with advice on how to deal with the pressure to have sex, and with messages that underline the importance of using contraception if they do have sex'.[26]

Local areas have already appointed 'teenage pregnancy co-ordinators' whose task is to pull together all the services that have a role in preventing teenage pregnancy. All local authorities and health authorities in England are jointly required to produce a teenage pregnancy strategy, stating the actions they intend to take to meet the national target for reducing teenage conceptions. The Family Education Trust analysed 23 such locally produced strategies and found a disappointing lack of originality. 'They all start from the basic premise that young women become pregnant because they are ignorant about the facts of life, and are either unable to obtain contraception or unaware of why it should be used. The answer, therefore, is seen to be more sex education and easier access to contraception.'[27]

5

All the strategies point out that sex education is already being delivered in schools in their area. 'The plan, therefore, is to take it lower down the age range, to primary schools, to make it more comprehensive within the school curriculum… This type of sex education is linked to the provision of contraception, and there is a stated intention in a number of these strategies to use school nurses and clinics for this purpose.'[28]

A national telephone helpline has been set up 'to give teenagers advice on sex and relationships and to direct them to local services'. A publicity campaign will tell young people 'they can talk to health professionals about sex and contraception in confidence'.[29] And teenagers who become parents 'should not lose out on opportunities for the future' and will be helped to finish their full-time education.[30] Funding of £60 million over the next three years has already been earmarked.[31]

Sex and Relationship Education Guidance (2000)

The Government's *Sex and Relationship Education Guidance* was issued to all schools and health authorities in England in July 2000. The guidance makes it clear that the objective is 'to help and support young people through their physical, emotional and *moral* development' and to help 'pupils deal with difficult *moral* and social questions'.[32] Young people should 'develop *positive* values and a *moral* framework that will guide their decisions, judgements and behaviour [my italics]'.[33] Sex education should focus on 'the building of self-esteem'.[34] Young people should learn 'the reasons for delaying sexual activity, and the benefits to be gained from such delay; and the avoidance of unplanned pregnancy'.[35] They should also 'understand the reasons for having protected sex'.[36] They should be provided 'with information about different types of contraception, safe sex and how they can access local sources of further advice and treatment'.[37] (In this context, 'treatment' means a prescription for contraceptives.)

The essence of the Government's approach is to give children a large amount of information about sex and invite them to make an informed choice between delaying sexual activity and having 'protected' sex. This approach is sometimes referred to as 'comprehensive sex education' in that it gives children all the inform-ation they need to make 'informed' sexual choices. So we see that an important dimension of sex education, despite its concern about the 'moralisers', is to deliver a *moral* message that influences the informed choice that children make with regard to their sexual conduct. In the next chapter we examine the moral philosophy that underpins sex education.

Another objective of school sex education is to teach that marriage and 'other stable relationships' are moral equivalents. The Government makes it absolutely clear that children are to be taught 'that there are strong and mutually supportive relationships outside marriage. Therefore pupils should learn the significance of marriage and stable relationships as key building blocks of community and society.'[38] The implication of this message is that marriage is but one type of stable relationship— other 'stable relationships' include cohabitation and same-sex relationships.

Sex education aims to help children to overcome their natural embarrassment and talk about sex. 'It is essential that schools can help children and young people develop confidence in talking, listening and thinking about sex and relationships. Teachers and other staff may need to overcome their own anxieties and embarrassment to do this effectively.'[39] The message is that it is important for teachers and children to overcome embarrassment so that they feel comfortable talking openly about sex.

Teaching children about contraception is at the heart of sex education. 'Knowledge of the different types of contraception, and of access to, and availability of contraception is a major part of the Government's strategy to reduce teenage pregnancy.' It follows that 'trained staff in secondary schools should be able to give young people full information about different types of contraception, including emergency contraception and their effectiveness... Trained teachers can also give pupils – individually and as a class – additional information and guidance on where they can obtain confidential advice, counselling and, where necessary, treatment.'[40] This means that children are to be given instruction in using contraception and emergency contraception, and teachers can give children confidential advice about where to obtain contraception. According to the guidance, 'young people need to know not just what safer sex is and why it is important but also how to negotiate it with a partner'.[41] The ability to negotiate 'safer sex' is an important skill that sex education hopes to impart to teenagers.

Contraceptives and the 'morning-after' pill for children

The Government's campaign to increase the use of both contraception and the 'morning-after' pill among children must be seen in the light of current patterns of usage. While sex education guidance creates the impression that children are having difficulty accessing contraception, and the Social Exclusion Unit claims that some young people actually think that it is illegal for them to use contraceptives, an examination of the statistics shows a different picture. During the last 25 years there has been a tenfold increase in the number of English girls under 16 using contraception (figure 1). In the year 1975, around 8 thousand girls were recruited into contraception; by the year 2001 the figure had risen to 80 thousand. In the same year, about 48 thousand 15-year-olds (that is, 16 per cent) attended family planning clinics.[42] Despite these alarming statistics the Government is doing all in its power to increase still further the use of contraceptives among children.

The use of the 'morning-after' pill (emergency contraception), which the Government is pushing so hard among under-age children, has shown an equally dramatic rise since it became available in the early 1980s. About two-thirds of prescriptions are issued by GPs and one third by family planning clinics, and by the mid-1990s the annual number of prescriptions for the 'morning-after' pill in England was just under 800 thousand. In the year 2001, family planning clinics issued nearly 26 thousand prescriptions for the 'morning-after' pill to girls under 16,[43] while the number obtaining GP prescriptions is not recorded.

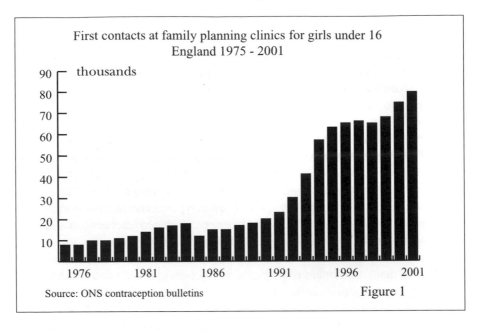

First contacts at family planning clinics for girls under 16
England 1975 - 2001

Source: ONS contraception bulletins

Figure 1

So how successful has contraception been in preventing teenage conceptions? How many of the 8 thousand under-16s who became pregnant in 2001, and how many of the 26 thousand under-16s who used emergency contraception in 2001 (because they thought they might be pregnant), were among the 80 thousand who had attended family planning clinics for contraception? Recent research of teenage pregnancies in general practice shows that most teenagers who became pregnant had discussed contraception (71 per cent) in the year before conception, and two-thirds (65 per cent) had been prescribed oral contraception before they became pregnant. Moreover, as this research was based solely on GP records and did not take account of contraceptives provided by family planning clinics, it under-estimates the total provision of contraception to pregnant teenagers.[44] So the true rate of contraception use prior to teenage pregnancy is likely to be even higher. Indeed, it is well known that the rate of contraceptive failure among children is high, hence the Government's campaign to provide emergency contraception. These disturbing figures suggest that while contraceptive based sex education has certainly encouraged children to use contraception it has not prevented them from becoming pregnant.

The age of sexual consent

The Government's policy of promoting contraception among under-age girls and teaching them how to negotiate 'safer sex' needs to be seen in the context of the law on the age of sexual consent. According to the law of the land, based on the Criminal Law Amendment Act 1885, and the Sexual Offences Act 1956, sexual intercourse between a man and a girl under 16 is a serious criminal offence so far

8

as the man is concerned. Parliament enacted these laws for the purpose of protecting young girls from sexual exploitation.

Despite the law on the age of consent, the British Government, in an attempt to reduce the rate of teenage pregnancies, issued a memorandum in 1974 that permitted doctors to prescribe contraceptives to under-age children without the knowledge or consent of their parents.

In 1979 *The Working Paper on the Age of Consent in relation to Sexual Offences*, produced under the chairmanship of Lord Justice Waller, emphasised the importance of the law in protecting under-age girls. 'In our opinion, sexually immature girls need protection from sexual intercourse on two grounds. First, when an immature girl has sexual intercourse with a man, her gradual development towards sexual maturity can be affected. She may be introduced prematurely into a world of adult feelings with only an adolescent's ability to control them. Secondly, an immature choice is not a free one. Immature girls are open to exploitation, particularly by older men, but also by boys of their own age or slightly older, who know what they want and are not deterred by using all kinds of psychological pressure to get their way. We think it is true that most girls are not eager to have sexual intercourse before they reach 16. The present law is, we consider, one factor strengthening their resolve to say "no".'[45]

In 1983 Mrs Victoria Gillick sought a High Court declaration that the Government's memorandum of 1974 was unlawful. Although she eventually lost her case on a split judgement in the House of Lords, over the course of her prolonged legal battle five judges found in her favour, against four who supported the Government. Two judges, in particular, cast considerable doubt on the lawfulness of the Government's position. In his ruling Lord Brandon wrote: 'It is sometimes said that the age of consent for girls is presently 16. This is, however, an inaccurate way of putting the matter, since, if a man has sexual intercourse with a girl under 16 without her consent, the crime which he thereby commits is that of rape. The right way to put the matter is that 16 is the age of a girl below which a man cannot lawfully have sexual intercourse with her. It was open to Parliament in 1956, when the Sexual Offences Act of that year was passed, and it has remained open to Parliament throughout the 29 years which have since elapsed, to pass legislation providing for some lower age than 16, if it thought fit to do so. Parliament has not thought fit to do so...' In his opinion, providing children with contraceptives is 'to undermine or circumvent the criminal law which Parliament has enacted', and this must be contrary to public policy.[46]

Lord Templeman ruled that an unmarried girl under the age of 16 did not, in his opinion, 'possess the power in law to decide for herself to practise contraception... Parliament has indicated that an unmarried girl under the age of 16 is not sufficiently mature to be allowed to decide for herself that she will take part in sexual intercourse. Such a girl cannot therefore be regarded as sufficiently mature to be allowed to decide for herself that she will practise contraception for the purpose of frequent or regular or casual sexual intercourse.'[47]

And so the question arises: is the Government, by encouraging the use of contraception among under-age children, undermining the criminal law? (The Gillick case is discussed in chapter 14.)

———————

The Government is now so confident of its approach that it has introduced a target to reduce the rate of teenage pregnancies by 50 per cent by the year 2010. The main weapons in its armoury are sex education, with its 'safer sex' message, and when that fails, emergency contraception. Reading the Government's guidance we could be forgiven for thinking that this is a new idea. In all its advice and guidance there is no mention of the fact that there has been a major sex education campaign in the UK since the early 1970s. There is not the slightest hint that the contraceptive based sex education of the last three decades may have been a failure. The proposition that promoting contraceptives among young people may be part of the problem is not even considered. In the mind of the Government, the problem is simply that the promotion of contraception has not been vigorous enough, that sex education messages have not been explicit enough and have not started at an early enough age. So after three decades of sex education we are asked to believe the Government's assertion that the underlying problem is that young people lack accurate knowledge about sex and contraception.

In this book I challenge the Government's assumption that the answer to the crisis in teenage pregnancy lies in yet more sex education and a yet more vigorous promotion of contraception among young people. I argue that comprehensive sex education is not only ineffective in achieving its stated objective of reducing sexual tragedies, but that it contributes to the problem. There is a better message for young people than that delivered by sex education, and the good news is that young people do not need to rely on contraceptives to avoid becoming pregnant. The so-called 'moralisers', so easily dismissed by the sex education lobby, do have something important to say. Because sex education raises profound moral questions, I approach the issue from a biblical perspective. Moreover, as over 70 per cent of the population still regard themselves as Christian, according to the latest census, it is important to examine the teachings of sex education in the light of biblical truth, the foundation of traditional morality in Great Britain. As we shall see, the real effect of sex education, whether by design or default, has been to liberate children from Christian standards that have formed the moral foundation of sexual behaviour in this country for over a thousand years.

Endnotes

1 *Teenage Pregnancy*, HMSO, London, June 1999, p4
2 Ibid. p4
3 Ibid. p5
4 *BBC News Online*, 27 June 2002, Pupils' contraceptive plan prompts fury
5 *The Mail on Sunday*, 4 November 2001, 'The card that lets children as young as 13 get free condoms', Ian Cross

6 *Contraception*, Barbara Hastings-Asatourian, Contraception Education Limited, 2001, p7

7 Ibid. p42

8 Ibid. p45

9 *Times Educational Supplement*, 26 October 2001, Contraception is a game of chance, Nic Barnard

10 *BBC News* website, 26 October 2001, School sex board game criticised

11 Exeter University website, 'A Pause For Health'

12 *BBC News* website, 21 February 2003, Sex lessons 'go too far'

13 *Times Educational Supplement* website, taken from Breaking News, 21 February 2003, Under-16s health course 'should have avoided the mention of oral sex'

14 *Times Educational Supplement* website, taken from News & opinion, 21 February 2003, The heart of the matter, Lynda Brine

15 *Daily Telegraph*, 16 March 2002, 'Tesco gives morning-after pill to teenagers', Becky Barrow

16 *Ananova News* website, 22 August 2002, Government supports Sainsbury's pill move

17 *The Sunday Times*, 7 January 2001, 'Under-age girls to be given morning-after pill at school', Adam Nathan

18 Ibid. *Teenage pregnancy*, p7

19 Ibid. p17

20 Ibid. p7

21 Ibid. p7

22 Ibid. p7

23 Ibid. p90

24 Ibid. pp40-41

25 Ibid. p95

26 Ibid. p8

27 *Why the Government's Teenage Pregnancy Strategy is destined to fail*, Family Education Trust, 2002, p4

28 Ibid. p8

29 Ibid. *Teenage Pregnancy*, p10

30 Ibid. p10

31 Ibid. p11

32 *Sex and Relationship Education Guidance*, DfEE, July 2000, Introduction, p3

33 Ibid. p20

34 Ibid. p9

35 Ibid. p5

36 Ibid. p20

37 Ibid. p10

38 Ibid. p4

39 Ibid. p22

40 Ibid. p15

41 Ibid. p18

42 *NHS Contraceptive Services, England: 2001-02*, bulletin 2002/20, Department of Health, ed. Lesz Lancucki, October 2002

43 Ibid.

44 Dick Churchill et al, Consultation patterns and provision of contraception in general practice before teenage pregnancy: case control study, *British Medical Journal*, 321, pp486-89

45 Working Paper on the Age of Consent in relation to Sexual Offences, HMSO, June 1979, cited from the article, 'A Lost Grandeur' in February 1999 edition of *Catholic Medical Quarterly*, catholicdoctors website.uk

46 *Butterworths LexisNexis Direct*, House of Lords, 17 October 1985, Gillick v West Norfolk, pp27-28

47 Ibid. p28

Chapter 2

The amoral ideology of sex education

Sex education guidance for schools; values clarification;

self-esteem and the morality of desire

We have seen the Government's confident claim that sex education is the answer to the sexual tragedies that are now so common in modern Britain. We are all familiar with headlines drawing our attention to the latest teenage pregnancy drama, reporting the birth of a baby to some unfortunate 12 or 13-year-old girl who did not know how to 'protect' herself. After the usual hand wringing, there is the inevitable cry from the experts for more sex education, and for it to start at an even earlier age. Except for a few voices advising that children should be taught the value of sexual abstinence, there are no alternative proposals as to how society should deal with these distressing tragedies. Although a recent publication by the Christian Institute, *Sex Lessons for Kids*, caused quite a stir among those who saw the explicit nature of the teaching materials, only a handful of parents have any idea about the messages that are being imparted by sex education. Furthermore, the majority of parents have put their faith in sex education and are quite content, even relieved, for their children to be taught about sex at school.

In order to understand the messages that are being delivered to children, in this chapter we examine some of the teaching techniques and materials used by those involved in sex education. Most of the materials have been produced by the Family Planning Association (FPA), the Brook Advisory Centres (Brook) and the Health Education Authority (HEA). While the HEA (it changed its name to the Health Development Agency in April 2000) is a Government quango, the FPA and Brook are registered charities which receive large amounts of public money to support their work in sex education. Brook's *Making sex education easier* is an example of a catalogue which provides sex education resources and literature 'to help teachers fulfil the requirements of the National Curriculum'.[1] Within the NHS, health promotion departments, attached to district health authorities, and more recently to primary care trusts, are responsible for delivering sex education at the local level. In most areas health promotion experts work closely with local educa-tion departments and schools, making available, for those schools that want them, the resource materials required for delivering sex education. In West Sussex, for example, the health promotion department produced a booklet, *Guide to Secondary School Sex Education Resources*, which listed a wide range of sex education materials available for use in local schools.[2] While many teachers make use of these resources, others do not, for each school is responsible for the type of materials used in their sex education lessons. Having said that, there is no doubt that the majority of resources that find their way into schools come from the HEA, the FPA and Brook.

Sex education guidance for schools

In 1994 the Conservative Government issued guidance which stated that sex education must not be value-free. 'Pupils should be encouraged to appreciate the value of stable family life, marriage and the responsibility of parenthood. They should be helped to consider the importance of self-restraint, dignity, respect for themselves and others, acceptance of responsibility, sensitivity towards the needs and views of others, loyalty and fidelity.'[3]

The FPA, while conceding that sex education could not be value-free, expressed the view that 'the question of what constitutes a moral framework for sex education in schools is an open one'. The problem, as the FPA saw it, was that 'teachers and governors sometimes feel under pressure to select and promote values which they, their pupils or the local community may not own or be comfortable with. People of all ages are caught in a moral dilemma... Perhaps they believe that everyone should wait to have sex until they are married or perhaps they want to celebrate the fact they are lesbian or gay. But in the real world, these values are not universally shared. So whose morals should teachers and governors be basing their framework on? Which values do schools actively wish to promote?' The problem is aggravated by the fact that there are 'many situations in life where what is "right" or "wrong" is not universally agreed'.[4] Clearly, the FPA did not agree with the set of values the Conservative Government wanted to impose on school sex education. This exchange shows that the FPA was unhappy with a moral framework for sex education that encourages children 'to appreciate the value of stable family life, marriage and the responsibility of parenthood'. They did not support sex education that was based on a single 'prescriptive' set of values.

As we saw in the previous chapter, the Labour Government's new guidance on sex education sets out to 'help and support young people through their physical, emotional and *moral* development', and to help 'pupils deal with difficult *moral* and social questions [my italics]'.[5] The draft guidance of the Welsh Assembly makes it clear that the aim of sex education is to develop attitudes, values and skills which influence the way children behave.[6] So we see that sex education,

13

like Christianity, aims, through its moral teaching, to influence the behaviour of children. In other words, the sex education that is being promoted by the Labour Government, in partnership with the FPA, is, in fact, an evangelical movement which aims to 'prepare young people for an adult life in which they can develop *positive values* and a *moral framework* that will guide their decisions, judgements and behaviour [my italics]'.[7] The fact that sex education teaches a 'moral framework' and 'positive values' is emphasised. Many people reading these words assume that the moral framework is based on Christian moral standards. Most people are reassured by the fact that sex education teaches 'positive values'.

The draft document of the Welsh Assembly outlines the way in which moral guidance should be taught. Under key stage 1, the moral aspect of sex education must ensure that pupils 'know what is fair and unfair and what they believe to be right and wrong'. Note that children are taught not what *is* right and wrong, but what they *believe* to be right and wrong. The implication is that right and wrong are a matter of opinion, depending on what each person believes, and not on any objective standard. This is the first step in introducing young children to the concept of moral relativism. Children are also taught 'that people have different preferences, views and beliefs'. Here the implication is that there is a range of views and beliefs to choose from, all of equal value, and so each child should choose the views and beliefs that suits them best.

Under key stage 2, children are taught to understand 'that people differ in what they believe is right and wrong'. In other words, right and wrong is a matter of choice—all views must be respected, for everybody is entitled to their own opinion, and it is inappropriate for a person to try to force their view of right and wrong on to anyone else. We must all be tolerant of other people's values. By key stage 4, sex education enables children to 'identify a set of values and principles by which to live'. So sex education is quite upfront about the fact that it aims to influence the sexual behaviour of children. Having explored the finer points of a range of moral options, children are in a position to identify their own set of values on which to base their sexual lives. And it doesn't really matter what set of values they choose (remember, there is no absolute right and wrong), so long as they feel comfortable with their choice.

Values clarification

The technique described above for enabling children to choose a set of values on which to base their sexual conduct is known as values clarification. In *Developing sex education in schools*, Gill Mullinar explains that a vital part of sex education 'involves encouraging young people to explore their own values and those of others. Values clarification requires participants to take an individual stance on an issue, for example "sex before marriage is wrong". The stance can be compared to another person's and then shared and discussed with the whole group.'[8] A technique for introducing values clarification into the classroom is called the values continuum. The teacher places a card with 'agree' on one side of the room and another with

14

'disagree' on the other side. The children are then presented with a moral statement, such as 'sex before marriage is wrong', and asked to move to the position between 'agree' and 'disagree' which is nearest the opinion with which they are most comfortable. Children then discuss the issue with someone with a similar view and then with someone of the opposite opinion. They are then asked if they want to change their position. 'The aim of the exercise is not to change other people's attitudes, but to hear and understand them. Thus participants are required to make a decision, justify it, and possibly change their view. A values continuum is also useful for establishing that people are entitled to their own views.'[9]

Values clarification aims to make children aware of their own feelings, their own ideas, their own beliefs, so that the choices and decisions they make are conscious and deliberate – some would say authentic – based on their *own* value system. In *Why are you losing your children?* Barbara Morris explains that the fundamental assumption behind values clarification is not a neutral point of view but rather a view known as moral relativism. Everything the child has been taught about morality is dissected, shaken and then clarified – sexual conduct, family, religious beliefs, feelings and attitudes. Nothing is too personal or sacred to be taken apart and challenged. 'The values you have passed on to your child – the values he comes to school with, must be clarified. They are not acceptable "as is", because you did the unforgivable – you decided for your child, because of your God-given responsibility and right – what values you want him to hold. Those imposed values, which he did not choose freely, must be clarified. He must decide, immature and unwise though he may be, whether or not he wishes to keep, modify or discard what you have taught him. Values clarification involves exposing the personal, private values of the child to the scrutiny of his peers in the classroom.' Morris argues that a child's values are forced through the 'meat grinder' of public exposure and group discussion. It's up to the child to decide, with the help of the pooled ignorance of his peers and the influence of the teacher, whose own value system may not coincide with that of the parents. She concludes that 'the effect of values clarification is to drive a wedge between parent and child, child and authority and between child and religious beliefs. It is a powerful vehicle for chaos and alienation. Without exaggeration, it sets up a battle between you and the school for the very soul of your child.'[10]

Values clarification places before children impossible dilemmas and forces them to make moral decisions about issues they do not yet fully understand. Paul Vitz has pointed out the five areas of bias associated with the technique. 'First, its exercises embody the moral ideology of a small, liberal segment of society... Second, its values are relative to individual tastes. Third, possible solutions to the moral dilemmas posed to students are limited to the most liberal opinions. Fourth, the exercises focus on the individual in isolation from family and society. And fifth, morality is construed simply as self-gratification. It is a simple-minded, intellectually incompetent system.'[11] Values clarification 'aggressively promotes a particular ethical view—moral relativism. It uses ambiguities to encourage agnosticism about universal moral rules. By posing extremely difficult problems to children untutored in ethical decision-making, values clarification destroys their confidence in moral absolutes.'[12]

The moral framework that is being promoted in schools through the technique of values clarification is moral relativism—a system that teaches that as there are no moral absolutes everyone is free to do as they like, and no one is to pass moral judgement on the behaviour of anyone else. The outcome of relative morality is that when faced with the same moral issue, such as having sex before marriage, one girl or boy may choose one thing and another girl or boy may choose the opposite. And no one can say that one choice is right and the other wrong—both choices are right for that individual at that time. The system of moral relativism is, in reality, a system that legitimises immorality.

Self-esteem

Another technique used in sex education is the promotion of self-esteem as a psychological tool to help children make positive sexual choices. Guidance from the Department for Education emphasises the importance of building self-esteem in children and young people in both primary and secondary schools.[13] Sex education 'enables young people to mature, to build up their confidence and self-esteem and understand the reasons for delaying sexual activity'.[14] The Teenage Parenthood Working Group claims that the reason young people make unhealthy sexual choices is because they have low self-esteem. 'Young people with positive self-esteem are much less likely to become teenage parents. Efforts to reduce teenage parenthood rates in both the short and long term must focus on improving self-esteem among young people.'[15] So sex education encourages young people to develop positive self-esteem as the basis for making healthy choices.

Most sex education manuals contain activities to help children develop positive self-esteem. For example, the sex manual for primary schools, *Knowing me, knowing you*, teaches that promoting positive self-esteem is an important aspect of sex education. The teacher is 'to offer a climate which develops self-esteem. If we feel good about ourselves, we are more likely to consider what we do and how we do it.'[16] The authors believe that 'sex education is about helping children to make responsible decisions about the relationships that they form with others. When considering ourselves in relation to others, the area of self-esteem also comes into play. Helping children to develop a positive sense of self will involve discussion about choice-making, assertiveness, self-expression and, in turn, respect for others.'[17] Sex education that promotes self-esteem is supposed to challenge the values, attitudes and taboos that have been formed by the culture with which we identify.[18]

The Northern Ireland sex education programme, *Love for Life*, is a classic example of a programme based on an appeal to self-esteem. It invites young people to make 'informed and mature sexual health choices' on the basis of information and positive self-esteem.[19] And 'self-esteem is when you feel good about yourself, and you feel confident that there are things you can do and do well. If you feel good about yourself, you have positive or high self-esteem. But if you feel bad

16

about yourself, you have negative or low self-esteem... Truly successful people are those with higher positive self-esteem.'[20] While *Love for Life* claims that its purpose is to encourage young people to delay sexual intercourse, it also believes that giving young people information about contraception and sexually transmitted diseases helps them to make an informed choice about whether or not to have sex.

The problem with the appeal to self-esteem as a guide to decision-making is that it ignores the moral dimension of life. While values clarification undermines traditional morality, the appeal to self-esteem simply ignores morality; those with positive self-esteem are empowered to make 'healthy' sexual choices, while those with poor self-esteem are likely to make 'unhealthy' choices. At the heart of the self-esteem approach is the idea that there are no right or wrong decisions, only 'healthy' and 'unhealthy' choices. So promiscuity is not wrong, but may be an 'unhealthy' choice. Some people feel that delaying sexual activity is a 'healthy' choice, while others may feel that for the young couple who truly love each other, and know how to use contraception, sexual intercourse can be an equally 'healthy' choice. After all, for those young people who practise 'safe sex' by using contraception, there is little threat to health. So the appeal to self-esteem persuades young people that their sexual choices should be made on the basis of how they feel about themselves and not on any objective moral standard. *Love for Life* reassures young people of 'the value and worth of each person' and informs them that they are 'special no matter what choices they make in any area of their lives'.[21]

In her study of the demoralisation of Britain, social historian Gertrude Himmelfarb draws a distinction between the current obsession with 'self-esteem' and the Victorian belief in 'self-help'. She makes the point that whereas self-help depends upon the individual's actions and achievements, self-esteem is presumed to adhere to the individual regardless of how he behaves or what he accomplishes. 'The current notions of self-fulfillment, self-expression, and self-realization derive from a self that does not have to prove itself by reference to any values, purposes, or persons outside itself—that simply is, and by reason of that alone deserves to be fulfilled and realized. This is truly a self divorced from others, narcissistic and solipsistic. It is this self that is extolled in the movement against "codependency", which aspires to free the self from any dependency upon others and, even more, from any responsibility to others.'[22] In other words, self-esteem is all about feeling good regardless of how I behave, and getting what I want, with no moral compass.

The self-esteem movement has its roots in the teachings of the secular psychologist Abraham Maslow. In his book *Towards a Psychology of Being* (1968), Maslow describes a positive, self-actualising force within each person that is struggling to assert itself. He believed that since our 'inner nature is good or neutral rather than bad, it is best to bring it out and encourage it rather than to suppress it. If it is permitted to guide our life, we grow healthy, fruitful, and happy'.[23] Maslow described a hierarchy of needs ranging from the lower, biological needs to the higher social needs. We need to become 'self-actualised' in order to experience wholeness, perfection, justice, richness, simplicity, beauty, goodness, uniqueness,

17

playfulness, truth and self-sufficiency. In *Unmasking the New Age*, Douglas Groothuis points out that although Maslow was an atheist, he invested humanity with the attributes of deity. 'Maslow's pathbreaking efforts cleared the way for an exodus from the old psychological view of humanity toward a new human that is essentially good and has within himself unlimited potential for growth. A whole host of thinkers – Erich Fromm, Rollo May, Carl Rogers and others – sound this call. In humanistic psychology the self is seen as the radiant heart of health, and psychotherapy must strive to get the person in touch with that source of goodness... This is the message at the core of New Age teaching.'[24]

There is now a massive self-esteem industry which uses a whole range of techniques for helping people develop positive self-esteem, including psycho-therapy, cognitive therapy, hypnosis, reiki and various other New Age techniques. The difficulty with the self-esteem movement from a Christian point of view is the focus on self. The idea that we should look within ourselves for empowerment to make positive choices is to deny the doctrine of original sin, to deny the truth that the human heart is deceitful above all things, and desperately sick (Jeremiah 17:9). While the Bible teaches that a moral decision is based on the objective truth of God's law, self-esteem teaches that a 'positive' choice is generated by subjective emotions—that which makes us feel good becomes a 'positive' choice. However, the self-esteem path is fraught with danger, for 'there is a way that seems right to a man, but in the end it leads to death' (Proverbs: 14:12).

Sex education literature

Over the last three decades the FPA, the Health Education Authority (HEA) and Brook have produced an array of sex education literature. Health authorities have been one of the main vehicles for distributing this literature, some of which is used in sex education lessons in school. I have analysed a sample of booklets and pamphlets to illustrate the moral philosophy promoted by sex education.

The morality of desire – only have sex because you want to

The pamphlet *Sexual health matters for young women* (HEA) explains that 'whether or not you have sex can be a difficult decision to make. But in the end it's what's right for you, and only you can answer that. If you've decided you're not ready for sex, then fine. Remember, it's your body, your choice and your right to say no. Only have sex because you want to.'[25] The young woman is offered a choice of whether or not to have sex, and her decision depends on what she *wants*, on her sexual desires, on how she feels at that moment in time, and not on any objective standard of right and wrong. Notice that if she does not *want* to have sex, then fine, it is her right to say no. The corollary is that if she does *want* to have sex, then fine, it is her right to say yes. The inference is that whatever she chooses is right for her. So the message is that, when it comes to sexual behaviour, young people should do what they *want*. A guide for gay and bisexual men puts it this way—'doing only what you want to do, what you enjoy and feel safe with'.[26]

According to the sex educators, the decision of young people to have sex is their own business and nobody should judge them—hence the idea of non-judgemental sex education. It is not difficult to see that this teaching leads to sexual anarchy, as each young person is encouraged to believe that they are free to do whatever they *want* to, whatever they feel to be right in their own eyes.

Well over one million copies of the pamphlet *HIV – Facts for Life* (1993), published by AIDS Care Education and Training (ACET), have been distributed. It tells the story of a young man, Steve, who is being pressurised by his friends, agonising over the question of whether he should have sex or not. His friends ask him, 'When did you first do it?' When he confesses that he has never done it, they laugh at him: 'Who are you saving yourself for, Steve?' and 'maybe he's scared of getting pregnant!' Steve reasons to himself that it's not the idea of sex that he finds embarrassing, and convinces himself that the real question is 'what I really want. It's your choice – no one else's.' When his friends taunt him, 'Come on Steve, admit it, you're just being a wimp!' Steve responds that 'at least I don't just go along with the crowd. At least I make my own decisions.'[27] The message is perfectly clear. A young man's decision to have sex depends on what he wants. There is no suggestion of right or wrong, simply what a young man *wants*. Here we have a classic example of morality based on desire, a morality which encourages young people to satisfy their sexual desires, if that's what they really want.

Teenage Living & Loving by James Hemming, published by the British Medical Association, explains that 'in matters of sex and love it is very important to be as frank as possible with one another and to act according to how you *really* feel and *really* want... Not so very long ago pre-marital relationships were condemned as utterly wrong. But ideas have changed a great deal, and many people today accept sexual relationships before marriage, provided that they are honest and caring. If a relationship is honest and caring, and the partners know each other well and trust each other, then whether or not they decide to have sexual relationships, when they feel ready for them, is their own decision.'[28] The booklet, having dismissed the idea that promiscuous sex is wrong, advises teenagers that their decision to have sex is based on what they *want*, guided by how they *feel* [my italics].

The booklet *Private & Confidential* (1994), published jointly by the British Medical Association, the Royal College of GPs, the FPA and Brook, has the aim of advising young girls under the age of 16 that they can get contraceptives from their GP without their parents knowing about it—'even if you are under 16, doctors still have to keep anything you tell them private, just as they would for an adult. So whether you ask for advice about a cold or something as personal as contraception or a sexual problem, your doctor will not tell anyone else what has been discussed.' Young girls are advised that 'it should be your choice to have sex. Think hard about the decision, don't jump into it before you're ready and never feel you have to do it because someone is pressuring you. It's really important to get contraception sorted out before you start having sex – or as early as possible in your relationship. Remember, you can get confidential help from a doctor even

19

if you're under 16 so there's no need to take any risks.'[29] Notice the casual, amoral approach to promiscuous sex—it's just something that young girls do, so what's the big deal? A teenage girl is advised 'it should be your choice to have sex', and if she decides she *wants* to have sex, her doctor will help her with contraceptives. So girls of 13, 14 and 15 are advised that they can choose to have sex if they *want* it. Notice the emphasis that teenagers should make up their own mind, free no doubt from the influence of their parents and the teaching of the Church, about their sexual conduct. One can only wonder how parents feel about this kind of advice being given to their daughters. Note too the false reassurance that 'there's no need to take any risks'—as if contraceptives removed all the risks associated with promiscuous sex.

Sexual abstinence

A consistent message of sex education ideology is that those who don't want to have sex should be encouraged to abstain until they feel they are ready. The booklet *One Love* (HEA) gives advice to young people who fall in love. It advises those who are 'tempted to go all the way' to talk about it with their partner. 'If you can talk to your partner about sex, then you'll probably enjoy it more than if you sleep with someone you don't really know. Your first time should be something to remember with pleasure – not embarrassment!' But 'if you're not ready it's your right to say no if you don't want to go all the way'.[30] The central message is that if a young girl is with someone she really likes then it is acceptable to have sexual intercourse if she feels that she *wants* to, but if she feels she does not *want* to go all the way, then it is her right to say no. So we see that the HEA advises those who are not ready that it is their right to delay the onset of sexual intercourse.

In the booklet *4 Boys: a below-the-belt guide to the male body* the FPA addresses the question of the right time to have sex. It points out that 'the average when both men and women first have sex is now 17. Many wait until they are older. If you have any doubts, or think that you'll regret it, then wait.' But if a couple 'think the time's right... try to make you and your partner's first sexual experience as good as possible'.[31] The message for those who are not ready for sex is to wait for the right time. A pamphlet for young men teaches that peer pressure can push people 'into having sex for all the wrong reasons. And if your partner isn't ready for sex, imagine how they feel if you keep pressuring them about it. So be fair to yourself and to your partner – only have sex if you both want to.'[32] The message is clear— if one partner does not want sex, then abstain from sexual intercourse until both partners want it.

The Sexuality Information and Education Council of the United States (SIECUS), the main organisation involved in sex education in the USA, is a keen advocate of abstinence. 'Some people feel sexual desire but choose not to be sexual with anyone else. That's just fine. The choice not to be sexual with anyone else is called sexual abstinence. It is a *good* choice and something you may choose at different times throughout your whole life. This can happen whenever you don't feel ready to be sexual with someone else, even when you have a partner you have been sexual with in the past. Abstinence is one possible choice... Abstinence from sexual relations has benefits for teenagers. It is the best way to prevent pregnancy and to prevent becoming infected with HIV and other STDs... Remember, for many young persons the choice to be abstinent is the *best choice.*'[33]

Advising young people to delay the onset of sexual intercourse, that is, to abstain until they feel ready to have sex, is central to sex education ideology. Most abstinence programmes promote self-esteem as the basis for making 'positive' or 'healthy' decisions. Virtually all sex education programmes advise those who feel they are not yet ready to say: 'No, I don't want to have sex with you now.' The essential characteristic of 'abstinence' education is that it is pro-choice, offering young people the choice between delaying sexual activity and 'safer sex'. Young people are presented with two options and invited to choose the one that makes them feel most comfortable, and whatever choice they make is right for them. Some people are misled into believing that this message, which encourages young people to delay the onset of sexual intercourse until they are ready, is consistent with biblical morality. But this is not the case. Delaying the onset of sexual intercourse, or abstinence, or learning to wait until the right moment, is a pragmatic decision based on the feelings and desires of the young people involved, and has nothing to do with what is right or wrong. Chastity, on the other hand, is a moral decision to remain chaste until marriage. There is a world of difference between these two positions. One is based on the morality of desire, the other on the morality of the Bible.

Moral philosophy of postmodernism

The above examples suggest a link between the message of sex education and the moral philosophy of postmodernism. In his *Guide to Contemporary Culture*, Gene Veith provides a useful summary of postmodernist thought. He explains that for postmodernists morality, like religion, is a matter of desire. 'What I want and what I choose is not only true (for me) but right (for me). That different people want and choose different things means that truth and morality are relative, but "I have a right" to my desires. Conversely, "no one has the right" to criticise my desires and my choices. Although postmodernists tend to reject traditional morality, they can still be very moralistic. They will defend their "rights" to do what they want with puritanical zeal. Furthermore, they seem to feel they have a right not to be criticized for what they are doing. They want not only licence but also approval. Thus tolerance becomes the cardinal virtue... postmodernist sins are "being judge-mental", "being narrow-minded", "thinking that you have the only truth", and "trying to enforce your values on anyone else". Those who question the post-modernist dogma that "there are no absolutes" are excluded from the canons of tolerance. The only wrong idea is to believe in truth; the only sin is to believe in sin. The morality of desire has wreaked havoc with sexuality.'[34]

Veith shows that in postmodern thinking meaning is not discovered in the objective world; rather, meaning is a purely human phenomenon. Because there is no ready-made meaning to life, individuals can create meaning for themselves. 'Since everyone creates his or her own meaning, every meaning is equally valid. Religion becomes a purely private affair, which cannot be imposed on anyone else. The content of one's meaning makes no difference, only the personal commitment… Moral values, like other kinds or meaning, are created by the self. The best example of an existential ethic can be found in some of those who advocate abortion but call themselves "pro-choice". To them it makes no difference what the woman decides, only that she makes an authentic choice to have or not to have a baby. Whatever she chooses is right—for her.'[35]

The guidance provided by sex education is based on the morality of desire. The guiding principle is what a child wants, and the child is taught that there is no clear distinction between right and wrong in matters of sexual conduct. The morality promoted by sex education is relative, a question of opinion, based on feelings of self-esteem—a child is taught that he is free to develop his *own* moral framework, to decide for himself what is right.

It is extraordinary that State sex education in England, a country which for the last thousand years has accepted the objective standard of biblical morality, should now encourage children to develop their *own* set of values. And when it comes to sexual conduct, it makes no difference what a young person chooses, only that he or she makes a 'positive' choice—and should their 'positive' choice lead to an unwanted pregnancy, that they make an 'informed' choice on whether or not to have an abortion. Whatever they choose is right for them, and no one has the right to criticise their choice. And if they choose to have sex, the important thing is for them to act 'responsibly' by using a condom.

Promiscuous sex

Consistent with its ideology that fails to distinguish between right and wrong, sex education teaches young people that they are free to choose any form of sexual lifestyle they desire, including promiscuous sex and homosexual sex. Having made it clear that young people are free to have sex when they want to, sex education explains the reasons why promiscuous sex might be a desirable choice.

The pamphlet *Lovelife* (HEA) records the thoughts of a teenage virgin: 'Seventeen and the only virgin in my class – I thought I was the last person in the world who'd never had it. Everybody's doing it – maybe I should too.'[36] Here sex education is using the classic propaganda technique of the bandwagon effect. Everybody's doing 'it', so you should be doing 'it' too. Teenagers are actually being persuaded to follow the crowd and have sex. The pamphlet advises the young virgin that 'being prepared doesn't mean taking the fun out of sex. And it doesn't mean you are planning to sleep around. It just makes sense.' And she can 'be prepared' by buying condoms 'from a machine or in a supermarket where you can get them off the shelf with other goods. Once you've bought them a few times you'll find it much easier.' The pamphlet goes on, 'You've bought the condoms – now how do you suggest using one? Talking about safer sex doesn't have to be difficult. Once you mention it you might find your partner is just as keen to talk about it as you are.'[37] Teenagers are advised that 'if you're likely to be in a situation where you may have sex – maybe after parties, pubs, clubs, raves – make sure you've got condoms with you.'[38] It's better to 'make sure you're carrying condoms'[39] than risk unsafe sex. The reason teenagers need to carry condoms is because they never know when they may have an opportunity for casual sex. In the amoral world of sex education it is unlikely that a teenager would refuse such an opportunity, so all must 'be prepared' for sex. This guidance gives a green light to promiscuous sex, for it suggests to impressionable teenagers that casual sex is acceptable provided they use a condom. The fact that most do not want to be promiscuous is ignored— the message is that *all* should 'be prepared' for sex.

The pamphlet *Play safe on holiday* (Brook) relates in cartoon strip the sexual adventures of two young women going on holiday. 'We'd saved all year for this holiday and nothing was going to stop us having a good time! Mandy had fallen straight into the arms of this guy (Jim) who'd sat next to us in the plane coming over.' After the second girl falls for Dan, one of the guys on the next balcony, the two young women get together to discuss their sexual adventures. 'I really fancy him, Mandy, but how on earth can I ask him to use a condom?' Mandy replies, with a happy smile, 'I've got all the colours of the rainbow with me – so I just asked Jim which he'd fancied!'[40] But her friend is despondent because Dan does not want to use a condom. 'It's no good – he thinks I think he's got something nasty! What shall I do?' Mandy advises her desperate friend, 'You could use a female condom yourself. Or you could play safe. Swimming naked together and massaging each other all over with suntan oil are about as sexy as you can get.' Notice the matter-of-fact way in which the pamphlet tells the reader that Mandy has already 'had sex' with Jim. The implication is that it is quite natural for a young woman to have casual sex with a man that she has just met, and what's more, it is sensible for a young woman who is going on holiday to be armed with a range of condoms. And Mandy's happiness has come about because she was prepared for sex. This pamphlet suggests to young women that casual sex is an exciting adventure. It encourages lustful thoughts, promoting the idea of casual sex as the norm. Teenagers reading it are led to believe that it is quite acceptable, even expected, for young women on holiday to have a good time by indulging in sex with the first man who is willing, provided they 'play it safe' by using condoms.

The booklet, *Learning to Live with Sex* (1972), produced by the FPA, describes chastity as 'not having sexual intercourse until you are married, and then only with that person... People's needs are different, and everyone has to make up his or her own mind about the value of chastity.'[41] The booklet explains that girls 'may be worried about having sex if they are not married... if you belong to a church and have definite religious beliefs there is no doubt that it will upset you a great deal if you do things which are against your conscience. Many people don't go along with those beliefs any more, but if your parents still believe them and think you should too, you may have a rather difficult time trying to sort out what is the right thing for you to do. If possible try and talk these over with someone outside your family. If you don't know anyone you can trust, try one of the organisations listed at the back.'[42] And the listed organisations include abortion, contraception and homosexual counselling agencies, the FPA and Brook.[43]

Learning to Live with Sex suggests that many young people no longer accept the traditional moral view held by the church and their parents that 'having sex if they are not married' is wrong. So instead of following the traditional view, indeed their own parents' view, teenagers are encouraged to make up their own mind about chastity—that is, they are being guided to do what they feel to be right in their own eyes. The booklet presents premarital sex as a morally neutral issue, simply a matter of choice, with teenagers free to decide for themselves how they should behave. Moreover, it invites children to reject chastity by suggesting that sexual intercourse among boys and girls is the norm: 'But it is important when a couple make love for the first time that the *boy* makes sure that the *girl* is relaxed and her vulva moist before he gently inserts his penis into her vagina [my italics].'[44] And if teenagers are confused about rejecting traditional morality they can phone the FPA for support.

There can be no doubt that teenagers reading the above pamphlets are being encouraged to believe that there is no moral objection to promiscuous sex—there is not even the slightest hint that promiscuity is wrong, or that it can have the most dire moral, emotional and physical consequences. Teenagers are being led to believe that, provided they use condoms, they can have sex whenever they like.

Homosexuality

Sex education literature also condones, and even encourages, homosexual relations. One of the books recommended by the FPA as being particularly helpful is *Girls and Sex*, written by Wardell Pomeroy, co-author of the Kinsey Reports on human sexual behaviour. This book provides young girls with the following advice: 'One thing that confuses a great many people is thinking of homosexuality as something separate and distinct from heterosexuality, which means sexual relations or attraction between members of the opposite sex. Because a girl is sexually aroused by or has relations with another girl doesn't mean she cannot have relations with boys, just as a girl who likes ice cream may also like pie.'[45] The book explains to girls that 'few people are able to accept the truth about themselves, which is that everyone is potentially capable of doing every act imaginable, including having homosexual relations, given the proper circumstances, conditioning and back-ground. Everyone has latent homosexual tendencies in one degree or another...'[46] Here Pomeroy is teaching that bisexuality is the norm, and that it is perfectly normal for a girl to be sexually attracted to, and have sex with, both girls and boys. In his mind, having sex has as much moral content as eating ice cream or pie.

According to *Learning to Live with Sex*, 'Many people in their teens find that they like members of their own sex much better than the other.' And 'because a man or woman is a homosexual does not mean he or she is perverted or carries out strange practices. For homosexuals, lovemaking is as natural as it is for anyone else.'[47] The pamphlet *Lovelife* informs young people that 'sexuality can be confusing at the best of times and if you're not sure which sex you're attracted to, you're not alone. Discovering your sexuality may take time, and you're the only one who can decide where your true feelings lie.' And if a teenager wants advice then they can phone the London Lesbian and Gay Switchboard for a private chat.[48] Sex education makes no moral distinction between heterosexual and homosexual sex—both are equally acceptable, it's simply a matter of choice.

The FPA booklet *4 Boys*, partly funded by the Department of Health, gives young men the following advice. 'Getting an erection when you are around other boys doesn't mean that you are gay. But you may be sexually interested in other men – or even men AND women. It's not a problem; your body is yours to share with whomever you choose.'[49] The booklet, *Is everybody doing it?* (FPA) gives this advice: 'Sexuality is not the same for everyone. Some people are attracted to people of the opposite sex, some to the same sex and some to both. Most people will grow up to be heterosexual (fancy someone of the opposite sex) but this doesn't mean that they are only attracted to the opposite sex all their lives.'[50] The clear implication of this advice is that both homosexuality and bisexuality are natural and should not be regarded as a problem. It is up to young people to choose with whom they want to share their body. And if they want to have sex with members of both sexes, then that is their choice, and nobody has the right to judge them. As we shall see in chapter 6, this advice is consistent with the ideology propagated by Alfred Kinsey, namely, that human sexuality is a continuum between heterosexuality and homosexuality with bisexuality being the norm.

The above examples make it clear that sex education regards all types of sexual orientation – bisexuality, heterosexuality and homosexuality – as moral equivalents; there is no moral distinction between having sex with members of the opposite sex, members of the same sex, or members of both sexes. Sex education simply helps teenagers to find their preferred sexual orientation.

'Safer sex' message

After encouraging young people to think and act sexually, sex education informs them that 'having sex' can have a few unfortunate side effects, such as sexually transmitted diseases and an unwanted pregnancy. The good news is that condoms can protect against these nasty side effects. The booklet *Is everybody doing it?* (FPA) recites the 'safer sex' mantra: 'Condoms protect against both pregnancy and sexually transmitted infections. Condoms can keep both you and your partner safe and allow you to relax and enjoy sex.'[51] According to *Lovelife* 'only condoms provide an "all-in-one" protection against pregnancy and sexually transmitted infections, including HIV'.[52] So all a teenager has to do is buy condoms or get them free from a family planning clinic and he is ready and prepared for his 'safer sex' adventures.

Say yes? Say no? Say maybe? (Brook) provides teenagers with advice on using condoms. It explains that although everyone feels a bit silly using a condom for the first time, there are three ways to get around this. 'First, have a giggle—who says lovemaking has to be deadly serious? As long as you're not laughing at him but at the condom, nobody gets hurt. Buy one of the coloured condoms and make like it's a party. Second, get over your giggles by using condoms at other times and getting used to them. Blow them up at parties—see who can burst theirs first or who gets them biggest. Third, practice makes perfect. Girls can practise opening a packet and putting them on their partner (use a banana as a model), and boys can practise putting them on and wanking.'[53] And to encourage girls to take the initiative in buying condoms, they are informed that 'one condom in three is now bought by women, so girls needn't feel shy or odd buying them. Make it an initiative test – the first one of you to pluck up courage has to be given tickets for a gig!'[54] Although the thought of teenage children playing party games with condoms is shocking to most parents, this is what children are being taught in the name of sex education.

The cartoon strip *The cool lovers guide to slick condom use* (Brook) shows Jon, a teenage boy, daydreaming about having sex with his girlfriend. When he realises that his girlfriend will expect him to practise 'safe sex', he searches for the condom attached to a leaflet he was given at the club. Jon mutters to himself, 'Now where's that "I'm a cool lover always carry a condom" condom gone?' Having found the mislaid condom the teenager comments, 'Let's have a practice run – I'd look a prat reading instructions in front of her.' The next day he tells his girlfriend, 'I got some condoms. I wanted everything to be OK.' His girlfriend responds, 'I've got some too when I went to the clinic.' She tells Jon that she has also practised using them on a roll-on deodorant bottle, an experience she found 'ever so sexy'.[55] And so the two sexually aroused children are 'prepared' for sex. And it's all so easy, so sexy, so exciting, so tragic.

Your Passport to Sexual Health, a booklet produced by Marie Stopes International, tells young people that 'a foreign holiday still holds promise of sun, sea and sex. But all too easily the romance can go sour, with irritating women's health problems and forgotten or lost contraceptives. Worse still, many women bring unwanted souvenirs home from their vacations – sexually transmitted disease and unplanned pregnancies.'[56] The booklet recommends that young people should have their contraceptives sorted out two or three months before they go on holiday, and gives some hints for a good time. 'The key to good holiday sexual health is condoms.' And 'condoms don't have to be a bore. They come in all colours, textures and flavours. They don't even have to smell rubbery – some condoms are made of plastic, making them thinner and stronger and odourless. Ask your GP or family planning clinic for free supplies of condoms. Then PACK THEM!!'[57] The advice continues, 'protection against pregnancy must be your first line of defence, but mistakes can happen. Condoms can come off or split, or you might just get carried away... But help is at hand. Emergency contraception can be used after unprotected sex.' And so Marie Stopes advises a young woman that to enjoy her holiday she needs to be well supplied with condoms, and even emergency contraception, in case her condoms fail.

According to *Lovelife*, 'the best way to make sure that you don't have unprotected sex is to plan ahead' by making sure you've got condoms with you. 'It is better to be prepared than risk unsafe sex. After all, you can easily hide condoms in your pocket or purse.' And if you're in a situation where you may have sex, make sure you take your condoms. And if you're going abroad remember to buy your condoms before you go.[58] The implicit message of these pamphlets is that casual sex is the norm; it's quite usual to have sex after parties, after going to the pub or when you go on holiday. The 'safer sex' message, however, seldom mentions the real danger of contraceptive failure. The sex educator does not emphasise the fact that condom failure rates of 14 per cent are reported among single young women. In other words, with typical use 14 out of 100 young women will become pregnant over the course of a year. Failure rates among deprived young women are even higher—almost one-quarter, that is, 23 out of 100, can expect to become pregnant during the first year of using condoms.[59] This is why so many young women who rely on 'safer sex' end up pregnant.

Sexually transmitted disease (STD)

After all the talk about 'safer sex' most teenagers could be forgiven for believing that, provided they use condoms, they are safe from sexually transmitted diseases. Alas, this is not the case. As the pamphlet *Lovelife* explains, 'the most important thing to realise about sexually transmitted infections is that anybody who is having sex can get them – young or old, male or female, straight, gay or lesbian'.[60] The implication is that 'unprotected' sex causes sexually transmitted diseases. So 'anybody who is having sex' can get infections such as gonorrhoea, chlamydia, herpes, genital warts and HIV. Notice that in categorising 'anybody who is having sex' the sex educator does not include the largest group, married couples. This remarkable omission shows how sex education propaganda presents a view of the world in which marriage is non-existent. It is only in this distorted view that 'anybody who is having sex' is at risk. In the real world, those who are faithful to their marriage partner are at no risk—they don't need to practise 'safer sex' to avoid sexually transmitted diseases. So the propagandist's claim, that 'anybody who is having sex' can get a sexually transmitted disease, is misleading.

To reinforce the need for 'safer sex' young people are informed that 'sexual infections are very common. Used properly, condoms can help protect against them.'[61] But the statement that sexually transmitted diseases are 'very common' is also misleading, for they are rare among married couples, who make up the majority of sexually active people in society. The truth that sex education is hiding is that sexually transmitted diseases are common among those who practise casual sex. After three decades of sex education propaganda and national 'safer sex' campaigns there is an epidemic of sexually transmitted diseases among the young people who have been taught that they can 'protect' themselves by using condoms. In the last five years the incidence of genital chlamydial infection in England and Wales has risen by 76 per cent, gonorrhoea by 55 per cent, syphilis by 54 per cent

27

and genital warts by 20 per cent, and the greatest increase has occurred among teenagers,[62] the age group targeted by sex education. The truth that young people are not taught is that sexually transmitted diseases are associated with sexual immorality—that is, promiscuous sex, multiple partners and homosexual sex.

According to *Lovelife*: 'The good news is that most sexually transmitted infections can be quickly and easily treated if they're discovered early on. But some can cause serious long-term problems, such as infertility in women, if they are not treated.'[63] Notice the reassuring statement that sexually transmitted infections can be treated quickly and easily, implying that they are trivial infections, nothing more than a minor inconvenience. All that young people need to do is go to a sexual health clinic for treatment. And young people are reassured that 'everything is completely confidential. Nobody will be told of your visit unless you say they can be told.'[64] Yet the truth is that all sexually transmitted diseases are serious, many are difficult to treat, and long-term complications in women include chronic pelvic inflammatory disease and infertility. There is no more distressing situation for a young girl than to be infected with gonorrhoea, genital herpes or pubic lice; she feels dirty, ashamed and betrayed.

We have seen that the Government's sex education programme aims to help schoolchildren develop a moral framework to guide their sexual behaviour. The moral guidance provided by sex education uses the dubious techniques of values clarification and self-esteem. Children are coaxed into rejecting absolute moral standards of right and wrong, which are portrayed as old-fashioned and no longer relevant in a modern world. When it comes to sexual conduct, children are taught that the decision whether to have sex or not is their choice, and theirs alone, and whatever choice they make is right for them. If they *want* to have sex, then provided they use a condom, that is a positive choice for them.

Sex education literature never teaches schoolchildren that any sexual conduct is wrong. To do so would be judgemental, or worse, moralising. The effect is to demoralise sexual behaviour in the eyes of children. Sex education literature promotes the idea that the purpose of sex is pleasure. Children and young people are left with the impression that sex is a game, something they do for fun: 'having sex' or 'having it off' has little more significance than going to the movies. Sex education seldom, if ever, mentions marriage and certainly does not teach that sexual activity should be confined to the marriage union.

We must not be deceived by the so-called 'positive' values that sex education claims to promote. According to the Pagan Federation one of the essential principles of paganism is the promotion of a *positive* morality, in which the individual is responsible for the discovery and development of their true nature. The pagan creed is often expressed as, 'do what you will, as long as it harms none' and it avoids a list of thou-shalt-nots,[65] a pejorative phrase for God's moral law. It does not take much insight to see that the ideology of sex education, which claims to teach children *positive* values, which ridicules the laws of God as judgemental thou-shalt-nots, and which encourages children to do as they *want*, is perfectly consistent with the pagan ethic.

In a debate in the House of Lords Baroness Gaitskell claimed that an important function of sex education is to reduce 'the ignorance and guilt which have been such a legacy from Victorian years'.[66] She was drawing attention to a conflict between Victorian sexual mores and the aims of the sex education movement. And she is absolutely right, for there is a vast difference between Victorian attitudes to sexual behaviour and what is being taught by modern day sex education. Many parents will be astounded at the large gulf between their own views of sexual morality and what their children are being taught. There is no denying that what is now being taught in the name of sex education represents a paradigm shift from the traditional moral views held in this country until only a few decades ago. There is no denying that the message propagated by sex education is light years from the moral standards of Victorian England, a largely Christian society which laid great emphasis on the virtues of modesty, chastity and fidelity.

How is it that we have so easily deserted the moral foundations that built Great Britain into a great Christian nation? How is it that we have moved so quickly from believing that sexual relationships should be confined to the marriage union? To understand the 'new morality' of sex education we need to see it within the historical context of Victorian England. We need to contrast the 'new' positive morality that is being taught by sex education with the traditional morality that it is so rapidly replacing. Only then will we be able to understand the extent of the moral devastation that is being visited on our children.

Endnotes

1 *Making sex education easier*, A guide to sex education resources, Brook publications, p4
2 *Guide to Secondary School Sex Education Resources*, West Sussex Health Authority
3 Department for Education, Circular 5/94, *Education Act 1993: Sex education in schools*, 1994
4 Gill Mullinar, *Developing sex education in schools: a practical guide*, Family Planning Association, 1994, pp38-39
5 *Sex and Relationship Education Guidance*, Department for Education and Employment, July 2000, p3
6 Draft *Sex and Relationship Education Guidance*, Welsh Assembly, January 2000, p 2
7 Ibid. *Sex and Relationship Education Guidance*, DfEE, p20
8 Gill Mullinar, *Developing sex education in schools: a practical guide*, Family Planning Association, 1994, p71
9 Ibid. p72
10 Barbara M Morris, 'Why are you losing your children?' cited from *Schools in Crisis: Training for Success or Failure*, Carl Sommer, Cahill Publishing Company, p210
11 Francis Beckwith and Gregory Koukl, *Relativism*, Baker Books, Grand Rapids, 1998, pp77-78
12 Ibid. p8
13 Ibid. *Sex and Relationship Education Guidance*, DfEE, p9, p10
14 Ibid. p4
15 *Myths & Reality: Teenage Pregnancy and Parenthood*, Report of the Teenage Parenthood Working Group.
16 Pete Sanders and Liz Swinden, *Knowing me, knowing you*, LDA, 1990, p21

17 Ibid. p3
18 Ibid. p3
19 Cited from Love for Life website, www.loveforlife.org.uk
20 Cited from Who's choosing, www.careincrisis.org.uk
21 Cited from Love for Life website, www.loveforlife.org.uk
22 Gertrude Himmelfarb, *The De-moralization of Society*, The Institute of Economic Affairs, 1995, p256
23 Abraham Maslow, *Towards a Psychology of Being*, Van Nostrand Reinhold, New York, p5
24 Douglas Groothuis, *Unmasking the New Age*, Intervarsity Press, 1986, p78
25 *Sexual matters for young women*, Health Education Authority, inside front cover
26 *Safer sex*, Terrence Higgins Trust, 1999
27 *HIV – Facts for Life*, ACET, 1993
28 James Hemming, *Teenage Living & Loving*, British Medical Association. pp24, 28
29 *Private & Confidential - talking to doctors*, The British Medical Association, General Medical Services Committee, Royal College of General Practitioners, Brook Advisory Centres and the Family Planning Association, 1994.
30 *One Love*, Health Education Authority and BBC Radio 1
31 *4 Boys: a below-the-belt guide to the male body*, Family Planning Association, 2000, p13
32 *Sexual matters for young men*, Health Education Authority, inside front cover
33 SIECUS website, For teens, Abstinence – what's right for me?
34 Gene Veith, *Guide to Contemporary Culture*, Crossway Books, Leicester, 1994, pp195-96
35 Ibid. pp37-38
36 *Lovelife* - Sexual health for young people, Health Education Authority, 1999, p2
37 Ibid. p6
38 Ibid. p8
39 *Sexual health matters for young men*, Health Education Authority, p3
40 *Play safe on holiday*, leaflet, Brook publications
41 *Learning to Live with Sex*, Family Planning Association, 1972, p16
42 Ibid. p25
43 Ibid. p59
44 Ibid. p29
45 Wardell Pomeroy, *Girls and Sex*, Penguin Books, first published 1969, 1986 reprint, p117
46 Ibid. p119
47 *Learning to Live with Sex*, Ann Burkitt, Family Planning Association, 1980, pp25-26
48 Ibid. *Lovelife*, p27
49 Ibid. *4 Boys*, Family Planning Association, 2000
50 *Is everybody doing it?* Your guide to contraception, Family Planning Association, 2000
51 Ibid.
52 Ibid. *Lovelife*, p4
53 *Say 'yes'? Say 'no'? Say 'maybe'?*, Suzie Hayman, Brook 1999, p13
54 Ibid. p16
55 *The cool lovers guide to slick condom use*, Leaflet, Brook publications
56 *Your Passport to Sexual Health*, Marie Stopes International, p1
57 Ibid. p6
58 Ibid. *Lovelife*, p6, p8
59 Haishan Fu et al, Contraceptive Failure Rates: New Estimates from the 1995 National Survey of Family Growth, *Family Planning Perspectives*, vol. 31, no2, March/April 1999
60 Ibid. *Lovelife*, p19
61 Ibid. *Sexual matters for young women*, p1
62 Trends in sexually transmitted disease in the United Kingdom, PHLS, summary p iv
63 Ibid. *Lovelife*, p19
64 Ibid. *Lovelife*, p21
65 The Pagan Federation website, paganfed.demon.co.uk
66 Hansard. Lords debate, 14 January 1976, c178

Chapter 3

Sexual morality in Victorian England

Influence of the Evangelical Awakening on the moral outlook of Victorian England

In the previous chapter we saw how sex education ideology demoralises sexual conduct, teaching young people in a climate that encourages promiscuity and homosexuality. Most parents will be amazed that the so-called 'positive values' of sex education are so different from the Christian view of sexual morality that has been a part of English culture for many centuries. There is no doubt that the approach of sex education is light years from traditional English standards of sexual conduct. We are all familiar, of course, with the accusation that the Victorians were sexual prudes and with the criticism levelled at their strict code of sexual conduct. Yet the Victorians were quite open in proclaiming the virtues of modesty, chastity and fidelity. So open, in fact, that they have been accused of hypocrisy because, their critics claim, they secretly indulged the pleasures of the flesh, and did not practise what they preached. Whether the Victorians were hypocrites or not, nobody was in any doubt about the strict standards of conduct they demanded. Even a superficial examination reveals a large chasm between the beliefs of the Victorian 'prudes' and the teaching of the modern sex educators.

An obvious example is the sex educators' insistence on sexual openness – children must develop confidence in talking, listening and thinking about sex – and the Victorians' renowned reticence to discuss sexual matters in public. In chapter 1 we heard the assertion that sexual ignorance, aggravated by the fact that most parents are silent about sex, is a prime factor behind the teenage pregnancy crisis. It is perfectly true that most British parents do not teach their children about sex, and this reluctance to talk about sex is widely regarded as a hangover from Victorian prudery, for our Victorian forefathers positively discouraged discussions about sex, which they considered to be both unnecessary and indecent. In nineteenth century England it was regarded as improper to make any reference to sexual matters in polite company, and the Victorians took extreme measures to suppress indecent literature. There is little doubt that most of the literature that is now distributed in the name of sex education would be condemned as obscene by our grandparents.

It is widely accepted that a major driving force behind the sexual revolution, which gained pace during the second half of the twentieth century, was the desire to be free from repressive Victorian attitudes. Many of the intellectuals who first took up the struggle for sexual liberation believed that they were fighting to free society from the unreasonable restraints imposed by the Victorians. Our starting point, therefore, must be to understand the Victorian beliefs about sexual conduct and why they have become so widely ridiculed. What was it about the Victorians' attitude towards sex that aroused the passion for sexual liberation? In this chapter we examine the beliefs that helped to develop the Victorian moral framework that has had such an impact on the sexual mores of England.

England in the eighteenth century

No study of Victorian England is complete without taking account of the evangelical awakening of the eighteenth century. At the beginning of the century England was in a moral quagmire. The restoration of the English monarchy in 1660 had brought with it a reaction against the Puritan regime of Oliver Cromwell, and Charles II, who had Cromwell's body ripped from the grave for public exhibition, contrived to have Puritans excluded from the ministry of the Church of England. After the Glorious Revolution of 1688, William and Mary, fearful of a Catholic revival, excluded from the national church those staunch Anglo-Catholics who could not find it in their conscience to switch allegiance from the deposed King James II. Within a generation the national church had been denuded of its most faithful churchmen and devoted Christians and the country was becoming increasingly decadent. Drunkenness was rampant and gambling was so widespread that one historian described England as 'one vast casino'. Bear-baiting and cock-fighting were popular sports, and executions were a source of public entertainment.[1] Social historian J Wesley Bready, author of a number of books on eighteenth century England, comments that 'at this period the trend of affairs was directed by materialism, self-seeking, and blatant paganism in high places. The age was one of moral and spiritual eclipse.' His book, *England: Before and After Wesley*, demonstrates the overwhelming impact of the evangelical revival on every aspect of life in Great Britain and in the English-speaking world. He concludes: 'No other movement has a comparable claim to be known as the moral watershed of Anglo-Saxon history.'[2]

In the year of John Wesley's conversion, 1738, Bishop Berkeley declared that morality and religion in Britain had collapsed 'to a degree that has never been known in any Christian country... Our prospect is very terrible and the symptoms grow worse from day to day.' Berkeley pleaded with all State officials to mend their ways and consider the future of their country, for 'the youth born and brought up in wicked times without any bias to good from early principle, or instilled opinion, when they grow ripe, must be monsters indeed. And it is to be feared that the age of monsters is not far off.'[3] Wesley Bready quotes an array of historians, from vastly different angles, as evidence 'of the moral and spiritual eclipse with which the earlier half of the eighteenth century was seriously threatened. Historians, too, of widely divergent schools, on this particular issue are singularly agreed... The fact then of a phenomenal social and moral degeneracy at this period is indisputable.'[4]

According to Bishop JC Ryle, writing a century later, the middle of the eighteenth century was characterised by corruption, jobbing and mismanagement in high places and purity was the exception. The state of the country from a religious and moral point of view was so painfully unsatisfactory that it is difficult to convey any adequate idea of it. He describes a nation overcome by spiritual darkness, a 'gross, thick, religious and moral darkness – a darkness that might be felt'.[5]

There was a growth of scepticism, and religion became chiefly a matter for intellectual discussion. Jesus Christ was reduced to the level of a mere ethical teacher, and the Bible came to be regarded simply as a religious book. With the Christian faith undermined, Christian morality was attacked at its roots. Popular literature of the time provides an example of the moral degeneracy prevalent in society. Sir Walter Besant, in *London in the Eighteenth Century*, writes: 'The coarseness prevalent in the eighteenth century, the gross indecency and ribaldry of its songs, of the daily and common talk, makes itself felt in the whole of its literature—in the plays, the poems, the essays, the novels... the grossness belonged not only to the poor wretch of a harlot, but to all classes alike.'[6] Along with ignorance, lawlessness, barbarism, and godlessness went also superstition, which was widespread during the reign of George I and George II.[7] The novels of the day were described as 'beyond imagination despicable, and had consequently sunk and degraded the whole department of literature'.[8] According to John Simon in *The Revival of Religion in England in the Eighteenth Century*, 'while mawkish women were enervating themselves with sentimentality, and besmirching their minds with the scenes and suggestions of infamous novels, their fathers and brothers pursued a more exciting form of pleasure. The men of the eighteenth century have an evil reputation for their passion for gaming. That passion was cultivated and inflamed by the rulers of the nation. The State lotteries affected thousands of men and women, and filled them with a burning desire for gain.'[9] The prevalence of drunkenness was widespread, affecting all ranks of society, and much of the literature was impure. England of the eighteenth century was a distinctly immoral society.

It was into this depressed land that the Christian evangelists, George Whitefield and John Wesley began their work of preaching the gospel of Christ to the English people. Even before the death of George II (1760), indeed by the middle of the century, new spiritual influences were stirring as England, at last, was regaining its soul. John Simon comments: 'On the accession of George III, Court life was sternly purged; for whatever the failings of this enigmatic sovereign, the moral standards of his home and Court were unimpeachable. This fact largely explains both the admiration of practical moralists, like Wesley, and the smouldering fury of "free-living" aristocrats who resented the introduction of what they styled a "puritanical Court".'[10] When George III came to the throne in 1760 England was slowly becoming a great world power. Its population was growing rapidly, and its manufacturing industry was the most advanced in the world. George III was a good and popular monarch; his character based on his Christian faith and his love for the Church of England. He was self-disciplined with a strong sense of duty. It was symbolic of his faith that he took off his crown before receiving communion at his coronation, and it was his practice to receive Holy Communion twelve times a year. As a devout Christian, he consistently opposed the vicious fashions of his age. Soon after his accession a royal proclamation appeared 'for the encouragement of piety and virtue'. The King had a long disagreement with his son and heir over the prince's sexual promiscuity, gambling and irresponsible behaviour. But these were troubled times as the American colonies battled for independence from British rule, and new radical ideas were in the air. The ideas associated with Romanticism produced a new restlessness and a desire for individual freedom.

The Evangelical Revival

The discerning historian understands the profound influence of the evangelical revival associated with the preaching of George Whitefield and John Wesley on the social, moral and religious condition of the country. The reawakening of Evangelical Christianity in England in the second half of the eighteenth century was an event that was to have national and international repercussions. According to Ryle, 'the men who wrought deliverance for us, a hundred years ago, were a few individuals, most of them clergymen of the Established Church, whose heart God touched about the same time in various parts of the country. They were not wealthy or highly connected. They had neither money to buy adherents, nor family influence to command attention and respect. They were not put forward by any Church, party, society, or institution. They were simply men whom God stirred up and brought out to do his work, without previous concert, scheme or plan... The movement of these gallant evangelists shook England from one end to the other.' They always taught the inseparable connection between true faith and personal holiness. A true Christian must always be known by his fruits, and these fruits must be plainly manifest and unmistakable in all the relations of life. 'They never shrunk from declaring, in plainest terms, the certainty of God's judgement and of wrath to come, if men persisted in impenitence and unbelief; and yet they never ceased to magnify the riches of God's kindness and compassion, and to entreat all sinners to repent and turn to God before it was too late... These were the doctrines by which they turned England upside down, made ploughmen and colliers weep till their faces were seamed with tears, arrested the attention of peers and philosophers, stormed the strongholds of Satan, plucked thousands like brands from the burning, and altered the character of the age.'[11]

George Whitefield was an extremely gifted and popular preacher. His powerful and eloquent presentation of the full gospel of Christ, however, caused offence to the establishment and church leaders soon openly denounced him. Unperturbed, he turned to preaching in the open air. In this way he reached thousands who would never dream of attending a place of worship. Ryle comments: 'The plain truth is, that the Church of England of that day was not ready for a man like Whitefield. The Church was too much asleep to understand him, and was vexed at a man who would not keep still and let the devil alone.' From 1739 to his death in 1770, Whitefield preached the gospel in virtually every town and city up and down England, Scotland and Wales. 'When churches were opened to him he gladly preached in churches, when only chapels could be obtained, he cheerfully preached in chapels. When churches and chapels alike were closed, or were too small to contain his hearers, he was ready and willing to preach in the open air. For thirty-one years he laboured in this way, always proclaiming the same glorious gospel, and always, as far as man's eye can judge, with immense effect.'[12] Ryle describes the effectiveness of Whitefield's ministry: 'He was the first to see that Christ's ministers must do the work of fishermen. They must not wait for souls to come to them, but must go after souls, and compel them to come in. He did not sit tamely by his fireside, like a cat on a rainy day, mourning over the wickedness of the land. He went forth to beard the devil in his high places. He attacked sin and wickedness face to face, and gave them no peace. He dived into holes and corners after sinners. He hunted out ignorance and vice wherever they could be found.'[13]

The ministry of John Wesley the preacher and Charles Wesley the hymn writer also had a massive impact on the spiritual and moral awakening of England. According to Wesley Bready the conversion of John Wesley, the one-time don of Oxford whose heart was 'strangely warmed' by God, was to produce 'a succession of results destined finally to change the whole trend of social history throughout the British Empire and the English-speaking world. Nor was the impact of this prophet, who claimed "the world for his parish", confined even within those spacious limits. Millions, of many colours, climes and tongues, inhabiting the four corners of the earth, have lived richer, happier, nobler and more serviceable lives because, in 1738, fire from off the altars of God purged and illumined the soul of a downcast and disillusioned English priest.'[14]

Professor Elie Halevy, the great French historian, in his volumes on the *History of the English People*, discovers in this spiritual awakening the only consistent explanation for the highest social and moral achievements of modern England. 'In the vast work of social organisation which is one of the dominant characteristics of nineteenth-century England, it would be difficult to overestimate the part played by the Wesleyan revival.'[15] Professor Thorold Rogers boldly asserts that he does 'not believe the mass of peasants could have been moved at all, had it not been for the spiritual and educational stimulus which they received from Methodist organisations.'[16] In a *Short History of the English People*, JR Green claims that the revival changed, after a time, the whole tone of English society. 'The Church was restored to new life and activity. Religion carried to the hearts of the people a fresh spirit of moral zeal, while it purified our literature and our manners. A new philanthropy reformed our prisons, infused clemency and wisdom into our penal laws, abolished the slave-trade, and gave the first impulse to popular education.'[17] The rationalist historian, WEH Lecky, states that the evangelicals gradually changed the whole spirit of the English Church. 'They infused into it a new fire and passion of devotion, kindled a spirit of fervent philanthropy, raised the standard of clerical duty, and completely altered the whole tone and tendency of the preaching ministers.'[18]

The revival reaffirmed and restated apostolic Christianity. The starting point of the preaching of both Whitefield and Wesley was a deep conviction that sin is a serious matter. Whitefield was an exceptionally gifted preacher with a powerful voice and the ability to hold the attention of a crowd. He was also an accomplished storyteller who preached extempore in an age when most preachers read their sermons. The large crowds who came to hear him preach in the open air trembled when he reminded them of God's wrath against sin, and wept when told of the Saviour's self-sacrifice on the Cross. At the heart of his gospel message was the need for repentance and a new birth through faith in Christ. His life was dedicated to the preaching of the gospel and he preached about a thousand times a year for nearly thirty years.[19]

The message that lay behind the great evangelical revival was the emphasis on both sin and righteousness. Both Whitefield and Wesley believed that sin was horrible in itself, and that it placed men under the condemnation of God. According to John Simon in *The Revival of Religion in England* the evangelists felt that nothing was done by their preaching so long as the conscience was unreached and the heart unmoved. 'So they set up the rigorous standard of the law in the midst of the people; they made them see the great white throne and Him who sat upon it; they spoke of hell as men who had been down to the iron gates and had gazed upon the horrors of death eternal.' John Wesley showed his audience 'that sin was an offence against God who was not only a Judge, but a Father whose infinite love for the world had been manifested by the gift of His Son... The one essential thing was that sin should be seen and bemoaned and hated, that it should drive a man to the cross of Christ and make him miserable until he realized the unspeakable joy of abundant pardon... As the conviction in respect of sin drives a man to the Saviour from sin, so the conviction in respect of righteousness impels him to enter on the quest after holiness; it fills him with a consuming desire to be as Christ was in this world.'[20]

John Wesley insisted on the necessity of new birth and taught that a faith that was not followed by a changed life was a delusion. Beginning from this point he continually preached the need for holiness. In his pamphlet *Advice to the People called Methodists* (1745), Wesley pointed out that they were to be distinguished as 'new people' by the strictness and purity of their life. Methodists were advised to abstain from worldly pleasures and to live pure lives. Dress was an expression of the inward man and Wesley taught his followers to always dress plainly. He believed that bright, gorgeous, gaudy attire bred vanity and tended to create and inflame lust. Wesley placed a strong emphasis on the moral significance of dress and wanted every man, woman and child to dress in clothes that were comfortable, neat, modest, and clean.[21] Wesley insisted on chastity among the single and on faithfulness to marriage vows. In his meetings men and women always worshipped separately. He gave to working men and women a new vision of what life could be and encouraged them in daily Bible reading.[22]

Charles Wesley wrote hymns full of Christian doctrine that were popular among the working people of the day. These hymns would change English worship as men and women in the thousands sang them in the market squares and on the hillsides and in the Methodist preaching houses. According to David Edwards in *Christian England*, John Wesley's marvellous organising ability taught the people to love singing hymns, and the 'multitudes, up and down the land, including many who once had been drunkards, prostitutes, wife-beaters, bruisers, gamblers, smugglers, sluggards and thieves, as they joined in the refrain: "My chains fell off, my heart was free, I rose, went forth, and followed Thee," were singing from the depths of a miraculous personal experience... And it was expressed in music at once lyrical, dignified, soulful and sweet. The Evangelical Movement gave the whole English-speaking world its richest heritage of sacred song.'[23]

One of the most outstanding results of the revival in evangelical Christianity was its effect on the Church of England. Gradually, despite an initial distrust, the doctrine and teaching of the Methodists gained ground in the Church of England as devout men recognised that a new and living piety was being kindled among the people. Moreover, nothing in the doctrinal teaching of the evangelists was in conflict with the doctrines of the Thirty-nine Articles of the established Church.[24] The tone of the Church's message on sexual conduct can be gleaned from a sermon by Edward Cobden, Archdeacon of London, delivered at St James's Palace in the presence of King George II. The Archdeacon used the attempted seduction of Joseph by Potiphar's wife to draw attention to the awfulness of sexual immorality. He based his sermon around Joseph's response, 'How then can I do this great wickedness, and sin against God?' (Genesis 39:9). The Archdeacon spoke of the heinous guilt and destructive consequences of adultery. Single people were apt to imagine that all obligations of chastity are confined to the marriage vow. But 'the crime of impurity is of a deeper dye, as it is attended with consequences more fatal and extensive: it is a breach of the strongest voluntary compact, as well as a transgression of that law of chastity which nature has engraven upon the hearts of all mankind...'

The Archdeacon continued that those who have received the pure and perfect law of the Gospel are clearly instructed to avoid impurity of every kind. 'We are raised to that original standard of chastity appointed by God in Paradise, and taught to restrain our passions of this sort within the pure and undefiled limits of conjugal affection. If we consider fornication with the unprejudiced eye of reason, before the passions have corrupted the judgement, I am persuaded there are few sins which people condemn more in their own breast; which they commit at first with more reluctance and recoilings of conscience; and which, upon cool reflection, fills them with more horror and keener censures of their own conduct. And would a man give himself leave to reflect upon the irreparable injury done to the unhappy female partner in the iniquity, it would open such a scene of misery to his view, as would be sufficient to check the most inflamed appetite of the most abandoned libertine.' The Archdeacon concluded that 'universal chastity, both in thought, word and deed is our undoubted duty; and to guard against all filthiness both of flesh and spirit, should be our continual care. It highly imports us therefore to fly all opportunities and temptations to immodesty.'[25] (Can you imagine what the Archdeacon would say about the literature of the sex education movement?)

George Whitefield and John Wesley were equally uncompromising in preaching the virtue of sexual purity, and by the beginning of the nineteenth century there was a clear consensus within English society that supported the Christian sexual ethic. Stated at its most simple, Christians believed in the virtues of modesty, chivalry, chastity and fidelity. This is not to say that all people lived to this standard, for many did not, but all agreed that it was the standard by which they ought to live. Modesty was accepted as the foundation for sexual purity, especially among women. 'Towards the end of the reign of George III (1820) women's dress had become more modest, with a higher neckline and fuller skirts with a greater number of petticoats. A new feeling of gentility and decorum was in the air...'[26] Victorian women dressed with propriety, taking care not to reveal more flesh than was considered decent. Most dresses were full length; shoulders were covered with a high neckline. It was unthinkable for a woman to dress in a manner that was sexually provocative, and every woman would be very careful not to behave in a way that put her reputation for sexual purity under the slightest doubt.

The moral foundations of Victorian England were firmly set in place during the spiritual awakening of the Church that resulted from the preaching of the great evangelists. Reviewing the characteristic of evangelical religion as he encountered it in the latter part of the nineteenth century, George Russell wrote in *Household of Faith*: 'I recall an abiding sense of religious responsibility, a self-sacrificing energy in works of mercy, an evangelistic zeal, an aloofness from the world, and a level of saintliness in daily life such as I do not expect again to see realised on earth. Everything down to the minutest details of action and speech were considered with reference to eternity... Money was regarded as a sacred trust, and people of good positions and comfortable incomes habitually kept their expenditure within narrow limits that they might contribute more largely to objects which they held sacred. The Evangelicals were the most religious people whom I have ever known.'[27]

A central aspect of the evangelicals was their belief in the all-sufficiency of the scriptures. This led to a passionate desire to read and understand the Bible, and to apply its teachings to their daily lives. According to Wesley Bready, 'Wherever the revival spread, its first avowed aim was to dispel religious illiteracy, and in so doing it became a mighty and ennobling educational force. To the individual convert, his much-underlined personal Bible was his handbook of moral and spiritual guidance; to the Evangelical household, the Family Bible was not only the sacred register of births, baptisms, marriages and deaths, it also was the medium of family worship wherein parents and children were daily lifted together to the Throne of Grace: to all Evangelical society, the Bible was both chart and compass in the voyage of life. Nor is it any accident that out of this movement sprang the British and Foreign Bible Society which, to date, has circulated the scriptures in hundreds of millions of copies in every quarter of the globe, while also it has translated them, in whole or in part, into over seven hundred different languages and tongues.'[28]

In *Wesley the Preacher*, John Pollock writes that Wesley, as he lay on his deathbed, could reflect 'that thousands upon thousands had heard from his lips or his pen about Christ, and many had responded. All over the country and overseas his Methodist societies were strengthening Christians in their daily lives. On an even wider scale, he had helped humble believers toward holiness, and he had set in motion a profound change in the moral climate of England, although this would not be obvious for another century.'[29] After John Wesley's death in 1791, *Gentleman's Magazine* paid the following tribute: 'By the humane endeavours of him and his brother Charles a sense of decency in morals and religion was introduced into the lowest classes of mankind... He was one of the few characters who outlived enmity and prejudice, and received in his later years every mark of esteem from every denomination... His personal influence was greater than any private gentleman in the country... Instead of being an ornament to literature he was a blessing to his fellows; instead of the genius of his age, he was the servant of God.'[30]

Victorian morality

At the beginning of the nineteenth century Methodism was a growing moral force especially among the lower classes. Its members were subject to strict moral discipline that was rescuing them from the irresponsibility and immorality of the traditional plebeian way of life.[31] In *Early Victorian Britain*, JFC Harrison made the point that the revival inspired by the preaching of Wesley 'was a primary factor in changing national attitudes and character, although the change was not widely evident for two or more generations. Victorian values (in the true sense of the word) are really Wesley's values, which are Christian values. Wesley saw what Britain needed: a strong Christian message and morality. He had the courage to endure hostility and unpopularity for what he believed to be right.'[32] The Victorian Church, greatly influenced by the evangelical movement, was marked by energy and strength, and had an effect on the community that extended well beyond the church doors. Of great significance was the new concept of a church which exerted a social effect on the whole community.[33]

Harrison concludes that Methodism had a major impact at the popular level in the early Victorian era. 'It is not an accident that almost every self-educated man in early and mid-Victorian England who came to write his memoirs, paid tribute to the beneficial influences of Methodism in his youth. The accounts of self-educated men show a pattern of Methodist domestic piety, help in a local Sunday school, conversion, membership of a Methodist class, preaching, and then (usually) a progression beyond the original Methodism to some new intellectual position... The impact which Methodism made upon working men was complex. In so far as it inculcated the goals of respectability and hard work it reinforced the puritan values of the middle classes.'[34] The early Victorian period was characterised by a strong growth in authentic Christianity. This did not mean that everyone went to church, although a majority of the population did, but that Protestant evangelicalism was a basic ingredient in the dominant ideology. Men's values and standards, their assumptions and attitudes, functioned within this context.[35]

The *Cambridge Social History of Britain* describes how evangelical Christianity has left its mark not only in Britain but throughout the Protestant world. In the Anglican Church the early evangelicals were not much concerned with ritual and sacraments or with church government, for they believed that no one should be allowed to intervene between God and man. 'Doctrines mattered more – the Bible as the Word of God, original sin, salvation by faith, the atoning sacrifice of Christ, God's forgiveness – even if they were neither new nor theologically sophisticated. But it was experience, and above all the experience of conversion – the "big change" – that was at the heart of evangelicalism: evangelicals were born-again Christians. They were also intensely moralistic. [Here we see the reason why the Victorians are so much despised by modern day sex educators.] Describing themselves as "serious" they saw life as a perpetual battle between right and wrong, in which every action, no matter how small, was to be subjected to moral scrutiny. The result was a religion not only of prayer and Bible reading but of active good works – not because good works were of the slightest help to anyone seeking salvation, but because God required them, because they might be taken as evidence of divine favour, and because they might help bring others to God. Evangelicals consequently were tireless do-gooders, organising and campaigning for a bewildering array of moral, philanthropic and missionary causes. The aims of the evangelicals could hardly have been more ambitious: to convert Britain, to roll back the Catholic Church and ultimately to carry their version of Christianity to every nation on earth.... The evangelicals' call for self-discipline, hard work and moral rectitude; their obsession with the use of time, their fetish of early rising and their strict accountability to God for every waking moment; their condemnation of idleness and frivolity: all these found a positive response in the middle-classes...'[36]

The evangelicals introduced to Britain a 'new moral economy' of sobriety, self-control, sexual restraint and respectability, which challenged both the hedonism of the aristocracy and the levelling and violence of the French Revolution. In the 1790s, when evangelicals (dissenting as well as Anglican) launched the modern missionary movement, they expected nothing less than the rapid and imminent conversion of the entire world.[37] The Victorian age was self-consciously religious.

Britain's greatness, Victorians believed – its prosperity, social stability, political liberties, and Empire – was rooted in Christian (and Protestant) faith.[38]

In *Victorian People and Ideas* (1973), Richard Altick argues that 'Evangelicalism is chiefly important in the history of English culture for the moral tone it lent society down to the last quarter of the century. Some of its characteristic moral standards, tastes, and avoidances are current today, though with ever-diminishing strength, as vestiges of what is popularly called Victorianism. In many ways, our abandonment of moral restrictions in favour of extreme permissiveness is simply the final phase of the reaction against Evangelical concepts of morality and value that began about a century ago.'[39] [I argue that much of this abandonment of moral restrictions is promoted by modern day sex education.] The evangelical ethos was diffused through most of the nation, and brought a morality that could be summed up in the single word 'respectability'. 'Respectability was not subject to private definition; its attributes represented a consensus. They included sobriety, thrift, cleanliness of person and tidiness of home, good manners, respect for the law, honesty in business affairs, and, it need hardly be added, chastity.'[40] The practical outworking of the evangelicals' faith was to influence public morality. They believed that public morality depended upon private virtue. In their zeal to save the souls of the lost 'they sought to impose their standards of right living (of whose absolute authority, residing in divine inspiration, they had no doubt) upon society as a whole'.[41]

A feature of the evangelicals was a love of reading that did much to widen the reading public. According to Richard Altick, 'Theirs was a veritable religion of print, resting as it did upon the Bible as the inerrant word of God. Daily communication with the Bible was necessary for salvation, for without its inspiration one could not achieve the faith requisite for divine grace. The ability to read therefore was highly prized, and the Evangelicals nurtured it in their educational activities. The large market they formed for improving literature encouraged the development of the cheap production and distribution techniques that revolutionised the Victorian book trade.'[42] The evangelical witness had a profound influence on the prose of the day, which was replete with biblical language and stories. 'From earliest childhood, consequently, on all levels of society, both at home and at school, the Victorians were accustomed to biblical language and biblical stories to an extent almost inconceivable today.' Richard Altick describes the custom of the reading circle in which most members of the family, children and adults alike, joined to hear one of their number, usually the father, read aloud from a book or magazine. And this custom had an enormous impact upon the content of Victorian literature, for the reading matter needed to be wholesome and pure. 'The Evangelicals suffered from an often neurotic anxiety lest the impressionable mind be sullied by impure thoughts. It was requisite, therefore, that all reading matter their hands took up, and paramountly that which was to be read aloud in a group including women and children, be devoid of the faintest impropriety of language or thought.'[43] Here we must note the contrast between the Victorian love of pure literature and the explicitness of sex education literature.

Perhaps the leading novelist of the Victorian period was Charles Dickens, a man in touch with the moral and social mores of his time. This was particularly true in his handling of sexual matters. In the opinion of a critic writing in *The Spectator* in 1857: 'In England nowadays novels are written for families; in France, they are written for men.'[44] Dickens never wrote anything that caused people to blush. He was eminently pure-minded and the purity of his novels reflected the moral climate of his time. After analysing the main features of Dickens' imagination, the French critic of English literature and observer of English life, Hippolyte Taine, commented: 'The counsels of this public taste are somewhat like this... Be moral. All your novels must be such as may be read by young girls... We believe in family life, and we would not have literature taint the passions which would attack family life.'[45]

The celebrated historian of the Victorian period, Gertrude Himmelfarb, recognises the powerful influence of evangelical Christianity on family values that were so much a part of Victorian England. She writes that 'it was these religious movements and the "moral reformation" inspired by them, as much as industrialism or capitalism, that made the home a haven not only from the pressures of the marketplace but from the temptation of sin and corruption.'[46] According to Himmelfarb 'the home was both a place of worship and an object of worship. The custom, among the middle classes especially, of assembling the family (including the servants) for prayers and Bible-reading was intended as much for purposes of moral edification as for religious observance.'[47] And the moral reformation was embraced equally by the working class family which was the repository of the conventional Victorian values; respectability, hard work, self-help, obedience, cleanliness, orderliness. These values were shared by the parents and consciously inculcated in the children.[48] Children were expected to have 'a clear idea of morality, or to behave on command in a moral way, without necessarily understanding the reason for their actions'.[49] Hippolyte Taine was impressed by the domesticity and sexual propriety of the English. He wrote that in England marriage was regarded with such profound respect that even in private conversation among men, adultery was regarded as a crime.[50]

In her book *A woman's place; An Oral History of Working Class Women, 1890 –1940*, Elizabeth Roberts explains that in Lancashire towns, premarital sex was condemned and great pains were taken to prevent it. A courting young couple would be accompanied by a younger brother or sister and were expected to return to the girl's home in the early evening.[51] The rigour of these rules was all the more remarkable – and perhaps all the more necessary – in view of the length of the courtships; they often went on for years, partly because the family was dependent upon the child's wages and partly because the young man could not afford to get married. There was no double standard; boys as much as girls were expected to 'behave themselves'. Among Catholics, 'keeping out of trouble' was taken more seriously than marrying out of the faith.[52]

In *Victorian Values*, James Walvin makes the point that 'female sexuality was assumed to take place within the confines of the family; but this had also been true for centuries. It was equally applicable to menfolk, though they, unlike their wives, had opportunities of sexual encounters outside marriage; the degree to which they took up these opportunities is unclear, and presumably varied enormously.' The concept of the 'fallen woman' was 'a fate imposed upon thousands of women by a society unwilling to tolerate, in public, free or "errant" sexual ways among women'.[53] Not surprisingly sex before marriage was unusual. Allowing for marked regional variations, illegitimacy rates were 6 per cent in the early nineteenth century, falling to 4-5 per cent late in the century.[54] It was widely accepted that sex outside marriage was wrong, and a virtuous woman would not put herself in a position in which she might sully her reputation. Consequently, the rate of illegitimate births was very low, and sexual purity was considered a noble virtue, especially for women.

It was in the middle classes that the Victorian religious boom had the biggest impact. A religious census of 1851 showed that half of the population attended church on the Sunday of the census. Over half of the children aged between five and fifteen attended or were enrolled with a Sunday school. And Sunday school was a significant factor in developing the social and moral ethos of Victorian society. Children were taught respect for authority, to obey their parents and the difference between right and wrong. In *Life in Victorian England*, WJ Reader comments that what gave certainty and drive to the Victorians' manifold activities was the backing of rigid notions about the right ordering of society and individual behaviour. While later generations have pointed out the repressive effect of some of these notions, what is often overlooked is that the weight of the Victorian conscience was not universally repressive. Although a few talented people found Victorian morality oppressive, 'the fact that unquestionable standards of right and wrong were generally held to exist, backed by the force of established authority, was an immense support to many people...'[55]

In the year 1859 a religious revival began in the United Kingdom, affecting every county in Ulster, Scotland, Wales and England, adding over a million new converts to the evangelical churches. The revival was associated with a great social uplift, and gave an effective impulse to home and foreign missionary activity.[56] Edwin Orr, writing in *The Second Evangelical Awakening in Britain*, concludes 'that the fifty years following 1859 constituted a distinct and definite period of the expansion of the Christian Church, in fact, a Second Evangelical Awakening comparable to its noted predecessor'.[57] While the preaching of Wesley and Whitefield moved a vast number of human beings, the second evangelical awakening moved an even greater number. 'Evangelistically, the Awakening of 1859 revived the older agencies raised up by the Evangelical Revival of the previous century. It also created new organisations of a permanent character, and increased the efforts of all Christians to fulfil the Great Commission to preach the gospel to every creature, at home and abroad... Socially, the awakening gave birth to a litter of active religious and philanthropic societies, which accomplished much in human uplift, the welfare of children, the reclamation of prostituted women, of alcoholics, of criminals, and the development of social virtues.'[58]

Victorian modesty

Starting in the last decades of the eighteenth century a plethora of books were written with the purpose of encouraging men and women to behave properly. Good manners and correct conduct were considered to be the essence of a good society. Most of these conduct books taught a way of behaviour that was consistent with Christian principles, with a large emphasis on the importance of modesty as a virtue among women. For example, *The Revolutions of Modesty* (1794) proclaimed: 'The genuine patroness of the fair sex is modesty. Under her banner they receive their first discipline, and according as more or less influenced by its dictates, either rise or sink in estimation. Therefore tender mothers, and pious governantes, make the word modesty the alarm-drum to young female hearts.'[59]

The Habits of Good Society informs its readers that the demeanour of man to woman should approach reverence. 'It should be the boast of every man that he had never put modesty to the blush, nor encouraged immodesty to remove her mask.'[60] And happy is the young lady who in all cases 'considers modesty the prettiest ornament she can wear'.[61] The book frowns at the fast young lady: 'An avowed flirt, she does not scruple to talk to her consorts, real or imaginary… By degrees, the assumption of assurance which has had its source in bad taste, becomes real; a hard blasé look; a free tongue; and above all, the latitude of manners shown to her by the other sex, and allowed by her, show that the inward characteristics have followed the outward, and that she is become insensible to all that she has lost of feminine charm and gained in effrontery. For the instant a woman loses the true feminine type she parts with half her influence. The "fast girl" is flattered, admired openly, but secretly condemned. Many a plain woman has gained and kept a heart by being merely womanly and gentle.'[62]

The Manners of Polite Society explains that 'women are happily endowed with a sense of propriety and a natural modesty which will generally guide them aright in their intercourse with the other sex, and the more perfectly well-bred and discreet you are in your intercourse with female friends, the easier it will be for you to acquit yourself well with your male ones'.[63] It follows that 'love in the heart of a woman should partake largely of the nature of gratitude; she should love, because she is already loved by one deserving her regard; and, if she never allowed herself to think of gentlemen in the light of lovers or husbands until asked to do so, she would escape much suffering'.[64] And there is advice for the way a gentleman should treat a lady. 'Towards ladies the most punctilious observance of politeness is due from a gentleman. Walking with them, one should, of course, assume the relative position best adapted to protect them from inconvenience or danger.'[65] When a woman alights from a cab or carriage, a gentleman should at once advance and hold the door open and offer his hand. In fact a gentleman should do all he can to be polite and protective toward women. He should never be forward or brash, and should never embarrass a lady by greeting her first. And when a gentleman loves a woman he treats her with the greatest care, and 'he would guard her person, her feelings, her reputation, everything precious to her. Let him not then, by the imprudence and frivolity of his conduct, expose her to the sneers and ridicule of vulgar and malicious persons.'[66]

The Victorian brochure *A Hint from Modesty* (1855) praises the domestic nature of English women as 'modest with a perfect untaught modesty'. But the author is concerned about a tendency of some to dress in a way that is careless of decent appearance. If only those who dressed immoderately knew that beauty guessed at was more engaging than beauty fully displayed. The woman who displays herself is likely to attract a man of fashion, an unworthy man 'with no thought beyond the gratification of self. She believes his protestations of love and is unaware of his character defects. In the long run she realises he is unworthy of her love, and she is miserable for life. The man of real worth, however, is suspicious of her indiscretion, and it takes him a long time to be convinced that innocence and indiscretion could travel together.' And so to the real question: 'What then gains she by the display? But she is of fine figure. Is that to be published to the world—which is rather jealous than admiring, and is more likely to hate than praise—or to be kept for home, where the love of one is worth more, far more, than all the admiration of the world?'[67]

In the *Young Lady's Friend* (1854) young women are warned against the moral danger of a low neckline. 'No woman can strip her arms to the shoulders and show her back and bosom without injuring her mind, and losing some of her refinement; if such would consult their brothers, they would tell them how men regard it.'[68] The novelist Charlotte Mary Yonge expresses the view in *Womankind* (1876) that 'exposure is always wrong; whatever be the fashion, it is the Christian woman's duty to perceive when indecency comes in and to protest against it by her own example'.[69]

In *Fictions of Modesty*, Ruth Yeazell explains that 'people living in England in the eighteenth and nineteenth centuries seldom discoursed on women's behaviour without elaborate attention to modesty. Much thinking about modesty centred on questions of middle-class marriage; and novels of the period take their most typical form as narratives of courtship… In its most general sense, modesty is a tempering of behavior that allows individuals to meet and come to terms with one another, whether for marriage or other purposes; and in this sense what we think of as a virtue can perhaps only be understood as a story. By adopting the modest woman as a subject for narrative, the novelists were able to represent modesty not as a set of rules but as a series of changing responses—not as a fixed condition but as a passage of time.'[70] She shows that modesty triumphs everywhere in classic English fiction, and offers the testimony of Anthony Trollope, who confidently assures the readers of his autobiography that the great English novelists have always taught modesty—he names Jane Austen, Maria Edgeworth, Scott, Thackeray, Dickens, and George Eliot. Trollope himself writes: 'I do believe that no girl has risen from the reading of my pages less modest than she was before, and that some may have learned from them that modesty is a charm well worth preserving.'[71] In his auto-biography Anthony Trollope underlines the moral tone of the British novel with the following claim: 'Can anyone by searching through the works of the six great English novelists I have named, find a scene, a passage, or a word that would teach a girl to be immodest, or a man to be dishonest? When men in their pages have been described as dishonest and women as immodest, have they not ever been punished?'[72] Trollope concludes, 'If the novelist, therefore, can so handle this subject [love] as to do good by his handling, as to teach wholesome lessons in regard to love, the good which he does will be very wide.'[73]

Marriage and the family

In his book *Untying the Knot*, Roderick Phillips describes how in seventeenth century England the family was seen as the basic unit of society, and order within the family was believed to be essential for social and political order. A vast literature emphasised the importance of marital and family stability for society and polity. Phillips goes on, 'Fundamental to these considerations was religion, for marriage was ordained by God, so that any behaviour that ran counter to harmony in marriage or the family not only threatened social stability but was also contrary to divine commandments.'[74] Consequently, conflict within marriage and marriage break-down was viewed with the greatest apprehension.[75] The English believed that marriage was indissoluble; there was no divorce with the right to remarry (except by a private Act of Parliament, of which there were on average about two per year) until 1858.

During the mid-Victorian period there was a great debate on divorce reform. Many in the House of Lords made the point that in the country at large marriage was held to be a sacred lifelong union. Most people took seriously the marriage vows they made in the presence of God as binding for life. The ideas conveyed in the old familiar words 'For better for worse, for richer for poorer... until death us do part' were part of the common conscience of the community. Lord Redesdale explained that the reason the marriage law was held more sacred in England than in any other country was because divorce had been withheld from the people at large.[76] The Bishop of Oxford (Samuel Wilberforce) maintained that there was a feeling among the people of England that marriage with any other person was impossible.[77] Speaking in the 1920s the Archbishop of York, Cosmo Lang, said that the words of the marriage service emphasised a notion of marriage that was not primarily a mutual arrangement for happiness, but an obligation of lifelong and faithful service.[78] The belief that marriage was for life was widely accepted as the basis of a good society, and divorce was an alien concept to ordinary Englishmen and women.

In my study of marriage and divorce, *The Great Divorce Controversy*, I conclude that one of the great triumphs of the Christian faith was its stabilising influence on English family life following the Reformation. 'Over the centuries the Church of England developed a marriage discipline that brought enormous blessing to the nation. Society was transformed as everyone – believers and unbelievers alike – accepted the biblical truth that marriage was a permanent union, only broken by death. The marriage service, based on the words of Christ, became a part of English culture and a clear witness to the lifelong nature of the marriage bond.'[79]

A characteristic of Victorian England was the consensus that moral standards were derived from the Bible. Consequently, there was a clear distinction between right and wrong conduct. It was right that women should be modest and chaste, and it was wrong, even shameful, for single girls to be sexually active. Everybody in society, with the exception of the 'new women' who openly challenged the sexual mores of their time, believed that sex outside marriage was wrong. For an unmarried man and woman to openly live together was unthinkable and condemned in no uncertain terms as 'living in sin'.

The historian Gertrude Himmelfarb decided that eminent Victorians were not only eminently human, with human failings and frailties, but also eminently moral. They did not take sin lightly, and they affirmed the principles of morality even if they did not always act in accordance with those principles.[80] David Edwards, in his three volumes on *Christian England*, concludes that Victorian England for all its faults 'was an age full of courage and creativity, one of the peaks of Christian civilisation; only people not fit to be compared with the Victorians will sneer at them'.[81] In the *Oxford History of England: England 1870–1914*, Sir Robert Ensor reaches the conclusion: 'No one will ever understand Victorian England who does not appreciate that among highly civilised, in contradistinction to more primitive countries, it was one of the most religious that the world has known. Moreover its particular type of Christianity laid a peculiarly direct emphasis upon conduct; for, though it recognised both grace and faith as essential to salvation, it was in practice also very largely a doctrine of salvation by works. This type, which had come to dominate churchmen and Nonconformists alike, may be called, using the term in its broad sense, evangelicalism.'[82]

This brief analysis of Victorian England demonstrates the powerful influence that the Christian gospel had on the moral framework of the nation. Of course not everybody accepted the teaching of the Christian faith, and many were nominal Christians, but there was a powerful witness within society to the moral standards taught in the Bible, and most in society felt that they ought to live by those standards. Moreover, the witness of Christian England, its commitment to marriage and the family, and its code of sexual conduct had an impact that extended well beyond its shores. Many other nations, especially English speaking nations, were influenced by the moral decency that was central to English society, by the moral purity that was a feature of English literature, by the English marriage service that witnessed to the indissolubility of the marriage union, and by the stability of the English family. Without question the Christian faith, the dominant factor influencing the moral standards of Victorian England, brought great blessing to the most powerful nation on earth.

And here we should pause for a moment to take in the massive gulf in moral outlook between Victorian Christians and modern day sex educators. Can you imagine the reaction of the Victorians to the sex education literature that we examined in the previous chapter? They would undoubtedly have been deeply shocked, condemning it as indecent, lewd and obscene. And can you imagine the reaction of the sex educators to the Victorians' view of morality? Here we have identified two implacable foes—the moral teachings of evangelical Christianity versus the amoral teachings of the sex education movement. Here is the battlefield for the hearts and minds of our children—this is what the sexual revolution is all about. The Bible makes it clear that men of depraved minds will oppose the truth (2 Timothy 3:8). We know that those who hate the light of biblical truth, which reveals moral decadence for what it is, will oppose the gospel of Christ. And so it was inevitable that there would be opposition to the Christian witness of the Victorians, and this is the story of the next chapter.

Endnotes

1 Evangelical Revival in England, *Glimpses*, Christian History Institute website, prepared by Ken Curtis et al.
2 J Wesley Bready, *England: Before and After Wesley*, Hodder and Stoughton, London, 1939, p14
3 Ibid. *England: Before and After Wesley*, cited from p19
4 Ibid. *England: Before and After Wesley*, p19
5 JC Ryle, *Christian Leaders of the 18th Century*, The Banner of Truth, 1885, reprinted 1997, p14
6 Ibid. *England: Before and After Wesley*, cited from p163
7 Ibid. p171
8 Jeffrey in *Essays*, cited from John S Simon, *The Revival of Religion in England in the Eighteenth Century*, Robert Culley, London, p80
9 John Simon, *The Revival of Religion in England in the Eighteenth Century*, Robert Culley, London, p81
10 Ibid. p126
11 Ibid. JC Ryle, *Christian Leaders of the 18th Century*, p28
12 Ibid. p40
13 Ibid. p48
14 Ibid. *England: Before and After Wesley*, p173
15 Elie Halevy, *History of the English People*, vol.1, p372, cited from Wesley Bready p179
16 *Six Centuries of Work and Wages* (1901 edition), p516, cited from Wesley Bready
17 JR Green, in *A Short History of the English People*, p736, cited from Wesley Bready
18 Ibid. *England: Before and After Wesley*, cited from p180
19 David L Edwards, *Christian England, From the 18th century to the First World War*, Collins, London, 1984, p50
20 Ibid. *The Revival of Religion in England in the Eighteenth Century*, pp293-297
21 Ibid. *England: Before and After Wesley*, pp259-60
22 Ibid. *Christian England, From the 18th century to the First World War*, pp65-66
23 Ibid. pp272-73
24 HDM Spence, *The Church of England. A history of the people*, vol. 4, Cassel and Company, London, 1898, p262
25 A sermon preached before the King, at St James's on the 11 December 1748, by Edward Cobden, Archdeacon of London. J. Lodge, MDCCXLIX.
26 Aileen Ribeiro, *Dress and Morality*, BT Batsford, London, 1986, p126
27 George Russell's *Household of Faith*, p232, cited from, *England: Before and After Wesley*, p295
28 Ibid. *England: before and after Wesley*, p296
29 John Pollock, *Wesley the Preacher*, Kingsway Publications, Eastbourne, 2000, p259

30 Cited from David L Edwards, *Christian England, From the 18th century to the First World War*, Collins, London, 1984, p50
31 Ibid. *Christian England, From the 18th century to the First World War*, p325
32 Ibid. *Wesley the Preacher*, p11
33 JFC Harrison, *Early Victorian Britain, 1832-51*, Fontana Press, London, 1988, p126
34 Ibid. pp128-29
35 Ibid. p133
36 *The Cambridge Social History of Britain 1750-1950*, edited FML Thompson, Cambridge University Press, 1990, pp321-22
37 Ibid. p326
38 Ibid. p328
39 Richard D Altick, *Victorian People and Ideas*, JM Dent & Sons, London, 1973, pp167-68
40 Ibid. p175
41 Ibid. p181
42 Ibid. p191
43 Ibid. p193
44 *Victorian Values*, 'Dickens and his readers', Philip Collins, edited by Gordon Marsden, Longman Group, 1990, p46
45 Ibid. pp48-49
46 Gertrude Himmelfarb, *The De-moralization of Society*, The Institute of Economic Affairs, 1995, p55
47 Ibid. p56
48 Ibid. p78
49 Elizabeth Roberts, *A woman's place; An Oral History of Working Class Women, 1890 – 1940*, Oxford, 1984, p12
50 Ibid. *The De-moralization of Society*, p71
51 Ibid. *A woman's place*, p73
52 Ibid. *The De-moralization of Society*, p79
53 James Walvin, *Victorian Values*, (A companion to the Granada Television series) Andre Deutsch, 1987, pp125-26.
54 Ibid. p126
55 WJ Reader, *Life in Victorian England*, BT Batsford, London, 1964, p6
56 J Edwin Orr, *The Second Evangelical Awakening in Britain*, Marshall, Morgan & Scott, London, 1953, p5
57 Ibid. p262
58 Ibid. p264
59 William Holbrooke, *The Revolutions of Modesty*, printed for M Cooper, at the Globe in Paternoster-Row, MDCCLVIL
60 *The Habits of Good Society: A handbook of etiquette for Ladies and Gentlemen*, James Hogg and Sons, London, p37
61 Ibid. p95
62 Ibid. p267
63 *The Manners of Polite Society or Etiquette for Ladies, Gentlemen and Families*, Ward, Lock, and Tyler, Warwick House, Paternoster Row, 1875, p245
64 Ibid. p249
65 Ibid. p4
66 Ibid. p 92
67 Fred Audax, *A Hint from Modesty to the Ladies of England on the Fashion of Low-Dressing*, FW Wheeler, 1855
68 E Farrar, *The Young Lady's Friend*, New York, 1854, pp 2-3
69 CM Yonge, *Womankind*, London, 1876, pp 110-11
70 Ruth Yeazell, *Fictions of Modesty*, The University of Chicago Press, London, 1991, preface p ix
71 Cited from Ruth Yeazell, *Fictions of Modesty*, The University of Chicago Press, London, 1991, preface p x
72 Anthony Trollope, *An illustrated Autobiography*, Allan Sutton, 1987, (first published 1883), pp159-60
73 Ibid. pp160-61

74 Roderick Phillips, *Untying the Knot*, Cambridge University Press, Cambridge, 1991, p28
75 Ibid. p29
76 Hansard. Lords debate, 3 July 1856, cc237-38
77 Ibid. 26 June 1856, cc1979-82
78 Ibid. 10 March 1920, cc362-76
79 Edward Williams, *The Great Divorce Controversy*, Belmont House Publishing, London, 2000, pp402-403
80 Ibid. *The De-moralization of Society*, p26
81 Ibid. *Christian England, From the 18th century to the First World War*, p9
82 RKA Ensor, *England 1870-1914*, in The Oxford History of England series, edited by Sir George Clark, Oxford University Press, first published 1936, reprinted 1968, p137

Chapter 4

The early sexual revolutionaries

The 19th century radicals and freethinkers;

Friedrich Nietzsche and Sigmund Freud

Victorian England was a deeply Christian nation. There was a belief within society that the Bible provided the moral standards by which people ought to live. But not everybody in society was willing to accept the Christian consensus—the radical freethinkers, the humanist philosophers, the utilitarians, the Neo-Malthusians, the Fabian socialists, the secularists and other liberals were all opposed to the Christian gospel. Although there was opposition throughout the nineteenth century, it gained ground in the 1880s and 1890s as the influence of the evangelicals started to wane. Among the most important groups were the freethinkers and 'new women' who were in favour of what they called 'free love' and sought sexual liberation from the repressive Victorian regime. They were in the vanguard of the sexual revolution that was to strike with such force in the second half of the twentieth century. Behind the 'free love' advocates were the radical thinkers, such as Friedrich Nietzsche and Sigmund Freud, who sought to provide an ideological justification for the revolution against Christian moral standards. In this chapter we identify some of the more important opponents of the Christian faith, and examine the ideas that formed the foundation for the sexual revolution.

Robert Owen (1771-1858) – father of British socialism

Robert Owen, generally accepted as the father of socialism in England, was among the first to openly attack marriage and the family. His rejection of the Christian faith while still a young man (he believed in a supreme being and in later life followed spiritualism) led to a rationalist philosophy for improving society, which perceived established religion as a singularly vicious opponent. The main point in Owen's philosophy was that man's character was formed by circumstances over which he had no control. It followed that education and social amelioration were the solution to man's problems. He disliked intensely the values of the 'old moral order' that he planned to destroy; his vision was of a new society with a new moral order.

Owen denounced the institution of marriage and the existence of private property. He believed that the human race needed to be liberated from a trinity of monstrous evils—private property, irrational religion and marriage.[1] Owen argued that the family was rooted in the values of the old immoral world and constituted a serious stumbling block to man's achievement. He saw the family as a cause of crime, tyranny and oppression, particularly of women. In his mind, the family was the cause of widespread misery.[2] It was the existence of the bourgeois family unit – the little commonwealth which looked only to its own interests and ignored those of its neighbours – which was the real barrier to social reform, rather than the power of the husband/father within the family.[3] He took part in public debates on marriage and divorce in which he argued that the individual and society were more important than the family, which he regarded as a divisive social unit. It is not difficult to see that the British socialist movement was founded on ideas that were hostile to marriage and the family.

Francis Place (1771-1854) and Thomas Malthus (1766-1834)

Francis Place was a political radical who started the birth control movement in England in the 1820s. His political friends included Jeremy Bentham, Richard Carlile, John Stuart Mill and Robert Dale Owen, the son of Robert Owen. He intensely disliked the growing influence of Christianity in the nation and was a committed secularist.[4] His apparent motive for promoting birth control was to help poor people limit the size of their families, although he had 15 children himself! His hatred of the aristocracy flowed from his belief that they deliberately oppressed working class people.

In 1803 Thomas Malthus, an English clergyman who later became a professor of modern history and political economy, wrote *An Essay on the Principle of Population*, in which he argued that the standard of living of the masses could not be improved because the power of population was infinitely greater than the power of the earth to produce subsistence for man. He added that moral restraint, late marriage and abstinence were factors that would limit population growth. It must be noted that Malthus would not have agreed with the views of those who later took the name Neo-Malthusian, advocating population control through the use of contraception.[5]

Francis Place eagerly accepted Malthus' reasoning on the need for population control, believing that the answer lay in contraception. In 1822 Place published *Illustrations and Proofs of the Principle of Population*, in which he was the first to advocate the case for birth control by contraception, and in 1823 he began a campaign to publicise his ideas about contraception. His aim was to explain to the common people that there were harmless and reliable methods of contraception that could be used to limit family size. He wrote and circulated anonymous leaflets, which became known as 'The Diabolical Handbills', that gave details of methods of contraception—the sponge as a vaginal tampon, though withdrawal was also mentioned.[6] He also wrote numerous letters and articles for newspapers promoting the idea of contraception. The periodical *Bulldog* accused Place of a 'most foul and devilish attempt at corrupting the youth of both sexes in this country: an attempt at making no less than catamites of the male portion of the youth, and of the females, prostitutes'. Place supported the idea of 'free love' and raised the question 'would it not be desirable that sexual intercourse should be free. I think it would.'[7] However, he kept his ideas on 'free love' to himself as he knew that the contraception campaign would be damaged by his radical views on sexual behaviour.

Richard Carlile (1790-1843) – author of the first sex manual

Richard Carlile was a freethinker, political radical, journalist and committed secularist. After reading Thomas Paine's *Rights of Man* he converted to radicalism and became a vigorous salesman of extreme radical literature. While in prison for blasphemous or seditious libel he was persuaded by Francis Place of the importance of the Malthusian overpopulation thesis and the need for contraception as the means of birth control. After his release Carlile became fully committed to the cause of birth control and its sexual ramifications. But like Place, he was critical of Malthus' prescription of sexual abstinence for the lower classes, and believed the answer to overpopulation lay in the public promotion of contraception. Carlile wrote and published an essay *What is Love?* in 1825, and a year later he published *Every Woman's Book*, the first popular sex manual which sold 10 thousand copies in the three years after publication. These two titles, in frank language, between them promoted both the pleasure of sex and three methods of preventing conception. The preferred method was a wet sponge with an attached thread inserted into the vagina; other methods were the sheath and withdrawal.[8] Carlile was adamant in his definition of love as no more and no less than sexual desire. To him, love was lust and lust was love, and that was all that there was to it.

In his essay, *The Rise of the Sex Manual*, Michael Bush makes the point that Carlile promoted a philosophy of love which saw sexual satisfaction as the basic source of health, beauty and happiness. 'Abstinence therefore had to be condemned, not commended; and, having the same sexual needs, men and women ought to stand as sexual equals. Given its importance, sexual intercourse should be accepted for what it was: not simply a means of reproduction but a self-fulfilling pleasure. Rather than repudiated as a vice, it ought to become the foundation of morality – not of immorality – and rather than be kept as the exclusive privilege of the married, it needed to be made the right of all who attained adulthood.'[9] Carlile aimed to create a new attitude to contraception as a means of freeing the pleasure of sex from the problem of unwanted pregnancies. He also challenged the sexual mores that were widely accepted by society, advocating a two-year trial marriage employing contraception before entering any binding commitment.

George Drysdale (1825-1904) – advocate of 'free love'

George Drysdale was a Scottish doctor and naturalist committed to the Neo-Malthusian cause. Following in the tradition of Richard Carlile he wrote *The Elements of Social Science* (1855) in which he describes his philosophy of sexual liberation. Despite its length (it was over 400 pages long) it sold over 90 thousand copies. Drysdale was a keen advocate of 'free love', believing that men and women had an obligation to exercise their sexual organs in order to prevent harming themselves by unreasonably repressing their animal passions. He regarded sexual fulfilment as more important than marriage, and saw sexual intercourse as a virtue even when unconnected with reproduction, claiming that it was as important as food for the well-being of mankind.[10] He believed that if a man and woman had a passion for each other they should be allowed to indulge it without binding themselves together for life. Sexual liberty meant that temporary sexual relationships were acceptable. According to Michael Bush, 'Drysdale went much further than Carlile, in rejecting monogamy and in encouraging juveniles to practise sexual intercourse, but he too was very much a moralist, his sexual philosophy springing from a deep hostility to masturbation and prostitution.'[11] As a consequence of Drysdale's work a Neo-Malthusian movement emerged which advocated contraception for the purpose of population control.

John Stuart Mill (1806-1873) – philosophy of utilitarianism

The liberal philosopher, John Stuart Mill, who had always been indifferent towards the Christian faith, developed a philosophy of utilitarianism, which asserted that the goal of ethics is to achieve the greatest happiness for the greatest number. From a young age Mill came under the influence of Francis Place and Richard Carlile, and so became involved with the birth control movement. As a 17-year-old, he was arrested for distributing Carlile's essay *What is Love?* and birth control handbills to unmarried young women.[12] He was found guilty in a trial before the Lord Mayor of London and sentenced to 14 days in prison. In his essay, *The Subjection of Women*, Mill discussed the legal servitude into which women are plunged upon getting married. Even those women who are well looked after by their husbands have sold their freedom in exchange for board and lodging. His view was that people who had failed in one attempt at happiness ought to be allowed a second try. Mill proposed that a marriage between equals is likely to be happier than one in which men hold all the power. He believed that women should demand greater freedom and equality in marriage.[13]

Mill converted the idea of liberty into a philosophically respectable doctrine in his book *On Liberty* (1859). He developed the idea of the free and sovereign individual, and was considered a radical because he advocated such measures as public ownership of natural resources, equality for women and birth control. While Mill was not a moral relativist, his ideas contributed to an atmosphere in which it became acceptable for people to do whatever pleased them, provided they did not harm others. His elevation of individual freedom led to an undermining of authority, and laid the foundation for the postmodernist belief that individuals are free to form their own value system.

The trial of Annie Besant (1847-1933) – birth control propagandist

Annie Besant is an icon of the sexual revolution because of her campaign to make contraception a public issue. In Victorian Britain the public discussion of contraception was considered to be indecent and against the mores of society. The idea of making contraception available to unmarried people was deeply shocking. But the radicals and freethinkers had different ideas. In *Annie Besant*, Anne Taylor explains that in England 'the impulse to disseminate [contraceptive] advice which the great majority of persons found offensive came from a philosophy which was concerned with achieving the greatest good for the greatest number—utilitarianism. It was as a disciple of its leader Jeremy Bentham that Francis Place distributed leaflets among the poor, in the 1820s, containing advice about limiting their families.'[14]

As a young woman Annie married a vicar of the Church of England, the Rev Frank Besant. Soon afterwards she started to have doubts about the deity of Christ—having studied the gospels she became convinced that Christ had denied his divinity. She saw herself as a heretic and, as a vicar's wife, in all honesty could not partake of Holy Communion. This led to problems in her marriage, and when she deserted her husband and two children, she was befriended by Charles Bradlaugh, a radical freethinker, avowed atheist and a prominent member of the Secular Society. She converted to socialism before herself becoming a committed member of the Secular Society. As a convinced atheist she made bitter attacks on Christianity.

In 1877 Annie Besant and Charles Bradlaugh set up the Freethought Publishing Company with the express purpose of publishing a book on contraception—*Fruits of Philosophy*. This book had been written by an American doctor, Charles Knowlton, who had been convicted of indecency when it was first published in the USA in 1832. When the book was published in England by Charles Watts, a fellow member of the Secular Society, he was charged with publishing obscene literature. Annie Besant strongly advised Watts that the publication should be legally defended. Despite advice from Besant and Bradlaugh that the book was defensible in court, Watts did not want to take the risk and pleaded guilty. This infuriated Besant, for she felt that the freedom of the press was at stake, and so she persuaded Bradlaugh to publish the book again and invite prosecution under the Obscene Publications Act.

Besant and Bradlaugh were duly charged with publishing material that was 'likely to deprave or corrupt those whose minds are open to immoral influences'. Their 'indecent, lewd, filthy, bawdy and obscene book' was likely to corrupt the morals of youth, and incite them and others to 'indecent, obscene, unnatural and immoral practices'. In a sensational trial, in which they conducted their own defence and sought as much publicity as possible, the prosecution asserted that those who 'published advice on contraception really intended that not only men but women should abandon chastity, to the utter ruin of society'.[15] Besant and Bradlaugh argued in court that 'we think it more moral to prevent conception of children than, after they are born, to murder them by want of food and clothing'. The jury found that the book in question was calculated to deprave public morals but at the same time exonerated the defendants from any corrupt motive in publishing it. The judge recorded a verdict of guilty, but the charges were later dismissed on a legal technicality. The trial generated enormous publicity for their campaign to make contraception a public issue. Within three months of the trial over 100 thousand copies of the Knowlton book were sold.

Friedrich Nietzsche (1844-1900) – the original immoralist

In the penultimate decade of the nineteenth century the German philosopher Friedrich Nietzsche developed a new way of thinking which was a direct assault on Christian morality. Much of his anti-Christian invective was directed at Victorian morality. Nietzsche produced his writings in the 1880s, as a relatively young man, and then suffered a mental and physical breakdown in 1889 at the age of 44 and disappeared from public life. He has subsequently emerged as one of the most influential, controversial and important figures in the history of modern philosophy. He believed that the basic ideas upon which Western civilisation was constructed were fundamentally flawed. The *Encyclopaedia Britannica* assesses Nietzsche's criticism of Christianity as follows: 'At bottom the charge is always the same: Christianity is born of weakness, failure and resentment and is the enemy of reason and honesty, of the body and of sex in particular, and of power, joy and freedom.'[16]

In his essay *The Madman*, Nietzsche announces the death of God, and invites the reader to listen for the noise of the gravediggers burying the decaying corpse of God. And having declared the death of God, Nietzsche asserts that man is liberated from the moral law of God and free to produce a moral framework that is to his liking. In *Ecce Homo* Nietzsche proudly proclaims himself as the first immoralist. He informs us that his truth is dreadful. 'I am the first *immoralist*: I am therewith the destroyer par excellence... At bottom my expression *immoralist* involves two denials. I deny first a type of man who has hitherto counted as the highest, the good, the benevolent, beneficent. I deny, secondly, a kind of morality which has come to be accepted and to dominate as morality in itself – *decadence* morality, in more palpable terms *Christian* morality.'[17] He continues the polemic, 'No one has yet felt *Christian* morality as *beneath* him... Have I been understood? – What defines me, what sets me apart from all the rest of mankind, is that I have *unmasked* Christian morality...'[18] In Nietzsche's view Christian morality is a malicious lie that is damaging mankind.[19]

In his essay, *Why I write such excellent books*, Nietzsche states that the 'preaching of chastity is a public incitement to anti-nature. Every expression of contempt for the sexual life, every befouling of it through the concept "impure", is the crime against life – is the intrinsic sin against the holy spirit of life.'[20] He explains the significance of his attack on Christian morality: 'The *unmasking* of Christian morality is an event without equal, a real catastrophe... He who unmasks morality has therewith unmasked the valuelessness of all values which are or have been believed in… The concept 'God' invented as the antithetical concept to life – everything harmful, noxious, slanderous, the whole mortal enmity against life brought into one terrible unity!'[21]

The influence of Nietzsche

Friedrich Nietzsche belongs among those very few thinkers – Karl Marx, Charles Darwin and Sigmund Freud are the others – whose ideas have had a massive influence on the life of modern Europe. (Freud knew and admired some of Nietzsche's psychological views.) Nietzsche is especially important because he is the father of existentialism, a system of thought which has formed the ideological basis for the moral philosophy of postmodernism. His writings came at a time when a number of radicals and intellectuals were looking for a philosophical basis for their challenge to Christian morality—Nietzsche was their philosopher.

In *The De-moralization of Society*, Gertrude Himmelfarb argues that in the twentieth century virtues ceased to be virtues and became, instead, values. She makes the point that Nietzsche was responsible for introducing this new vocabulary into the discussion of moral issues. And this 'new vocabulary, which was so radical a departure from the old and which constituted in itself a revolution in thought, passed without notice'. It was in the 1880s that Friedrich Nietzsche 'began to speak of "values" in its present sense—not as a verb, meaning to value or esteem something; not as a singular noun, meaning the measure of a thing (the economic value of money, labour, or property); but in the plural, connoting the moral beliefs and attitudes of society. Moreover, he used the word consciously, repeatedly, indeed insistently, to signify what he took to be the most profound event in human history.' Himmelfarb then draws the obvious conclusion that a philosophy that is based on the central idea that God is dead 'would mean the death of morality and the death of truth—above all, the truth of any morality. There would be no good and evil, no virtue and vice. There would be only values. And having degraded virtues into values, Nietzsche proceeded to de-value and trans-value them, to create a new set of values for his "new man".'[22]

Gertrude Himmelfarb describes the way Nietzsche's philosophy undermined the meaning of virtue, replacing it with the subjective idea of 'values'. The issue is that Christian virtues were developed from the Bible and had an enduring absolute quality. Virtues were good. Himmelfarb argues that so long as morality was couched in the language of 'virtue', it had a firm, resolute character. The term values, on the other hand, brings with it the assumptions that all moral ideas are subjective and relative, that they are mere customs and conventions that have utilitarian purposes for certain societies at certain times. 'One cannot say of virtues, as one can of values, that everyone's virtues are as good as anyone else's, or that everyone has a right to his own virtues. Only values can lay claim to moral equality and neutrality. This impartial, "non-judgemental", as we now say, sense of values – values as "value-free" – is now so firmly entrenched in the popular vocabulary and sensibility that one can hardly imagine a time without it.'[23] Victorians believed that virtues were fixed and certain, and 'when conduct fell short of those standards, it was judged in moral terms, as bad, wrong, or evil, not, as is more often the case today, as misguided, undesirable, or (the most recent corruption of our moral vocabulary) "inappropriate".'[24]

The ideas that flowed from Nietzsche's atheistic philosophy promoted the notion that there is no objective truth, and, therefore, there are no absolute moral standards—the concepts of right and wrong have been discarded, and no act is intrinsically evil. As there is no absolute moral law it is absurd to say that what is right for one person is proper for another. His thinking introduced the ideas that would develop into the ideology of postmodernism, in which each person is free to decide their own truth and their own morality. What they want, if it feels good, is right for the moment. This philosophy opened the gateway for the sexual revolution. Having removed the absolute moral laws of the Bible, people were free to decide their own values, to set their own standards. Having asserted that God was dead, morality was also dead, and so were the biblical virtues of modesty, chastity and fidelity. Man was now free to make his own arrangements for sexual conduct. The sexual revolutionaries, following Nietzsche's atheistic philosophy, encouraged the idea that people, and even children, are free to develop their own set of sexual values, without regard to an absolute moral standard.

The sexual philosophy of Sigmund Freud (1856-1939)

Sigmund Freud took up the baton of promoting an amoral world-view from Nietzsche. His voluminous writings have had a massive influence on Western thought. He was deeply sympathetic to the ideas of Nietzsche, and wrote that Nietzsche was a 'philosopher whose guesses and intuitions often agree in the most astonishing way with the laborious findings of psychoanalysis'.[25] Freud was strongly attracted to Darwin's theories of evolution 'for they held out hopes of an extraordinary advance in our understanding of the world'.[26] He gathered around him a set of disciples who were committed to his radical ideas and determined to spread the message through the techniques of psychoanalysis. He delved into the hidden depths of the unconscious mind and claimed to have uncovered the secrets of human sexual behaviour. At the heart of Freud's work was his hostility to the Christian faith; his motivation was to provide an interpretation of human sexuality that disregarded biblical morality. He was the father of the psychoanalytic movement that has spread Freudian philosophy across the Western world.

The influence of Freud was pervasive and far-reaching. According to JN Isbister, in *Freud – An introduction to his life and work*, the psychoanalytic movement, instigated by Freud after the turn of the century, from its humble beginnings as the Wednesday Society with its handful of interested practitioners, grew to an international movement with supporters in virtually every continent and every sphere of influence. 'Politicians, poets, scientists, doctors, all were represented in the portals of psychoanalysis by the time that Freud died. In that sense his insistence on maintaining the purity of his doctrines paid off in the end – he established both a thriving profession, and a group of sympathetic, interested supporters.'[27] One of Freud's more talented younger disciples was Wilhelm Reich, author of *The Sexual Revolution* (discussed in chapter 7), who believed that health depended on orgastic potency and advocated full and free sexual gratification.[28]

Although Freud did most of his work in Austria, he was acquainted with the thinking of Havelock Ellis, and his ideas were readily absorbed into English intellectual circles. Ernest Jones, a devoted follower and Freud's authorised biographer, began propounding the ideas of psychoanalysis in England in 1908. Freud developed links with the Bloomsbury Set when James and Alix Strachey visited Vienna for analyses shortly after World War I. He was not slow in spotting their literary talents as translators. The Stracheys were old friends of Virginia and Leonard Woolf, and used their influence to persuade Leonard, who was then founding the Hogarth Press, to take a lead in publishing and promoting the writings of Freud in English.[29] Leonard Woolf played an outstanding role in the dissemination of Freud's ideas in the English-speaking world.[30]

The Oedipus Theory

The analytical work of Freud led him to surmise that all children were sexual beings, with sexual desires directed towards their parents. His Oedipus theory postulates that in the first years of infancy 'boys concentrate their sexual wishes upon their mother and develop hostile impulses against their father as a rival, while girls adopt an analogous attitude. All of the different variations and consequences of the Oedipus complex are important; and the innately bisexual constitution of human beings makes itself felt and increases the number of simultaneously active tendencies.'[31] It follows 'that a child's first object choice is an incestuous one'.[32] Freud claimed that the sexual life of man is biphasic in onset. After his early 'efflorescence of sexuality passes off' the sexual impulses are overcome by repression and during a period of latency 'the reaction-formations of morality, shame and disgust are built up'.[33] Freud concluded that sexual development in humans occurs in two phases, and 'so far as we know, nothing analogous is to be found in man's animal relatives'.[34] In *Seductive Mirage*, Allen Esterson explains that Freud's findings 'in regard to the sexual nature of young children rest largely on the shifting sands of the highly speculative phantasy theory and his equally doubtful interpretative technique'.[35]

Freud states that the Oedipus complex offers the child two possibilities of satisfaction, in accordance with his 'bisexual constitution'. 'He could put himself in his father's place... and have intercourse with his mother as his father did... or he might want to take the place of his mother and be loved by his father, in which case his mother would become superfluous.'[36] Freud explains that 'even in boys the Oedipus complex has a double orientation, active and passive, in accordance with their bisexual constitution; a boy also wants to take his mother's place as the love-object of his father—a fact which we describe as the feminine attitude.'[37]

The Oedipus complex in a girl is much simpler in that 'it seldom goes beyond the taking of her mother's place and the adopting of a feminine attitude towards her father... Her Oedipus complex culminates in a desire, which is long retained, to have a baby from her father as a gift—to bear him a child.'[38] In his *Three Essays on the Theory of Sexuality* Freud writes, 'Every new arrival on this planet is faced by the task of mastering the Oedipus complex; anyone who fails to do so falls a victim to neurosis. With the progress of psychoanalytic studies the importance of the Oedipus complex has become more and more clearly evident; its recognition has become the shibboleth that distinguishes the adherents of psychoanalysis from its opponents.'[39] The key theoretical idea of the Oedipus complex – which suggested that young children entertain wishful sexual desires for their parents – was seen by Freud as the most important discovery he had made.[40]

Female sexuality

In his early writings Freud asserted that the first attachment of female infants is to their father. He later changed his mind and claimed that in both girls and boys the mother is the original object. At the Oedipal stage girls abandon the mother and take their father as a sexual object. Freud contrasts the reaction of boys and girls—'when a little boy first catches sight of a girl's genital region, he begins by showing irresolution and lack of interest' but the suggested threat of castration 'arouses a terrible storm of emotion in him'. This 'leads to two reactions... horror of the mutilated creature or triumphant contempt for her'.[41] But the little girl behaves differently at the sight of the male genitals. 'She makes her judgement and her decision in a flash. She has seen it and knows that she is without it and wants to have it.'[42] According to Freud, this leads to a 'castration' complex which 'is of the profoundest importance in the formation alike of character and of neurosis'.[43] The strong desire in young females for a penis 'may put great difficulties in the way of their regular development towards femininity, if it cannot be got over soon enough. The hope of some day obtaining a penis in spite of everything and so of becoming like a man may persist to an incredibly late age and may become a motive for strange and otherwise unaccountable actions.' Alternatively, 'a girl may refuse to accept the fact of being castrated, may harden herself in the conviction that she does possess a penis, and may subsequently be compelled to behave as though she were a man'. The psychological consequences of penis envy are various and far reaching: 'After a woman has become aware of the wound to her narcissism, she develops, like a scar, a sense of inferiority... she begins to share the contempt felt by men for a sex which is the lesser in so important a respect, and, at least in holding that opinion, insists on being like a man.'[44]

Freud's homosexuality

In *Freud – An introduction to his life and work*, JN Isbister concludes that Freud was involved in a homosexual relationship with Wilhelm Fliess.[45] He writes that on the evidence of the published material we can conclude that Freud had a homosexual love for Fliess which dominated his life in the 1890s and early 1900s. All of the passion of his adolescent friendships and engagement days was present in this relationship. 'Hitherto Freud's biographers have sought to suppress this passionate aspect of the relationship and attempted to suggest that Fliess was just a "father figure", or a sounding board for his ideas; such a playing down of this relationship cannot be continued – it was an expression of Freud's "dominant sexual disposition".'[46]

Isbister argues that the presence of these two elements in his sexual constitution – heterosexuality in his marriage and homosexuality in his relation to Fliess – was no great theoretical problem to Freud, for in their theories of sexuality both men affirmed the diverse, and frequently contradictory nature of the libido. Both Fliess and Freud believed that 'human nature was fundamentally bisexual and that the development of a unisexual disposition is always only partially successful'.[47] In the words of Freud's *Three Essays* of 1905, bisexuality was the decisive factor, for 'without taking bisexuality into account I think it would scarcely be possible to arrive at an understanding of the sexual manifestations that are actually to be observed in men and women'.[48] Moreover, Freud believed that homosexuality 'scarcely deserved' to be labelled a perversion, for 'it can be traced back to the constitutional bisexuality of all human beings and to the after-effects of the phallic primacy'.[49] He claimed that psychoanalysis pointed to a trace of 'homosexual object-choice in everyone'.[50]

Freud and Christianity

Underlying all Freud's thinking was a deep hostility to the Christian faith. In a letter to Fliess he describes how deeply upset he was by the Christian influence he perceived during a visit to Rome. Freud was disturbed by its meaning, and incapable of putting out of his mind his own misery and all the other misery which he knew to exist. 'I found almost intolerable the lie of the salvation of mankind which rears its head so proudly to heaven.'[51] According to Isbister this intense dislike of Christianity produced in Freud an inner conviction, 'the pursuit of which became the dominant, but covert, aim of his life – to expose the "lie of salvation" and show it to be just that, a lie'.[52] He concludes that Freud hated Christianity and 'all that it stood for—anti-Semitism; the hypocrisy of "Christian" civilisation; the stern demands of its morality; and the suggestion that man's destiny was ultimately linked with an eternal purpose. From 1900, his opposition to Christianity, hitherto mostly expressed as caustic comments in his letters, found an increasing outlet in his theories and in the movement they spawned... Freud's overt aims may well have been scientific – furthering the new science of depth psychology – but his covert aims were far more subtle and complex – to conquer the source (as he saw it) of Christianity, Rome, to accomplish that which Hannibal failed do... the covert aspects of his mission become clearer as the history of the psychoanalytic movement unfolds.'[53]

The influence of Freud

In a feature article entitled *Dr Fraud*, Roger Scruton criticised Freud's theories as his revenge against ordinary decent humanity. He argues that what Freud is really offering is a new and subversive morality, wrapped in scientific garments. 'He is asking us to see children as intrinsically sexual beings who, from the first moments of consciousness, are engaged in strategies of seduction, and whose unconscious thoughts are constantly directed to their sexual parts. And his account of sexual desire is constant with this. Desire, according to Freud, proceeds from the "libido", which is an instinctive and impersonal force...' Scruton declares that Freud has squeezed personal love from the picture and replaced it with an obsession with the genitals. 'Freud's theory has contributed substantially to the corruption of sexual morals in the modern world... it is now orthodoxy to think that children are sexual beings, that their sexual feelings are malleable and can flow in any direction, that what we mean by chastity is merely repression, and that innocence is another name for unconscious desire. These assumptions underlie the repulsive lessons in sex education that the national curriculum is now forcing on children—lessons designed to facilitate sexual activity long before personal love is possible...'[54]

Freud constructed a psychological theory that dehumanised people. In his eyes, humans are simply evolved animals, without dignity, purpose or value. The penis is the totem around which human life revolves; the organ that explains human existence. Little boys, triumphant possessors of a penis, are contemptuous of the mutilated creatures (girls) who do not have a penis. And the absence of a penis, which causes womankind to suffer from a 'castration' complex, is the dominant factor in the development of their character.

Flowing from his low view of mankind, Freud constructed a view of sexual behaviour that was devoid of a moral dimension. In all his writings there is not the slightest suggestion that any sexual act is wrong or immoral. People are driven by unconscious, innate sexual desires over which they have little control, and suppressing these desires is supposed to cause neurosis. Life can be explained in terms of the sexual impulse, the libido, which is bisexual in direction. His greatest 'discovery' was infantile sexuality. In his mind, children from the earliest ages had hidden desires to have sex with their parents—an idea that was to be developed and expounded by Alfred Kinsey. Freud's contribution to human thought was to demoralise sex, to separate it from human love, marriage and reproduction. His psychoanalytical movement propagated an interpretation of life that separated sex from morality and relationships. After Freud had pronounced his theories, people were encouraged to think about sex without moral constraints—the gateway to the sexual revolution was now opened wide.

Endnotes

1 John Butt, *Robert Owen, Prince of Cotton Spinners*, David & Charles, Newton Abbott, 1929, p45
2 Roderick Phillips, *Untying the Knot,* Cambridge University Press, New York, 1991, p165
3 Barbara Taylor, *Eve and the New Jerusalem,* Virago, London, 1983, p39
4 Herbert Schlossberg, *How Great Awakenings Happen*, in First Things, 106, October 2000, p46-51
5 *Encyclopaedia Britannica*, Malthus, Thomas Robert, William Benton, 1963, vol. 14, p745

6 Francis Place, *Illustrations and Proofs of the Principle of Population*, cited from C Wood and B Suitters, *The Fight for Acceptance: A history of contraception*, Medical and Technical Publishing, 1970, p134
7 Jeremy Wickens, *An overview of Francis Place's Life, 1771-1854*, A web of English History, The Peel Web
8 *Early Victorian Feminism*, Warwick University history teaching course, lecture 8, www.Warwick.ac.uk
9 Michael Bush, 'The Rise of the Sex Manual', *History Today*, February 1999, vol. 49, issue 2, p36
10 Michael Bush, *What is Love? Richard Carlile's Philosophy of Sex*, Verso, 1998, p144
11 Ibid. Michael Bush, 'The Rise of the Sex Manual', p36
12 Ibid. Michael Bush, *What is Love?*, p129
13 JS Mill, *On Liberty*, Pelican Classics, Penguin Books, reprint 1977, pp155-158
14 Anne Taylor, *Annie Besant*, Oxford University Press, Oxford, 1992, p108
15 Ibid. p115
16 *Encyclopaedia Britannica*, 'Nietzsche, Friedrich', William Benton, 1963, vol. 16, p435
17 Friedrich Nietzsche, *Ecce Homo*, 'Why I am a destiny', Penguin Books, translated RJ Hollingdale, 1980, p127-28
18 Ibid. p131
19 Ibid. p132
20 Ibid. *Ecce Homo*, 'Why I write such excellent books', p77
21 Ibid. *Ecce Homo*, 'Why I am a destiny', p133
22 Gertrude Himmelfarb, *The De-moralization of Society*, The Institute of Economic Affairs, London, 1995, p10
23 Ibid. pp11-12
24 Ibid. p13
25 Sigmund Freud, Standard Edition (SE) XX, *An Autobiographical Study*, Hogarth Press, London, 1968, p60
26 Ibid. p8
27 JN Isbister, *Freud – An introduction to his life and work*, Polity Press, 1985, p191
28 Paul Roazen, *Freud and his followers*, Da Capo Press, New York, 1992, p503
29 Ibid. p345
30 Ibid. p347
31 Ibid. Freud, SE XX, *An Autobiographical Study*, p36
32 Ibid. p37
33 Ibid. p37
34 Sigmund Freud, SE VII, *Three Essays on the Theory of Sexuality*, p234
35 Allen Esterson, *Seductive Mirage*, Open Court Publishing Company, 1993, p136
36 Sigmund Freud, SE XIX, *Dissolution of the Oedipus complex*, p176
37 Ibid. Freud, SE XIX, *Anatomical Sex-distinction*, p250
38 Ibid. Freud, SE XIX, *Dissolution of the Oedipus complex*, pp178-79
39 Ibid. Freud, SE VII, *Three Essays on the Theory of Sexuality*, notes on p226
40 Ibid. *Freud – An introduction to his life and work*, p167
41 Ibid. Freud, SE XIX, *Anatomical Sex-distinction*, p252
42 Ibid. p252
43 Ibid. Freud, SE XX, *An Autobiographical Study*, p37
44 Ibid. Freud, SE XIX, p253
45 Ibid. *Freud – An introduction to his life and work*, p91
46 Ibid. p92
47 Ibid. p94
48 Ibid. Freud, SE VII, *Three Essays on the Theory of Sexuality*, p220
49 Ibid. Freud, SE XX, *An Autobiographical Study*, p38
50 Ibid. p38
51 Letter to Fliess, 19 September 1901 (no. 146), *The Origins of Psycho-Analysis: Letters to Wilhelm Fliess*, Drafts and Notes 1887-1902, Basic Books, 1954, pp335-36
52 Ibid. *Freud – An introduction to his life and work*, p178
53 Ibid. pp179-180
54 *Sunday Times*, News Review, Dr Fraud, 8 April 2001, Roger Scruton

Chapter 5

New men, new women and a new morality

The revolt of Edward Carpenter, Havelock Ellis, Lytton Strachey and the Bloomsbury Set against traditional morality

Towards the end of the nineteenth century, while Nietzsche and Freud were developing their amoral philosophies in Europe, a small group of 'new men' and 'new women' were emerging in England who were determined to liberate society from repressive Victorian morality. Consistent with Nietzsche's amoral philosophy, with which they were no doubt familiar, they sought liberation from the old moral code as it applied to sexual behaviour. Prominent among the group were Edward Carpenter, Havelock Ellis, Olive Schreiner, HG Wells, Rebecca West, Mona Caird, Eleanor Marx, and Oscar Wilde. What they had in common was a rejection of the sexual conventions and mores of the time. The moral climate was changing, the subject of sex was increasingly coming into the public arena, and many intellectuals were proposing a new sexual ethic.

The Christian consensus on sexual morality was under threat as the 'new women' insisted on alternatives to the traditional roles for women. They felt restricted by what they regarded as the stifling prudery of the time and sought a new freedom to do their own thing. They saw the home as a place of oppression and boredom. Some of the more radical 'new women' regarded marriage as little more than legal prostitution, a hateful yoke under which women conceived and bore children in a sense of duty, not love. The emerging 'new women' were confined mainly to the middle and wealthy classes. They were advocates of a revolution against the 'repressive' sexual ethic of the time—they wanted sexual freedom, what they called 'free love'. But the 'new women' and the promoters of 'free love' were only a fringe group in society whose views were roundly condemned as immoral. They were, in fact, the pioneers of the sexual revolution.

Edward Carpenter (1844-1929)

Edward Carpenter is a significant figure in the revolution against Christian morality, for he was one of the early advocates of homosexual rights, a strong opponent of traditional marriage and a supporter of female liberation. After completing his studies at Trinity Hall, Cambridge, Carpenter entered the Anglican Church as a curate in 1869. But his heart was not committed to the gospel, and before long he renounced the Church, becoming more interested in Eastern religions and mysticism. Having obtained a good inheritance from his wealthy father, he was able to spend time on his writings. Much of what he wrote was a plea for homosexuality to be made socially acceptable. His book *The Intermediate Sex* (1908) presented homosexuality in a positive light, defended eroticism between males, and referred to homosexuals as sensitive and artistic men.[1] In his utopian mind Carpenter longed for 'love' that was untrammelled by laws. He had a vision of a lost sexual utopia which worshipped sex and life, and practised group marriage.[2]

His book *Love's Coming-of-Age* (1896) revealed his intense dislike for traditional marriage, which he described as a form of serfdom for women. Marriage was a life and death struggle in which the frail and delicate female is supposed 'to cling round the sturdy form of her husband – as of the ivy with the oak – forgetful of the terrible moral, namely, that (in the case of the trees at any rate) it is really a death-struggle which is going on'.[3] He opposed marriage of 'the common prayer book type' that made a woman subservient to her husband. Such marriages were a detestable lopsided alliance in which women endured the arrogant lordship and egoism of men. As long as women were economically dependent on men they could not stand up for themselves and insist on the rights which men had withheld from them.[4]

In his opinion, marriage needed to be freer, more companionable, and a less pettily exclusive relationship. The odious marriage law, which bound people together for life, without scruple, and in the most artificial and ill-sorted unions, needed to be abolished or at least modified.[5] He believed that it was possible 'in some cases, for married people to have intimacies with outsiders, and yet to continue perfectly true to each other; and in rare instances for triune and other such relations to be permanently maintained.'[6] He predicted that in the future people would not consent to pledge themselves irrevocably for life.[7]

In *Love's Coming-of-Age*, Carpenter carefully avoided naming the sexual organs. Twenty years later Marie Stopes, the mother of the family planning movement, would read his book as she was working on her manuscript for *Married Love*.[8] Carpenter is an icon of the sexual revolution, for his underlying motivation was his rejection of Christian marriage and his desire to make homosexuality socially acceptable. His ideology made him a strong opponent of traditional morality, and in his later years he became vehement in his anti-Victorian rhetoric.

Havelock Ellis (1859-1939)

Havelock Ellis was a British intellectual and writer on sexual psychology who became an important figure in the revolt against traditional morality. He was a congenial friend of Edward Carpenter with whom he shared a sense of being engaged in a common purpose. He strongly influenced Margaret Sanger who was a devoted disciple. As a young man Ellis had considered the Church as a career path before he rejected the Christian faith. In 1897 he published the first of seven volumes in *Studies in the Psychology of Sex*. Entitled *Sexual Inversion*, the book was initially published in Germany because English publishers were afraid of being charged under the obscenity laws. In the book Ellis claimed that homosexuality was a congenital variation and not a disease. He rejected the notion that 'inversion' was a crime and openly supported it as a legitimate lifestyle. When a radical bookseller, George Bedborough, sold a copy of the book in England he was arrested and charged with distributing obscene literature. The judge who reviewed *Sexual Inversion* concluded that it was a filthy book and asserted that the 'strong arm of the law should be used to stop all such efforts to break up the morals of the English public'.[9] Bedborough pleaded guilty.

Ellis married Edith Lees, a lesbian who for some of their married life lived with a woman lover. Ellis seemed to accept the situation as part of the 'new moral order' that he was advocating. He believed that the 'new man' and 'new woman' should be free from the old moral codes of self-restraint and chastity. In an essay, *The Meaning of Purity* (1920), he wrote: 'It is passion, more passion and fuller, that we need. The moralist who bans passion is not of our time; his place these many years is with the dead. For we know what happens in a world when those who ban passion have triumphed. When Love is suppressed Hate takes its place.'[10]

Ellis, like Freud, was familiar with the writings of Nietzsche and believed that he 'was in the first rank of the distinguished and significant personalities our century has produced'.[11] He saw Nietzsche as a great freethinker, a great moral teacher. 'Progress is thus a gradual emancipation from morals. We have to recognise the services of the men who fight in this struggle against morals, who are crushed into the ranks of criminals... In renewing our moral ideas we need also to renew our whole conception of the function and value of morals. Nietzsche advised moralists to change their tactics: "Deny moral values, deprive them of the applause of the crowd, create obstacles to their free circulation; let them be the shamefaced secrets of a few solitary souls: *forbid morality!*" '[12]

Ellis had an affair with the author Olive Schreiner (probably platonic, for Ellis was notably deficient in sexual desire and potency), one of the original 'new women'. Her popular novel, *The Story of an African Farm* (1883), convinced him that growing up female was a 'curse', with its rigid restrictions, and that marriage could be a form of entrapment. Schreiner believed that true love could only exist outside marriage, in a state of perfect freedom.[13] Ellis's own sexual experience was unusual. Impotent for most of his life, he suffered from urolagnia (sexual excitement at seeing a woman urinate). Although he was helpful and generous to Marie Stopes, she disliked Ellis's concentration on the abnormal. Reading him, she said, was 'like breathing a bag of soot; it made me feel choked and dirty for three months'.[14]

Writing an introduction for the book *Sex in Civilization* (1929), Ellis expressed his support for the revolt against traditional sexual morality. 'A century or so ago the very nature of sex attitudes would have thwarted such a project... The first intellectual revolt against this old attitude is to be found in the work of Freud and his followers, who some think rediscovered sex. Just as the revolt against civilization has taken on numerous forms, each more complex than the other with advancing change, the revolt against old sex attitudes has followed the same evolution. Revolt has become the characteristic of our age. The intellectuals are in revolt against an entire civilization. The revolt against the old sex attitudes, with their silences and stupidities, is a vital part of this entire revolt against a decaying culture.'[15]

Herbert George Wells (1866-1946)

The popular English historian and novelist HG Wells was highly influential in breaking down the nineteenth century outlook in morals and religious belief. Wells is remembered chiefly as the prophet of optimism, a writer who vividly expressed the sense of release from the conventions of Victorian thought. His influence was enormous, both on his own generation and that which followed. Few did more to incite revolt against Christian dogma or against the accepted codes of behaviour, especially in matters of sex, in which, both in his writings and in his personal life, he was a persistent advocate of an almost completely amoral freedom.

In his novel *Ann Veronica* (1909) Wells creates a rebellious young woman who rejects the safe and protected life of the suburbs for one of sexual and intellectual independence in London. The novel was regarded as deeply shocking at the time. It was roundly condemned for its sexual immorality and banned in public libraries. A review in *The Spectator* referred to 'this poisonous book' because of his apparent approval of the heroine's illicit sexual behaviour. Wells responded that the book shocked because he had depicted a woman who 'wanted a particular man who excited her and she pursued him and got him. With gusto...'[16] Another review in *T.P.'s Weekly* (October 22, 1909) condemned *Ann Veronica* as a 'dangerous novel' because the heroine regarded her defiance of the 'old morality' as 'glorious'.[17]

According to social historian Gertrude Himmelfarb, Wells was a notorious philanderer. During the thirty years of his second marriage he engaged in one affair after another. He had two sons by his second wife and two illegitimate children by other women. At one time he was involved with two women at the same time. His most celebrated affair was with the novelist Rebecca West, a 'new woman' who bore his illegitimate child. She and her 'love' child were tucked away in a cottage in the countryside, without friends and for long periods, without the companionship of Wells.[18]

Lytton Strachey (1880-1932)

Another important figure in the revolt against morality was Lytton Strachey, author of *Eminent Victorians* (1918). Strachey's book dealt cynically with the lives of four famous Victorian public figures, making fun of what he saw as their personal absurdities, artificial pieties and moral failures. His book cultivated the idea that the single word 'Victorians' stood for all that had been wrong with British society for the past fifty years. The notion of Victorian hypocrisy became widely accepted, arousing almost hysterical enthusiasm among the liberal elite, an enthusiasm that remains to this day. Today it is widely believed that the Victorians were hypocrites and prudes, who preached morality while secretly indulging in the pleasures of the flesh. The man who did more that any other to cultivate the idea of Victorian hypocrisy was Lytton Strachey.

In his third year at Trinity College, Cambridge, Strachey was elected to the most notorious of all university societies, the Cambridge Conversazione Society, better known as the 'Apostles'.[19] It was as a member of the Society that Strachey cultivated his deep dislike of all things Victorian. In a paper to the Society he symbolised Caliban as freedom from restraint and Christ as the repression of the nineteenth century. In essence his paper was a polemic against a Victorian society which he believed had turned its back on his own deepest problems and classed him an outcast.[20] In another speech he expressed his belief in the disintegration of Victorian society: 'But if external help is lacking, is there no chance of some swift internal disintegration? Is there no possibility of a break-up so general and so complete that the entire reorganisation of society would be a necessary sequence? Personally, I welcome every endeavour, conscious or unconscious, to bring about such an end. I welcome thieves, I welcome murderers, above all I welcome anarchists. I prefer anarchy to the Chinese Empire. For out of anarchy good may come, out of the Chinese Empire nothing.'[21]

Strachey and Maynard Keynes saw Victorian society as a hostile world in which they were searching for an alternative sexual code. They repudiated the customary morals, conventions and traditional wisdom. Strachey wrote in 1906 to his friend Keynes, 'We can't be content with telling the truth – we must tell the whole truth; and the whole truth is the Devil. Voltaire abolished Christianity by believing in good. It's madness of us to dream of making dowagers understand that feelings are good, when we say in the same breath that the best ones are sodomitical. If we were crafty and careful, I dare say we'd pull it off. But why should we take the trouble? On the whole I believe that our time will come about a hundred years hence, when preparations will have been made, and compromises come to, so that, at the publication of our letter, everyone will be, finally, converted.'[22]

In his biography, *Lytton Strachey*, Michael Holroyd comments on the correspondence between Strachey and Keynes, 'with its frequent references to buggery and rape, its oscillation between higher and lower sodomy... What they were looking for almost as urgently as sexual licence and homosexual love was freedom of speech as a sympathetic source of disclosure. Often they were nervous of their letters going astray, for according to the law they were both criminals – hideous criminals in the public's opinion.'[23] By 1911 Beatrice Webb described the Apostles as 'a pernicious set... which makes a sort of ideal of anarchic ways in sexual questions'.[24] There can be no question about the long-term aims of Strachey – it was a revolution in sexual behaviour that would overturn the old ideas of morality that were so important to the hated Victorians. And he had the foresight to predict that the ideas he was implanting in society would take a long time, perhaps a hundred years, to mature, and then society would finally be free.

Michael Holroyd describes Strachey's intellectual growth while at Cambridge, and concludes that 'he had grown to be so much of an intellectual force that his influence is said to have left its mark on three generations of undergraduates... Evidence of his influence upon other undergraduates comes from their letters in which they aimed at a style of semi-pornographic humour. His reputation for decadence was gaining notoriety.'[25] According to Holroyd, James Strachey, Lytton's brother, made the following evaluation. 'My own view is that Lytton's Cambridge years had an important effect on the subsequent mental life in England; especially on the attitude of ordinary people to religion and sex. The young men in my years (though also interested in socialism) were far more open-minded on both those topics than their predecessors – and I believe they handed on what they derived from Lytton, and this (taken in conjunction with Freud, who was totally unknown till much later) is, I think, what has resulted in the reform of the general attitude to sex.'[26]

In his book *Eminent Victorians* Lytton Strachey cultivated the idea of Victorian hypocrisy. He parodied the values and personal lives of four great Victorian personalities, Cardinal Manning, Florence Nightingale, Dr Arnold and General Gordon. Strachey's real targets were those aspects of Christian culture from the recent past that had emerged from the evangelical faith. Historian GM Trevelyan was appalled by the supercilious and dismissive tone of *Eminent Victorians*. 'He hated its zestful iconoclasm and self-conscious irreverence, thought its impressionistic approach the height of scholarly irresponsibility, and disliked the unsympathetic treatment of his subjects' private lives. Trevelyan believed in great men and women, and he was enraged that Lytton cut them down to size in such a sneering and dishonest manner... Lytton had poisoned history, traduced the Victorians.'[27] And Edmund Wilson wrote the following comment: 'Lytton Strachey's chief mission, of course, was to take down once and for all the pretensions of the Victorian Age to moral superiority... But neither the Americans nor the English have ever, since *Eminent Victorians* appeared, been able to feel quite the same about the legends that had dominated their pasts. Something had been punctured for good.'[28]

Michael Holroyd concluded that what Strachey wanted to do was 'to infiltrate his libertine and libertarian beliefs through literature, into the bloodstream of the people, and by such oblique methods that readers accepted it all quite naturally. The polemics of *Eminent Victorians* had been created by the war; in *Queen Victoria* he had carefully laid down a subversive sexual subtext; and then, more boldly in

Elizabeth and Essex, written sexual deviation into the mainstream of English history.'[29] Strachey believed that the influence of Freud and Marx appeared to be advancing the 'New Age' to which he was committed. In their ideas Strachey saw 'a renewed opportunity for escaping the "superstition that hangs over us and compresses our breathing and poisons our lives". And if, by helping to release homosexuality from legal danger and social disgrace, he could change the future destinies of people like himself, then his secret ambition would be accomplished.'[30]

Bloomsbury Set

The Bloomsbury Set was a group of intellectuals who revelled in the 'new morality'. They flaunted convention, scoffed at Christianity and practised 'free love'. Most of the group had been undergraduates at Trinity or King's College, and some had belonged to the Cambridge 'Apostles'. Lytton Strachey was one of the original group, others were a left-wing political journalist Leonard Woolf who married Virginia Stephen, Maynard Keynes who became a world famous economist, eminent author EM Forster, art critic Clive Bell, artist Rodger Fry, and Desmond MacCarthy, a dramatic critic.[31] Both Strachey and Keynes were practising homosexuals, while EM Forster seems to have become an active homosexual after the two younger men had made their propensities known.[32] The Bloomsbury Set was said by Dorothy Parker to comprise pairs who had affairs in squares. Their relationships were complicated, promiscuous, and frequently homosexual or bisexual. They wrote about themselves and their friends at inordinate length, first in their diaries and later in their memoirs.[33]

The Bloomsbury group met on most Thursday evenings in the house of Virginia Woolf for intellectual discussions. Part of the Bloomsbury ethos was the desire to challenge social norms and rebel against what they saw as Victorian hypocrisy. According to Keynes: 'We repudiated entirely customary morals, conventions and traditional wisdom. We were, that is to say, in the strictest sense of the term immoralist. The consequences of being found out had, of course, to be considered for what they were worth. But we recognised no moral obligation on us, no inner sanction, to conform or to obey. Before heaven we claimed to be our own judge in our own case.'[34] According to Virginia: 'Sex permeated our conversation. The word bugger was never far from our lips. We discussed copulation with the same excitement and openness that we had discussed the nature of good. It is strange to think how reticent, how reserved we had been and for how long... Now we talked of nothing else... we listened with rapt interest to the love affairs of the buggers. We followed the ups and downs of their chequered histories, Vanessa sympathetically; I – it is one of the differences between us – frivolously, laughingly.'[35]

In her essay 'A Genealogy of Morals: From Clapham to Bloomsbury', social historian Gertrude Himmelfarb shows the link between the Clapham 'sect' and the Bloomsbury group. 'Where Clapham had inspired a moral and spiritual reformation, Bloomsbury sought to effect a moral and spiritual liberation—a liberation from Clapham itself and from those vestiges of Evangelicalism and

Victorianism that still persisted in the early twentieth century.'[36] She points out that the true revelation about the Bloomsbury Set was the compulsive and promiscuous nature of their homosexuality. 'Bloomsbury itself marvelled at the "permutations and combinations" of which it was capable. In 1907, for example, Strachey discovered that his lover (and cousin) Duncan Grant was also having an affair with Arthur Hobhouse, who, in turn, was having an affair with Keynes. The following year Strachey was even more distressed to learn that Grant was now having an affair with Keynes as well.'[37] The 'higher sodomy', as Bloomsbury called it, 'seemed to be not only a higher form of sexuality but a higher form of morality. In sex as in art they prided themselves on being autonomous and self-contained, free to experiment and express themselves without inhibition or guilt.'[38] Himmelfarb concludes that Lytton Strachey was the essence of Bloomsbury. 'And we can also appreciate the contrast between the generation of Strachey and that of his elders— those late Victorians whom Strachey, and Bloomsbury, so mercilessly derided.'[39]

The author DH Lawrence had little time for the Bloomsbury Set. He wrote in a letter: 'To hear these young people talk really fills me with black fury: they talk endlessly, but endlessly—and never, never a good thing said. They are cased each in a hard little shell of his own and out of this they talk words. There is never for one second any outgoing of feeling and no reverence, not a crumb or grain of reverence. I cannot stand it. I will not have people like this—I had rather be alone. They made me dream of a beetle that bites like a scorpion.'[40]

According to Dora Black, the second wife of Bertrand Russell, 'The claim of Bloomsbury to shaping the future lay as much in its views on sex, the marriage laws and women's life in this aspect, as in political power and economics… The efforts of men and women of my generation to strive for these ideals in human relations and for women's emancipation brought conflict and even tragedy into our private lives.'[41] In *Hope and glory: Britain 1900-1990*, Peter Clark comments on the homo-erotic bond between Lytton Strachey, Duncan Grant and Maynard Keynes. He writes, 'this clearly helped reinforce the revolt against the respectable late-Victorian conventions, which Strachey's volume of biographical essays *Eminent Victorians* (1918) subjected to an exquisite literary assassination by a thousand digs. The book had an amazing success and inspired countless 'debunking' biographies in its wake.'[42]

Roots of the sexual revolution

The last two decades of the nineteenth century and the first decades of the twentieth century were a time when the Christian moral framework was being seriously challenged by a small group of radical intellectuals. 'Free love' was the expression which encapsulated the ideas of the sexual revolutionaries. They wanted the freedom to express themselves sexually without the restraints imposed by Christian morality, and many wanted homosexuality to become socially acceptable. The 'new men' and 'new women' had been skilful in their denunciation of Victorian morality, and especially what they labelled as Victorian prudery. There was a growing fashion of scorning all things Victorian spreading like a virus from its hotbed in Cambridge to the rest of the country. The autobiographical novel *The Way of All Flesh* by Samuel Butler, published in 1903, was extremely influential in cultivating anti-Victorian ideas in the young. He threw a subversive brick at the smug face of Victorian domesticity, using irony, wit and sometimes rancour to savage contemporary values and beliefs.[43] HG Wells, in his novel *Ann Veronica*, was another who disparaged Victorian respectability. By the end of the Great War anti-Victorian sentiment was a settled condition of English intellectual culture.[44] The *New Statesman* carried an attack on the period which was particularly notable for its venom and swagger—'as an era, it may have been good, but it was good in a wicked way. By 1918 the *Times Literary Supplement* was voicing an attitude that went strikingly beyond mere detestation of the Victorian age...'[45]

Many British intellectuals had taken up the fight for a new moral order. A number of books and articles appeared that criticised the hypocrisy of the Victorians, urging society to take a more enlightened approach to moral issues. But while this ferment of ideas was gaining ground among the intellectuals, the population at large was still influenced by the familiar ideas of Christian morality. In other words, while the intellectuals were winning the battle of ideas, the general population was slow in taking up the new freedoms, for they were accustomed to the old tried and tested ways. But the seeds had been sown and slowly they started to take root and grow. Slowly, ordinary people started to believe the incessant clamour of the intellectuals that repressive Victorian morality had done enormous harm by fostering a climate of sexual ignorance. By the 1960s and 1970s, as the result of the radical ideas implanted by Edward Carpenter, Friedrich Nietzsche, Sigmund Freud and his disciples, Lytton Strachey and his Bloomsbury friends, the revolution was in full bloom and flourishing.

According to historian Gertrude Himmelfarb, 'in contemplating the sexual anarchy of the late nineteenth century, one can hardly fail to see in it portents of the sex revolution of the late twentieth century. There are indeed significant resemblances between that time and ours. But there is also one overriding difference. A century ago the advanced souls were just that, well in advance of the culture, whereas now they pervade the entire culture. This is the significance of our "sexual revolution": it is a revolution democratized and legitimized.'[46] The driving force behind the revolution was the belief that the people of England needed to be liberated from the restraints of Victorian morality in order to express their natural sexuality. The revolutionaries believed that society needed to be open about sex and the hope lay in sex education.

Endnotes

1 Edward Carpenter, *The Intermediate Sex*, 'The Place of the Uranian in Society'
2 Michael Mason, *The Making of Victorian Sexuality*, Oxford University Press, 1994, p12
3 Edward Carpenter, *Love's Coming-of-Age*, First edition 1896, reprinted 1948, George Allen & Unwin Ltd, London, 1948, p100

4 Ibid. pp103-104
5 Ibid. p118
6 Ibid. p122
7 Ibid. p123
8 June Rose, *Marie Stopes and the Sexual Revolution*, Faber and Faber, London, 1992, pp93-94
9 Journal of the American Medical Association, 1899, 32, 135
10 Havelock Ellis, *On life and sex*, 'The meaning of purity', WM Heinemann, London, 1948, p39 [First published 1920]
11 Havelock Ellis, *Selected essays*, 'Nietzsche', in Everyman's library, edited by Ernest Rhys, JM Dent & Sons, London, 1936, p54
12 Ibid. pp39-40
13 Ibid. June Rose, *Marie Stopes and the Sexual Revolution*, p137
14 Ibid. p112
15 *Sex in Civilization*, ed VR Calverton and SD Schmalhausen, G Allen and Unwin, 1929, with introduction by Havelock Ellis
16 Sheila Rowbotham, *A Century of Women*, Penguin Books, 1997, p7
17 Cited from Karl Beckson, *London in the 1890s. A cultural history*, W. W. Norton & Company, 1992, p158
18 Gertrude Himmelfarb, *The De-moralization of Society*, The Institute of Economic Affairs, London, 1995, p204
19 Michael Holroyd, *Lytton Strachey*, Chatto & Windus, London, 1994, p76
20 Ibid. p79
21 Ibid. p80
22 Ibid. p92
23 Ibid. p105
24 Ibid. p92
25 Ibid. p101
26 Ibid. p101
27 David Cannadine, *G. M. Trevelyan. A life in History*, HarperCollins, 1992, pp43-44
28 Edmund Wilson, Lytton Strachey, *New Republic* 72 (21 September 1932), pp146-48, collected in *The Shores of Light: A Literary Chronicle of the Twenties and Thirties*, 1952, p551-56, cited from Michael Holroyd's *Lytton Strachey*
29 Ibid. Michael Holroyd, *Lytton Strachey*, p633
30 Ibid. p642
31 George Spater and Ian Parsons, *A marriage of true minds*, Jonathan Cape and the Hogarth Press, London, 1977, p28
32 Ibid. p34
33 *Beneath a Rougher Sea*, Virginia Woolf's Psychiatric History, website, Ourworld
34 John Maynard Keynes, 'My Early Beliefs' in *Two Memoirs*, New York, 1949, pp97-98, cited from Gertrude Himmelfarb, 'A Genealogy of Morals: From Clapham to Bloomsbury', in *Marriage and Morals among the Victorians*, Ivan R Dee, 2001, pp34-35
35 Virginia Woolf, cited from George Spater and Ian Parsons, *A marriage of true minds*, Jonathan Cape and the Hogarth Press, London, 1977, p41
36 Gertrude Himmelfarb, 'A Genealogy of Morals: From Clapham to Bloomsbury', in *Marriage and Morals among the Victorians*, Ivan R Dee, 2001, p30
37 Ibid. p43
38 Ibid. p45
39 Ibid. p49
40 John Maynard Keynes 'My Early Beliefs' in *Two Memoirs*, New York, 1949, p76, cited from *Marriage and Morals among the Victorians*, p47
41 Dora Russell, *The Tamarisk Tree*, Vol. 1, My Quest for Liberty and Love, p69
42 Peter Clark, *Hope and glory: Britain 1900-1990*, Allen Lane, Penguin Press, 1996, p166
43 Samuel Butler, *The Way of all Flesh*, Penguin Books, First published 1903, reprint 1986, back cover
44 Ibid. *The Making of Victorian Sexuality*, Oxford University Press, 1994, p10
45 Ibid. p10
46 Ibid. Gertrude Himmelfarb, *The De-moralization of Society*, p218

Chapter 6

Beginnings of sex education

Marie Stopes founds the FPA; the Education Act of 1944

Alfred Kinsey's research into human sexual behaviour

In Victorian England sex was not a subject discussed in polite society. The mores of the day demanded decency in language, modesty in behaviour, purity in thought and there was a strong taboo against lewdness and obscenity. But the discrediting of Victorian morality in the early decades of the twentieth century, especially the accusations of prudery and hypocrisy, were slowly changing the way society viewed sexual conduct. Some prominent intellectuals, such as Lytton Strachey, Edward Carpenter, Havelock Ellis, Bertrand Russell and HG Wells, were arguing the case for a more 'enlightened' approach to sexual matters. To overcome the sexual ignorance that was such a feature of Victorian society the English needed to be more open about sex and contraception. Marie Stopes was the first person to commit her life to the sex education of the British people.

Influence of Marie Stopes (1880-1958)

It is probably true to say that the sex education movement in England started with the publication of Marie Stopes' book *Married Love* in March 1918, eight months before the end of the First World War. This sex manual was to sell over a million copies and make its author world famous as an expert in sex education. She had worked on the book for the past four years, at the very time that she was seeking an annulment of her first marriage on the grounds of her husband's impotence and failure to consummate the marriage, a claim strongly disputed by her husband. The book, which was supposed to be directed at married couples, was unique in that it described in explicit language the physiology of the sex act. Stopes admits that she was saying 'things about sex which have not been said by anyone else, things which are of profound importance to men and women who hope to make their marriages beautiful'.[1] And this was done in the apparent belief that married women, in particular, were ignorant about the physical side of sex, and this meant that they were unable to experience a truly fulfilling married life. In the preface to *Married Love*, Stopes explains that in her first marriage she paid such a terrible price for sexual ignorance that she felt the knowledge she had gained should be placed at the service of humanity.

Ideologically, *Married Love* was consistent with the thinking of Edward Carpenter, Havelock Ellis and Olive Schreiner. Stopes believed that society could be changed on a foundation of satisfactory orgasms and a renewal of sexual tenderness that was once instinctive.[2] Yet such was the explicit nature of her writing that it was considered shocking by publishers and academic colleagues who were still influenced by Victorian attitudes to sex and women.[3] Despite the writings of 'freethinkers' who were ardent supporters of the idea of sexual liberation, the large majority of the population still believed in the Christian sexual ethic. Although Carpenter, in his book *Love's Coming-of-Age*, had carefully avoided naming the sexual organs or referring to sexual anatomy, Marie Stopes had no such inhibitions for she believed that explicit language was necessary to get her message across. Carpenter was intrigued by her explicit language, something that he had been too nervous to try.[4]

Married Love rapidly became a best seller, selling over two thousand within a fortnight. According to Marie it crashed into English society like a bombshell. 'Its explosive contagious theme – that woman like man has the same physiological reaction, a reciprocal need for enjoyment and benefit from union in marriage distinct from the exercise of maternal functions – made Victorian husbands gasp.'[5] A week or two after publication all London was talking about *Married Love*, and while it was received enthusiastically by a section within society, others were outraged by the explicit nature of the book. A distinguished psychiatrist commented that Marie's book was read extensively and secretly in girls' schools and by boys in the same spirit that indecent literature in general is enjoyed.[6] Members of the public were equally outraged. One married woman wrote to Stopes that the details of sexual behaviour were absolutely unnecessary. 'Your book is written for married people but you cannot control its distribution... Personally much of the book simply disgusts me and spoils other parts.'[7] Another mother was even more upset, 'As a 30-year-old married and, I hope, broad-minded woman, mother of six children, I read your *Married Love* and was disgusted with the filth. Your two or three pages on contraception are, and have been, known to most of my acquaintances for years and all the other pages of muck demean you... [that] you take upon yourself to teach us what surely nature herself does is an insult to all decent people and I fail to see the use at all except to excite people and cause a deal of immorality.' A private letter enquired whether it was the desire to put bank notes in her pocket that had made her write such a book. 'Do you really think that my wife and I... are sadly in need of such dirty advice as you offer?'[8] Although *Married Love* was widely reviewed, *The Times* refused to advertise the book.

Marie Stopes was careful not to let her views about sex outside marriage become public knowledge. She was too clever a propagandist to allow herself to be openly associated with the sexual revolution and the idea of 'free love'. According to June Rose in *Marie Stopes and the Sexual Revolution*, 'Marie herself had doubts about the value of the pristine purity of the virgin state.'[9] She pondered whether too much emphasis was placed on the woman retaining her virginity before marriage. 'This plan for "free love" and sexual equality, Marie sensibly kept to herself. Had she not insisted emphatically that the sexual knowledge that she had made available was intended only for married couples, her book would have been declared obscene and the author and publisher prosecuted.'[10] Her views on sexual morality were consistent with her rejection of the Christian faith. She despised the Catholic Church because of its opposition to her views. She believed 'the Catholics were plotting against her – in the sense that she herself was plotting the overthrow of Catholic dogma and Christian thinking generally'.[11] In a speech at the Criterion Theatre, Marie claimed, 'I am out for a much greater thing than birth control. I am out to smash the tradition of organised Christianity, and to enthrone Christ's own tradition of wholesome, healthy, natural love towards sex life.'[12]

Marie Stopes met Margaret Sanger in London in 1915. The radical American birth control propagandist, having been indicted for violating USA postal obscenity laws, was unwilling to risk imprisonment and so she jumped bail and set sail for England. As Marie listened intently to Sanger's story of the struggle for birth control in the USA she was persuaded to start a similar campaign in Great Britain. Around the time of her second marriage in 1918 (her first marriage having been annulled on ground of failure to consummate) she produced *Wise Parenthood*, a 32 page booklet on the technique of birth control. Although Stopes was not medically qualified, this did not stop her from offering advice on the technique of contraception. Her advice, that a certain device could be safely left in place for several days or even weeks, was criticised by some members of the medical profession, who pointed out the potential problems of doing so. Nevertheless, she was increasingly becoming recognised as an expert in the delicate matter of birth control and was paid to write for the *Sunday Chronicle*, an opportunity she used to promote *Wise Parenthood*. According to June Rose, 'The result of this open propaganda for birth control agitated her publisher to a panic' for it had been agreed that her booklet would be directed towards young married couples. Her publisher, AC Fifield, was so deeply upset by the situation that he wrote, 'It certainly is disgusting to me to receive furtive letters from illiterate young unmarried girls asking me to send the book along "in plain wrapping".'[13] The *New Witness* was disparaging of *Wise Parenthood*. It decided that 'a thundering attack would please this most unpleasant woman almost as well as ardent support… The peculiar horror of her book is that it is couched in pseudo-scientific terms and is addressed to the married woman.'[14]

Marie Stopes realised that for her campaign to promote contraception to the masses to really succeed it needed to gain the support of the Church, and when the Anglican bishops gathered for the 1920 Lambeth Conference she saw her opportunity. Believing herself to be to be a prophetess bearing God's message, she wrote to the bishops a message she claimed to have received from God. She called her message *A New Gospel to All Peoples: A revelation of God uniting physiology and the religions of man*. Marie's *New Gospel* began: 'My Lords, I speak to you in the name of God. You are his priests. I am his prophet. I speak to you of the mysteries of the union of man and woman...' She refuted Paul's teaching on marriage saying, 'Paul spoke to Christ nineteen hundred years ago. God spoke to me today.' According to Marie, God commanded that couples should use the best means of birth control discovered by science. She advised the bishops that they must teach their flocks that 'the pure and holy sacrament of marriage may no longer be debased and befouled by the archaic ignorance of centuries...'[15] The reaction of the bishops to the prophetess of birth control is not on record. The Conference did, however, pass a resolution which condemned 'the teaching which, under the name of science and religion, encourages married people in the deliberate cultivation of sexual union as an end in itself'.[16]

Marie Stopes founded the first birth control clinic in London in 1921, funded by her second husband, HV Roe. When the clinic was opened only a few small newspapers covered the event as the family newspapers considered the subject 'inappropriate for discussion or publicity'.[17] The clinic was not the roaring success that Marie hoped as at first only a trickle of women attended. Over the next few years a number of other birth control clinics were opened in various parts of the country.

In 1922 the editor of *John Bull* launched a powerful attack on the writings of Marie Stopes. The editorial noted that in the name of science 'Dr Stopes has unloaded on to the market a series of books – *Married Love, Wise Parenthood, Radiant Motherhood*, and the like – which contain the frankest and most intimate discussion of sexual matters that has ever been permitted in this country. I write not as a prude or a puritan, but as a man of the world with a fairly easy tolerance in matters of this kind... The whole tendency of this raging, tearing propaganda... is profoundly mischievous. Its sole practical effect, as far as I am able to judge, is to impart a knowledge of "birth control" methods to people who ought to have no use of them... and while I cannot possibly gauge the feelings of this gifted author as she sees her scientific works paraded for sale in the company of pornographic French novels and other accessories of vice, I should be wanting in candour if I did not point out the plain moral implications of these things.'[18]

By now Marie Stopes was recognised as the national expert in the matter of sex as her books became widely read. June Rose concludes that she became the nation's first acknowledged advisor on sexual problems. 'The Welsh Education Board asked her to give schoolchildren advice on sex that summer and the Oxford University Press invited her to write a book on the subject addressed to medical practitioners.'[19]

One of her aims was to persuade local authorities to allow advice on contraception to be given at maternity welfare centres. In 1927 the Women's National Liberal Federation passed a resolution that information should be available to those who asked for it at maternity centres controlled by the Ministry of Health. This would enable the poorest members of the community to obtain information to which the wealthier classes already had access. Advocates of birth control tried to gain support from the 1927 Labour Party conference for a resolution which would remove a ban on the giving of birth control information at public maternity centres. But the resolution was strongly opposed because it was seen as an issue which deeply divided religious convictions. Some argued that to pass such a proposal would be a disaster for the Labour Party.[20]

Undeterred by this minor setback the birth control campaign, led by the Labour Party, held a public conference in 1930. Attended by health workers, welfare officers, councillors, medical officers of health, women's organisations and birth control organisations, the conference passed a resolution requesting the Ministry of Health to make birth control advice available to married people. Three months later the Ministry responded by sending a memorandum to maternity and child welfare authorities. However, the content of the memorandum was considered to be so sensitive that it was not sent to the press or to Local Authorities. According to June Rose in *Marie Stopes and the Sexual Revolution*, 'Only maternity and child welfare authorities received the memorandum, which squirmed round the subject with obscure wording. First of all, it reaffirmed that it was not the centres' function to provide birth control advice. Only in cases where there were medical grounds, where further pregnancy would be detrimental to health, could such advice be given. And then, as if the very topic were contaminating, the advice has to be given at a separate session.'[21] Nevertheless this was a major triumph for the birth control movement. It was the thin end of the wedge. The State had taken on responsibility for providing contraceptive advice to married women, and there would be no going back. Next would be single women, and when the time was right, the State would take on the role of providing contraceptive advice to children.

By 1930 there were a dozen or so voluntary birth control clinics around the country, and a number of societies promoting the cause of birth control. When the clinics decided to unite to form a national council, Marie Stopes was invited to propose the motion to establish the National Birth Control Council, which would change its name to the Family Planning Association (FPA) in 1939. The reasoning behind the new name was that the FPA would in future help women to have wanted children in the same spirit as it would help them to avoid having unwanted children. The Malthusian League, which had been active in promoting birth control in order to limit family size for economic and eugenic reasons, was disbanded in 1927 as it believed that birth control had become well accepted by society. So the propaganda role for promoting contraception in Great Britain was now firmly in the hands of the newly established Birth Control Council. Its main function was to co-ordinate the work of a number of organisations that were involved in the struggle to promote contraception among the public. The birth control movement received a huge boost from the 1930 Lambeth Conference when the bishops of the Anglican Church, who ten years previously had voiced moral opposition to contraception, now passed a resolution that recognised that there was moral justification for birth control in certain circumstances.

The enormous influence of Marie Stopes can be judged from the fact that she had become known worldwide for her work in the cause of educating women about sex and contraception. In 1935 a group of American academics, assessing the most influential books published during the last fifty years, voted *Married Love* as the sixteenth most influential book from a list of twenty-five.[22]

Marie Stopes's contribution to the sexual revolution was to cultivate the myth of sexual ignorance, to legitimise the use of sexually explicit language, and to involve the State in the provision of contraception. She propagated the idea that the public was ignorant about sex and this ignorance could only be overcome by explicit sexual information; as an expert propagandist she used every means of publicity to promote her ideas. *Married Love* was the first publication to use explicit sexual language and the effect of her writings was to undermine modesty in the minds of those who read her books. Although most in society were shocked by the explicit description of sexual intercourse, her writings helped to make explicit language acceptable. Her other contribution to the sexual revolution was to found the Family Planning Association, the organisation that today is in the forefront of the sex education movement. The organisation that bears her name, Marie Stopes International, is now active in 35 countries promoting the ideals of the sexual revolution. It has moved a long way from Stopes's original claim that she was promoting contraception for the benefit of married couples. The organisation's website responds to a question about the right time for first sexual intercourse: 'Have sex when you really feel ready, never mind what anyone else says.'

Education Act of 1944

Despite the efforts of Marie Stopes, who wrote and campaigned for information about sex and contraception to be made more widely known, in the first half of the twentieth century there was little public discussion of sex, and no sex education in schools. Indeed, most school textbooks on biology were discreet when it came to the sex organs and reproduction. In 1927 the Board of Education recommended that schools should provide sex education, but it was discretionary, and most schools carefully avoided the subject. In 1943 the Board of Education, acknowledging public concerns about the sexual conduct of young women in particular, produced a pamphlet, *Sex Education in Schools and Youth Organisations*, commenting on the need for suitable instruction in schools, with parental backing, before strong emotions developed. The pamphlet acknowledged that, as sooner or later children gained an understanding of the process of human reproduction, it was important that they should be given answers to the fullest extent that the child was capable of understanding. 'It appears that a substantial proportion of parents either have some reluctance to give such knowledge to their children, or feel the need of some guidance on how best to deal with the matter.'

The pamphlet pointed out that, as many parents were absent from home because of the War, the parental advice that might have been given was not available. 'As a result, there is an increasing sense among teachers that they have a degree of responsibility for seeing that their pupils shall have some simple measure of sex education before leaving the school. Many teachers have approached the subject with diffidence in view of its nature and what they feel to be their own inadequate training or capacity to undertake it: others, for these and other reasons, have not ventured to embark on it at all.'[23] Few teachers felt well enough prepared to carry out the recommendations and on the eve of the Education Act of 1944 about one third of secondary schools made some provision for special lectures which aimed to inculcate a general respect for married life and condemned extramarital sex or deviant sex.[24]

The 1944 Education Act made schools responsible for providing education that contributed to the spiritual, moral, physical, and mental development of the community and made religious education and a daily act of worship a statutory requirement. It is interesting to note that over fifty years ago it was acknowledged that parents were reluctant to discuss sex with their children. Moreover, teachers were confused about what constituted sex education.

Alfred Kinsey – the fraudulent researcher of sexual behaviour

Like a bombshell the Kinsey Reports burst upon the relative innocence of the early 1950s. The publication of *Sexual Behavior in the Human Male* (1948) and *Sexual Behavior in the Human Female* (1953) heralded a major advance for the sexual revolution. The two reports received massive publicity and rapidly became international best sellers. *Esquire* magazine referred to Alfred Kinsey as the 'patron saint of sex', the man whose reports set in motion 'the first wave of the sexual revolution', while Albert Deutsch's article in *Harper's* asserted: 'The Kinsey survey explodes traditional concepts of what is normal and abnormal, natural and unnatural in sex behavior.'[25] There is no doubt that Kinsey's research has had a massive impact on public morality and the popular understanding of human sexual behaviour. It has also had a powerful and far-reaching influence on sex education policy in the USA and the UK.

According to Kinsey's associate, Wardell Pomeroy, Kinsey became an atheist while a college student when he discovered a basic incongruity between science and religion.[26] As a consequence, Kinsey, in setting up his research programmes, was careful to avoid selecting staff who believed in God. In his mind, America's repressive sexual attitudes were based on its religious beliefs.

In *The Family in America*, Jack Douglas provides the following assessment of Kinsey's philosophy: 'Alfred Kinsey asked questions and analysed their answers statistically in ways which implicitly assumed that all forms of "sexual outlets" are the same in meaning, value, emotional power, consequences and everything else... Kinsey literally reduced all human sexuality to the single dimension of orgasmic "outlet". In his behaviourist metaphysics, the number of "outlets" alone has meaning. His revolutionary zeal knew no bounds. His casual pronouncement on animalism shows the monomaniacal zealot at work.'[27]

In *Kinsey, Sex and Fraud* (1990) Dr Judith Reisman and her co-authors document the sinister spirit behind the work of Kinsey and his carefully selected group of like-minded researchers. Dr Reisman goes to great pains to demonstrate that the samples used by Kinsey were seriously biased—the male sample was largely made up of volunteers; that is, people who were willing to be interviewed about the details of their sexual life, and so were clearly not representative of the American population. The male sample was also heavily reliant on prison inmates and sex offenders. The statistical handling of the data is suspect and it is, therefore, misguided to generalise from the findings of Kinsey's survey to the population of the USA as a whole. The results are therefore not only meaningless, but potentially misleading. The authors reached the following conclusion: 'In view of Kinsey's grossly and knowingly unrepresentative interviewee populations, his use of data from illegal sexual experimentation on children, his history of deception in other endeavours, his predetermined bias and selection of like-minded co-researchers, his unethical and deceptive omission of data injurious to his own hypotheses, and his lucky coincidence in finding out about human sexuality exactly what he wanted to find out, we believe Kinsey's research to be worse than worthless—we believe the evidence over-whelmingly points to fraud.'[28]

Dr Albert Hobbs provides the following summary of the inconsistent and unscientific nature of Kinsey's methodology: 'Kinsey, in his studies of sexual behaviour, violated all three of the precepts necessary to scientific procedure. He denied, flatly and repeatedly, that he had any hypothesis, insisting that he merely, in his words, "presents the facts." Yet to any observant reader, Kinsey obviously had a two-pronged hypothesis. He vigorously promoted, juggling his figures to do so, a hedonistic, animalistic conception of sexual behaviour, while at the same time he consistently denounced all biblical and conventional conceptions of sexual behaviour. He refused to publish his basic data. He kept secret not only his hypotheses, but also refused to present the basic facts on which his conclusions rested. He refused to reveal the questionnaire which was the basis for all of his facts. In addition, it is possible to derive conclusions opposite to Kinsey's from his own data.'[29]

The research of Alfred Kinsey

Kinsey was insistent in his claim to be an objective scientist searching for scientific truth. He claimed that his research 'represents an attempt to accumulate an objectively determined body of fact about sex which strictly avoids social or moral interpretations of the fact. Each person who reads this report will want to make interpretations in accordance with his understanding of moral values and social significances; but that is not part of the scientific method and, indeed, scientists have no special capacities for making such evaluations.'[30] But, as we shall see, this claim was really a smokescreen to hide his revolutionary aims. He was, in fact, using 'science' to support his beliefs about sexual behaviour, and imposing his own moral interpretations through his writings.

He argued that the real scope of human sexual behaviour was unknown because 'our laws and customs are so far removed from the actual behaviour of the human animal that there are few persons who can afford to let their full [sexual] histories be known' because of the prejudices and taboos in Western society.[31] Only objective research could uncover the true nature of the sexual behaviour of the human animal. Because cultural factors had inhibited the human animal, because humans felt too ashamed or inhibited to reveal their true sexual nature, Kinsey always assumed that everyone had engaged in a particular type of sexual activity,[32] unless they specifically and repeatedly denied that they had done so. He was building into his research method a potential source of bias that would ensure that it produced results that fitted his own presuppositions.

Kinsey's hypothesis – the basic mammalian pattern of sexual behaviour

Kinsey and his co-researchers claimed that in many instances 'variant types of behaviour represent the basic mammalian patterns which have been so effectively suppressed by human culture that they persist and reappear only among those few individuals who ignore custom and deliberately follow their preferences in sexual techniques. In some instances sexual behaviour which is outside the socially accepted pattern is the more natural behaviour because it is less affected by social restraints. The clearest picture of learning in sexual behaviour is to be found in the homosexual; and if the homosexual had been ignored in the present study, we should not have realised that similar learning processes are involved in the development of the heterosexual.'[33] Kinsey's underlying presupposition was that human sexual activity would follow that of other mammals were it not for repressive human culture. And in Kinsey's mind the repressive culture inhibiting human sexuality was the one based in biblical morality.

The sexual nature of children

Kinsey had a special interest in the sexual nature of children. He claimed that sexual play is a common feature of childhood and that even the youngest children are capable of experiencing a sexual orgasm. 'Most of the [sex] play takes place with companions close to the subject's own age. On the other hand, the boy's initial experience is often (although not invariably) with a slightly older boy or girl. Older persons are the teachers of younger people in all matters, including the sexual. The record includes some cases of pre-adolescent boys involved in sexual contacts with adult females, and still more cases of pre-adolescent boys involved with adult males.'[34] A most remarkable finding was that 'about half of the older males (48 per cent), and nearer two-thirds (60 per cent) of the boys who were pre-adolescent at the time they contributed their histories, recall homosexual activity in their pre-adolescent years.'[35] He claimed that his research showed considerable sexual capacity among pre-adolescent boys. 'These records are based on more or less uninhibited boys, most of whom had heard about sex and seen sexual activities among their companions, and many of whom had had sexual contacts with one or more adults. Most of them knew of orgasm as the goal of such activity, and some of them, even at an early age, had become definitely aggressive in seeking contacts. Most boys are more inhibited, more restricted by parental controls.'[36]

Kinsey reported that 'the females in the sample who had had pre-adolescent contacts with adults had been variously interested, curious, pleased, embarrassed, frightened, terrified, or disturbed with feelings of guilt. The adult contacts are a source of pleasure to some children, and sometimes arouse the child erotically and bring it to orgasm. The contacts had often involved considerable affection... If a child were not culturally conditioned, it is doubtful if it would be disturbed by sexual approaches of the sort which had usually been involved in these histories. It is difficult to understand why a child, except for its cultural conditioning, should be disturbed at having its genitalia touched, or disturbed at seeing the genitalia of other persons, or disturbed at even more specific sexual contacts. When children are constantly warned by parents and teachers against contacts with adults, and when they receive no explanation of the exact nature of the forbidden contacts, they are ready to become hysterical as soon as any older person approaches, or stops and speaks to them in the street, or fondles them...'[37]

Kinsey concluded that children are sexual beings, capable of enjoying sexual contacts with other children and adults. He implied that it is unfortunate that natural childhood sexual activity was being suppressed by a moral code which prohibits sex with children. He was, in his mind, providing the evidence that it is natural for children to enjoy sexual contact with adults, and that it is only cultural conditioning that prevents children from enjoying genital sex. These views represent an open encouragement to paedophilia.

The total sexual outlet

Turning to adults, Kinsey recorded 'the frequency and sources of sexual outlet in the biological mature male, that is, in the adolescent and older male'. He measured human sexual capacity by the number of sources of sexual orgasm and the frequency of orgasm that resulted from each source—taken together they produced what he called the 'total sexual outlet'. 'The sexual activity of an individual may involve a variety of experiences, a portion of which may culminate in the event which is known as orgasm or sexual climax. There are six chief sources of sexual climax. There is self-stimulation, nocturnal dreaming to the point of climax, heterosexual petting to climax (without intercourse), true heterosexual intercourse, homosexual intercourse, and contact with animals of other species.'[38] Kinsey made the point that there were 'both theoretically and in actuality, endless possibilities in combining these several sources of outlet and in the extent to which each of them contributes to the total picture.'[39]

According to Kinsey the variations in frequency of sexual activity are of great social importance. Our sexual conventions, and especially marriage, assume that people have similar sexual needs and therefore can conform to a moral code of behaviour. But this does not recognise the large variations in sexual capacity. 'Even in such an obvious sexual situation as marriage, there is little consideration, under our present custom, of the possibility that the two persons who have mated may be far apart in their sexual inclinations, backgrounds, and capacities.'[40] The implication is that in the marriage union one or other partner is likely to be sexually deprived because of innate differences in sexual capacity. It follows that the moral code, which does not recognise variations in sexual capacity, can lead to sexual repression and frustration as the more active partner is deprived of finding another outlet to satisfy their needs. The solution, in Kinsey's eyes, is for the deprived partner to engage in an extramarital outlet.

No sexual activity abnormal or perverted

Kinsey sees the range of human sexual behaviours as a continuous curve, and argues that evaluating the frequency of sexual outlet as 'normal' or 'abnormal' serves no purpose. 'The most significant thing about this curve is its continuity... At the best, abnormal may designate certain individuals whose rates of activity are less frequent, or whose sources of sexual outlet are not as usual in the population as a whole; but in that case, it is preferable to refer to such persons as rare, rather than abnormal. Moreover, many items in human sexual behaviour which are labelled abnormal, or perversions, in textbooks, prove, upon statistical examination, to occur in as many as 30 or 60 or 75 per cent of certain populations. It is difficult to maintain that such types of behaviour are abnormal because they are rare.'[41] Here Kinsey is developing the argument that because certain types of sexual activity, such as homosexuality, are relatively common according to his research, they cannot be labelled as abnormal or perverted. Other activities, such as paedophilia and bestiality, although rare, are only so because of restraints imposed by social and religious conditioning.

The despised Victorian moral code

Throughout his writings Kinsey reveals a deep dislike of Christian morality, which he refers to as the 'ancient English moral codes', almost as if he is reluctant to use the word Christian. He expresses his frustration that 'scientific classifications [of sexual behaviour] have been nearly identical with theological classifications and with the moral pronouncements of the English common law of the fifteenth century'. As a consequence of this despised English moral code, 'present day legal determinations of sexual acts which are acceptable, or "natural," and those which are "contrary to nature", are not based on data obtained from biologists, nor from nature herself... In no other field of science have scientists been satisfied to accept the biologic [sic] notions of ancient jurists and theologians, or the analysis made by the mystics of two or three thousand years ago.'[42] Here Kinsey is suggesting that science, and not biblical morality, should determine which sexual acts are acceptable. He was intensely irritated that the sexual laws of Western civilisation were based on biblical morality, and he saw it as his mission to change the laws which made certain forms of sexual behaviour illegal.

Having declared that all types of sexual activity are normal, Kinsey identified Victorian sexual morality as the major cause of sexual repression in England and America. He claimed that adolescent sexual activity was almost universal in Western Europe throughout the eighteenth century until the Victorians interfered. He comments that there is every indication in European literature, both sober and erotic, that 'the high [sexual] capacity of the younger male was recognised and rather widely accepted until near the Victorian day in England. The problem of sexual adjustment for the young male is one which has become especially aggravated during the last hundred years, and then primarily in England and in America, under an increasing moral suppression which has coincided with an increasing delay in the age of marriage.'[43] Kinsey saw the Victorian code of sexual behaviour as the chief cause of sexual suppression in Western society.

Kinsey identifies three conflicting views of sex. The first is found in 'cultures and religions which have inclined to the hedonistic doctrine that sexual activity is justifiable for its immediate and pleasurable return'. The second is based in religions 'which have accepted sex primarily as the necessary means of procreation, to be enjoyed only in marriage, and then only if reproduction is the goal of the act'. The third view interprets 'sex as a normal biological function, acceptable in whatever form it is manifested'. He laments that this amoral view is unacceptable to most people in society, and he knows where to lay the blame. 'By English and American standards, such an attitude is considered primitive, materialistic or animalistic, and beneath the dignity of a civilised and educated people.'[44] And so the battle lines are drawn between the biblical view of sex, which links sexual intercourse with marriage and fidelity, and Kinsey's biological, animalistic view, which sees sex as no more than a biological function devoid of all moral considerations.

Kinsey is profoundly hostile to the sexual conventions, morals and laws of England and America. 'Specifically, English-American legal codes restrict the sexual activity of the unmarried male by characterising all premarital, extramarital, and post-marital intercourse as rape, statutory rape, fornication, adultery, prostitution, association with a prostitute, incest, delinquency, assault and battery, or public indecency—all of which are offences with penalties attached.' In addition to establishing restrictions by way of the statutory and common law, 'society at large, and each element in it, have developed mores that even profoundly affect the frequency of sexual activity and the general pattern of behaviour'. The effect of these mores on the individual who conforms 'is strongly to limit his opportunity for intercourse, or for most other types of sexual activity, especially if he is unmarried, widowed, separated or divorced.'[45]

In the above polemic Kinsey is acknowledging the powerful influence of biblical morality on the sexual behaviour of England and America. 'There is nothing in the English-American social structure which has had more influence upon present-day patterns of sexual behaviour than the religious backgrounds of that culture… Our particular systems certainly go back to the Old Testament philosophy on which the Talmud is based, and which was the philosophy of those Jews who first followed the Christian faith.' Furthermore, the sex law of English common courts, formulated between the twelfth and fifteenth centuries, was based on biblical law, 'and irrespective of the specific statutes which the several states have written to control sexual behaviour, the decisions of American criminal courts today are primarily based upon the precedents of those common courts.'[46]

The main problem, from Kinsey's point of view, is that Christian teaching on sexual morality had influenced the whole of society. 'The church, however, exerts a wider influence on even non-devout individuals, by way of the influence which it has had throughout the centuries upon the development of the sexual mores of our Western European-American culture. The religious codes have always and everywhere been the prime source of those social attitudes which, in their aggregate, represent the sexual mores of all groups, devout or non-devout, churchgoing or non-churchgoing, rational, faithful to a creed, or merely following the customs of the land… In theological terms, such systems are ascribed to divine revelation…'[47]

Kinsey observed that the effect of moral teaching was to restrict the sexual activity of the human animal. This is why the 'average frequencies of sexual outlet for the human male are distinctly below those which are normal among some other anthropoids and which would probably be normal in the human animal if there were no restrictions upon his sexual activity.'[48] In other words, if the restrictions imposed by biblical morality could be removed, human beings would be free to achieve their optimal level of sexual activity.

Premarital sex

Kinsey presented the arguments for and against premarital sexual intercourse. He asserted that the arguments in favour 'have rarely been marshalled, perhaps because of the general disapproval in our culture'.[49] Among his twelve reasons in favour were factors such as satisfying a physiological need for a sexual outlet; becoming a source of immediate physical and psychological satisfaction; increasing one's ability to function more effectively in other, non-sexual fields; providing training in the sorts of physical techniques that may be involved in marital coitus; and testing the capacity of two persons to make satisfactory sexual adjustments after marriage.[50]

According to Kinsey, the only undesirable physical after-effects are 'an occasional unwanted pregnancy, a rare instance of venereal disease, or a very rare instance of physical damage'.[51] The main problem is seen as conflict with the social organisation of which the individual is a part, which can generate guilt, and neurotic disturbances. However, when premarital sexual intercourse is accepted by the culture then it does not generate psychological conflicts. So the major source of psychological and social problems among those who engage in premarital sex is the condemnation that comes from a society which has labelled such behaviour as immoral. Kinsey's assessment that premarital sex is associated with an 'occasional' unwanted pregnancy and a 'rare' instance of venereal disease shows how little he really knew about the consequences of his ideology. It is significant that as his views have become more acceptable in society, sexual tragedies have become increasingly common.

Extramarital sex

Kinsey comments that although extramarital sexual intercourse is generally desired, it has seldom worked in society as it is constructed at present. He appears to be disappointed that only an occasional writer has suggested that extramarital sex can be utilised for human needs. Nevertheless, Kinsey is interested in the question that naturally flows from his view of sex: 'Is it inevitable that extramarital intercourse should lead to difficulties, or do the difficulties originate in the mores of the group...? Do extramarital relations ever contribute to the effectiveness of a marriage? What effect does such activity ultimately have upon the personalities of those who are involved? Certainly society may be concerned with securing objective answers to these questions.'[52] And he claims that his survey showed that 'there are some individuals among our histories whose sexual adjustments in marriage have undoubtedly been helped by extramarital experience. Sometimes this depends upon their learning new techniques or acquiring new attitudes which reduce inhibitions in their marital relations.'[53] Kinsey was disappointed that there was still such a strong taboo against adultery. He encouraged the idea that adultery could, in fact, be beneficial, but once again the obstacle to such benefit was the sexual mores of society.

Homosexual outlet

Kinsey informs his readers that 'exclusive preferences and patterns of behaviour, heterosexual or homosexual, come only with experience, or as a result of social pressures which tend to force an individual into an exclusive pattern of one or the other sort'. He concludes that, considering the mammalian background of human behaviour, 'it is not so difficult to explain why a human animal does a particular thing sexually. It is more difficult to explain why each and every individual is not involved in every type of sexual activity.'[54]

Kinsey claims that homosexuality is extremely common. According to his definition (of physical contact to the point of orgasm) 'the data in the present study indicate that at least 37 per cent of the male population has some homosexual experience between the beginning of adolescence and old age. This is more than one male in three of the persons that one may meet as he passes along a city street. Among the males who remain unmarried until the age 35, almost exactly 50 per cent have homosexual experience between the beginning of adolescence and that age.'[55] In addition, 'about 60 per cent of the pre-adolescent boys engage in homosexual activities, and there is an additional group of adult males who avoid overt contacts but who are quite aware of their potentialities for reacting to other males'.[56] And among females, by the age of 30 'a quarter of all females had recognised erotic responses to other females'.[57]

Despite the fact that over half the male population is homosexual or bisexual, according to Kinsey's reckoning, homosexual contacts only account for 8 to 16 per cent of total male orgasms among unmarried males. This suggests that men are being sexually deprived, for they are missing out on homosexual contacts. Kinsey continues, 'These low rates are in striking discord with the fact that homosexual contacts could in actuality be had more abundantly than heterosexual contacts, if there were no social restraints or personal conflicts involved. The sexual possibilities of the average male in his teens or twenties are probably more often assayed by males than by females, and younger males who are attractive physically or who have attractive personalities may be approached for homosexual relations more often than they themselves would ever approach females for heterosexual relations. A homosexually experienced male could undoubtedly find a larger number of sexual partners among males than a heterosexually experienced male could find among females.'[58] His argument is that men are being deprived of a major source of sexual gratification by not indulging in more homosexual contacts.

According to Kinsey, 'long-time relationships between two males are notably few. Long-time relationships in the heterosexual would probably be less frequent than they are, if there were no social custom or legal restraints to enforce continued relationships in marriage.'[59] The implication is that short-term sexual relationships, both homosexual and heterosexual, are natural, and that it is marriage that forces couples into unnatural lifelong sexual relationships.

Heterosexual-homosexual balance

Kinsey is concerned that 'a great deal of the thinking done by scientists and laymen alike stems from the assumption that there are persons who are "heterosexual" and persons who are "homosexual", that these two types represent antitheses in the sexual world, and that there is only an insignificant class of "bisexuals" who occupy an intermediate position between the other groups. It is implied that every individual is innately—inherently—either heterosexual or homosexual.'[60]

But Kinsey, who regarded himself as a great sexual scientist, proposed a new theory of human sexual behaviour. 'The histories which have been available in the present study make it apparent that the heterosexuality or homosexuality of many individuals is not an all-or-none proposition. It is true that there are persons in the population whose histories are exclusively heterosexual, both in regard to their overt experience and in regard to their psychic reactions. And there are individuals in the population whose histories are exclusively homosexual, both in experience and in psychic reactions. But the record also shows that there is a considerable portion of the population whose members have combined, within their individual histories, both homosexual and heterosexual experiences and/

or psychic responses. There are those whose heterosexual experiences predominate, there are those whose homosexual experiences predominate, there are some who have had quite equal amounts of both types of experience... The living world is a continuum in each and every one of its aspects. The sooner we learn this concerning human sexual behaviour the sooner we shall reach a sound understanding of the realities of sex.' On the basis of his findings Kinsey presents his heterosexual-homosexual rating scale, which shows human sexuality as a continuum.[61] As humans are bisexual in nature, it is perfectly natural for males and females to have sex both with members of the same sex and with members of the opposite sex.

Kinsey concludes that 'the homosexual has been a significant part of human sexual activity ever since the dawn of history, primarily because it is an expression of capacities that are basic in the human animal'.[62] In his mind, the problem for society is not homosexuality, which he regarded as a natural expression of human sexuality, but the moral standards that condemn homosexuality as a perversion.

Animal sexual contacts

Kinsey also challenges the widely held belief that human sexual contact with animals is unnatural. 'In the animal kingdom as a whole, is it to be believed that the sources of sexual attraction are of such a nature that they provide stimuli only for individuals of the same species? For the scientist it does not suffice to be told that nature allows nothing else but intraspecific mating because she considers reproduction to be the objective of all sexual activities.' It is only those people who have not had sexual contact with animals who view with abhorrence 'intercourse between humans and animals of other species'.

Kinsey states that human sexual contacts with animals are relatively frequent. 'Ultimately, 14 to 16 per cent of the rural males of the grade school level, 20 per cent of the rural males of the high school level, and 26 to 28 per cent of the rural males on the college level have had some animal experience to the point of orgasm.'[63] Moreover, 'in not a few cases the animal contacts become homosexual activities. Masturbating the male animal, whether it is a dog, horse, bull or some other species, may provide considerable erotic excitement for the boy or older adult. He senses the genital similarities between the male animal and himself, and he recognises the relationship between the animal's performance and reactions and his own capacities.'[64]

'In rural communities where animal contacts are not infrequent, and where there is some general knowledge that they do commonly occur, there seem to be few personal conflicts growing out of such activity, and very few social difficulties. It is only when the farm-bred male migrates to a city community and comes in contact with city-bred reactions to these activities, that he becomes upset over the contemplation of what he has done... The clinician who can reassure these individuals that such activities are biologically and psychologically part of the *normal mammalian picture* [my italics], and that such contacts occur in as high a percentage of the farm population as we have already indicated, may contribute materially toward the resolution of these conflicts.'[65]

Kinsey concludes that despite the moral issues involved, 'and however long-standing the social condemnation of animal contacts may have been throughout the history of Western European civilisations, the easy dismissal of such behaviour by characterising it as abnormal shows little capacity for making objective analyses of the basic psychology that is involved'. So in Kinsey's *amoral view* of sexual behaviour even animal contacts cannot be labelled as abnormal or unnatural, for they constitute another useful sexual outlet.

Kinsey and the sexual revolution

In their essay 'The Kinsey Grand Scheme', Edward Eichel and Gordon Muir argue that the ultimate purpose of the Kinsey Reports was to prove a theory and establish a new morality.[66] In his passion to promote a new scheme of human sexuality, Kinsey initiated a two-part strategy. 'First, he advocated the establishment of bisexuality as the balanced sexual orientation for normal uninhibited people. In effect, the objective was to get heterosexuals to have homosexual experiences. This was the basic step in obliterating the heterosexual norm of sexuality, with the traditional protective family structure, values and conventional sexual behaviour (heterosexual intercourse) implied. This would open the way for the second and more difficult step—the ultimate goal of "cross-generational sex" (sex with children).'[67] The authors conclude that 'while adult-child sex is identified as a major objective of the Kinsey "grand scheme", arriving at such a goal will not be easy'.[68] But 'the challenge is being met with a subtle and comprehensive campaign affecting society's most-prized belief systems, professions and institutions'. Key aspects of the campaign include the following:

* encourage gay activist movements, and establish homosexuality as a normal sexual orientation
* declare paedophilia a sexual orientation and add adult-child sex to the agenda
* promote widespread promiscuity to create a sexual anarchy, where so many are implicated that the distinction of paedophilia might seem insignificant
* promote the sexual rights of children, to open the way for paedophilia
* attack religion to undermine the Judeo-Christian concept of sin and eliminate the distinction between right and wrong
* redefine family to break the heterosexual model of a nuclear family with a mother and father.[69]

From the above analysis it is clear that Kinsey was not an objective scientist, as he claimed, but a dedicated sex revolutionary. At the centre of his research was a fascination with the sexual response of children. He used his research to cultivate the idea that even the youngest children are sexually responsive, and that sexual contacts with adults are a source of pleasure to some children. He propagated the idea that the reason children were not more overtly sexually active was because of the negative influence of societal restraints and cultural inhibitions. Kinsey's research provided the 'scientific' foundation for the belief that children benefit from becoming sexually active at an early age – with the help of adult 'partners'.[70]

At the heart of his ideology is a profound rejection of biblical morality. Sex is no more than a natural biological instinct and therefore people should be encouraged to choose their sexual outlets free from any cultural or moral inhibitions. His approach is strictly amoral—nothing is right or wrong, no form of sexual outlet is abnormal or harmful and there is no such thing as sexual perversion since every type of sexual activity, even bestiality, is natural. Kinsey demoralised every aspect of sexual behaviour to the extent of claiming that there is no difference between human and animal sexual behaviour. Males are presented as predatory sexual playboys who seek as many sexual 'outlets' as possible; females are portrayed as sexually promiscuous playmates; premarital sex is promoted as beneficial for overcoming unnatural sexual inhibitions. In Kinsey's amoral world no conduct is off-limits; the frequency of the climax and the quality of the source is all that counts.

Kinsey realised that true sexual liberation would only be achieved when the last vestiges of Christian morality, which he identified as the main cause of sexual repression, had been purged from society. He was in no doubt that the moral teachings of the Bible stood in the way of the sexual revolution that he longed for. In Kinsey's mind the Victorians were the real culprits, for they had established a society based on the biblical virtues of modesty, chivalry, chastity and fidelity and had spread their beliefs across the English speaking world, and especially to the USA.

Kinsey's writings are important because they have had a significant influence on sex education policy, particularly in the USA, but also in the UK and other English speaking countries. The sex education movement has eagerly grasped his ideas and many of the human sexuality programmes, designed to educate sex educators, are committed to the homosexual orientation of the Kinsey school of thought. We have already seen, in chapter 2, that sex education literature in the UK is consistent with Kinsey's ideas on homosexuality. Moreover, the sex education books of Kinsey's co-worker, Wardell Pomeroy, have been enthusiastically promoted by the FPA as being 'particularly helpful to family planners and sex educators'. *Boys and Sex*, discussed on page 136, is described by the FPA as providing adolescent boys with practical advice 'on how to achieve a happy, guilt-free sex life'.[71]

Endnotes

1 Marie Stopes, *Married Love*, Putman & Co, 24th edition, London, 1940
2 Ruth Hall, *Marie Stopes, a biography*, Andre Deutsch, London, 1977, p131
3 June Rose, *Marie Stopes and the Sexual Revolution*, Faber and Faber, London, 1992, p100
4 Ibid. pp93-94
5 Marie Stopes, *Marriage In My Time*, Rich and Cowan, 1935, p44
6 Ibid. June Rose, *Marie Stopes and the Sexual Revolution*, p114
7 Ibid. p114

8 Ibid. p131

9 Ibid. p118

10 Ibid. p118

11 Ibid. Ruth Hall, *Marie Stopes, a biography*, p260

12 *Daily Mirror*, 16 March 1925, cited from Ruth Hall, *Marie Stopes*, p260

13 Ibid. June Rose, *Marie Stopes and the Sexual Revolution*, p124

14 *The New Witness*, 12 September 1919, cited from *Marie Stopes and the Sexual Revolution*, p130

15 Marie Stopes, 'A New Gospel to All Peoples', AL Humphreys, London, 1922, cited from June Rose, *Marie Stopes and the Sexual Revolution*, p136

16 Lambeth Conference 1920, report

17 Ibid. June Rose, *Marie Stopes and the Sexual Revolution*, p144

18 *John Bull*, 8 April, 1922, cited from *Marie Stopes and the Sexual Revolution*, p157

19 Ibid. June Rose, *Marie Stopes and the Sexual Revolution*, p119

20 *The Times*, 6 October 1927

21 Ibid. June Rose, *Marie Stopes and the Sexual Revolution*, p204

22 Ibid. p209

23 Board of Education, *Sex Education in Schools and Youth Organisations*, Educational Pamphlet no. 119, 1943, HMSO, cited from Ofsted Report, *Sex and Relationships*, Office for Standards in Education, 2002, p33

24 Mike Davis, *Sex, lies and stereotypes*, Chartist Magazine website

25 Cited from Judith A Reisman, Edward Eichel, John Court, Gordon Muir in *Kinsey, Sex and Fraud*, A Lochinvar-Huntington House Publication, 1990, p2 and p3

26 Wardell Pomeroy, *Kinsey and the Institute for Sex Research*, Harper & Row, New York, 1972, p53

27 Jack Douglas, *The Family in America*, The Rockford Institute, Mount Morris, Illinois, May 1987, pp1-8, cited from *Kinsey: Crimes & Consequences*, Judith Reisman, 2nd edition, 1998, The Institute for Media Education, p16

28 Judith A Reisman, Edward Eichel, John Court, Gordon Muir, *Kinsey, Sex and Fraud*, A Lochinvar-Huntington House Publication, 1990, p219

29 Albert H Hobbs, unpublished manuscript, cited from Judith Reisman, *Kinsey: Crimes & Consequences*, The Institute for Media Education, 2000, p54

30 Alfred Kinsey, Wardell Pomeroy, Clyde Martin, *Sexual Behavior in the Human Male*, WB Saunders Company, 11th printing, 1953, p5

31 Ibid. p44

32 Ibid. p53

33 Ibid. p59

34 Ibid. p167

35 Ibid. p168

36 Ibid. p177

37 Alfred Kinsey, *Sexual Behavior in the Human Female*, WB Saunders, 1953, London, p121

38 Ibid. *Sexual Behavior in the Human Male*, p157

39 Ibid. p193

40 Ibid. p197

41 Ibid. pp199-201

42 Ibid. pp202-203

43 Ibid. p222

44 Ibid. p263

45 Ibid. pp263-265

46 Ibid. p465

47 Ibid. pp486-87

48 Ibid. p468

49 Ibid. *Sexual Behavior in the Human Female*, p308

50 Ibid. pp308-309

51 Ibid. p320

52 Ibid. *Sexual Behavior in the Human Male*, p591

53 Ibid. p593

54 Ibid. *Sexual Behavior in the Human Female*, pp448-451
55 Ibid. *Sexual Behavior in the Human Male*, p623
56 Ibid. p610
57 Ibid. *Sexual Behavior in the Human Female*, p453
58 Ibid. *Sexual Behavior in the Human Male*, p632
59 Ibid. p633
60 Ibid. p637
61 Ibid. pp664-65
62 Ibid. p666
63 Ibid. p671
64 Ibid. p676
65 Ibid. p677
66 Ibid. *Kinsey, Sex and Fraud*, p217
67 Ibid. p205
68 Ibid. p213
69 Ibid. p214
70 Ibid. p217
71 The Family Planning Association, Book List 1972

Chapter 7

The permissive 1960s

Ideology of Margaret Sanger and the IPPF; Wilhelm Reich

and the Sexual Revolution; the establishment of

Brook in the UK and SIECUS in the USA

Following the enthusiastic reception of the Kinsey reports by the mass media and liberal intelligentsia, the sexual revolution, which had been put on hold during the Second World War, was slowly beginning to gain momentum. Kinsey's research had laid a firm foundation for sex education. He had shown that there was no 'scientific' basis for labelling any form of sexual activity as abnormal or perverted. Indeed, the only reason people did not partake of every type of sexual activity imaginable was because of cultural and religious restraints. Therefore, if people could be educated in a way that helped them overcome their sexual repression they would be free to express their true sexuality. To be truly liberated they also needed to understand the benefits of their bisexual nature, and grasp the profound 'truth' that no sexual activity could be proved to be wrong, perverted or evil.

In England, meanwhile, Marie Stopes had succeeded in placing birth control on to the national agenda, while in the USA, Margaret Sanger, founder of the birth control movement, was busy insinuating the ideas of the sexual revolution into mainstream American thought. Her vision was to spread the message of birth control worldwide.

Ideology of Margaret Sanger and the IPPF

The formation of the International Planned Parenthood Federation (IPPF) in 1952 in Bombay was the first step towards a worldwide birth control movement. The eight founding members included national organisations from the USA, England, Sweden, India and the Netherlands. Margaret Sanger, who by now was world famous as the pioneer of birth control, was a principal force behind the creation of the Federation and one of its first co-presidents. Her mission was to persuade the government of member nations to take on the responsibility of providing birth control for their population.

A fundamental objective of the IPPF was to get family planning, legal abortion and sex education accepted as human rights. This objective is embedded in the constitution of the IPPF as a fundamental principle on which its worldwide network of membership is based. Since its inception it has striven to make birth control a human right for all people.[1]

The IPPF sees itself in the role of family planning pioneers, taking the birth control message to nations that have not yet heard it. By sending family planning motivators into a country the IPPF stimulates interest in its cause. Their aim is to influence public opinion, thereby encouraging a country to form its own family planning association—by 1961 the IPPF already had 32 members. According to a pamphlet produced in 1971, the IPPF encourages 'the formation of national associations to pioneer family planning services in each country of the world and to bring about a favourable climate of public opinion in which governments can be persuaded to accept responsibility'.[2]..The idea is for FPAs to provide a nucleus of staff around which an expanded government programme can be built.

Controlling population growth is another important aim. Actions to reduce the birth rate include the following: the restructuring of the family so as to postpone or avoid marriage; altering the image of the ideal family; promoting policies that make married people pay more taxes than single people, and encouraging women to work.[3] This is one of the reasons why the taxation regime in the UK is so unfavourable to married couples. According to Patricia Morgan, in her book *Farewell to the Family*, the decreasing ability of men to make provision for families 'has probably played a pivotal role in generating high rates of non-marriage, family breakdown and a rising proportion of children without fathers on both sides of the Atlantic'. Unemployment, low paid jobs and 'a tax system progressively disinclined to recognise family responsibilities, have produced a momentous change in the marital as well as the economic opportunities of populations'.[4]

In 1976 the IPPF set out a *Strategy of Legal Reform – and how FPAs are interpreting it*.[5] Strategic aims to improve the status of women include a woman's 'right' to abortion, sterilisation, tax reform, relaxed divorce laws, a lower age of consent for birth control services and, of course, compulsory sex education. The IPPF encourages governments to accept responsibility for establishing State controlled family planning, such as we have in the UK. By the year 2000 the IPPF had a network of FPAs in over 180 countries actively engaged in spreading its ideology of 'safer sex', 'safe abortion' and sex education.

To understand the IPPF it is necessary to understand the ideology of its founder Margaret Sanger, the woman who devoted her life to the promotion of contraception, and who coined the term 'birth control'. She believed that preventing conception helped to liberate women from the bondage caused by bourgeois morality, laws and superstitions.[6] In *Birth Control in America*, David Kennedy describes how the young Margaret was influenced by a group of New York radicals, including the redoubtable anarchist Emma Goldman who was an outspoken advocate of voluntary motherhood.[7] 'When Freud came to Clark University in Worcester, Massachusetts, to lecture in 1909, his was only the most dramatic in a long series of importations of radically new sexual ideas from England and Europe. The United States had known Havelock Ellis's researches in sexual psychology for a decade. Margaret Sanger had certainly read them. She had also read Edward Carpenter, whose *Love's Coming-of-Age* had a wide circulation in America after 1911.'[8]

Margaret Sanger admired Nietzsche for his attack on Western morality, which she saw as the foundation on which the repressive Church and State were built. She rejected the Christian ideal in favour of a new ethic which emphasised life in its fullness. Emotion played a large role in the new morality Mrs Sanger advocated.[9] 'Those who restrain desire', she wrote, 'do so because the desire is weak enough to be restrained.'[10] She was an open and ardent propagandist for the joys of the flesh and believed that traditional attitudes towards sex were infantile, archaic, and ignorant. She believed that the birth control movement freed the mind from 'sexual prejudice and taboo, by demanding the frankest and most unflinching re-examination of sex in its relation to human nature and the bases of human society.'[11]

David Kennedy concludes that Margaret Sanger, as the foremost propagandist for sexual reform in twentieth century America, exemplified a critical shift in sexual attitudes from those of the nineteenth century.[12] She identified the objective of her activities as 'unlimited sexual gratification without the burden of unwanted children'.[13] She had absorbed and believed every last word written by the sexual revolutionaries of the nineteenth century. When she visited England in 1914 she met Charles Drysdale and his wife, leaders of the English Neo-Malthusian League; she also met Edward Carpenter and her hero Havelock Ellis to whom she developed a strong attachment. Her discussion with the leaders of sexual liberation in England had a strong impact on her thinking. According to David Kennedy, 'The Drysdales, and especially Havelock Ellis, insisted that she concentrate on one issue, birth control, and leave the denunciations of capitalism, churches and matrimony aside... With Havelock Ellis's guidance, Margaret Sanger began to shape the ideas she had assimilated into a systematic, even philosophic, justification for birth control.'[14]

Margaret Sanger was totally committed to the ideology of the sexual revolution, and this ideology was the motivating force behind the IPPF, a vehicle that would deliver her revolutionary ideas to the world. She had understood that for her vision of worldwide birth control to succeed, the IPPF needed to infiltrate the ideals of the sexual revolution into governments in order that governmental organisations, backed up with State funding, could be used to promote the message.

Today the IPPF has divided the world into six regions from which it delivers its operations. It also works closely with the United Nations Population Fund, the United Nations Children's Fund, the World Health Organisation and the World Bank. The IPPF is funded by grants from the wealthy nations, such as the USA, the UK, Canada, Japan and Sweden, and also receives donations from a number of private foundations, including the Rockefeller Foundation. The strength of the IPPF is that it is a federation of national FPAs, which, while operating within their own cultural and legal setting, are committed to the ideology of the Federation. It acts as the conscience of the family planning movement in tackling controversial issues which Government departments are unwilling to deal with, such as the distribution of new methods of contraception and sex education. As the financial resources of IPPF have grown, it has been able to support FPAs in developing countries around the world.

A key objective of the IPPF is to safeguard the right of individuals to make free and 'informed choices' in regard to their own sexual health. It has always campaigned to make family planning and access to 'safe' abortion a human right. In countries which permit abortion, the IPPF objective is for women to be informed of their legal rights and provided with confidential information on how to obtain an abortion. National FPAs are advised that any political, administrative or social barrier to this right should be condemned. The IPPF also campaigns for the rights of young people to be provided with contraceptive information and services, and specialises in using the mass media to defend these rights. It helps FPAs use every opportunity to influence Government policies, and strives to remove all barriers and opposition. The IPPF aims to 'educate' government policy-makers on the need for a national commitment to family planning and sex education.[15]

The IPPF Youth Manifesto declares that young people must have education on sexuality and the best possible sexual health services, including contraception, which must be confidential, accessible and free from judgement. Young people must be supported by laws that allow them to act freely in the way they choose to live their lives. Obstacles that make young people feel uncomfortable about themselves, their bodies and their relationships must be removed. Society must recognise the right of all young people to enjoy sex and to express their sexuality in the way that they choose.[16]

The IPPF believes that it is always a mistake for FPAs to enter into debates on questions of morality. Instead, the approach of those who advocate family planning, abortion and sex education should be to insist on free and informed choice.[17] This is an interesting admission for it shows how the IPPF, and its constituent FPAs, are afraid of moral debates and therefore strive to demoralise all discussions on contraception, abortion and sex education. It follows that those who would oppose the ideology of the IPPF should do so on moral grounds, and not fall into the trap of demoralising the debate on abortion and sex education.

Although the ideas developed during the last decades of the nineteenth century and first part of the twentieth century had laid the foundation for the sexual revolution, it did not occur immediately for it took time for the ideas to gain acceptance among the English people who were still largely conservative in their attitudes to sexual matters. The first half of the twentieth century had been racked by two world wars, and people had other things to occupy their energies. At the end of the Second World War, the traumatised people were only too happy to abide by the old traditional values with which they were so familiar. Many people had depended on their Christian faith for comfort and security during the difficult war years, and national days of prayer at critical points had been observed nationwide. Shattered lives were being restored and marriage and the family were really important. The old morality was convenient and reassuring in our time of need. And so the 1950s were a time of rebuilding that brought with them a sense of security and peace. The Crowther Report on education, *Fifteen to Eighteen* (1959), in tune with the moral outlook of the 1950s, proposed the use of sex education to teach the values of chastity, marriage and family. The report went so far as to suggest that the incentive for girls to equip themselves for marriage and home-making was genetic.

But once life was on an even keel, and prosperous times were upon us, the desire for the new freedoms offered by the sexual revolution grew during the restless 1960s, and the scene was set for the revolt against traditional morality. When the FPA approved the use of oral contraception in 1961, it became easier to separate sex and reproduction—recreational sex was a tempting possibility. Now the ideas implanted by the philosophy of Friedrich Nietzsche, Sigmund Freud, Edward Carpenter, Havelock Ellis, Lytton Strachey, Marie Stopes and Alfred Kinsey, to mention some of the more important sexual revolutionaries, would take root and bear their inevitable fruit. The reprinting in English of *The Sexual Revolution* by Wilhelm Reich was a portent of the sexual revolution that was to spread like a cancer through society during the permissive decades of the 1960s and 70s. The dark cloud of sexual immorality was slowly starting to descend on Great Britain.

Ideology of Wilhelm Reich (1897-1957)

The Sexual Revolution, written by Wilhelm Reich, a disciple of Freud, is an important book for it provides a clear statement of the objectives of the sexual revolution. Reich makes it clear that the aim of the revolution is to produce people who are sexually free to enjoy genital gratification. This required a radical transformation of human sexual behaviour as society was sexually repressed by what he labelled 'compulsory morality'. His fight was to destroy 'compulsory morality' in order to develop what he called a sex-affirming society. He claimed that sexual repression formed the basis for the patriarchal authoritarian society.[18] 'The existence of severe moral tenets always proves… that the biological needs, particularly the sexual needs, are not being gratified. Every kind of moral regulation is *per se* sex-negative, condemns or denies the natural sexual needs. Any kind of moralism is life-negative, and the most important task of a free society is that of making possible for its members the satisfaction of their natural needs.'[19]

Reich's analysis identified a struggle between, on the one side, Christian sexual morality, which he saw as the cause of sexual repression, compulsory marriage and the authoritarian family, and, on the other side, what he called 'natural' morality. What he was advocating was a 'natural' morality based on self-regulation, for such a morality would establish a society that was free from sexual repression. The two kinds of morality are in conflict. The 'morality' which everybody affirms as a matter of course, such as not to rape, not to murder and so on, can be established only on the basis of full gratification of the natural needs. The other 'morality', which teaches sexual abstinence for children and adolescents and compulsory marital fidelity, is refuted by Reich as, in itself, pathological, for it 'creates the very chaos it professes to control. It is the archenemy of natural morality.'[20] Compulsory morality, as illustrated in marital duty and familial authority, 'is the morality of cowardly and impotent individuals who are incapable of experiencing through natural love what they try to obtain in vain with the aid of the police and marriage laws. These people try to put all humanity into their own straitjacket because they are incapable of tolerating natural sexuality in others.'[21] The moralist simply does not understand that 'sexual misery is an integral part of the social order which he defends'.[22]

Reich encouraged the idea that a couple should have sex before they considered marriage, for they need to 'convince themselves that they are matched in the basis of their life together, that is, in their sexual life'.[23] While acknowledging that at the time it seemed absurd, he was in favour of children of 15 or 16 having sex and predicted that 'in a few more years it will be as much a matter of course as is today the right of the unmarried woman to have a sexual partner'.[24] This prediction, which seemed ridiculous at the time, has now become reality.

According to Reich, the reason for the slow progress to sexual reform was the failure to recognise the links between marriage, the family and sexual behaviour. He had discovered that it was the institution of marriage that acted as the brake on sexual reform. It was the sexual repression inherent in marriage which helped to maintain extramarital chastity and marital fidelity. Moreover, the compulsive family was the educational apparatus that inculcated into children the ideas of 'compulsive morality'. In Reich's mind the family was 'the foremost breeding ground of traditional morality'. It deprived women and children of their sexual rights, and educated people in the ideals of lifelong, monogamous marriage; and the patriarchal family demanded sexual abstinence of youth as the logical measure. The links between chastity, lifelong marriage and the family meant that there was a 'contradiction between the desire for sexual reform and conservative marriage ideology'.[25] Reich recognised that marriage was the main obstacle to a sexually free society, and so for the revolution to succeed marriage needed to be undermined.

He addressed the issue 'as to whether morals are necessary or should be abolished'.[26] He argued that as we lose our 'compulsive morality' we develop a 'natural morality' which allows us to become 'genitally healthy'.[27] After the sexual revolution had succeeded 'a free society would not put any obstacles in the path of the gratification of the natural needs. It would, for example, not only not prohibit a love relationship between adolescents; it would give its full protection and help; it would not only not prohibit infantile masturbation; it would deal severely with any adult who would prevent the child from developing its natural sexuality. ...For example, if a boy of 15 were to develop a love relationship with a girl of 13, a free society not only would not interfere, it would affirm and protect it.'[28] Reich would undoubtedly have given his wholehearted approval to the policy of the British Government, which assists a 'love relationship' between a boy of 15 and a girl of 13 by providing them with free contraception. But even Reich would have been amazed that a future British Government would go to the extreme of providing contraception free of charge to a girl of 13 without the knowledge or consent of her parents.

Reich saw that it was the institution of marriage that led sex reform into a blind alley. All sexual misery 'can be logically reduced to the ideology of marriage by way of which authoritarian society decisively influences all sexual activity'.[29] He believed that extramarital chastity and marital fidelity on the part of the woman could not be maintained for long without a considerable degree of sexual repression. The two cornerstones of reactionary sexual morality were premarital chastity and strict fidelity of the married woman, which, by creating a sex-negative structure, helped to support authoritarian marriage and the family. And still worse, the demand of premarital chastity deprived the male youth of love objects.[30] Conventional morality, as the cornerstone of the authoritarian institution of marriage, was at variance with sexual gratification and presupposed a sex-negative attitude.[31]

Reich had definite ideas about the sex education of children. 'Before tackling the question of sex education at all one must first take an unequivocal stand for or against sex-affirmation or sex-negation, for or against the ruling sexual morality. Without clarity about one's own standpoint in this question any discussion of the sexual problem is fruitless; it is the prerequisite of any agreement in these matters.'[32] A key question was 'whether one should accustom them [children] to the sight of the naked human body, more specifically, of the human genitals'.[33] He believed that repressing the impulse to observe and display the genitals led to either neurotic symptoms or to exhibitionism. It was anti-sexual to object to nakedness as a crucial part of sex education. The vital question was 'whether the sexes should lose their shyness to expose their genitals and other erotically important parts of their bodies. More concretely: whether educators and pupils, parents and children, when bathing and playing, should appear before each other naked or in bathing costumes; whether nakedness should become a matter of course.'[34] Reich reasoned that if 'one is not ashamed of appearing naked before a child it will not develop sexual shyness or lasciviousness; on the other hand, it will undoubtedly wish to have its sexual curiosity satisfied.'[35] He believed that to evade the child's request to watch sexual intercourse would restrict a sex-affirming attitude.[36]

Reich made the point that 'with our approval of nakedness, with our sexual education—dealing not with the fertilisation of flowers, but of humans!—we are pulling one stone after the other from the edifice of conservative morality; that the ideal of virginity until marriage becomes as hollow as that of eternal monogamy, and with that the ideal of conventional marriage in general. For no sensible person will contend that people who have had a sex education which is serious, uncompromising and based on science, will be able to conform to the prevailing compulsive customs and morality.'[37] Reich saw that a key element of sex education, which was geared towards breaking down the edifice of conventional morality, was explicit sexual nakedness and exposing the sexual organs. And Reich acknowledged that those parents who educated their children in this way should know that 'they will have to renounce many things which ordinary parents value most highly in their children, such as attachment to the family beyond puberty, and a sexual life of their children which is considered as decent by today's standards'.[38]

Reich claimed the family reproduced itself by crippling people sexually. By perpetuating itself, the patriarchal family also perpetuated sexual repression, and created people who were afraid of life. The family also deprived women and children of their sexual rights. Unfortunately, despite the misery and hopelessness of the marital situation and family constellation, many people continued to defend it. 'The social necessity of doing so makes it necessary to hush up the actual misery and to idealise family and marriage; it also produces the widespread family sentimentality and the slogans of "family happiness", "the home as the castle", "the quiet harbour" and "the haven of happiness" which the family allegedly represents to the children.'[39]

Here we can summarise the aims of Reich's sexual revolution. In essence, it is a revolt against Christian morality that aims to create a new moral order based on self-regulation. The purpose of sex is to obtain genital gratification. In order for people to experience maximum gratification they need to live in a society that is sex-affirming and so does not make them feel guilty. At the heart of a sexually repressed society is the institution of legal marriage and the authoritarian family. Marriage denies the sexual rights of women and children. The family, which is the main vehicle for providing children with a traditional moral foundation, perpetuates sexual repression. It follows that traditional marriage and the family need to be destroyed before people can achieve true sexual liberation. Sex education is important for inculcating into children the ideals of sexual freedom. Children who receive explicit sex education will no longer accept traditional morality. So to be really effective sex education must be explicit. Nakedness is of great value for it enables children to overcome feelings of sexual guilt and embarrassment.

Situation ethics

The sexual revolution received great encouragement from the BBC's Reith lectures in 1962, when Professor George Carstairs condemned traditional morality as 'a wasteland, littered with the debris of broken convictions' and questioned whether a sexual morality which appeared to consist entirely of sexual restraint was tackling the moral problems raised by social change. He noted that the moral norms were shifting rapidly, especially among the young. Chastity no longer seemed 'the supreme moral virtue'; seeing sexual relationships as a source of pleasure was 'turning our own society into one in which sexual experience, with precautions against conception, is becoming accepted as a sensible preliminary to marriage'; people now saw marriage as 'a mutually considerate and mutually satisfying partnership', in marked contrast to the 'unromantic compromise between sensuality and drudgery which has been the lot of so many British husbands and wives in the past 60 years'.[40]

The Bishop of Woolwich, John Robinson, provided further moral support to the sexual revolution in his book *Honest to God* (1963). In a chapter entitled 'The New Morality' he warned against the danger of identifying Christianity with the 'old traditional morality'. He approved of the revolution in ethics which he believed was becoming established, involving the rejection of an ethic based on absolute, objective moral values. Rejection of the old morality was a significant shift as it cleared the way for various kinds of ethical relativism. Commenting on the 'new morality' he noted that times were changing and that Christianity must rethink its position in morals as in faith. According to his new morality, 'nothing can of itself always be labelled as wrong'.[41] The seeds of situation ethics had already been sown in Joseph Fletcher's 1959 lecture, *The New Look in Christian Ethics*, published in the Harvard Divinity Bulletin. In 1965, Joseph Fletcher, professor of Ethics at the Episcopal Theological Seminary, explained the essence of his new morality in a lecture to 80 teenagers. 'It all depends on the situation. In certain circumstances unmarried love could be infinitely more normal than married love. Lying could be more Christian that telling the truth. Stealing could be better than respecting private property.'[42] As far as sexual conduct is concerned, his book *Situation Ethics* (1966), makes it plain that no behaviour is right or wrong in itself. The whore who by the services she provides helps a man to shed his sexual inhibitions is to be commended for her contribution to the 'love ethic'. According to Fletcher, 'Whether any form of sex (hetero, homo, or auto) is good or evil depends on whether love is fully served.'[43] This so-called 'new morality' provided the justification for permissive sexual conduct with the apparent approval of liberal theologians.

Dr Alex Comfort, author of *Sex in Society* (1963) and *The Joys of Sex: A Gourmet Guide to Lovemaking* (1972), which sold 12 million copies, was a dedicated advocate of the sexual revolution. He was appalled by what he referred to as the 'sexual ignorance' of the average Englishman. 'For several centuries open discussion of some forms of sexual conduct has been restricted or prohibited by convention and by religious belief, and the scope of this prohibition widened during the early nineteenth century to include almost all aspects of the subject.'[44] Dr Comfort believed that Victorian society had censored the discussion of sex, and therefore was responsible for the 'sexual ignorance' of Englishmen and women. He put forward the humanist view 'that no form of sexual behaviour can be regarded as unacceptable, sinful, or deserving of censure unless it has demonstrable ill effects on the individuals who practise it, or on others'.[45] He predicted that 'we may eventually come to realise that chastity is no more a virtue than malnutrition'. He advocated that children should be taught the sport of sexual intercourse and he was insistent that parents should teach their children how to masturbate. On television he defined a chivalrous boy 'as one who takes contraceptives with him when he goes to meet his girlfriend'.[46] Speaking about marriage, Dr Comfort said that fidelity between husband and wife was an outdated concept and due for some radical rethink.

BBC – the shop window of the sexual revolution

The BBC had no qualms about making a hero figure of Alex Comfort even though he was a self-acclaimed anarchist, whose views were diametrically opposed to the accepted norms of society. Under Director General Hugh Greene, the BBC sought to encourage controversy, challenging conventional ideas by giving radical views a platform. Those who supported sexual permissiveness were given plenty of airtime, while those who supported traditional morality were seldom given the opportunity to present their case. The tone of programmes would invariably be sympathetic to the idea of 'free love'. The BBC believed that it had an obligation towards tolerance and the maximum liberty of expression—authority was to be questioned rather than accepted.[47] It became a shop window for the sexual and moral libertarians of the 1960s, and Mary Whitehouse responded with fury to the lax attitude of the BBC towards moral issues. 'If anyone were to ask me who, above all, was responsible for the moral collapse which characterised the sixties and seventies, I would unhesitatingly name Sir Hugh Carleton Greene, who was Director General of the BBC from 1960 to 1969. He was in command of the most powerful medium ever to affect the thinking and behaviour of people – television. His determination to give the freedom of the screen to the protagonists of the new morality, to open the doors to foul language, blasphemy, excesses of violence and sex, had the most profound effect upon the values and behaviour patterns of the day. And although he made a great thing of his desire to "open the windows" of the Corporation and let in what he was pleased to call "reality", he had no hesitation whatsoever in shutting the doors against those like myself who questioned both his policy and the wisdom of the new moralists.'[48]

In *Sexing the Millennium* Linda Grant describes the new sexual freedom that was transforming the moral fibre of Great Britain. 'Topless dresses, mini-skirts, hipster trousers, edible knickers, see-through blouses, nudity on stage, streakers, a four letter swear word first heard on British television – all the ephemeral images of Swinging London said that Britain had abandoned conventional morality and replaced it with the most frivolous forms of hedonism.'[49] In *Dress and Morality* Aileen Ribeiro describes the sexual nature of the fashions that characterised the 1960s. 'The look of the sixties was brash, violent, and blatantly sexual; it is perhaps no accident that the dress of prostitutes, partly in reality and wholly in popular images, derives from the cruder aspects of the dress of that decade – short skirts, the legs emphasised by fishnet tights, shiny fabrics of the most artificial kind. It is a paradox that such styles have lasted so long, although the signals conveyed are of the "use-me", "throw-away" kind.'[50] One of the main characteristics of the growing sexual revolution was the way that some women, having lost all sense of modesty, were on sexual display.

The 1960s produced a plethora of books on sex education. Rose Hacker wrote *Telling the Teenagers* (1957) and *The Opposite Sex* (1963); Julia Dawkins produced *Teach your child about Sex* (1964); *Love and Sex in Plain Language* by Eric Johnson (1968) was published by Andre Deutsch. Other books included: *A Textbook of Sex Education* (1967) and *Young People and Sex* (1967); Colin Wilson produced *Sex and the Intelligent Teenager* (1966); Claire Rayner produced *A Parent's Guide to Sex Education* (1968), in which she exhorts parents 'to teach children about sex, to discuss it freely'. Alan Harris wrote *Questions about Sex* (1968), which includes clear representational diagrams of the sexual organs, including a male with an erection; C Macy edited *Let's Teach Them Right* (1969), in which Alan Harris asks whether the need for young people to experiment sexually should be openly recognised. The British Medical Association published *So Now You Know About Family Planning* (1969) written by Margaret Smyth. In *Boys and Sex* (1970), Wardell Pomeroy gives details of early sexual experience and concludes 'it isn't what you do sexually that matters, as long as you're not hurting someone else; it's how you feel about what you're doing'. In *Sex Telling it Straight* (1970), Eric Johnson explains that 'there are lots of ideas about the place of sex in life. You have to decide for yourself which ones are right. No one can decide for you, but others can help you learn and understand so that you can make good decisions.'[51]

The Archdeacon of Chesterfield, Talbot Dilworth-Harrison, was alarmed at the growth of sex education in schools and warned of the danger of providing children with contraceptives. He wrote in his parish magazine: 'Perhaps we shall never know the educationists who were guilty of the crass stupidity of decreeing that intimate sex instruction should be given in our schools. I say without any hesitation that, failing the duty of parents to teach their own child, I would far rather that children discuss these things in their own way – as most do – and retain a sense of shame than that they should be taught officially, often by teachers whose outlook is inevitably that of the world. When we read of the rapid increase of girls becoming mothers from the age of 12 upwards, when we hear of contraceptives being frequently the property of schoolboys, the country is reaching a lower stage of degradation than has ever been envisaged before.'[52]

Another ray of hope was the report *Half our Future* (1963) produced by the Central Advisory Council for Education, under the chairmanship of John Newsom, which dealt with the issue of spiritual and moral development in schools. Research showed that most boys and girls wanted to be what they call 'being good', and knew what this meant in the personal situations which confronted them. And they also wanted to be told the truth. The authors of the report believed that 'it is wrong to leave the young to fend for themselves without guidance, and wrong to conceal from them (as if we could) the differences on this issue which separate men and women of real moral sensitivity. For our part we are agreed that boys and girls should be offered firm guidance on sexual morality based on chastity before marriage and fidelity within it. We believe, too, that this is predominantly the standpoint of the schools.'[53] Remarkably, even as the sexual revolution was gaining pace, this review of education took the stance that schoolchildren should be taught the Christian virtues of chastity and fidelity.

In 1963 a working party of the Family Planning Association (FPA), under the chairmanship of Professor F Lafitte of Birmingham University, recommended the promotion of a parliamentary bill to provide for free advice on family planning under the NHS, possibly including arrangements to charge for contraceptives as for other prescriptions.[54] (The phrase 'free advice on family planning' is a euphemism for sex education.) An editorial in *The Times* acknowledged that a large section of the community was opposed to the work of the FPA at a fundamental level and that the differences would continue to be entrenched.[55] In December 1964 the Minister of Health in the newly elected Labour Government, Mr Kenneth Robinson, visited the FPA and expressed support for family planning. In the keynote speech at the FPA national conference (1966) he said that planned parenthood promoted happiness and that lack of planning, often due to ignorance of effective methods of contraception, might lead to misery, ill-health and, in some cases, to criminal abortion. As the law stood local authorities were empowered to provide family planning only for those for whom pregnancy would be detrimental to their health. He believed that there was a large body of opinion that would like to see family planning made more widely available through local authorities.[56]

Brook Advisory Centres established

A clinic offering contraceptive advice for young *single* people was opened in Walworth, London, in the autumn of 1964, with plans for four other clinics. The inspiration for the clinics came from Mrs Helen Brook, a member of the Islington FPA and a director of the Marie Stopes advisory clinic, which had been running an advice centre for unmarried young people for about a year. Mrs Brook explained that she had seen teenagers coming to clinics for help and being sent away. She went on, 'We have had no virgins coming for advice, and we cannot therefore feel that we are encouraging licence.' An anonymous donor was financing the clinics.[57] Up until this point family planning was regarded as providing a service for those married women who wished to control the size of their family. With the setting up of the Brook Centre the pretence that contraceptives were meant for planning families was finally put to rest—Brook made it absolutely clear that their aim was to make contraception available to *single* young women to help them prevent pregnancy. Brook specialises in providing contraceptives for children under the legal age of consent, without informing their parents; GPs are only informed if the child gives her consent. The Brook manifesto *Safe Sex for Teenagers* (1978) made it clear that the underlying philosophy for staff appointments is that the customer is always right. 'We must be prepared to challenge our established attitudes that sexual activity in young people is dangerous… There are still too many workers in birth control clinics who believe, consciously or subconsciously, that sex before sixteen is sinful.'[58]

An integral part of the service is to provide on-the-spot pregnancy testing, followed by pregnancy and abortion counselling with a social worker and doctor. Where an abortion is indicated, in the view of the clinic doctor, Brook arranges for a speedy referral, either through the GP or direct to a NHS hospital or private agency.[59] The 1973 Brook annual report stresses that young people are put off from attending by the thought that their parents may find out. 'Confidentiality is crucial. If young people fear that their parents or general practitioner will be told, without their permission, that they have come to the centre, they will not come.'[60]

There are now approximately 18 Brook Centres scattered around the UK, funded largely by local health authorities, with an annual attendance of about 60 thousand. The brochure *Making sex education easier* assists schools in delivering their sex education syllabus. Brook believes that sex education should enable young people 'to make informed choices about their personal and sexual relationships so that they can enjoy their sexuality without harm'.[61] It produces a range of sex education literature, including resource packs for schools, and leaflets and booklets for young people.

Sex Information and Education Council of the USA (SIECUS)

In America sex education was also taking off, and in 1964 a group of prominent professional 'sex experts' created the Sex Information and Education Council of the United States (SIECUS). Among the founders were Dr Mary Calderone, former medical director of the Planned Parenthood Federation of America and Dr Lester Kirkendall, emeritus professor in the Department of Family Life at Oregon State University. Other board members included Kinsey's co-author, Wardell Pomeroy, and David Mace. The mission statement of the new organisation was 'to assure that all people – including adolescents, the disabled, sexual minorities, and the elderly – have the right to affirm that sexuality is a natural and healthy part of their lives'. A significant early policy development was to change the term 'sex' education to 'sexuality' education.

During the last four decades SIECUS has been in the forefront of promoting sexuality for all people, and of protecting the right of individuals to make 'responsible' sexual choices. It also aims to defend sex education against attack. It produced the *Guidelines for Comprehensive Sexuality Education: Kindergarten – 12th Grade*, and a number of sex education study guides. The study guide *Sex Education*, says that it must be thought of as being education, not moral indoctrination. 'Attempting to indoctrinate young people with a set of rigid rules and ready-made formulas is doomed to failure in a period of transition and conflict.'[62] According to the study guide *Premarital Sexual Standards*, 'The choice of a premarital sexual standard is a personal moral choice, and no amount of facts or trends can "prove" scientifically that one ought to choose a particular standard.' The guide *Sex, Science and Values* openly accepts situation ethics as the common ground for professionals to stand on in dealing with the subject of morality in the classroom: 'The strict Judeo-Christian codes inherited from the past, in which chastity is prescribed, are being challenged. Rational enquiry is replacing blind faith… A so-called new morality is being ushered in…' The guide characterises the traditional Christian position as dogmatic, a morality of commandment based upon the assumption that transcendental powers and eternal truths exist. But those who follow the relativistic position 'do not see right and wrong as eternal entities; rather they distinguish between what is wise and foolish in actions that vary according to time, place, and circumstances'. This approach 'seems to offer most hope for consensus under modern conditions'.[63]

The SIECUS guide *The Sex Educator and Moral Values*, written by Isadore Rubin, describes a version of morality based on four core values which he believes should be used as the ethical framework for making sexual decisions. Briefly stated they are: respect for truth, respect for the basic worth of each individual, co-operative effort for the common good, and recognition of the individual's right of self-determination. 'Applied to sex conduct, these values suggest the right of the individual to engage in any form of sex behaviour within the limits of social obligation and welfare and except where exploitation, violation of another's personality, or cruelty is involved.' Rubin advises teachers that their 'acceptance of truth as a core value would also imply that the effect of all sex practices would be described as objectively and scientifically as possible, whether or not the results conformed to the official mores or to a particular social code'.[64]

Comprehensive Sex Education

In 1990 SIECUS convened a national task force to develop Guidelines for Comprehensive Sexuality Education. According to the guidelines comprehensive sex education has four primary goals. The first is to provide accurate information about human sexuality, giving young people information on a range of subjects including human reproduction, anatomy, physiology, masturbation, pregnancy, sexual response, sexual orientation, contraception, abortion, HIV/AIDS and other sexually transmitted diseases. The second is 'to provide an opportunity for young people to question, explore and assess their sexual attitudes in order to understand their family's values, develop their own values and increase self-esteem…' The third goal is 'to help young people develop interpersonal skills including communication, decision-making, assertiveness and peer refusal skills, as well as the ability to create satisfying relationships. The fourth goal is 'to help young people exercise responsibility regarding sexual relationships, including addressing abstinence, how to resist pressure to become prematurely involved in sexual intercourse, and encouraging the use of contraception and other sexual health measures'.[65]

According to SIECUS the guidelines are based on 'values that reflect the beliefs of most communities in a pluralistic society'. Values inherent in the guidelines include: sexuality is a natural and healthy part of living; all persons are sexual; every person has dignity and self-worth; young people should view themselves as unique and worthwhile individuals within the context of their cultural heritage; all persons have the right and obligation to make responsible sexual choices; young people develop their values about sexuality as part of becoming adults; abstaining from sexual intercourse is the most effective method of preventing pregnancy and STD/HIV; young people who are involved in sexual relationships need access to information about health-care services.[66]

Comprehensive sex education is central to SIECUS ideology. An essential dimension is that it is pro-choice. This means that young people are provided with all the factual information they require in order to make informed decisions with regard to their sexual behaviour. The crucial point is for young people to decide for themselves what they want on the basis of their own values, guided by positive self-esteem. SIECUS teaches that 'adolescents should be encouraged to *delay sexual behaviours* until they are physically, cognitively and emotionally ready for mature sexual relationships and their consequences [my italics]'. Therefore 'helping adolescents to *postpone sexual intercourse until they are ready* for mature relationships is a key goal of comprehensive sexuality education [my italics]'. An effective sex education programme 'includes a *strong abstinence message* as well as information about contraception and safer sex [my italics]'.[67] In other words, SIECUS teaches that young people should be encouraged to delay sexual intercourse until they are ready, and that they should be given information about contraception so that they know how to practise 'safe sex' when the need arises.

On the issue of sexual orientation SIECUS provides teenagers with the following explanation: 'Our sexual orientation is who we are attracted to – it is not a choice we make. You may be bisexual, and attracted to people of both sexes. You may be heterosexual and attracted to people of the other sex. You may be homosexual (often called lesbian or gay), that is, attracted to people of your same sex. For many young people, exploring their sexuality with someone of the same sex is a natural part of growing up. These normal feelings may continue through your adult lives. If you are struggling with questions about your sexual orientation, be sure to speak with a trusted adult and/or gay or lesbian organisation in your area. A lot of people think that some sexual activities are just for heterosexual people, or that others are just for lesbians and gay men. The truth is that all people, regardless of their sexual orientation, may do all things. The difference is that gay men and lesbians do these activities with people of the same sex as themselves. Heterosexual people do these activities with people of the opposite sex. Lesbian and gay relationships, like heterosexual relationships, can be fulfilling and can last a very long time. All of these sexual orientations are part of being human.'[68] It is not difficult to see that SIECUS is committed to Kinsey's view of sexual orientation.

SIECUS view of the sexual revolution

Writing about the sexual revolution in 1976, David Mace, a founder member of SIECUS, makes the point that while human communities have dealt with the problem of sexual behaviour in a great variety of ways, basic to all of them have been marriage and the family in one form or another. 'Our own Western culture has developed a particularly rigid system, largely imposed by the Christian church. Individual sexual rights have been officially confined to marriage and even there regarded as mildly reprehensible unless procreation was deliberately intended. Women have been protected from premarital sex and extramarital sex by the threat of severe penalties.' But a new knowledge of sex, women's emancipation, the democratic ideal of individual freedom and other influences have combined in a revolutionary challenge to the entire traditional system, ushering in a process of change that has been in operation for about a century. 'Like all true revolutions, it began with radical changes in the realm of ideas and is now being progressively implemented in action.'[69]

Mace describes a world in which the views of the sexual revolution have been put into practice. 'In such a world, a child would from the beginning be encouraged to enjoy to the full all the sensual libidinal experiences which Freud described as infant sexuality. The child would be fully exposed to adult sexuality. It would be commonplace for him to witness heterosexual and homosexual encounters, and other sexual experiences covering the whole range of what we now divide into normal and abnormal. Sexual language would be part of his means of communication as soon as he began to speak, and any sexual curiosity he displayed would be at once fully satisfied. No restraint would be placed upon the sexual play of children, including attempts to simulate intercourse.

'On reaching puberty, boys and girls would freely gratify their sexual urges as they arose, and would be free to do so throughout the rest of their lives… It would be entirely proper to invite any other person, of either sex or age group to participate in any kind of sexual experience—on a couple or group basis. The other would of course be entitled to decline without causing offence. Everyone in the population would be very well informed about all aspects of sexual behaviour, because this would be a central subject of basic education from early childhood.

'Any group of two or more persons could, by common consent, enter into a lasting relationship that would be equivalent to the marriage of today. Such relationships could be embarked upon for life; but there would be no obligation involved other than the agreement made between the persons concerned; and there would be no obligation for anyone to enter into such a relationship at all if he preferred not to do so. These relationships would have no legal or economic conditions attached to them—they would be entirely voluntary.'[70]

Mace's interpretation of the sexual revolution stresses the importance of childhood sexuality and the importance of educating children in all aspects of sex. He believed that children should be taught a sexual language, and would undoubtedly have been a strong advocate of the sex word games that are now so common among modern sex education programmes. Sexual gratification, especially among children, is at the heart of the revolution. Once again a variety of sexual relationships replace traditional marriage, and the traditional family disappears.

NHS Family Planning Act – 1967

The permissive 1960s were a time of great progress for the FPA. Oral contraceptives became available in clinics in 1961 and the intrauterine device was approved for use four years later in 1965. In February 1966 the Ministry of Health sent a circular to local authorities urging them to provide family planning services free of charge to those women whose health would be detrimentally affected by pregnancy. Local authorities were also expected to give all help and encouragement to the FPA and other similar voluntary bodies. The FPA was naturally delighted with this circular and responded that it hoped that family planning would soon take its part in the NHS.[71] According to the circular, 'An adequate family planning service, fully integrated with other community services, will not only contribute to the dispersal of ignorance and fear and to the increase of happy family life, but will also relieve the burdens placed on other local authority services by the physical ill health and mental distress which so frequently arise from lack of knowledge and advice.'[72]

In early 1967 the Government indicated its support for the Private Member's Bill, sponsored by Mr Edwin Brooks, that aimed to extend State funding for family planning clinics. Under existing law the State could only fund contraceptive services for those women to whom a further pregnancy would be detrimental to their health.[73] The State was now keen to provide contraceptive services to women on social grounds. An editorial in *The Times*, with great foresight, noted that such a provision could become an instrument of great social change: the Bill proposed that assistance should not be limited to the married, and this raised the moral question as to whether the State should endorse the official extension of contraceptive aids to the unmarried. 'In the sense that the State represents a parental figure, it should not.'[74] The National Health Service Act (Family Planning) became law in 1967 and conferred permissive powers on area health authorities to provide birth control advice regardless of whether the person was married or not. In other words, health and local authorities were now encouraged to provide advice and contraceptive supplies to *single* women. And health authorities were allowed to use the FPA as their agent if they so wished. This heralded the beginning of collaboration between the NHS and the FPA that continues to this day—the NHS had the money and the FPA had the 'expertise'. Working together they would change the sexual attitudes of the people of Great Britain. The IPPF's strategy of infiltrating Government had been implemented to perfection.

The first sex education school TV programmes, produced by Granada and designed for schoolchildren aged 15-16, were shown in three Independent Television areas in May and June 1966. In a foreword to the teacher's notes, Sir John Newsom, chairman of Independent Television, congratulated Granada for tackling the problem with frankness and with a respect for the human personality. He claimed that parents are not always the best people to help their children with such matters, and children prefer to discuss some subjects outside the family. The six programmes, entitled *Understanding*, were shown in the north, the West Country and Wales.[75] A further significant development occurred in 1967 when the Ministry of Education put forward recommendations for sex education in all secondary schools and proposed introductory courses in junior schools. The

Government was now accepting in principle that children needed to be educated about sex in the school classroom, and there was a growing confidence in the ability of contraceptives to solve the problems of unwanted pregnancies. The doctor of Aston University, Birmingham, Dr Philip Cauthery, was typical of this attitude. He said that contraceptive pills should be made easily available to girl students at universities and colleges to stop the terrible waste of taxpayers' money which resulted from the large number of girls who became pregnant and had to give up their studies. He explained, 'You cannot control the sexual behaviour of young people. But there is a safe contraceptive method which costs only a few pence, and which would prevent this situation from arising at universities.'[76]

Abortion Act – 1967

The Abortion Act of 1967 was a watershed in the gathering revolt against traditional morality. The legalisation of abortion would have a massive effect on the lives of hundreds of thousands of women and lead to a substantial reduction in the national birth rate as over 170 thousand legal abortions are now performed each year. In Victorian times the Offences Against the Person Act of 1861 had made it a criminal offence to procure an abortion in any circumstances. But the changing sexual mores of the sexual revolution brought with them a desire for women to have the right to choose whether they wanted a pregnancy to continue or not. During the permissive 1960s there had been four unsuccessful Private Member's Bills to legalise abortion when in 1966, David Steel, a young Liberal MP, came third in the ballot for a Private Member's Bill and agreed to sponsor the Abortion Reform Bill. Behind David Steel was the Abortion Law Reform Association which had been set up in the 1930s by a group of socialist feminists. A number of prominent figures in the Labour Party were supporters of abortion reform, including the Minister of Health, Kenneth Robinson, who had put his own Private Member's Bill to Parliament in the early 1960s. Labour's tacit support in allowing extra parliamentary time was essential to the success of the Bill.

Key personalities behind the pro-abortion campaign were Alastair Service, a highly effective parliamentary lobbyist, and Dilys Cossey, the secretary of the Abortion Law Reform Association, both of whom would in future play prominent roles in the FPA. In a recent seminar of the Institute of Contemporary British History, Dr David Paintin said that the Act, by making abortion a treatment decided upon by doctors, made the abortion decision difficult to challenge by the police or in the courts. If a man 'has attempted to stop his partner having an abortion the judge has had to explain: "The abortion has been recommended by her doctors, it is a medical matter and neither you nor I have any power to interfere." A further benefit is that medical control over termination of pregnancy gives women some protection from the vehement groups who oppose abortion on moral grounds: the women tend to be portrayed as victims and the doctors – who are more able to absorb the stress – as the wrongdoers who have allowed her, who have even "encouraged" her, to have the termination. The fact that the law made abortion a medical treatment has been important in convincing health authorities that access to abortion is an essential part of women's health care, and something that should be provided free of charge by the NHS.'[77]

Helene Grahame, who worked for the FPA during the 1960s, explained how careful the FPA were in keeping secret their support for abortion reform. When she attended meetings of the pro-abortion Birth Control Campaign, she was not listed as an attendee. 'Everything I said or agreed to do was credited to somebody else, so that it would have been impossible for anybody from the Department of Health to discover that the FPA has played any part in the organisation.'[78] Caroline Woodroffe was the director of Brook at the time of the Abortion Act. She explained that Brook 'slid quite easily into incorporating pregnancy testing and referral for abortion into our services, which continued to be paid for by the NHS under contracts. We simply included referral for abortion in with our service.'[79]

One implication of the Act was that contraceptive failure could now be 'treated' by legal abortion on the NHS, and within a few years tens of thousands of teenagers would avail themselves of this 'treatment'. Moreover, in the future the family planning lobby would use the same tactic of labelling contraceptives a 'treatment' and so give doctors the authority to 'treat' children with contraceptives without the consent of their parents.

A decade of progress for the FPA

The annual report of the FPA (1968) emphasised that there was no evidence to suggest that giving contraceptive advice to the unmarried increased sexual promiscuity in any age group. (This claim would become a slogan for the sex education lobby over the next three decades, together with the mantra that contraceptives reduce the number of sexual tragedies.) Although the Family Planning Act of 1967 enabled local authorities to provide family planning services if they wished, only one in six authorities in England and Wales were fully implementing the Act. The annual report argued that a private medical service like that provided by the FPA clinics was an anachronism, and should be handed over to local health authorities as quickly as possible, so that family planning could become an integral part of the NHS. In June 1968 the FPA had opened its 800th clinic.[80]

Mr Richard Crossman, Secretary of State for Social Services, told the FPA's national conference in London (1969), that he did not want Britain to be known as the capital of abortion. Rather, it should be known as the place where family planning was so much part of national life that abortion was unknown. He gently chided local authorities over their apparent reluctance to take on family planning services. Out of 204 local authorities, only 34 had an adequate service, and 129 had restricted services. Lady Alma Birk, Chairman of the Health Education Council, told the conference that as far as contraception was concerned Britain was an undeveloped country,[81] while Mr Michael Schofield gave three steps for improving health education. The first was to establish the right of every child to get basic information about health education. The next was to get across the idea that sex was delightful but could be dangerous, and the third was to make it clear that sex is not something that just comes naturally. On premarital sex he asked the question, 'Are we really asking young people to believe that no one has sex for fun? Are we to say it is not possible to have sex for fun and not regret it afterwards?'[82]

The FPA was delighted with the progress that it had made during the 1960s. 'The whole of the past decade has been a period of great expansion and innovation for the FPA, but with the final months of the sixties came an unprecedented upsurge of public and political demand for comprehensive birth control.'[83] To overcome what it saw as widespread ignorance about family planning and sex education the FPA launched its 'Every Child a Wanted Child' campaign in the summer of 1969. The aim of the campaign was to spread information about birth control and raise money for a massive educational programme – involving the use of films, filmstrips, sound tapes, books, booklets and other visual aids – throughout the country. In November 1969 the FPA made an approach to the Department of Health and Social Security (DHSS), recommending that it assume central responsibility for family planning and that it use the FPA as its agent. The Association, for its part, would continue to extend family planning until it was available to all who wanted it, free of charge to those who could not afford to pay, and would also assume responsibility for training doctors and nurses in contraceptive techniques. As an indication of its support for the work of the FPA, the Government made an annual grant of £20,000 for training doctors and nurses in contraceptive techniques. The FPA claimed that withholding contraceptives from single girls with an established sexual relationship only produced unwanted babies, illegal abortions, high illegitimacy rates and forced marriages. It made a policy decision to provide contraceptive advice for men and women over the age of 16, irrespective of marital status, from April 1970.[84]

The end of the 1960s was characterised by a large increase in sexually transmitted diseases among young people. The total number of patients attending clinics in England for all sexually transmitted diseases in 1969 was 203 thousand, an increase of 77 thousand in just five years. There was a lot of comment about the epidemic, and a furore broke out when a doctor informed the parents of a 16-year-old girl that she had been put on the pill by a contraceptive clinic. The Health Education Council, which was running a campaign particularly aimed at young people to reduce the incidence of sexually transmitted diseases, was concerned that they would be deterred from going for treatment because they were afraid their parents would be told. This same Health Education Council, apparently so concerned about the epidemic of sexually transmitted diseases among young people, had recently put out an advertisement which showed Casanova on his knees beside a bare-breasted girl with the caption—'Casanova never got anyone into trouble'. This was the example being presented to young people by sex education propaganda—a sexual libertine who knew how to avoid getting his women pregnant.[85] Alarmed by the increase in sexually transmitted disease, Baroness Summerskill informed the Lords that the FPA proposed to distribute a pamphlet about the availability of contraceptives with an added page on secrecy, bypassing the children's parents.

The FPA commented that the page had been added solely to reassure teenagers that confidences would continue to be respected. 'There was never any intention to distribute the pamphlet individually. It was always intended it should be handed out through local education authorities and head teachers.'[86]

Coinciding with the epidemic of sexually transmitted disease was an equally alarming rise in abortions among young people. The latest abortion figures, for the first nine months of 1972, were a blow to Government officials and the sex education lobby. The most disturbing increase was among the very young. Abortions for schoolgirls age 15 and under rose by more than 20 per cent from 1,838 to 2,227. For those aged 16-19, abortions were up from 15,850 to 20,537—an increase of 30 per cent during the nine-month period.[87] The rising rate of sexually transmitted disease and abortion among teenagers at the end of the 1960s was a national scandal—and the revolution was just beginning.

Endnotes

1 *The Human Right to Family Planning*, International Planned Parenthood Federation, 1984, p6
2 *Her Future in the Balance* (pamphlet), International Planned Parenthood Federation, October 1971
3 *Activities Relevant to the Study of Population Policy for the US*, Memorandum from Frederick S Jaffe to Bernard Berelson, 11 March 1969. Cited from *Sex and Social Engineering*, Valerie Riches, Family and Youth Concern, 1986
4 Patricia Morgan, *Farewell to the Family*, IEA Health and Welfare Unit, London, 1995, p61
5 *Strategy for Legal Reform and how FPAs are interpreting it*, IPPF News, July/August 1976
6 David Kennedy, *Birth Control in America*, Yale University Press, London, 1970, p1
7 Ibid. p9
8 Ibid. p13
9 Ibid. p14
10 Margaret Sanger 'Journal', entry for November 3-4, 1914, cited from *Birth Control in America*, p14
11 Margaret Sanger, *The Pivot of Civilization* (New York: Brentano's 1922) p244, cited from *Birth Control in America*, p127
12 Ibid. *Birth Control in America*, p128
13 Margaret Sanger, *The Woman Rebel*, reprinted in Woman and the New Race (1922)
14 Ibid. *Birth Control in America*, pp30-31
15 International Planned Parenthood Federation, Strategic Plan, IPPF website, about strategi
16 *IPPF Youth Manifesto*, developed by the youth committee between April and October 1998, IPPF website, youth manifesto
17 *The Human Right to Family Planning*, International Planned Parenthood Federation, 1984, p32
18 *The Sexual Revolution*, Wilhelm Reich, translated by Theodore Wolfe, Vision Press, 1969, p10
19 Ibid. p25
20 Ibid. p28
21 Ibid. p29
22 Ibid. p31
23 Ibid. p27
24 Ibid. p27
25 Ibid. p32
26 Ibid. p23
27 Ibid. p23

28 Ibid. p24
29 Ibid. p51
30 Ibid. p35
31 Ibid. p39
32 Ibid. p63
33 Ibid. p61
34 Ibid. p63
35 Ibid. p63
36 Ibid. p64
37 Ibid. p66
38 Ibid. p67
39 Ibid. p73
40 George Carstairs, 'This Island Now', The BBC Reith Lectures, 1962, Hogarth Press, p55, p50, p51, cited from *Rules of Desire* by Cate Haste, Chatto & Windus, London, 1992, p183-84
41 John Robinson, *Honest to God*, 1963, p118
42 *The Living Church*, 18 July, 1965, cited from *Whatever happened to sex?*, Mary Whitehouse, Hodder and Stoughton, London, pp10-11
43 Joseph Fletcher, *Situation Ethics*, 1966, p139
44 Alex Comfort, *Sex in Society*, Penguin Books, 1963, p10
45 Ibid. p15
46 *Daily Mirror*, 15 June, 1963.
47 Cate Haste, *Rules of Desire*, Chatto & Windus, London, 1992, p195
48 Mary Whitehouse, *Whatever happened to sex?*, Hodder and Stoughton, London, p15
49 Linda Grant, *Sexing the Millennium*, HarperCollins Publishers, London, 1993, p88
50 Aileen Ribeiro, *Dress and Morality*, BT Batsford, London, 1986, p168
51 Eric W Johnson, *Sex Telling it Straight*, Bantam Books, 1970
52 *The Times*, 7 August 1961, Sex instruction in schools attacked
53 *Half our Future*, A report of the Central Advisory Council for Education (England), Department of Education and Science, HMSO, 1963, p54
54 *The Times*, 25 October 1963, Birth advice by NHS urged
55 Ibid. editorial
56 Family Planning Association, *Free and Good*, January 1973, pB5
57 *The Times*, 1 June 1964, Clinic to be opened for the unmarried
58 *Safe Sex for Teenagers*, Brook Advisory Centres, 1978, pp23,24,27
59 Brook Advisory Centres Annual Report, 1973, p2
60 Ibid. p3
61 *Making sex education easier*, Brook publications, p6
62 Cited from, *The SIECUS Circle*, Claire Chambers, Western Islands, 1977, p41
63 Ibid. pp44-45
64 Isadore Rubin, 'The Sex Educator and Moral Values', SIECUS Study Guide 10, 1969, pp6-9, cited from *The SIECUS Circle*, Claire Chambers, Western Islands, 1977, p4
65 SIECUS website, Guidelines for Comprehensive Sexuality Education Fact Sheet
66 Ibid.
67 SIECUS, Adolescence and Abstinence Fact Sheet, published in SIECUS Report, vol. 26, no.1, November 1997
68 Cited from SIECUS website, For teens, What is sexual orientation?
69 David R Mace, 'Sex in the Year 2000', in *Sexuality Today and tomorrow*, ed Sol Gordon and Roger W Libby, Duxbury Press, 1976, p396
70 Ibid. p402
71 *The Times*, 21 February 1966, Contraception guidance welcomed
72 Ministry of Health, Circular 5/66, February 1966, cited from *Free and Good*, Family Planning Association, January 1973, pB6
73 *The Times*, 4 January 1967
74 *The Times*, 6 January 1967, Editorial
75 *The Times*, 29 March 1966, TV sex talks for children
76 *The Times*, 24 April 1967, Let students use the pill
77 David Paintin, in 'The Abortion Act 1967', seminar held 10 July 2001, Institute of Contempo-

rary British History, 2002, www.icbh.ac.uk/icbh/witness/abortion/, p49
78 Ibid. Helene Grahame, p52
79 Ibid. Caroline Woodroffe, p57
80 *The Times*, 15 November 1968, More choose birth control pill at family planning clinics
81 *The Times*, 26 June 1969, Delays in family planning
82 *The Times*, 27 June 1969, Teachers are best to tell about sex
83 Family Planning Association, Annual Report 1969-70, p3
84 Ibid. pp14-15
85 *Daily Telegraph*, 25 March 1971
86 *Daily Telegraph*, 23 March 1971
87 *Daily Mail*, 14 November 1972

Chapter 8

_____

Sex education into the 1970s

Explicit sex lessons on the BBC; the trials of Dr Robert

Browne and Colin Knapman; the Longford Report

on pornography

Undeterred by the rising trends in abortion and sexually transmitted disease among young people, the sex education movement was gaining in confidence as the 1960s drew to a close. At the annual conference of the National Association for Maternal and Child Health in 1970, chairman of the Health Education Council, Lady Alma Birk, made an impassioned plea for more sex education for young people. She told the conference that contraception should be provided by the NHS, and suggested that to do so might save money for other social services. She said that an expansion of sex education was also urgently needed.[1]

The FPA, at its annual conference in 1970, acknowledged that most of the religious, medical and political barriers against which it had struggled for years had been overcome. 'Concern over the great demand for abortion has focused attention on contraception as part of preventive medical care. Many of the FPA's former opponents, spurred on by debates over abortion and pollution, now agree on the need for a massive extension of contraception services. The Association is now allowed to advertise on television, and the Government has publicly stated that the provision of birth control is a priority task. Two new FPA clinics open each week, and the Association has well over 600,000 patients... the once remote possibility of freely available birth control services within the NHS now seems almost inevitable.'[2] The FPA was now desperate to devolve its one thousand contraceptive clinics to the NHS so that it could put all its efforts into sex education. It was becoming increasingly clear that the Health Education Council and FPA were pushing on an open door, for the Government was now convinced of the need to develop sex education.

Sex education on television

Meanwhile the BBC was eager to use radio filmstrips and television for delivering the messages of sex education to schoolchildren. And so in 1970 the Schools Broadcasting Council of the BBC beamed a series of sex education programmes to schools across the nation. These powerful visual programmes, delivered with the full authority of the BBC, undoubtedly influenced the values of many young people and set the tone for sex education in the UK. The radio filmstrip *Where do babies come from?* was given a late night preview on television before being broadcast on Radio 4 during school hours. Among the first to criticise the filmstrip was Mrs Mary Whitehouse, head of the National Viewers' and Listeners' Association. She argued that the BBC's sex education programmes for primary schools were educationally and psychologically unsound. Her main complaints were that at no time was the word love mentioned and that the woman in the filmstrip shown having sexual intercourse was clearly not wearing a wedding ring.[3]

A more detailed criticism was contained in a letter to *The Times*, signed by Peter Bevan and eight other medical practitioners. 'Now that the BBC have completed their series of previews of sex education films for primary schools, teachers and parents will be making up their mind whether or not to expose their children to them. Before doing so we recommend them to consider the following facts: The initiative for these teaching methods came not from parents and teachers as a whole, but from the Schools Broadcasting Council. To the best of our knowledge this body has received no mandate from any national teaching organisation to recommend televised sex instruction of this kind. Nor have they produced any statistical evidence to show whether such teaching is necessary or even desirable.

'Evidence of the long-term effect of sex-teaching for the very young is freely available from such countries as Sweden and America, where it was introduced supposedly to offset the rise in promiscuity, VD, and illegitimacy. But in Sweden, for instance, where primary school sex education in its fullest and frankest terms has been compulsory for 15 years, it is now reckoned that for every 20 births there are one legal and four illegal abortions; 35 per cent of brides are pregnant on their wedding day; venereal disease figures are soaring and it is common for boys to have had over 200 sexual partners. Last July, 140 leading educationalists and doctors petitioned the Swedish Government to reverse its policy on sex education, which, they believed, was one of the chief causes for this state of affairs.

'In America the situation is even worse. There, sex education has been used as a pretext for introducing hard-core pornography into the schools in the guise of sex manuals. As a result of numerous protests from the public, more than 20 state legislatures are now considering drastic changes in their sex education policy.

'The BBC sex-teaching films show what we regard as an unhealthy preoccupation with the purely physical aspects of human reproduction. Sex is concerned with love, feelings, emotions and mutual responsibilities. It is something that children should learn progressively over a number of years, preferably from their parents. It should not be thrust upon them in one short course at so tender an age. We are seriously concerned about the long-term effects of these films and of those likely to follow them, bearing in mind Swedish and American experience.'[4]

Defence of the sex education films came from a surprising quarter – the Chief Officer of the National Marriage Guidance Council. Nicholas Tyndall responded: 'Mr Bevan and others show natural parental concern about the sex education of young people, but in making a valid point draw a conclusion which should be challenged. It is indeed desirable for parents to encourage "a healthy and responsible attitude to sex" among their children, but many parents lack not only the factual information, but also the verbal capacity or the confidence in their relationship with their children to enable them to do so. Schofield in 1965 found that 67 per cent of boys and 29 per cent of girls never received advice about sex from their parents. Adults need not only information but also help in creating mature relationships with young people in which intimate matters can be discussed frankly, sympathetically and responsibly... Sex education should not be a question of either advice from parents or instruction from books and TV. Both should complement the other. Similarly parents, teachers and other adults, such as Marriage Guidance counsellors, also have a part to play in guiding young people away from the uncertainty based on rumour and salacious stories to the possibility of responsible conduct based on facts and helpful relationships.'[5]

A year later, after widespread use in schools, Margaret Thatcher, Secretary of State for Education, told a selected audience in a BBC 1 programme that she did not know whether sex education was being handled with sufficient care. She said that love and marriage ought to form part of the education and implied that to leave them out could further encourage permissiveness in society.[6] A number of women MPs, in a letter to the *Daily Telegraph*, supported Mrs Thatcher's stand on the ethics of sex education in schools. 'The majority of children are born in wedlock but apparently our new educationalists seek to persuade the young that this is an unnatural state and that the religious ethics of marriage and the security of good family life are something to be ignored and decried.'[7] This letter reflected the common complaint that the BBC films and filmstrips went out of their way to avoid the word marriage, and the reason, according to the producers, was that full consideration had to be taken of unmarried mothers whose children might be embarrassed by the husband and wife concept. A school headmaster expressed the view that the BBC sex education films would prove irreparably harmful to young minds. 'We now learn that parents have no legal right even to the option of withdrawing their children from viewing these visual programmes. This is monstrous indeed. It cannot be argued that head teachers "know best" what, in this delicate sphere, is best for every child. It must be clearly held that parents have the right and duty to decide in the context of their children's development and personality as to the timing and method of this education.'[8]

119

Where do babies come from?

So why were these programmes so controversial? I have used the teacher's notes to develop the following account of the radio-vision filmstrip *Where do babies come from?* The target audience is schoolchildren aged 8 and 9. A slide showing a mother holding her baby, wrapped up warmly in its shawl, together with the baby's father, represents the family group. (The words husband and wife are not used.) The film explains that a woman has a womb. The way out of the womb is through the vagina, which ends in an opening between the woman's legs (slide of a naked woman), where the hair is in the picture. Boys have a penis, and it can sometimes become stiff and then instead of hanging down it stands up at an angle (slides show a naked man). And the vagina is just the right size for the penis to fit into, especially when the penis is stiff and firm (slide shows man lying on top of a woman). If the sperm from the man has got to an egg in the woman's body a baby begins to grow. The filmstrip then shows a picture of a baby being born and explains to the children that all the people in the world were made in the way they've been shown. The filmstrip does not mention the words marriage, husband or wife. A clear inference is that it is not necessary for a man and woman to be married before they have a baby. Indeed, children viewing the filmstrip may quite logically conclude that there is no link between producing babies and marriage. The filmstrip presents a number of facts about conception and child birth, but does so without any moral guidance.

Merry-go-round television films

The *Merry-go-round* series of films also raised controversy about the type of sex education that was being delivered to schoolchildren. In these films marriage was again not mentioned, and Mary Whitehouse was deeply concerned about their explicit nature. The third film was obsessively preoccupied with the sex organs, including full frontal nudity. It shows small boys standing naked at the edge of a swimming bath, before the camera zooms on to their genitals already perfectly obvious in the distant shot. Another shot shows a male model posing naked, while 'the commentator makes reference to his pubic hair and penis and, once again – even though it is already quite apparent that he possesses both! – the camera zooms, concentrating the attention. One can only assume that those who produce such programmes have themselves been conditioned into insensitivity by the sexual explicitness of the culture in which they work… Children brought up to accept educational practices of this kind will find it a small step indeed to the crudities of the "girlie" press. What is more, they are totally destructive of the natural modesty which serves to protect the child from over-stimulation and exploitation and which preserves the wonder and mystery, so important a part of life.'[9] A mother expressed her anger at the explicitness of the films. 'What concerns me is this: why, why, why the need for *visual* sex education? The children are shown a man's penis, and then its erection diagrammatically; today watching the particularly messy birth, we were then shown (again unnecessarily) a long clear shot of the mother's stretched and swollen pubis. After this, is it such a big step to saying "We have been so very frank up to a point, lest anyone still be in any doubt or ignorance at all, shouldn't we be totally frank and show coitus...?" '[10]

In May 1971 the BBC produced a report defending its decision to produce sex education films. The report claimed that in the middle years of junior school children are generally becoming objectively interested in facts and in how things work and are relinquishing fantasy. 'During the preparation of the programmes and subsequently one question recurred in discussion, though, significantly, it occurred very rarely in the schools which used the programmes. This is that in the broadcasts no mention is made of marriage, and ethical and moral questions are not discussed. However, the dependence of the young on the loving care of the parent is clearly demonstrated throughout the programmes. This is because children of 8, 9 and 10 are too young to understand the moral and social codes and conventions of the family and marriage.' [But apparently not too young to understand the significance of sexual intercourse.] 'After the broadcasts many teachers with an unusually high proportion of children from unconventional families expressed relief that orthodox marriage had not been emphasised.' [11]

However, there were a number of pointers in the BBC report to the controversial nature of the programmes. Nearly 40 per cent of primary schools which bought the sex education programmes decided not to use them. The main objections were that the school was usurping the right of parents, the audience was too young, and no mention was made of love and marriage. Of the *Merry-go-round* films it was admitted that 'in some schools the parents had been approached and had proved hostile. In other schools the staff were deeply divided.' [12] Teachers who decided against the programmes were said to have feared 'a situation which seemed to them, at that time, contrary to their educational, moral or religious principles'.[13] There was no discussion in the report of the propriety of using compulsory education to show children material to which some parents were known to be hostile, and the BBC continued to rebroadcast the films to captive audiences of children for years, until the colour version appeared in 1976, which both parents and teachers were refused a chance to preview.

The *Learning about Life* (BBC Radio 4) series of programmes promoted the idea that teenagers were responsible for developing their own 'personal values'. Dr Martin Cole, a sexual revolutionary who was producing his own sex education film showing a couple having sexual intercourse (discussed below), took part in the radio programme *Sexual Feelings* which discussed in detail masturbation for boys and girls. According to the programme one technique is for children practising masturbation to think sexual thoughts. The programme produced an angry response and eight MPs tabled a House of Commons motion deploring it. The BBC was so much on the defensive that it refused to make a script of the programme available to the education correspondent of the *Daily Telegraph*.[14] Apparently, the programme was confidential despite having been broadcast to thousands of schoolchildren. Responding to the criticism the BBC's Director of Public Affairs, Kenneth Lamb, commented that the policy for this particular series of programmes had been reviewed and endorsed by the specialist programme committee of the Schools Broadcasting Council. 'However, we well appreciate that people outside the schools can listen to this service, whether by accident or by design, and that they may sometimes be surprised by what they hear—for education, like everything else, does not stand still.' He said that it was important for those who happen to 'eavesdrop' on schools programmes to realise that the usual practice is for teachers to tape-record these programmes, study them, decide whether they wish to use them, and only then play them back to their pupils.[15]

The programme *Falling in Love* gave a precise description of sexual intercourse, and the word 'partner' was used to describe the man and woman involved. Detailed instructions were given of various methods of contraception. The ITV programme *This Week* (February 1975) showed Dr Elphis Christopher of the FPA talking to a class of 14-year-olds about contraception. Mary Whitehouse describes the film: 'She illustrated her talk by showing the children various types of contraceptives, and gave a graphic description of how a sheath – hold it well up so the children can see it – should be fitted on to an erect penis. Heaven help us – and them! The image of that device swinging between the doctor's fingers remains for me a graphic symbol of the gross insensitivity of the hot-gospellers of the contraceptive society. There is a bigotry, almost fanaticism, about them which makes one feel they – so often well intentioned – are the victims of their own propaganda.'[16]

Dr Martin Cole's sex education film

Dr Martin Cole, a genetics lecturer at Aston University and sexual freethinker, hijacked the debate on sex education films. He produced a 20-minute colour film, *Growing up*, that showed full frontal nudity, a fifteen-second sequence of sexual intercourse and sequences in which a married woman of twenty-three and a boy of fifteen masturbate before the camera. At its London preview before an audience of over 500, made up of press reporters, teachers, health education specialists, politicians and children, Dr Cole claimed that many of the crises confronting adolescents resulted from sexual guilt, and that his film went some way towards dispelling the guilt. In reply to a question from Lord Longford, Dr Cole said that premarital sex was not a bad thing and that it would be presumptuous for either him or Lord Longford to dictate to young people what they should do. The film upset Mary Whitehouse who complained that Dr Cole's amoral approach was turning people into animals. She predicted that no school would be interested in showing the film. While the feeling among those teachers who had seen the film was mixed, Dr Cole claimed there was fantastic interest from teachers and health education authorities. Two 16-year-old girls at the preview said they liked the film.[17]

In a report prepared for the Archbishop of Canterbury, Dr Arthur Ramsey, Canon DJW Bradley reached the conclusion that Dr Cole's film had been produced with genuine educational motives in mind. The Canon said he did not think there was anything pornographic in the film, nor was there anything gratuitously provocative.

He was anxious to make the point that he did not want to be associated with unqualified condemnation of the film. His main quibble was that the commentator committed himself to a view that is unacceptable to the Christian, namely the suggestion that masturbation and premarital intercourse were norms of human sexuality.[18]

At a special meeting Birmingham City Council recommended that the film should not be shown in its schools. The council deplored Dr Cole's intensive public activities in relation to sexual matters and advised him that his film was causing great public annoyance. The council rejected it as repugnant and too extreme for the majority of their citizens.[19] The Modern Churchmen's Union, however, were apparently so taken with Dr Cole's ideas that they invited him to speak at their annual conference. Dr Cole used this platform to suggest the need for youth camps where young people could be promiscuous provided they used contraception. He argued that society should accept that a certain number of young people are promiscuous, and by accepting the situation, unwanted pregnancy could be avoided. It would do an enormous amount of good for those who needed sexual exploration and would lead to their entering better relationships afterwards.[20]

There is no doubt that Dr Cole was a true sexual revolutionary. In the past he had advocated free brothels and the promotion of a sex supermarket. In an article in the *Guardian* he described the presumption that sex should only be taught as part of a loving relationship as an 'iniquitous philosophy'.[21] He argued that the purpose of sex education should be to encourage teenagers to accept their own sexuality and take precautions against unwanted pregnancy. He wrote: 'I think teenagers should be promiscuous, I think being promiscuous can, in many cases, be a vitally important part of growing up.'[22]

The growing use of sex education films in schools had aroused a great deal of anxiety among those parents who were aware of their content. An editorial in the *Daily Telegraph* made the point that many parents must be very uneasy about what was being done to their children in the name of sex education. 'This may take various forms: talks by teachers or by itinerant "experts", films or broadcasts or any combination of these, all at the schools' or local authorities' discretion. Parents will not be reassured by the realisation that whatever type of sex education is selected is, unless the head graciously gives way, compulsory.' The editorial pointed out that while the 1944 Act gave them the right of withdrawing their children from religious instruction, they had no such right in the field of sex education, presumably because no one in 1944 could foresee the post-war boom in this industry. The editorial argued that the right to withdraw should clearly be given to parents; yet, even if it were, many may be hesitant to exercise it, for fear of exposing their children to ridicule or even pedagogic displeasure.[23]

And this was a very real problem for parents who objected to the moral tone of the sex education that was on offer. The experience of one such family is described in a letter to *The Sunday Times*. The father, Jack Proom, wrote: 'Parents have no rights: people are very reluctant to criticise school material when their children are held hostage. Our experience is proof of the tyranny involved. My wife and I believe that modesty, chastity and fidelity are virtues. We aim for excellence in life and had sent our four daughters to a "good" school at considerable financial sacrifice. Both my wife and my sister had been pupils of the school and there was nothing to warn us that the headmistress was to become a keen exponent of school sex education. Even so, this could have had our support, had not the underlying philosophy of some school material proved repugnant to conscience. This material included the widely used BBC films, which the Longford Report later described as visually pornographic. The school doctor was called in to teach our 14-year-old family planning—without her request or our consent... My wife and I both wrote gently to the headmistress and our questions were ignored to the point of rudeness. When eventually I wrote demanding that parents' views be taken into account, I was invited to find another school for our children. I submit that it is an abuse to use the compulsory education system to teach children sexual attitudes known to be contrary to some parents' moral principles (as the BBC have admitted their films to be). It damages the family, the basis of our society.'[24]

The booklet 'Sex Education: The Erroneous Zone'

In 1970 the National Secular Society published a booklet intended for parents and teachers, *Sex Education: The Erroneous Zone*. Written by two primary school teachers, it criticised sex education literature as being obscure, moralistic or euphemistic. The authors believe 'that the condemnation of all forms of sexual expression for young people was an attitude totally divorced from reality. Sexual feelings cannot be switched off by cold showers.'[25] The FPA regarded the booklet so highly that it was included in the 1972 book list, marked with an asterisk to indicate that it was particularly helpful to family planners and sex educators. This booklet is important because it presents a modern version of the ideology of the sexual revolution.

The authors argue that sex education, which does not contain moralising, should be provided in all schools. At the appropriate age children should be given all the physical *facts* of sexual development, puberty, stimulation, love-making, copulation, variations of sexual expression, conception, pregnancy, birth, contraception, abortion, disease, and the various problems that young people may encounter as their bodies develop. A basic aim is to help children experience sex for what it is, 'a normal and delightful aspect of human behaviour – and to enjoy it without guilt, fear or danger'.[26] The authors say that children should be given 'all the information and help they need to form satisfactory relationships in adolescence, and this includes freedom to experiment'. They argue that it is possible for society 'to make sex lovely and joyful, but first we have to remove the anti-sex attitudes of traditional immoral codes, and particularly the influence of the churches'.[27]

124

According to the authors, those who oppose sexual freedom often claim that it would result in a great increase in the number of illegitimate children and in cases of venereal disease. But there can be no doubt that silence on the subject of contraception is responsible for many of the unwanted pregnancies that are caused by *ignorance*. 'It is, however, precisely the inadequate and repressive nature of most sex education which is responsible for a large proportion of unwanted pregnancies and cases of VD.' The argument is that those parents who really want to protect their children should see to it that their sons and daughters are fully informed about sex, and particularly about efficient methods of contraception.[28]

The booklet argues that it is wrong to condemn promiscuous sex, for 'it seems that the normal development of many individuals involves a necessary period of exploration and experiment followed by a stable attachment to one loved person. If this is so, there is no sense in condemning the early stage. Nor is there any good reason, given consent and safety, why a stable love relationship should not exist side by side with other, less intense relationships.' To support their case the authors quote from *Sexual Morals* produced by the Student Humanist Federation: 'copulation between lovers is especially satisfying, but copulation between mere good friends is also well worthwhile, and if you reject the latter you are less likely to achieve the former.'[29] The authors conclude that 'it should be recognised that those who find their greatest sexual satisfaction with a loved partner are not therefore superior to those many others who enjoy sexual experiences with a number of partners with whom they have no deep emotional ties. Apart from the problem of contraception and disease already dealt with above [by using condoms] there is no reason why they should not seek mutual satisfaction in their own way. Provided both partners understand what is happening, they should be free to take pleasure in each other, without being ostracised, discouraged or condemned. Most of our writers pretend that love is possible only in marriage, that sex outside marriage must be "promiscuous", and that procreation and love are the only valid reasons for copulation. Many young people know from experience and from observation that all this is not so. They are not likely to listen to advice from people who will not be honest with them.'[30]

With regard to morality the authors quote the two cardinal rules from Alex Comfort's book *The Joys of Sex*: 'Thou shalt not exploit another person's feelings. Thou shalt not negligently risk producing an unwanted child.' On the basis of this moral approach, the authors no longer believe in telling the young what to do, but 'if we were asked for advice on this topic we would say something like this: "Make love if you both feel like it. But first make sure you are safe… Remember too that the powerful excitement of love-play may lead to copulation even when it is not at first intended. Your only safe course, therefore, is to go to a clinic (FPA or Brook Advisory Centre) and get advice on contraception. Making love is normal, healthy and pleasurable, and a means of communicating delight between human beings. Providing you are sincere with each other, and safe, then if you feel like sex [here the booklet uses a four-letter word] do it with a clear conscience; and we hope you enjoy it".'[31]

With regard to homosexual sex, the authors have this advice for young people: 'Homosexual relationships in adolescence are normal, and provided there is no exploitation of one person by another, there is no harm in them. What may be harmful is the attempt to suppress your desires and to substitute guilt and fear for love, affection and friendship. If you are attracted to a member of your own sex, and if you both want to give physical expression to your feelings, then do so; and we hope you enjoy it.' They continue: 'Of homosexual and bisexual adults we would say that they should discard any false sense of guilt which has been imposed on them. If society does not yet accept them, it is society that is at fault.'[32]

The authors make the following suggestions, 'not on the basis of an arbitrary "moral code", but as an attempt to draw rational conclusions from the *facts*. Sex education should not: conceal *facts*, discourage the expression of affection and love, use the threat of disease or unwanted pregnancy to frighten the young for moralistic purposes, attempt to create guilt by claiming that sexual activity ought to occur only within marriage, imply that the only respectable life-aim for girls is to become wives and child-bearers.

'Sex education should: give full and honest factual information about the physical and emotional aspects of sex, help to remove guilt and fear from sexual activities, give information about means of contraception (which should be free) and encouragement to practise it, give information about the transmission, symptoms and treatment of venereal disease, within this framework of knowledge and freedom, encourage young people to make their *own decisions* about their behaviour, where advice is given, base it on the *facts* and on reason, not personal tastes or sectarian codes [my italics].'[33]

Although *Sex Education: The Erroneous Zone* later disappeared from the FPA book list when its amoral approach was criticised in the House of Lords, it is an extremely important booklet because it gives a modern account of the underlying objectives of the sexual revolution in that the authors are open and straightfoward about their ideology.

Here again we should note some of the key objectives of the revolution. The first priority of sex education is to remove what it regards as the 'anti-sex attitudes' of traditional moral codes, and particularly the influence of the churches. Second, is the insistence that young people should be given a large amount of factual information about sex—the more *facts* about sex the better, and from every conceivable angle. Third, is the denial that any type of sexual behaviour is wrong. Both promiscuity and homosexual sex are defended as acceptable, even desirable forms of behaviour. Fourth, sex education is pro-choice. So young people are invited to make their *own* decisions, based on the facts and free from moral considerations. They are free to do whatever they *want*, whatever feels good, whatever gives them pleasure. Fifth, unintended pregnancies and sexually trans-mitted diseases are caused by sexual *ignorance* and especially the inability to use contraception properly. Lastly, teaching young people that sexual activity ought to occur only within marriage makes them feel guilty.

The remarkable trial of Dr Robert Browne

A remarkable incident occurred in early 1971 when the Birmingham Brook Advisory Centre complained to the General Medical Council (GMC) that a family doctor had broken confidentiality by telling a father that his 16-year-old daughter had been prescribed oral contraceptives by the Brook clinic. As a result of the complaint Dr Robert Browne was accused of serious professional misconduct, a charge which carried the maximum penalty of being struck off the medical register. The case against Dr Browne was that he was guilty of improper conduct for disclosing to a father that oral contraceptives had been prescribed to his daughter, despite the fact that Brook had given him this information in confidence. According to the charge, Dr Browne had neither sought nor received his young patient's permission to make this disclosure.[34]

The story is as follows—Dr Browne had been the family doctor for over twenty years and had been present at the birth of their 16-year-old daughter, who had been his patient all her life. When the young girl formed a relationship with a boy, unbeknown to her parents or Dr Browne, she went to the local Brook clinic where Dr Philip Hamilton, without consulting Dr Browne, prescribed oral contraceptives. The clinic, having obtained consent from the young girl, sent a letter to Dr Browne, informing him that his patient was on oral contraceptives. Dr Browne now faced the dilemma of whether or not he should take the parents into his confidence and let them know that their daughter was using contraceptives. When the father came for a check-up Dr Browne, after careful thought, decided to let the father see the letter sent to him by the Brook clinic. The father asked what it meant and whether he should discuss it with his wife. Dr Browne suggested that to do so would be a wise course of action.

Before the trial a colleague of Dr Browne spoke of the doctor's dilemma. 'Should a doctor be compelled to keep information of a schoolgirl's pill-taking secret from the parents? It is an issue of the greatest interest and importance, not only to doctors, but to thousands of worried parents.' Dr Browne received overwhelming support from colleagues and local people, and a petition carrying thousands of signatures was delivered to the Prime Minister by Stirchley Residents' Association, who were staunch supporters of the doctor.

During his trial before the GMC, Dr Browne explained from the witness box that when he received a letter from the clinic it sounded an alarm bell in his mind. 'I was concerned that a girl of only 16 – just 16 years of age – had been placed on a contraceptive pill without prior knowledge or consultation with me as her family doctor.' The doctor said that, in his opinion, taking account of the family circumstances, he thought that the parents were the best people to counsel their daughter. 'I also felt that if she was keeping a secret to herself she might have a sense of guilt which could have a harmful effect on her emotionally.' Under cross-examination Dr Browne said that his interest was primarily for the patient. 'I have no other interests than what is best for her.' Asked if he would have used moral arguments to try and persuade the girl not to take the pill if medical arguments failed, Dr Browne replied, 'I would have explained to her the long-term course of her action.' Asked if he would make a decision on medical or moral grounds he replied, 'Medical, psychological, social and moral are all intertwined. It is very difficult to dissociate one from the other.' He considered the girl's interests and that was his sole concern.

Mr George Jonas, who appeared for Brook, said of the doctor: 'No one minds what moral views he may have in a private capacity. He is fully entitled to hold whatever views he pleases. The burden of the complaint in this case is that he let those views interfere with his objectivity as a professional man.' The issue was of concern to Brook and the FPA, for they believed that it was vital for family doctors to keep confidential the information passed on to them about children who had been given contraceptives without the knowledge of their parents.

Brook issued a statement during the proceedings, expressing its absolute determination to continue assisting unmarried women of any age who showed a responsible attitude by choosing to consult its experts in order to avoid the risks of unwanted pregnancy and abortion. Brook was aware of increasing evidence of a need for contraceptives and sexual advisory services to be made available to the younger members of the community. Brook's executive committee believed that such services would only be used if the utmost secrecy were maintained. It therefore guaranteed the strictest confidence to all its clients. The statement said that Brook advised each client to give consent for her general practitioner to be informed.[35]

Dr Browne was cleared of the charge of improper conduct. The GMC found that in the particular circumstances of this case – and the chairman emphasised that the finding applied to this particular case – the committee did not regard the doctor's action in disclosing information to the parents as improper. Interestingly, by the time of the hearing the young girl had ended her relationship and wrote to the doctor expressing her sorrow for what had happened. 'I realise now that in telling my parents you were doing what you believed was the best for me, not because you wanted to get me into trouble with my mother and father, but because you cared about what happened to me.'[36] The FPA and Brook were furious at the outcome of the case. But there was a great deal of popular support for the doctor, as most people believed he was an honourable man who had acted with great courage in the best interests of the whole family. Many people were amazed that anonymous organisations, like Brook and the FPA, had such power over the lives of children. If these organisations had their way, the parents who had nurtured and loved their daughter since birth would have been kept in ignorance of the fact that she was facing a crisis, fraught with danger and unhappiness.

Shortly after the verdict of the GMC, the FPA produced a sex education pamphlet with an added page on confidentiality, which advised children that they were entitled to receive contraception without their parents being told. The Chief Education

Officer of Norfolk County Council was incensed by the action of the FPA. 'As one who has been actively concerned in the field of sex education in schools may I deplore the action of the FPA. I well understand their sense of defeat following the decision of the GMC and the widespread approval of that decision. None the less the distribution of a pamphlet to schools in which there are children for whom sexual intercourse is illegal, and especially with its added page on secrecy, must cause considerable concern. Many will see in this a new aggressive advocacy of a permissive society and an attempt to disrupt families. Our objective should surely be a sympathetic planning of the effective family unit which involves much more than birth control. The publicity given to this proposed action by the FPA could well undermine the efforts of many who are now working in schools to help children to a responsible attitude in these matters.'[37]

Following the GMC's verdict there was a flood of letters to the newspapers. Elizabeth Mitchell, Chairman of Marie Stopes Memorial Centre wrote: 'Such a finding is extremely disturbing to those of us who have to do with birth control clinics where unmarried girls are seen… What assurance can our patients now have that their general practitioner will not betray their confidences? It seems that clinics may have to reconsider this practice—the patient's interests after all must take precedence over medical etiquette.'[38] The response was brisk: 'Yes indeed. And who is likely to be the best judge of the patient's interests—the family doctor who has known and attended her for years, or the clinic doctor for whom she is just another young female organism to be dosed with a pill or fitted with a device?'[39] And another correspondent: 'What is in question is not the interpretation of medical etiquette, but the far more serious matter of family relationships. Mrs Mitchell rightly says the patient's interests must take precedence, and surely the interests of a 16-year-old of either sex are better served if the parents are made aware of the problems confronting their children than if she is left to deal with them alone, with only the advice of strangers, however well-intentioned, to help and guide her.'[40] And yet another: 'The attitude of some of those concerned with family planning should strike terror into the hearts of anyone concerned with our strength and stability. That any girl of 16 should be supported by some "clinic" without her parents knowledge in her wish to be able to indulge in intercourse with her boyfriend without fear of unwanted pregnancy is irresponsible and degrading. The emotional damage which can be caused by such conduct is enormous.'[41]

The prosecution of Colin Knapman: November 1971

Within a few months there was another sensational court case, this time over a parent's objection to the type of sex education that was being taught to his children. The Exeter Education Committee published *The Scheme of Education in Personal Relationships* (1970), a booklet aimed at helping teachers address the issue of sex education in Exeter schools. The booklet made it clear that its moral framework for sex instruction was not Christian; rather, morality was interpreted as 'belonging to conduct, supported by evidence of reason or probability'.[42] It followed that 'the question of what is right and what is wrong should be dealt with on the grounds of consequences rather than of didactic rule'. In matters of sexual conduct 'young people need to discover by reasoned argument their own solutions to the problems which may arise. Such self-evolved solutions are likely to be much more lasting and effective than dogmatic rules laid down by their elders who may not appear to be fully aware of the changing pattern of social ethics.'[43] Children need to be able to discuss sexual matters 'with adults who will be prepared to explain and advise without condemnation, preaching or dogmatising'.[44]

The booklet leaves little doubt that parents are a part of the problem, because they do not give their children adequate sex education. As many parents 'contract out of their responsibility through lack of interest, insufficient knowledge, inability to communicate, or sheer embarrassment, it becomes increasingly the responsibility of teachers, as professional educationists, to ensure that every child is given this very important instruction and guidance'.[45] And that's not the only problem with parents. The pre-school child's natural sexuality is 'too often adversely affected by the inhibitions of the parents. What does it matter if children go round the home unclothed?'

The booklet informs teachers that healthy attitudes in infant school can be cultivated by encouraging children 'to change their clothes completely for physical education and there is no logical reason why boys and girls should not strip together at this stage in the same room... Some parents and teachers may fear that such a practice might stimulate an unhealthy interest among children in the sex organs but, on the contrary, children soon accept the situation as a normal one. They revel in the sense of freedom from restrictive clothing and develop a healthy attitude towards their bodies.'[46]

With regard to homosexuality, the booklet teaches that 'relationships with members of the same sex are homosexual in nature but are not necessarily harmful, on the contrary they often provide lasting and enriching experiences... It is increasingly realised that the inculcation of a guilt complex is far more distressing and damaging to the developing boy or girl than any slightly illicit homosexual escapade. Similarly with masturbation... those who do not, never discover the function of their sexual organs.'[47]

Colin Knapman, a practising Christian, was amazed when he read in the booklet that right and wrong were to be decided only according to consequences. As he read more it became increasingly clear that the sex education booklet was rejecting the Christian religion as the basis of sexual morality.[48] Mr Knapman was particularly disturbed by the assertions that homosexual relationships were described as 'not necessarily harmful', often provided 'lasting and enriching experiences', and that those who did not masturbate 'never discover the function of their sexual organs'. While he was not opposed to sex education in general, he found the suggestions abhorrent, and against the moral standards he was teaching his daughters. He informed the headmaster of his concerns and warned that he would withdraw his two daughters, aged 8 and 11, if the programme of sex education went ahead as laid out in the booklet. When he failed to receive any assurances he withdrew his daughters from school and was prosecuted by Exeter Council for non-attendance. The prosecutor appealed to the court not to allow one individual to use the court as a forum for putting forward his own views on education. Mr Knapman was found guilty and without comment the magistrate fined him £10 with £25 costs.[49] He still refused to send his children to a State school, and had them educated privately at considerable personal cost. After the case the Director of Education said that the booklet would continue to be used in Exeter's schools, and commented that the vast majority of parents were perfectly happy with the scheme.

The Bishop of Exeter, Dr Robert Mortimer, gave his unqualified support to the controversial sex education booklet. In his diocesan leaflet he wrote of the difficulties parents experienced in broaching the subject of sex teaching. They were prone to make a mess of it and there was a strong case for providing sex education in schools. The bishop justified the booklet's approach to homosexuality, believing that 'homosexual activity, while young, is likely to prove very transient and to have few if any lasting ill effects'. He was grateful for 'the wise, responsible and pastoral advice and help contained in this booklet. And I hope that what I have written may reassure and encourage the parents of our children.'[50] Despite the bishop's praise for the booklet, a later version contained considerable changes, including a recommendation that teachers study the chapter in *Half our Future* (1963), produced under the chairmanship of John Newsom, which supported chastity before marriage and fidelity within it.

Longford Report on pornography

The *Longford Report* (1972), which investigated the growing menace of pornography in the UK, included a section on broadcasting, led by Malcolm Muggeridge. According to the report, 'Pornography is evil in itself, and not as a matter of degree; and its tolerance or rejection is primarily a question of the individual conscience rather than of social legislation. As the Apostle Paul put it, in circumstances very similar to our own, in his letter to the Christians in Rome: "To be carnally minded is death, but to be spiritually minded is life and peace." Such an attitude, central to the Christian position through the twenty centuries since it was first propounded, leaves no room for pornography in any form or guise. It follows that recognising the harm pornography inflicts, and the evil that it is, does not depend on statistical research, or any other external "evidence", but on the experience of its corrupting power in our own lives. No one can say he is immune to this corruption. Indeed, pornography's assault on human sexuality reaches into the very centre of human activity and of the human persona, and must therefore be considered as being evil in its darkest form.'[51]

In dealing with the issue of television sex education, the report described a *Panorama* programme in which a schoolmaster demonstrated the use of a contraceptive to a class of adolescent boys. 'There was no suggestion in anything he said that the sexual experiences the contraceptive was designed to facilitate had any connection with marriage, procreation or love. They were just for excitement or pleasure, and the contraceptive would enable this to be experienced without any anxieties about untoward consequences like a pregnancy or other entanglements. It is difficult to imagine a more wicked proposition that could be put to an adolescent mind, and with the immense persuasive power of television and the authority of the BBC behind it. Perhaps a millstone might be added to the Corporation's insignia.'[52]

The report considered the visual aspect of sex education resources. The materials used were of two kinds: commercially sponsored sex education manuals, and the programmes produced by the BBC at the request of the Schools Broadcasting Council. In their opinion the visual techniques employed were considered to be pornographic, in differing degrees, for the following reasons. First, the visual presentation of images of sexual organs and activities is likely to induce voyeurism and alienation. Second, 'the photographs in many commercially sponsored sex education manuals are obviously intended to sell the manuals, and serve no instructional purpose. To obtain these photographs the boys and girls whose bodies are used must have been stimulated and posed in a sadly degrading manner. The deadpan presentation of these pictures to other boys and girls must tend to destroy their sense of respect for the human body and its God-given organs.'

Third, 'as it is widely practised, sex education is the tacit encouragement of sexual activity without the restraints of a moral order and without any sense of personal responsibility. It reduces what should be the most intense expression of human love into mere technique.' The report commented that the BBC sex education programme designed for 8 to 10-year-olds contained an illustration of a woman having intercourse who was not wearing a wedding ring. The Schools Broadcasting Council's statement contained the ambiguous sentence that it 'would not wish to overemphasise the question of marriage, particularly in programmes for younger children...'[53] Fourth, 'in the field of sex education, as many witnesses testified, the risk that the material may take a pornographic form or seem in the eyes of children, must be very great. In this respect the increasing visual presentation of sex education material becomes a dangerous tyranny. Parents may hesitate to withdraw their children from classes for fear these children will be ridiculed and isolated.'[54]

In a letter to *The Times* Mrs Sarah Curtis claimed that the *Longford Report's* section on sex education 'is not only misleading, it is irresponsible'. She argued that the object of sex education in schools 'is not to initiate the young into premature relationships but to open their eyes to the risks and pressures to which they are exposed in our commercial and sex-orientated culture'.[55] Mrs Valerie Riches disagreed. 'I am afraid that is exactly what it is doing. Recent statistics show that there is an alarming rise in abortions and venereal diseases in little girls hardly out of puberty... By teaching our children about sex as though they are a group of little animals, the educationists are destroying the finest spiritual sensitivities associated with sex life. Being only children, they are experimenting with their new found information with the very same lack of foresight and self-discipline one rightly associates with their immaturity.'[56]

The verdict of the authoritative *Longford Report* that the visual sexual images being shown to schoolchildren were pornographic in nature was a shocking indictment of the growing sex education industry. The unthinkable had occurred—images that Victorians would have called lewd and obscene were being used to 'educate' schoolchildren. Sex education, with the connivance of the BBC, had succeeded in legitimising pornography. Victorian 'respectability' was now well and truly a thing of the past as the sexual revolution gathered pace.

Endnotes

1 *The Times*, 25 June 1970, Call for sex teaching
2 Family Planning Association, Annual Report 1969-70, p3
3 *The Times*, 14 January 1970, Attack on TV sex film
4 *The Times*, 20 March 1970, letter, Peter Bevan and eight others
5 *The Times*, 23 March 1970, letter, Nicholas Tyndall, Marriage Guidance Council
6 *Daily Telegraph*, 22 March 1971
7 *Daily Telegraph*, 24 March 1971
8 *Daily Telegraph*, 20 March 1971, letter, BJ Murphy
9 Mary Whitehouse, *Whatever happened to sex?* Hodder and Stoughton, 1978, p57
10 Ibid. p60
11 *School broadcasting and sex education in the primary school*, BBC publications, May 1971, pp24-25.
12 Ibid. p22
13 Ibid. p38
14 *Daily Telegraph*, 12 February 1971
15 *Daily Telegraph*, 12 February 1971, letter
16 Ibid. *Whatever happened to sex?* pp62-63
17 *The Times*, 17 April 1971, Frank film on sex gets mixed reception, Christopher Warman
18 *The Times*, 28 April 1971, 'Growing up' made with real educational motives, Dr Ramsey told
19 *The Times*, 7 May 1971, Sex education film fails to impress delegates at festival
20 *The Times*, 30 July 1971, Promiscuity camps suggested.
21 *Guardian*, 1st May 1971
22 Cited from Mary Whitehouse, *Whatever happened to sex?* p33
23 *Daily Telegraph*, 10 March 1971
24 *The Sunday Times*, 9 November 1975, letter, John Toft (pseudonym for Jack Proom)
25 *The Times*, 12 November 1970, Moralistic sex education
26 Maurice Hill and Michael Lloyd-Jones, *Sex education: The Erroneous Zone*, National Secular Society, 1970, p2
27 Ibid. p12
28 Ibid. pp12-13
29 Ibid. p17
30 Ibid. p18
31 Ibid. p20
32 Ibid. p23
33 Ibid. p27
34 *The Times*, 25 February 1971
35 *The Times*, 6 March 1971, Pill case GP defends right to tell parents
36 *The Times*, 8 March 1971
37 *The Times*, 16 March 1971, letter, F. Lincoln Ralphs, Chief Education Officer, Norfolk County Council
38 *The Times*, 9 March 1971, letter, Elizabeth Mitchell, Committee Chairman, Marie Stopes

Memorial Centre
39 *The Times*, 11 March 1971, letter, KJT Elphinstone
40 *The Times*, 12 March 1971, letter, Betty Lewin
41 *The Times*, 12 March 1971, letter, C Anthony Prince
42 *The Scheme of Education in Personal Relationships*, Exeter Education Committee, 1970, p5
43 Ibid. pp9-10
44 Ibid. p10
45 Ibid. p5
46 Ibid. p7
47 Ibid. p10
48 Ibid. *Whatever happened to sex?* pp29-30
49 *Daily Telegraph*, 19 November 1971, Sex book row father keeps girls at home
50 The Exeter Diocesan Leaflet, January 1972, Asst. Ed. Rev John Parkinson
51 *Pornography: The Longford Report*, Coronet Books, Hodder Paperbacks, London, 1972, p215
52 Ibid. p229
53 Ibid. pp231-32
54 Ibid. p232
55 *The Times*, 23 September 1972, letter, Sarah Curtis
56 *The Times*, 26 September 1972, letter, Valerie Riches

Chapter 9

House of Lords debates sex education

Government increases funding for the FPA; arguments for

free contraceptives on the NHS; the Lords' debate

Sir Keith Joseph, Secretary of State for Social Services, concerned about the high rate of abortions in the early 1970s, announced more money to encourage the growth of local authority family planning, and particularly visits by teams of 'experts' to homes where the idea of family planning was unknown. In a parliamentary debate David Steel, the main sponsor of the 1967 Abortion Act, said that there was growing evidence that the demand for abortion is caused by lack of provision for family planning.[1] Meanwhile, the number of FPA contraceptive clinics had now increased to around a thousand, spread across the country. In 1971 Sir Keith announced an extra £100,000 for the FPA, half of which would be for an experimental project to provide saturation family planning services in selected areas of need.

A delighted Mr Caspar Brook, Director of the FPA, explained that a pilot project was to be set up in which two towns would be saturated with family planning. He said that if, after a reasonable period, saturation reduced the number of unwanted pregnancies, there would be an irresistible case for making family planning freely available throughout the country.[2] The two areas selected for the saturation project were Runcorn in Cheshire and Coalville in Leicestershire, both of which met the criteria of being self-contained communities of about 30 thousand.[3] Caspar Brook forecast that the project would save £500,000 in health and welfare costs by preventing the births of unwanted children. In September 1972 the project opened a family planning shop in Coalville, and everything possible was done to saturate the area with contraceptive advice. Publicity was sought through contact with local newspapers and interviews were held with the *Guardian* and *Radio Leicester*. Family planning leaflets were distributed to three thousand houses and details of the clinics were widely distributed in the community; posters were placed in dance halls, bingo clubs and libraries. Speakers were made available for schools, youth clubs and other interested organisations.[4]

A key aspect of the FPA's activities was distributing literature to teach young people how to avoid unintended pregnancies. The leaflet, *Straight facts about sex and birth control* (1971) advised that 'there is only one way to make sure you do not get pregnant, unless you have decided you want a baby – use a reliable method of birth control'. In 1972 the FPA produced its booklet for young people, *Learning to Live with Sex,* which sold over 90 thousand copies within two years. This booklet is significant for it gives an account of the FPA's ideology. The original 1972 version was heavily criticised in that it described sexual intercourse in terms of boys and girls, and did not mention marriage.

In 1972 the medical director of the FPA, Dr Janet Evanson, set up an experiment in community sex education in the London boroughs of Camden and Islington— the Grapevine project. The idea behind the project was to get the message of sex education to young people by going out to meet them on the streets, instead of waiting for them to visit family planning clinics. Grapevine used what it called 'alternative methods' for conveying the message to children out of school hours. For example, the project made use of volunteers, mainly young people aged around 20, who went out on to the streets, into clubs, pubs, coffee bars and discotheques, the highways and byways, to spread the message. Like sex missionaries, they sought out young people to discuss anything to do with sex in an unembarrassed way.[5] The volunteers were trained to explain to young people their sexual 'choices' and then to leave them to make up their own minds on how to act. During the two years of the project over two thousand young people were contacted and 50 thousand leaflets distributed. Grapevine also went into schools and youth clubs to meet with groups of young people.[6] The project, however, attracted adverse publicity and the FPA decided to discontinue it when the funding period was completed.

The book list of the FPA, issued in 1972, showed a strong commitment to the ideology promoted by Alfred Kinsey and Wardell Pomeroy, co-authors of the Kinsey Reports. *An Analysis of the Kinsey Report on Human Sexual Behaviour* provided a review of the famous report by sixteen experts. Pomeroy's two sex education books, *Boys and Sex* and *Girls and Sex* were marked with an asterisk to indicate that they are particularly valuable for sex educators. *Boys and Sex* received a glowing tribute as a book which 'gives practical advice to adolescent boys on how to achieve a happy, guilt-free sex life'. Consistent with the message of the Kinsey reports, both books were sympathetic to homosexual relationships in children. For instance, Pomeroy writes that 'sometimes boys get started in sex with other boys for no better reason than because it is the easiest thing to do and boys are much more available... A boy knows without being told what is pleasing to himself must be pleasing to other boys. When he masturbates himself, for example, it is easy for him to transfer the knowledge of this pleasure to another boy, but it is naturally much more difficult for him to understand a girl's sexual feeling because he is not a girl.'[7] *Boys and Sex* advises that 'any of the farm animals may become a sexual object – ponies, calves, sheep, pigs even chickens or ducks. Dogs are also commonly used, but cats rarely. Intercourse with animals is usually infrequent among those boys who practise it, but there are some who build up a strong emotional attachment to a particular animal and will have intercourse with it on a regular basis…'[8] Having sex with 'the adult male animal, whether it is a dog, horse, bull, or some other species, may provide considerable erotic excitement for the boy or older adult… His enjoyment of the relationship is enhanced by the fact that the male animal responds to the point of orgasm…'[9]

Girls and Sex is recommended by the FPA as a book that explains 'to teenage girls the physical changes and urges they will normally encounter during adolescence'. In this book, discussed in chapter 2, Pomeroy promotes the view that bisexuality is the norm.[10] It follows that it is perfectly normal for a girl to be sexually attracted to, and have sex with, both girls and boys. Both of Pomeroy's books are devoid of any moral content; in fact, they openly promote Kinsey's ideology that it is natural for children to be sexual active.

Unplanned Pregnancy Report of the RCOG

In the early 1970s a working party of the Royal College of Obstetricians and Gynaecologists (RCOG), under the chairmanship of Sir John Peel, investigated the problem of the rapidly rising number of pregnant women requesting abortion.[11] The working group, which included the chairman of the Health Education Council, Lady Alma Birk, published *Unplanned Pregnancy* in February 1972. The report claimed that knowledge of contraception was 'very widely disseminated', and expressed 'both surprise and concern that the effectiveness of contraception in preventing unplanned pregnancies is, in fact, very disappointing'.[12] The majority of those who gave evidence to the working party 'stated emphatically that they regarded 16 as the lowest age at which contraception should be made available'.[13] With regard to the provision of contraceptives to under-age children, the report stated: 'Clearly, in the interest of family life and its stability, parental consent should be obtained in the case of any girl under the age of sixteen…'[14]

It was universally agreed that sex education was really the responsibility of parents. However, 'many parents were either unwilling or incapable of fulfilling this role so that it had to become a joint responsibility of parents and schools'. Acknowledging that 'practically nothing is known about the effects of sex education programmes, either in regard to the future health and happiness of the individual children or in relation to unplanned pregnancy',[15] the working party recommended a joint committee between the departments of Health and Education, and the Health Education Council, 'to study the content of school health educational programmes, and the extent to which they are being put into practice, and the best ways and means to determine their effectiveness'.[16] Despite the important observation that contraception was very disappointing in preventing unplanned pregnancies, the working party strongly recommended 'that a comprehensive contraceptive service should be established within the National Health Service'.[17]

Argument for free contraceptives on NHS

A Government review of family planning services within the NHS concluded that a substantial expansion was necessary to reduce the number of unwanted pregnancies. In a statement to the House of Commons in December 1972, Sir Keith Joseph said that 'with modern contraceptive methods available there should be fewer abortions and much less unhappiness and ill health which results from unplanned pregnancies'. There were three areas in which family planning services needed to be improved. First, was the need to expand the clinic services, which would become the responsibility of new health authorities in April 1974. There would be more clinics, more easily accessible, giving free advice on contraceptive methods, and the domiciliary services would be further expanded to enable those who needed advice in their home to receive it. Second, was the need to do more to inform the public about the services available and to encourage them to use them, and so Sir Keith announced extra funds for the Health Education Council to expand information and education programmes. Third, he concluded that there should be free contraceptive supplies for those with special social needs who would be unlikely to undertake effective contraception.[18]

Mr Alastair Service, chairman of the Birth Control Campaign, responded to the announcement of the Secretary of State by claiming that evidence from the London boroughs showed that a totally free service could reduce abortions by 50 to 75 per cent.[19] There was now growing pressure to increase the availability of contraceptives on the pretext that it would reduce the number of abortions and teenage pregnancies. And so a week later, when the House of Lords considered clause 4 of the National Health Service Reorganisation Bill, Lady Llewelyn-Davies (Labour) moved an amendment to provide free contraceptives on the NHS for all without qualification.[20] The Bishop of Bristol spoke in favour, saying that he sympathised 'because the amendment is aimed at diminishing human misery, and not least that particular kind of misery which the abortion rate indicates'. Baroness Macleod also supported the amendment. 'I feel very strongly about it; indeed, I think this is the turning point of the whole Bill, and future generations will commend us if we pass this amendment.' Baroness Gaitskell agreed: 'If it is passed it will mean that everything we have said and done over the last fifty years will have had a really good effect. If the Government do not accept the amendment, they will be taking a huge step backwards.'[21] The House of Lords' amendment passed by 76 votes to 51, and the British Government was on course for providing free contraceptives to all, without qualification.

Press comment was generally in favour of free contraceptives on the NHS. The argument was simply that free contraceptives were a good thing because they would reduce the number of unwanted pregnancies. The *Daily Mail* declared that 'free birth control will not increase immorality. But it will reduce the need for abortion. And it will reduce the number of unwanted children born in our world.'[22] *The Scotsman* argued that spending another £20 million over four years on family planning would be an efficient social investment. 'State family planning would pay a better dividend than most forms of public planning.'[23] The *British Medical Journal* said that discussion had moved away from theorising about morals and concentrated on the practical problems of reducing the number of unwanted pregnancies. It claimed that there were several good reasons for believing that a policy of free contraception would help cut the numbers of unintended pregnancies. The first reason was that changes in contraceptive techniques were leading to more people consulting their doctors, and the second reason was growing medical anxiety about the numbers of abortions, many of which were performed on young girls. 'If contraception were given the same volume of propaganda as abortion law reform received and every impediment to its use, including cost, removed, then there might be some real prospect of cutting the numbers of illegitimate births and teenage terminations.'[24]

House of Lords debate – 1973

The introduction of the Bill for the reorganisation of NHS in February 1973 provided an opportunity for a debate in the House of Lords on the issues of sex education and family planning. The Bill proposed that the NHS would become responsible for providing advice on contraception (that is, sex education) and for providing supplies of contraceptives to all, free of charge. Another aim of the Bill was to transfer the running of family planning clinics from the FPA to the NHS. The debate in the House of Lords is important for it shows the arguments of two opposing camps—those in favour of supplying children with contraceptives in order to prevent sexual tragedies, and those who believe that supplying children with contraceptives is a part of the problem. A number of amendments were introduced by those who were concerned both about the role of the FPA in providing sex education, and about the free provision of contraceptives to children under the age of 16.

Baroness Elles moved an amendment which proposed that it should be the duty of the Secretaries of State for Health and Education 'to approve the content of any sex education programme for children in schools which shall be given only by the teachers or by such organisations as they may approve'. In proposing the amendment the Baroness explained the deep anxiety that a number of Lords felt about sex education. 'Sex education for children is a matter of such vital importance, affecting the whole of a generation, that it ought to be considered in the context of the reorganisation [of the NHS] and especially in connection with the family planning advisory service which is being set up under clause 4 of the bill.'[25] At the time the agencies involved with sex education were the Health Education Council, which had a subcommittee which dealt entirely with sex education, the FPA and Brook.

Baroness Elles expressed her concern about the moral stance of the FPA. She drew attention to the response of the FPA to a question about its view of traditional morality. 'Our job is simply to help people avoid unwanted pregnancies. We cannot stop anything. We do not know what society's view of morality is. Do you? Everyone has their own view of morality, and what we do is seek to realise the aims and objectives of our Association which includes this, to educate the public in the field of procreation, contraception and health, with particular reference to personal responsibility in sexual relations.'[26] Baroness Elles noted that the effect of the last five years of sex education had been an 'enormous increase in the cases of VD, together with the enormous increase in the number of abortions and in the number of illegitimate children being born to girls under 20. I cannot of course prove – nor do I think anyone else can – that there is any close connection with the kind of sex education that has been given, but it must be open to anybody to have certain doubts.'[27]

The Baroness mentioned that the report of the Royal College of Obstetricians and Gynaecologists made the point that practically nothing was known about the effects of sex education programmes. The report suggested 'that wrongly orientated sex education could be having a result which was exactly the opposite of what it was desired to achieve, in that it was arousing curiosity and the desire to experiment. The rapidly rising incidence of unplanned pregnancies in the young age group gives some support to this idea.'[28] She pleaded for a reassessment of the kind of sex education made available to children.

Baroness Macleod of Borve argued that many parents were either unwilling or unable to teach their children about sex, and were thereby abrogating their responsibilities. Viscount Ingleby made the point that the kind of sex education that was being taught allowed children to do as they liked so long as they took the proper precautions. He mentioned an interview with the columnist of the magazine *Petticoat* on the BBC in which she stated that she could not advise anyone not to make love. 'A feature article in the magazine *Nineteen* assured readers that venereal disease was an inevitable by-product of our liberated sexual attitudes.' He said that this kind of advice was partly responsible for the increase in births to girls under 16, and was also partly responsible for the increase in venereal disease. 'It is this kind of advice that is destroying family life. If you have free love before you are married, although all things are possible under the grace of God, what are the chances of your forming a happy and stable marriage afterwards?'[29] He said that if they destroy family life they destroy the country and he raised the question 'ought we not set before young people the ideals of chastity before marriage and faithfulness afterwards?'

Baroness Gaitskell placed great emphasis on sex education. She said that no one should be afraid to give children sex education. 'It is the only way in which we shall get a generation of parents who will be able to educate their own children about sex. Nowadays, parents are not able to educate their own children about sex.' She quoted the number of pregnancies and abortions that occurred to under-age girls. 'My Lords, are these girls to be abandoned, with the exhortations to be good if they cannot be careful? Are they not to be helped and instructed in birth control and sex education? Is it more responsible not to teach them birth control?'[30]

The Earl of Lauderdale commented that some of the FPA material simply treated sex as a pleasant activity without any reference to marriage. He said that the attitude implicit in some of the FPA literature, or the attitude evident at the 1971 conference of the Health Education Council, was that 'sex outside marriage is wholly legitimate and in no way to be discouraged, provided care is taken to make sure that there is no VD or unwanted pregnancy as a result'. He warned that they should not accept at face value the raucous propaganda of humanists and the misplaced view of some churchmen 'that contraception by itself and contraceptive instruction and free availability of both in all forms, for use outside marriage, is the only cure for the rising VD and abortion rates'.[31] Following the debate the amendment of Baroness Elles was withdrawn.

A further debate took place around clause 4, which dealt with family planning services and which proposed making contraception available free of charge on the NHS to all, irrespective of age or marital status. Lord Stamp moved an amendment that contraception should be made available on the NHS only for 'married persons or unmarried persons over 16 years of age'. He was concerned that the proposal to extend the facilities for providing birth control not only to the married, but also to the unmarried, irrespective of age, would have a negative effect on the health and welfare of the teenage girl. Speaking as a bacteriologist, he drew attention to the rapidly rising incidence of venereal disease, with a threefold increase in numbers attending VD clinics since 1959. He claimed that 'more premarital sex, which surely must follow on increased facilities for contraception, is only too likely to result in greater promiscuity – which will certainly result in more VD'. He then turned his attention to abortion, showing that there had been a large increase over the last three years. 'It has been generally assumed that more freely available contraception would effect a reduction. It is said that teenage girls who want to will have sex relationships anyway, so that everything must be done to protect them from pregnancy. This may seem the obvious solution, but is it the right one? On balance, the provision of free contraception might, far from reducing the abortion rate, have the opposite effect, bearing in mind that on the one hand protection is far from 100 per cent, owing to imperfections in the mechanical methods and the improper use of the pill (which is particularly likely in the case of the teenager) and, on the other hand, the lack of restraint in teenage sex relationships that such provision would encourage.'[32]

Lord Stamp continued, 'the health of the teenager is not solely a question of medical aspects; there is the moral and sociological side... If the State accepts schoolboy and schoolgirl sex relationships, which can so easily be construed as condoning or even encouraging them—an idea which I should have thought would have been utterly repugnant to most parents—where do you draw the line? Even the age of 16 means little when one considers how eager younger girls are to copy their elders. Knowledge of contraceptive methods would soon get about even among the early teenagers, without even the benefit of the counsel that older girls, in the most favourable circumstances, might receive. I know I am speaking for very many in the education field when I emphasise that they are fighting an uphill battle against deteriorating moral standards among teenagers; and their position will be infinitely more difficult if schoolboy and schoolgirl sex relationships are in effect condoned by the State provided that no pregnancy follows. That may not be the intention of this legislation but it will be its effect—and one which no amount of advice by counsellors on sex matters can fully counteract.'[33]

Baroness Summerskill asked whether it was wise to supply contraceptives to schoolchildren, and reminded the House that they had legally increased the school leaving age to 16. She mentioned the case of Cathy, who was found in a bedsit dying of haemorrhage and shock after having delivered herself of a baby. Cathy had left her home in Wales, desperate and afraid and hid herself in London. 'How times have changed? It may be that a film star can declare to the world that she has had a child outside marriage; but for the schoolgirl—and we are speaking of schoolgirls now—the prospects for an unmarried mother are fraught with tragedy. She thinks of the business of having an abortion, all the time full of shame, generally deserted by the boyfriend who, after he has impregnated her, is no longer interested.' She said they could not reconcile the idea of a fuller, better life for children with the provision of contraceptives to 15-year-olds.[34]

Lord Avebury said that the rise in illegitimacy was a dreadful thing. 'It is ghastly that there are so many abortions. But is there not an element of schizophrenia in the thinking of some people who, with one breath, say that they will deny contraceptive facilities to the young, and who, with the next breath, are complaining about the alarming increase in the number of abortions about which we have been reading recently. They cannot have it both ways. If you have an efficient and comprehensive family planning service, then the abortion figures will begin to decline and the tragedies, such as the noble Baroness, Lady Summerskill, has referred to, will no longer take place.' He said that the 'increasing figures of abortion are evidence of the failure of the contraceptive services in this country. If you have a free and comprehensive family planning service, and you do not attempt, as this amendment suggests, to deny it to girls below the age of 16, then you will begin to get somewhere.'[35] In conclusion he said that the under-16 age group was more in need of professional advice than any other category of people. 'I know it is difficult for many of your Lordships to accept that young people under the age of consent are having regular sexual intercourse, but if you make access to contraception more difficult it will not solve the problem; on the contrary young people need to be made aware that skilled and sympathetic advice is regularly available.'[36]

(Here Lord Avebury was stating the dogma of the family planning lobby that easy access to contraceptives was the solution to the problem of teenage pregnancies. He claimed, in unequivocal terms, that the objective of a comprehensive family planning service was to reduce unwanted teenage pregnancies and abortions. Yet after three decades it is clear that comprehensive family planning has failed to reduce teenage pregnancies. This is why the current Government, in order to meet its objective of reducing teenage pregnancies, is promoting the use of emergency contraception among teenagers with such vigour.)

The Bishop of Bath and Wells (Edward Barry Henderson) said that 'the basic position of the Church, which is fairly well known, is more and more widely rejected by the majority of the community. Therefore one feels slightly that one is disqualified from taking part in the debate.' But he made clear that the Church's position was 'that sexual intercourse should take place only within the stable and lasting relationship of marriage'. Nevertheless, 'we feel that we should do everything possible to encourage people of all ages to seek advice in sexual matters; and this particularly concerns the young'. He said that the advice provided by family planning clinics 'does much to assist the young, in particular, in sorting out their ideas on sexual matters... I think the Board of Social Responsibility of the Church of England would wish to encourage the provision of full, free family planning services, and would oppose any financial or other restriction that would inhibit people from using them. This includes restrictive regulation as to the minimum age of people who may benefit from the services of such clinics.' He said that to restrict the provision of the family planning service to single people who are over 16 years of age would simply ensure that a proportion of those young people at risk of pregnancy would not be reached by the counselling services.[37]

Viscount Barrington said that if he were accused, along with those who supported the amendment, of shutting the gates of mercy on mankind, 'perhaps I should say womankind or girlhood – I would take the line that we could be doing the opposite'. He reminded the House that no method of contraception was completely reliable. 'If one is encouraging people on the understanding that it is their privilege and right to indulge in what I would call miscellaneous experimental copulation, then in my view the result is bound to be an increase in the number of unwanted pregnancies.'[38]

Baroness Gaitskell said that she believed that the high rate of unwanted pregnancies among the under-16 age group was 'probably due to their having had no sex education and no birth control education at all, no contraceptive education. Again I ask: is it more responsible to deny knowledge of birth control to the young and unmarried than to give them contraceptive advice?' Baroness Elles responded that they were all agreed as to the end they wanted to achieve, namely, the protection for the under-16s from illegitimate children, venereal disease and abortions. 'But I think we are perhaps in two minds as to how to achieve this. We can all quote figures, but all we can see is that there has been, in the last five years, a very rapid increase in premarital intercourse, and it is this that is worrying people who say we should not have free contraception readily available for people of all ages, including those under 16. I think that is the basis of our argument. We say that to allow contraceptives to be freely available to people under 16 will encourage them to have more intercourse, and will therefore encourage them to have the kind of consequences which, as we all know, can be the result of sexual intercourse.'[39]

Lord Aberdare, speaking on behalf of the Government, opposed the amendment. He said that those engaged in providing contraceptive services consistently say that the unmarried girl who seeks contraceptive help is nearly always already sexually experienced and has a steady boyfriend. 'When one considers how the rise in illegitimate pregnancies started a long time before the pill was generally available, one can see that the present standards of sexual behaviour are part of a

143

general code of conduct and have been affected little, if at all, by the making available of contraceptive services to unmarried people. What we believe is most important is that contraceptive services should be provided in the context of personal counselling... We are not talking about handing out contraceptives on a plate to all young unmarried girls. If we want to help solve the problem of unwanted births to young unmarried girls under 17, surely what we need to do is make advice and counselling readily available in conjunction with treatment and supplies.'[40]

Baroness Llewelyn-Davies of Hastoe reminded their Lordships that they were not the only ones asking for free contraceptives and a comprehensive family planning service. The British Medical Association had also recommended an absolutely free and comprehensive service that should be available to all women of childbearing age. The Royal College of Obstetricians and Gynaecologists also strongly recommended a comprehensive service within the NHS, and all the leading serious newspapers applauded the decision.[41] Lord Stamp withdrew his amendment with the plea that the only solution was to encourage, by every possible channel, self-restraint in the young – in other words, morality.[42]

Following the debate in the House of Lords, the Chairman of the FPA, Florence Tewson, defended the organisation in a letter to *The Times*. 'The most important single fact is that the vast majority of young people who come to the FPA and to their clinics for advice and help are already sexually active. No amount of moralising will erase this fact. The FPA believes that whilst most ordinary parents recognise that they should be responsible for the sex education of their children they also recognise how ill-equipped they are for this... It is the considered view of the FPA that the case for an entirely free family planning service is irrefutable on humanitarian, economic and medical grounds.[43] Valerie Riches from the Responsible Society responded: 'The FPA says that most ordinary parents recognise how ill-equipped they are to be responsible for the sex education of their children. Does she believe that her association is better equipped to be responsible to do it for them? Let us examine one FPA leaflet addressed to "boys and girls" (*Straight facts about sex*). They are told "sex is yours to enjoy" and that there is only one way to avoid unwanted pregnancy, and that is to use birth control "every time you have sex". Why is no mention made of contraceptive failure rates (up to 20 per cent, and more in some cases)?'[44]

Another correspondent was equally unconvinced by the special pleading of the FPA. 'Judging by some FPA pamphlets, publications and now cartoons, younger and still younger members of society are encouraged to believe that not only is it irresponsible to copulate without thought for a possible pregnancy but that premature sexual indulgence is expected of them. By a sin of omission this propaganda subverts the very fabric of society by ignoring love, marriage, personal responsibility and self-discipline in sexual relationships.'[45] Another correspondent argued that 'the basic objection to the policies of the FPA is that they create the very problems they profess to solve'. He then compared two years – 1930 and

1970, which had virtually identical crude birth rates of around 16 per 1000. 'In 1930 there were no free contraceptives, or contraceptive advice for the young especially, no pills and no free abortions. The total illegitimate births were 27,000 out of 630,000 [4.3 per cent]. There was no abundant sex education. In 1970 there was abundant sex education, freely available contraceptives, and free abortions, and the total illegitimate births was 64,000 out of a total of 789,000 live births [8.1 per cent]. There were also 120,000 abortions of which the majority were undertaken on young people. Morality is very much a matter of social climate, and in the social climate of the thirties (when I was young) the majority of teenagers did not sleep around, and sex was regarded as the privilege of marriage. The policies of the FPA will only produce even greater suffering than they now inflict.'[46]

In November 1973 the FPA set up an education unit to organise courses for sex educators. One of its main objectives was to develop sex education courses for teachers and students at colleges of education and universities. Professor N Wagner, an American psychologist and sex educator, who spent his sabbatical year as a consultant to the FPA, held courses in London and Manchester with the aim of training 50 sex educators to become tutors for the training of schoolteachers in the skills of sex education.[47] But the FPA's vision extended well beyond the shores of Great Britain; the annual report (1973-74) acknowledged the important role in the future of fund-raising 'both for ourselves and for the International Planned Parenthood Federation. The world is shrinking and the FPA in Great Britain can no longer be concerned only with what happens here. It must play an increasing part in international plans for worldwide family planning.'[48]

It is interesting to note that during the first five years of the 1970s, when the TV sex education programmes were being broadcast to schools, when the FPA and Health Education Council were producing a vast quantity of literature providing advice on contraception, when the number of contraceptive clinics for young people were increasing rapidly, the rate of teenage abortions did not decline, as was widely predicted by the promoters of contraception, but, in fact, doubled. Among teenage girls aged 12-18, the number of abortions increased from 11.3 per 1000 in 1970, to 21.8 per 1000 in 1975. Slowly but surely the sex revolution was bearing its inevitable fruit.

Endnotes

1 *The Times*, 24 February 1971, Parliament, 23 February 1971, House of Commons.
2 *The Times*, 21 July 1971, Abortion on request
3 *The Times*, 24 February 1972
4 Family Planning Association, Annual Report 1973-74, p5
5 *The Times*, 5 April 1974, I heard of it on the Grapevine
6 Family Planning Association, Annual Report 1975, p11
7 Wardell Pomeroy, *Boys and Sex*, Penguin Books, 1971, p58
8 Ibid. p134
9 Wardell Pomeroy, *Boys and Sex*, A Pelican Book, New York, 1981, pp134-135

10 Wardell Pomeroy, *Girls and Sex*, Penguin Books, first published 1969, 1986 reprint, p117
11 Report of the Working Party of the Royal College of Obstetricians and Gynaecologists, *Unplanned Pregnancy*, February 1972, London, p7
12 Ibid. p51
13 Ibid. p52
14 Ibid. pp53-54
15 Ibid. p82
16 Ibid. p92
17 Ibid. p91
18 Hansard, Commons debate, 12 December 1972, Sir Keith Joseph
19 *The Times*, 13 December 1972, Contraceptives to be free only on social or financial grounds
20 *The Times*, 20 December 1972
21 Hansard, Lords debate, 19 December 1972
22 *Daily Mail*, 13 December 1972
23 *The Scotsman*, 13 December 1972
24 *British Medical Journal*, 20 January 1973
25 Hansard, Lords debate, 12 February 1973, c1285
26 *Daily Mail*, 6 February 1973
27 Ibid. Hansard, Lords debate, cc1284-1287
28 Ibid. c1287
29 Ibid. c1290
30 Ibid. cc1291-92
31 Ibid. cc1307-09
32 Ibid. cc1326-32
33 Ibid.
34 Ibid. cc1335-38
35 Ibid. c1338
36 Ibid. cc1339-40
37 Ibid. cc1341-42
38 Ibid. cc1344-45
39 Ibid. cc1350-52
40 Ibid. cc1353-57
41 Ibid. c1357
42 Ibid. c1358
43 *The Times*, 5 April 1973, letter, Florence Tewson, Chairman, FPA
44 *The Times*, 16 April 1973, letter, Valerie Riches, Responsible Society
45 *The Times*, 24 April 1973, letter, Arthur Wigfield
46 *The Times*, 27 April 1973, letter, W Corbishley
47 Family Planning Association, Annual Report 1973-74, pp5-6
48 Ibid. p2

Chapter 10

Free contraceptives for children on the NHS

Doctors allowed to presribe contraceptives for under-age

children without the knowledge or consent of their parents

In 1974 the British Government became responsible for supplying contraceptives to children. The NHS Reorganisation Act, which came into force in April 1974, made contraceptives available free of charge, irrespective of age or marital status, on the National Health Service. What would have been unthinkable to the Victorians had happened—it was now Government policy for the State to provide contraceptives to children under the age of sexual consent. Henceforth, a child of 14 or 15, or for that matter even as young as 11 or 12, could go to a NHS clinic, drop-in centre or Brook clinic to receive his or her supply of contraceptives. This Act of Parliament represented a massive change in social policy and was a landmark decision in favour of the sexual revolution. The British State was now responsible for ensuring that children could participate in an active sexual life, without the worry of the girl becoming pregnant. And this major change in social policy, that was to have an enormous influence on the sexual mores of the British people, had occurred without the general population really being aware of what was happening. In effect, the family planners had achieved a parliamentary coup d'etat. Under the guise of an Act to reorganise the NHS the sexual mores of Great Britain had been subverted, with few people understanding the full implications of this sea change in social policy.

And the most shocking aspect of the Act was that it allowed doctors to prescribe contraceptives to children without the knowledge or consent of their parents— and hardly anybody outside the Department of Health or the family planning lobby was aware of this fact. According to the Department of Health Memorandum of Guidance implementing the Act: 'It is for the doctor to decide whether to provide contraceptive advice and treatment, and the Department is advised that if he does so for a girl under the age of 16 years he is not acting unlawfully provided he acts in good faith in protecting the girl against the potentially harmful effects of intercourse.'[1] Contraceptives for children, like abortion, were now in the hands of doctors. Few people realised that this guidance meant that doctors working in family planning clinics now had the right to prescribe contraceptives for children, and to keep the fact secret from their parents. Parliament had effectively subverted the authority of parents—the State now had the right to 'treat' children with contraceptives without the knowledge or consent of their parents.

The FPA rejoiced in what it regarded as a triumph for the birth control movement, and its chairman, Florence Tewson, in her preface to the annual report in 1974, wrote: 'The FPA has worked towards this end for over 40 years and is proud of its success. The devoted work and forward-looking approach of the pioneers of the movement and of thousands of workers all over the country has achieved this aim – a completely free public service available to all. It is to our credit that birth control is now considered respectable and those seeking it responsible. This does not mean that the FPA can – or wish to – sit back on its laurels. From April 1974 the Association will act as the agent of the NHS, providing a service in 944 family planning clinics throughout the country... But that is not the end of the story. Indeed it is only the end of one chapter and the beginning of another. There is a great deal more important work to be done: we must tackle apathy, ignorance, fear, misinformation and distortion – about birth control, about sexual relationships, about sex education. We must continue to concern ourselves that the public family planing service remains not only free but good. We must continue to explore and develop new fields – we are currently turning our attention to *sex education* [my italics].'[2]

Policy of free contraceptives for children criticised

A few people were deeply unhappy about this change in social policy. Ronald Butt, assistant editor of *The Times* and erudite critic of the FPA, was scathing in his condemnation. He commented that Mrs Castle (Secretary of State for Social Security) had hastily set about fulfilling Labour's election manifesto pledge to provide free 'family' planning (if 'family' is the right word in so widened a context). She had done so without regard either to age or marriage. Responding to a sustained campaign by a persistent minority, she had decided to enforce a policy which in the long run was likely to influence the behavioural attitudes of young people in a way that was conducive to their unhappiness. Butt made the point that the campaign for indiscriminate birth control was closely linked with the campaign for sex education in schools, which the FPA was to make one of its main roles, now that the State was taking over its clinic work. 'In the area of sex and contraceptive education the FPA are now to act as the agent for the Health Education Council and any resistance to the type of sex teaching that is offered provokes scorn and anger. A spokesman of the FPA complained bitterly to me recently that schools were far too unresponsive to their efforts in this field and that some heads, in their old-fashioned blindness, were content to leave it to simple biological lessons and to parents. When I said quite gently that perhaps many parents would understandably not care for the moral assumptions and attitudes which informed the FPA's sex teaching, she exclaimed: "Parents! They're the most dangerous people of all!" And that, I suppose, is really the attitude that inspires the iceberg campaign of which Mrs Castle's diktat is only one tip.'[3]

A leading gynaecologist accused the Department of Health and Social Security (DHSS) of irresponsibility, for giving doctors *carte blanche* to prescribe the contraceptive pill to young girls without insisting that the doctors should give adequate advice of the risks involved. Speaking at a Royal Society of Health conference, Sir John Stallworthy, Emeritus Nuffield Professor of Obstetrics and Gynaecology at Oxford University, said that a draft memorandum from the Department of Health was not nearly forceful enough about educating young people on sexual dangers. 'It would have been more arresting, but a correct interpretation… if it had stated at the outset that the family planning services were to be available to men, women and children. Such a frank statement of what is at present obviously officially intended would no doubt have caused a public outcry with vociferous supporters on both sides.'[4]

Cardinal Heenan, the Archbishop of Westminster, warned that free contraceptives would lead to increased promiscuity and a dramatic spread of venereal disease. He said that Barbara Castle's announcement of a free contraceptive service for the unmarried, including schoolchildren, called for immediate notice. He appreciated that the Minister was carrying out a policy agreeable to many members of Parliament irrespective of party and was motivated by the desire to reduce the alarming growth of abortion. 'It must, however, be said that this official action is bound to promote promiscuity among the young. Educationally it is a policy of despair to provide the means for self-indulgence instead of teaching self-control. It is insulting to the young to take for granted that they are incapable of refraining from fornication. It is a fact of experience that many women seeking abortions have used contraceptive devices. It is therefore highly likely that the pregnancy rate among schoolgirls will continue to rise and the number of abortions to increase. In addition it is virtually certain that there will be a dramatic spread of venereal disease. We believe that the abandonment of Christian standards of sexual morality will have an eroding effect on the moral health of the whole community.'[5]

The Bishop of Norwich, Maurice Wood, wrote in a letter in *The Times* that 'contraception freely offered "without regard to marital status" must surely promote extramarital physical relationships, and these Christians believe to be sinful, whether they are heterosexual or homosexual, and many outside organised religion recognise that they are disruptive of stable family life. "Without regard to age" must surely encourage the lecherous to harm those below the age of consent. Young people, already under assault from the commercial interests profiting from the exploitation of sex, will be in greater danger… I have a great regard for the good sense and courage of young people today trying to live clean, full and self-forgetful lives, and they deserve a responsible Government that believes in chastity, not immorality; in self-control more than self-indulgence; and in the sanctity of marriage rather than the hurt of promiscuity.'[6]

Dr Margaret White, an eminent Croydon GP, commented that 'there is no evidence that a free contraceptive service will lead to a decrease in the number of unwanted pregnancies, paradoxically the evidence points the other way. In Aberdeen contraception has been free since 1966, but the illegitimate pregnancies rose from 262 in 1966 to 480 in 1971... The answer to the problem of unwanted pregnancies is education in responsible sexual behaviour.'[7] Dr David Short believed that the proposal to provide a free contraceptive service for schoolchildren was a serious mistake and one which would actually aggravate the problem it was designed to solve. He wrote, 'The fact that the Government itself promotes free contraceptives is bound to be taken by young people as a sanction, and indeed an encouragement to promiscuity. There can be no doubt that this will lead to an increase (rather than a decrease) in the number of pregnancies among schoolgirls – since there is abundant evidence that knowledge of contraceptive technique does not prevent pregnancy. It is equally certain that there will be a further increase in the incidence of venereal disease. But the most serious damage will be in the character training of young people. They will be officially encouraged to self-indulgence when what is desperately needed in society today is an increase in self-control. Many teach that self-control in the realm of sexual activity is impossible and even harmful; but this is simply not true... From every point of view, therefore, the provision of a free national contraceptive service can only be regarded as a prescription for national dissolution.'[8]

Dr Rhodes Boyson, Conservative MP for Brent North, pointed out that over the last 15 years there had been a steady increase both in sex education in schools and in the easier availability of contraceptives. 'The result has simply been a doubling in the percentage of illegitimate births, an increase in abortions and more than a doubling in the figure for venereal disease. That any Government on this negative evidence could decide to give out free contraceptives irrespective of age must presumably be the result of the work of another of the minority permissive pressure lobbies which have done so much harm to this country over the past ten years. Government sponsored promiscuity will make the present position worse.'[9]

The DHSS Memorandum of Guidance issued to area health authorities in May 1974, mentioned above, described the arrangements that were necessary for a comprehensive family planning service within the NHS. The guidance made it clear that not only should family planning be available for all within the reorganised NHS, people should also be free to choose their source of advice – either a family planning clinic or a general practitioner. Health authorities were instructed to give particular attention to the development of family planning services because 'of the benefits to be obtained from enabling people to avoid unwanted pregnancies, and from the reduction which may be achieved in the large number of abortions, unwanted illegitimacies and unwanted premarital conceptions that occur each year and which result in so much distress and unhappiness'.[10]

To ensure that the service was available to everybody who might need contraception, DHSS guidance authorised the provision of contraception to girls aged 15 years and younger, although Brook had already been providing contraception to under-age girls for some time. The advice of the DHSS was that a doctor who provided contraceptives to an under-age girl would not be acting unlawfully, provided he acts in good faith in protecting the girl against the potentially harmful effects of intercourse.[11] The legality of this guidance was later to be challenged by Victoria Gillick in the courts. Nevertheless, it was now possible for any child, no matter how young, to obtain free contraception from the State. The guidance, repeating the mantra of the sex education lobby, claimed that ignorance about contraception and the unavailability of family planning services had been shown to lead to unwanted pregnancies. For this reason it was necessary for family planning services to receive widespread publicity, so that children knew where to go to get their contraceptives. To help overcome ignorance, the Health Education Council would mount national campaigns to inform the public about contraceptive methods and services, while area health authorities were responsible for providing local publicity about their services.

In 1975 general practitioners joined the NHS family planning service on an item for service payment scheme, which meant that GPs would receive a special fee every time they provided contraceptives to a patient. This became a potential lucrative source of income and the vast majority of GPs, about 23 thousand, entered into contracts to provide contraceptive services.

So we see that way back in 1974, almost three decades ago, the Government was claiming that ignorance was the cause of teenage pregnancies, and that a comprehensive family planning service would reduce the incidence of sexual tragedies. To ensure that children had easy access to contraceptives, doctors were allowed to prescribe them without parental consent. How ironic that after three decades of free contraception for children provided by the State, the UK has not only a high rate of teenage pregnancies, as those who opposed the policies predicted, but the highest in Western Europe! Any reasonable person would conclude that the policy has failed—that the promotion of contraceptives is not the answer to teenage pregnancies. Why then does our Government persist with the policy of promoting contraceptives among children, a policy that is clearly not meeting its stated objectives?

FPA develops its role in sex education

The reorganisation of the NHS had been a triumph for the FPA. It was delighted at the policy that allowed doctors to provide contraceptives to children, for this was consistent with its ideology. And further, passing the management of its contraceptive clinics to the NHS meant that the FPA could devote its energy and time to promoting sex education, and so in March 1974 the FPA announced a fundamental change in its role. Having shed the burden of running its contraceptive clinics (by the second half of 1976 all FPA clinics had been taken over by the NHS) it was now free to devote itself to its real mission—the sex education of the British people. 'The Family Planning Association has traditionally been involved primarily in contraception. But its officers believe they should take on the job of sex education because family planning workers so often find shame, fear, ignorance, distortion and misinformation shrouding unwanted conception. The reason that six out of ten brides go to the altar pregnant is because they feel they cannot talk to their parents about sex. There is a much greater freedom of discussion and questions are asked where sex education is given in the classroom either by a regular teacher or by a visiting sex educator.' In order to achieve this objective the FPA planned to recruit teachers to teach methods of sex instruction.[12]

David Holbrook responded to the announcement of the FPA in a letter to the *Daily Telegraph*. 'The FPA is now part of a network of people who are motivated by a simplistic humanist approach which is seriously out of date.' He pointed out that the only youth representative on the Health Education Council, with which the FPA was closely connected, was a representative of IPC magazines. 'Parents should read the articles on sex in magazines like *Honey* and ask if they would wish their children to be taught sex by such people. I believe that these journals may be accused of exploiting young people by titillation. And one of their most serious faults is to try to turn children against their parents. This will no doubt be a feature of the new FPA sex education. Yet the public is largely unaware of what is happening. There are also connections with the pro-abortion lobby, while some members of the FPA have asked for the age of consent to be lowered or abolished. Do we really want to give over the teaching of sex to such people?'[13]

In August 1974 Mrs Valerie Riches was critical of the Population Countdown Campaign of the FPA in a letter to *The Spectator*. She wrote that the family planners and contraceptive distributors were motivated by a desire 'to create a "copulation" explosion in our own country'. She referred to the crude activities of the area representatives of the Population Countdown Campaign who hawked 'around suitcases of condoms on their fund-raising tours', and mentioned a newspaper report that 'soon the Family Planning Association's "Population Countdown" will be at school gates to tell schoolchildren where to get contraceptive advice… They are intent on casting their nets wide enough to capture all the youth.' She concluded that 'these attempts to pressurise and incite sexual activity among the young, even children, are but manoeuvres to connive, collude and condone the breaking of the law of the age of consent, and bring the population campaigners into disrepute.'[14]

The FPA took such strong exception to Valerie Riches' criticism that their solicitors wrote to *The Spectator* informing them that, in their opinion, the letter 'is gravely defamatory of them and that they are likely to succeed in obtaining substantial damages should they commence legal proceedings against your periodical and Mrs Riches'.

152

Patrick Cosgrave commented on the threatened legal action in an article in *The Spectator* entitled 'The politics of sex education'. 'I will say at once that I have never concealed – indeed, I have broadcast – my personal view that the Family Planning Association is a body the effects of whose propaganda and activities generally are almost unmitigated evil, whatever their intentions. I hold this view because I believe that the logic of any pressure group so organised tends to lead towards the meanest end of the spectrum in which it exists: the Family Planning Association is not an association for the planning of families, but one for the planning of control – that is, the prevention – of birth, and it is an abuse of the language, apart from anything else, to suppose otherwise. The main effect of the Association's activities and literature is, in my informed opinion, to equate love with sex – an inaccurate equation – and then sex with pleasure – another inaccurate equation – and then pleasure with pleasure without responsibility – a third and final inaccurate equation... What the FPA are devoted to is not simply a divorce between a human activity and a human feeling – between sex and love – but the elevation of a technique – the capacity to prevent conception mechanically – into an end in itself. Once the technique is allowed to become the be-all and end-all of a massive propaganda campaign, in part financed through the impersonal machinery of the State, and once politicians accept that, where they do not openly support such campaigns in the name of enlightenment and progressivism, they at least, like, alas, Sir Keith [Joseph], accept that they should neither interfere with nor attempt to judge the consequences of such a campaign, the very fabric of society itself is threatened. And the threat thus posed should command immediately the liveliest response and the most energetic debate.'[15]

In a statement issued with their annual report in 1974, the FPA said that they saw sex education as one of the most important ways of fulfilling their aim of preventing poverty, hardship and distress caused by unwanted conception. While recognising the role of parents in sex education, the FPA believed that parents alone are often inadequately prepared and children are often resistant to receiving sex education from them. Moreover, according to the FPA there was no truth in the claim that sex education increases precocious sexual behaviour. The statement laid down guidelines for sex teachers, who must accept that sexuality is an integral part of the total personality and that people have a right to full, objective information about it.[16]

Ronald Butt again commented on the activities of those he referred to as family planning missionaries. He wrote that in the congeries of influences that were sapping away at the values of young people, the missionaries of the so-called 'family planning' lobby were playing an increasingly active part. Since the State had taken over responsibility for what was theoretically the free supply on demand of contraceptive supplies and advice, they had achieved a new ebullience. In family planning clinics for teenagers, schoolgirls under 16 were being given free sheaths to hand to their boyfriends on the argument that if they did not get them, they would come back pregnant. 'It is for the politicians, who are the public's representatives, to find out whether the official attitude of the FPA (which is in the role of something like a government agent in these matters) is that of its former press officer, Mrs Wendy Smith, who wrote in a teenage magazine: "There is no reason why a girl shouldn't carry a sheath around with her all the time, so if the situation arises when she wants to sleep with a boy, she can ensure that he wears one…" It is also the business of the politicians, who provide the birth control missionaries with public money, to ascertain precisely what counselling is given to very young people in clinics. Is an immature girl warned about the dangers of VD, the advantages of self-restraint, the possible side effects of the pill?'

Butt then turned to the business of sex education in schools. He made the point that the FPA, expecting to offload to local authorities its functions (and no doubt its attitude) in contraceptive distribution, was now anxiously trying to get into schools to make sure that children were well prepared to use these facilities by sex education. They were battering at the doors of schools with specious arguments that either children were ignorant of the 'facts' or that they were already 'sexually active'. 'Yet the Department of Education and Science has no responsibility in this matter; even heads of schools may not be aware of what is being precisely said in the classrooms by the sexologist's representatives, or of the value-free context in which contraceptive instruction is often given.'[17]

Mr John Geffen, director of the FPA, emphasised the utopian aims of the Association. 'Divested of our clinics, we will continue our endeavours to ensure that all have the knowledge and the means to plan the children they want, in the belief that this will lead to happier and more stable families, and to fewer abortions, illegitimacies and broken marriages.'[18]

At a press conference Mr Alastair Mackie, director general of the Health Education Council, announced a national campaign to remind women and children that contraceptives were freely available. The Council had produced a 45-second film costing £97,000, which was to be shown in more than a thousand cinemas. The film showed a middle-aged woman, who had four children crying at her skirts and two babies in a pram, telling a pretty teenage girl to 'be careful'. It concluded with the advice: 'Don't listen to old wives' tales about family planning… look in the phone book under Family Planning.'[19] In response to the criticism that audiences often treated advertisements on contraception in cinemas with ribaldry and laughter, Mr Mackie said that such films were cost-effective, and expressed the hope that the film would be seen by about five million people, many of whom would be in the 14 to 24 age group. The idea was to reach young women who did not seek expert advice on contraception.[20]

By 1976 concern about the activities of the FPA was so great that an all-party group of MPs and peers wrote to the Charity Commissioner asking that its charitable status be withdrawn. In an open letter the Family and Child Protection Group, chaired by Mrs Jill Knight, cited a number of grounds for ending the FPA's charitable status—a charity should not be a commercial venture nor have political objectives; a charity should not assist in and connive at the breaking of the law, nor have the mere increase of knowledge as its purpose. Moreover, the FPA was connected with a separate trading company marketing contraceptives, which had no charitable status but whose profits helped to finance the FPA. The FPA also operated as a pressure group. The Charity Commissioner, however, was not convinced by these arguments and made it clear that a charity may legitimately engage in political pressure as a secondary function.[21]

Endnotes

1 Memorandum of Guidance, *Family planning services*, HSC(IS) 32, Department of Health and Social Security, May 1974

2 Family Planning Association, Annual Report 1973-74, p1

3 *The Times*, 5 April 1974, Putting family planning before family happiness, Ronald Butt

4 *The Times*, 17 January 1974, Ministry accused of irresponsibility over pill for under-16s

5 *The Times*, 8 April 1974, Cardinal attacks free family planning

6 *The Times*, 10 April 1974, letter, Maurice Norvic

7 *The Times*, 11 April 1974, letter, Dr Margaret White

8 *The Times*, 16 April 1974, letter, Dr David Short

9 *The Times*, 17 April 1974, letter, Dr Rhodes Boyson

10 Ibid. Memorandum of Guidance, *Family planning services*, May 1974

11 Ibid.

12 *Daily Telegraph*, 26 March 1974

13 *Daily Telegraph*, 3 April 1974, letter, David Holbrook

14 *The Spectator*, 3 August 1974, letter, Valerie Riches

15 *The Spectator*, 31 August 1974, The politics of sex education, Patrick Cosgrave

16 *The Times*, 27 September 1974, Sex lessons the best way to prevent poverty

17 *The Times*, 24 October 1974, The link between public money and public morality, Ronald Butt

18 *Daily Telegraph*, 4 December 1974

19 *The Times*, 11 November 1975

20 Ibid.

21 *The Times*, 25 August 1976, All-party group challenges charity status of FPA

Chapter 11

A 'libellous attack' on the FPA

Lord Lauderdale: 'Do the Government agree that sex education must be coupled with instruction in right and wrong?'

By the beginning of 1976 the FPA was undoubtedly the driving force behind sex education. The NHS was running its contraceptive clinics and the Government was committed to ploughing even more money into developing what it called a 'comprehensive family planning service'. Contraceptives were freely available to all, including children under the age of sexual consent, and guidance from the Department of Health allowed doctors to prescribe contraceptives to girls under 16 without the knowledge or consent of their parents, although few parents were aware of the fact. In addition, the FPA was receiving a large Government grant and had considerable influence within the NHS. Freed from running contraceptive clinics, the FPA could now put all its efforts into sex education, and particularly into educating the educators. Moreover, its initiatives had the full support of the British Medical Association and the Royal College of Obstetricians and Gynae-cologists. What the FPA now wanted was more influence in schools, and it was starting to campaign for sex education to become part of the national curriculum. The way was wide open for the FPA and its acolytes to propagate their ideology of comprehensive sex education.

Yet some people were becoming increasingly concerned about the activities of the sex education lobby. Why should a campaigning organisation like the FPA be given such power over the lives of children? Moreover, the type of literature that was being used was disturbing to many people. It was in this climate that members of the House of Lords called for a debate on the subject of sex education. This debate is important for it again presents views from both sides of the ideological divide. I have selected from a number of speeches to summarise the essential arguments.

House of Lords debate – 1976

Baroness Elles, introducing the debate in the House of Lords, called attention to problems involved in the sex education of children. She said that the subject was of fundamental importance to families with young children in schools as well as for future generations. Sex education was rightly of deep concern to head teachers and their staff, to parents, and, indeed, to young people. Most of her remarks dealt with children under the age of 16. She acknowledged that her religious faith (she was a member of the Church of England) influenced her views. Unlike the teaching of other subjects, sex education influenced a child's pattern of behaviour. It did not deal only with sexual matters, it also dealt with moral education. 'It can have the effect of bringing up children to live according to the rules accepted by society as being reasonable and in the best interests of all within society, or it can be directed to changing the climate and mores of society.' She noted that the FPA and Brook were moving more directly into the dissemination of sex education and were receiving large grants from the Department of Health. 'A member who was one of the leading forces in the Abortion Law Reform Association way back in 1967 and who was highly successful, also served on the Divorce Law Reform Association and is now chairman of the managing committee of the FPA.' She drew attention to a report of the Monopolies and Mergers Commission, which showed that London Rubber Industries allowed the FPA a 5 per cent retrospective rebate on all purchases 'because the FPA's educational activities widen the market for contraception'.

Talking about the FPA she mentioned what appeared to be deliberate misrepresentation of the facts to encourage the young to use contraceptives. 'I have seen rather too much literature on this matter lately. For instance, there is a booklet called *Learning to Live with Sex*, and various other publications with enticing titles. In this literature there are no notices of the failure rates of the non-medical supplies which they are purporting to give or which they are encouraging the young to use.'[1]

Lord Wells-Pestell, Labour Party spokesman for the DHSS, said that four Government departments had an interest in the subject. He addressed himself mainly to those aspects of sex education which affected the various professions within the NHS. 'The question is, how much can sex education do for boys as well as girls, when offered in a controlled situation, with due sensitivity, to avoid much of the misery caused by the unwanted pregnancy?' He said that many members of the profession felt that doctors should work with health educators to help reduce the number of casualties of sex. He noted that health education officers were now being appointed to area health authorities and therefore 'we can hope for an expansion in the field of sex education in the NHS'. He stressed the important role of school nurses and health visitors, who were able to teach and promote health in schools. 'The Department of Health and Social Security (DHSS) is at the present time sponsoring from central funds an experimental course on sex education for health visitors. This is being run by the FPA in conjunction with the Health Education Council and the Central Council for the Education and Training of Health

Visitors. The FPA is also involved in arranging sex education courses for teachers, health educators and community workers, in co-ordinating youth work, and it is not the only voluntary body doing this. The courses attempt to discuss sex education in a very wide context. Topics include the history and philosophy of sex education and the role of sex in personal relationships as well as the more detailed aspects of sexual behaviour and contraceptive practice. The DHSS is meeting the costs of the Association in running these courses.'[2] The Earl of Lauderdale interrupted the noble Lord to ask him whether 'he or the Government considered that sex education must be coupled with instruction in right and wrong, in the principles of chastity before marriage'. Lord Wells-Pestell replied he did 'not know that it has ever been considered in the way in which the noble Earl has raised it'. The tone of this speech demonstrated the Government's total commitment to sex education, and its determination that all the resources of the NHS should be used to educate children about sex and the importance of using contraception.

Earl Ferrers said that the subject of sex education concerned the moulding of people's minds, the inculcating, or deliberate exclusion, of ideas into the thoughts of children, which determine the nature of the child and its behaviour and attitude to society, both as a child and when the child emerges as an adult. Speaking about sex education, he said that the word 'educate' was used because it sounded better than 'inform'. 'It gives the impression that children will emerge more balanced, sensible and happy, the children of choice, not indoctrination. But I wonder whether they are more happy and more balanced.' He said that they had decided to tell the children everything, with no holds barred. 'We tell them what a unique and wonderful thing sex is, and, having instructed them as best we possibly can on how at the same time both to copulate but not to procreate, is it not surprising that the children then go and try it out?' But mistakes are made and pregnancies ensue, leaving a trail of scarred emotions and bruised, even ruined, lives in its wake.

The Earl mentioned the new breed of avant-garde teachers who take the view that contraceptive education has to be given very young and that it is almost too late when children get to puberty. 'So we have the sight of children of five years old, six years, seven years or eight years old, being taught all about the facts of life and contraception in order that, having learned it all, they should know they should not use it. To me, this approach is both pathetic and wholly wrong. What is one of the greatest attractions of children if it is not the innocence of youth? It goes soon, and I believe it to be almost a desecration of youth to destroy it prematurely because the "expert" says that the child will be the better for it. The evidence does not point that way.' He quoted figures to show that the number of abortions in girls aged under 16 had trebled since 1969, and there had been a fourfold rise in abortions among young people aged between 16 and 19. 'If sex instruction has anything to do with these figures, they point not to the success but to the failure of the methods used. Yet as the figures get worse, so the pressure to intensify the effort increases.'

The noble Lord said that some of the material put out by the FPA, a body which the Government supported, was wholly unsuitable and even mischievous. He described a leaflet produced by the FPA, called *Getting it on*. 'It depicts in cartoon form, and in a vulgar and pornographic manner, the advantages of wearing a condom, and ends with the caption, "if you have it off, have it on". I am frankly amazed that such a serious and personal matter can be treated in such a flippant and offensive manner by a body which expects public respect and which commands public money. Such a publication does nothing other than to invite, and, by inference, to condone, promiscuity. So also does a large advertisement, inserted in the newspaper by the same Association, of a half-naked girl and a young man, with bold letters, saying, "Play safe, ask your chemist for contraceptives". The whole advertisement implies intercourse between young unmarried couples. It correlates sexual intercourse with playing, or commendable relaxation, and it infers that if you do this with sheaths purchased from the FPA then you will be safe. Safe from what? Pregnancy? That is not so. Disease? That certainly is not so. Reprimand? Well, even nowadays that could happen. Or emotional upheaval? They do not say anything about that. In all these instances this advertisement is shamefully misleading, and I venture to suggest is socially irresponsible and debasing. Yet this is too often what the children, and even adults, are subjected to under the mantle of education.'

He drew attention to the fact that the Department of Health was taking over the FPA clinics and asked if the same personnel and the same methods would be employed by the DHSS as were at present employed by the FPA. Are the views of the FPA to become the accepted policy and practices of the Department, and therefore of the Government? He concluded his speech by reminding the House that what will destroy Great Britain is not the hydrogen bomb but the inability to discern between right and wrong. 'My Lords, it is the ability to discern between right and wrong over which we, the adults, need to give the children the greatest help and which the children, believe it or not, look to us, and want us, to give.'[3]

Baroness Gaitskell, who confessed to not being a Christian, deplored what she felt was 'the almost libellous attack by the noble Baroness, Lady Elles, on the FPA. I use these strong words because I have supported the FPA for over 50 years...' She believed that 'many parents have shirked their responsibility. They have left their children to acquire like vagabonds their knowledge about sex.' She said that the debate in the Lords was 'not setting about reducing the ignorance and guilt which have been such a legacy from Victorian years'. She said that most people regarded sex education for children as a dangerous thing. 'It is dangerous only when we do not answer their questions and satisfy their curiosity honestly and plainly. For most parents this is not an easy thing to do. There seems to be a dearth of educators, and we still suffer not only from the sins of our fathers but from the silence of our fathers and mothers. We must look elsewhere for educators, for people who are less personally involved and who have less fear than have parents in this matter.' The time had come for people to stop saying that sex education for children was either pornographic or a passport to promiscuity. By maintaining this attitude they were eroding their responsibilities. 'Pontificating and moralising will not solve the difficulties we are in. We have to be frank with our children, and we have to answer their questions when they ask them. "Is it right to have sex outside marriage? Is it right not to be faithful on occasions? Must marriage last a lifetime?" All these questions must be answered frankly and there must be far less hypocrisy about the whole subject.'[4]

Lord Alexander of Potterhill (he was a Director of Education in the 1930s and 1940s) made the point that thirty years ago a considerable amount of money was made available from Government sources, following the last war, for sex education. Three years ago his own organisation made available 200 sources of information on sex education, all of them prepared by responsible organisations, some from the Department of Education. 'So it would be idle to suggest that there has not been substantial effort made… but I share the view of the noble Earl, Lord Ferrers, that it has failed.'[5]

The Earl of Longford concentrated on the question of what kind of sex education ought to be offered to children. He said that sex education may do good as well as harm, although some people believe 'that you have only to call something sex education for some kind of magical effect to take place. I submit that it is impossible to provide a sex education that does not impart values of some kind, positive or negative; in other words, *sex education which does not place sex in a moral context teaches immorality* [my italics].'[6] He then discussed 'the question of whether it is or is not possible to discuss sexual relationships without indicating that some are morally permissible in our view and some are not'. He mentioned that Lady Gaitskell had raised certain moral questions, such as, is sex permissible outside marriage? But she did not answer them. 'She said that these questions should be dealt with frankly. I believe that that word "frankly" can be misleading and, indeed, dangerous. One can deal with something rightly or wrongly but to say that one deals with it frankly is ambiguous, to say the worst. Let us take a subject like promiscuity. One may regard it, as I think most would regard it, as damaging on physical grounds, or on psychological grounds, or on moral grounds, or on all three grounds; but if we can agree as far as that, then surely we ought to discourage it as far as possible in sex education… I hope that we could also discourage adultery and fornication. Those who receive instruction in sexual matters without being taught that these activities are wrong will quickly conclude there is nothing wrong about them.'

Lord Longford said that many people believed that sexual intercourse between young people is acceptable so long as contraceptive devices are used. 'In other words, so long as contraceptive devices are used there is no such thing as irresponsibility. There is no mention by such people – and I am afraid they have wielded a lot of influence in recent years – of venereal disease, of the failure rate of every type of contraceptive or of the health hazards of many such contraceptives. There is no worry about the danger, the emotional damage that may be done in so many different ways.

'Those who advise our young people in the press or in schools frequently fail to reveal any of the vast body of knowledge which demonstrates that promiscuity is psychologically damaging, particularly for the woman. Such people deliberately conceal the fact that the long-term stable commitment of marriage is the only proper way in which sexual relations can be meaningful and can find joyful fulfilment. Those facts are concealed by many of those who are most active in what is called sex education, either in administering it or promoting it. Real responsible activity must be something different. Sexual intercourse is the signing seal of the complete mutual self-giving which starts a new social unit – the family. The responsibility is simply the recognition of the potential riches of this unique relationship and its unique physical expression. It represents an understanding of the value of family and home, and a willingness to explain these relationships to growing young people. That can be put in different words – more elegant ones – but that is the gist of the responsibility as I see it, and as most Christians and others who believe in the family, would see it.' The Earl ended his speech with an appeal to all 'who believe that if we destroy the family we destroy the country itself. There are forms of sex education which will bring this disaster close; some of them may be bringing it close already.'[7]

The Marquess of Lothian declared that his position was an orthodox Christian attitude to sex education which advocated chastity before marriage. He referred to Brook, the Birth Control Campaign and the FPA as organisations which 'favour the indiscriminate sale of contraceptives through mail order, slot machines or in supermarkets with no questions asked about age and no warnings given as to the failure rates of contraceptives; so, in fact, children of any age can – and indeed do – obtain these without any form of control.' He quoted a statement from the Order of Christian Unity which drew attention to sex education advertisements which advised young people to 'play safe' but gave no warnings of contraceptive failure. He said that 'such misleading information draws children today into a commercial circle in which they become increasingly imprisoned. First of all, they are advised to buy protectives as being sure and safe and then, when such protectives result in failures, they are drawn into the pregnancy testing and abortion net, and then after abortions they are again counselled to buy protectives. So it is not really surprising that this type of sex education results in increasing teenage tragedies such as abortion and the terrible problem of venereal disease. Surely it is up to Parliament and to Government to do all they can to protect young people, particularly those under 16, from any deceptive sex education; because I am perfectly certain that the majority of parents, teachers and indeed children both need and want sound sex education.' He expressed concern that as the Department of Health was absorbing so many family planning clinics and personnel in the new National Family Planning Service, this must inevitably result in the FPA acquiring an even greater influence from within the NHS. 'Therefore there are dangers that ideological extremes, such as we have heard criticised today, are now even more likely to influence a future generation. Indeed, the captive audiences in schools may be getting sex education from FPA teachers.'[8]

Lady Ruthen of Freeland spoke as the Vice-President of the FPA. She said that the FPA was trying to provide more courses to teach teachers about how to introduce their pupils to the delicate area of sex education and the responsible attitude towards sexual relationships which children need. This did not mean that sex education should be given by teachers; sex instruction 'should be given by the father, or mother, or both. Throughout my life, however, I have found that fathers and mothers are more shy of talking about such subjects as sex to their own children than they are of talking to somebody else's children.' She did not accept that sex education, provided it was done in the right way, would lead to an increase in promiscuity. She mentioned the high proportion of unwanted pregnancies and abortions among young people. 'If we are ever to reduce such figures to the very low numbers that we would hope to see it is clearly necessary that these young girls – and the young men – should be taught at school age the responsibility which they are undertaking in starting a close relationship, and informed of the consequences if they enter a sexual relationship without contraceptive precautions.' She went on, 'we must take all possible steps to educate young people about their sexual responsibility and the avoidance of unwanted children. The FPA is concentrating on educating the educators. That is to say it teaches school teachers and youth workers the way in which they could do something about the situation I have just described.'[9]

Baroness Summerskill said that most parents find it difficult to speak to their own children on sex because they are identified with it. She believed that 'the place for sex education is outside the home, preferably in school, but by a special instructor who is wise enough not to concentrate on the physical aspect of the relationship between the sexes, but to emphasise the satisfaction derived from a true companionship stemming from the sharing of matters of mutual interest.' She argued that sex education in the schools is not enough. It should be provided in all women's organisations.[10]

The Duke of Norfolk said that he did not believe that the sex education that was being given in schools was on the right lines. 'In my view, it is too progressive in relaxing the wise restraints which were inherited by us from the Victorian Christians. The sex education that is now being given tends, in my opinion, to encourage promiscuity.'[11]

Lord Sudeley commented that many of the proponents of sex education believed that it reduced the rate of abortion, venereal disease and illegitimacy, 'so I should like to put before the House some facts and statistics which show that, on the contrary, the increase of sex education has coincided with the growth in the rates of illegitimacy and venereal disease'. He made the point that it was 'in 1967 that the Ministry of Education put forward recommendations for sex education in all secondary schools and proposed introductory courses in junior schools. It was also in 1967 that the BBC began its spate of programmes on sex education.' Corresponding with these developments the rate of gonorrhoea amongst girls aged under 16 had almost doubled and the rate of illegitimacy had more than doubled.

'I should like also to say something about the political overtones of the promotion of sex education and contraception, which assist in promoting sexual relations outside marriage. Many advocates of sex education promote it in the belief that sex may be indulged in freely and without the rules of previous ages. In this conviction they are the spokesmen of our time.' He commented on the commercial interests of those organisations who promoted sex education. He said that 'the FPA, as agents of the Health Education Council in the field of sex education, enjoys a discount on products of London Rubber Industries, because London Rubber Industries regards the educational activities of the FPA as widening the market for contraceptives. The FPA also enjoys a brisk trade in the sale of sex books and the hiring out of audio-visual aids.' He concluded by saying, 'Let us have sex education, but not as an education in contraception. Stripped of its commercial connotations, sex education must be given within the context of Christianity and marriage.'[12]

Lord Somers asked if sex education was really necessary, and, if so, why? He said that sexual intercourse if used properly could be of great benefit and lead to great happiness: if it was used outside the marital relationship it could lead to disaster. 'But the FPA are teaching the exact opposite. They are teaching our young people, many of them under 16, that sexual intercourse is a very desirable thing, giving great excitement and benefit, and that you have not really fulfilled yourself until you have experienced it. They divorce it entirely from the love motive, or from marital status for that matter, neither of which two things seem to be of very much importance to them.

'They also distribute all these contraceptives to the young, but—and this is very important—they give no warning whatsoever to the young of the failure rate of these contraceptives, which in some cases is quite considerable. Nor do they warn young girls that the taking of the pill can lead to very undesirable effects... My Lords, this organisation is leading our young people down the slippery slope of amorality, the only result of which can be a totally degenerate population. Is there no one who can come to their aid? They need our help. How can they defend themselves when they are not told the true facts? Another thing the FPA has not told them is that sexual promiscuity very often leads to venereal disease.' He said that he believed that the ideal teachers were a child's own parents. 'But we have to recognise the fact that not all parents are as responsible as they might be and therefore we must make some provision for it... I am convinced that this instruction should emphasise the virtue of Christian morality and should make it quite plain that a departure from this is not only morally wrong, but physically dangerous.' He said that young people needed to know that 'sexual intercourse is not a thing to be played with. It is a thing to be taken seriously. When it is properly used it can bring enormous joy and benefit to the family; but when it is abused it can be very dangerous and degenerating.' He concluded by saying that children needed protection from organisations which for commercial purposes were trying to delude them with false and dangerous propaganda.[13]

Lord Clifford of Chudleigh stated that the international socialists and their allies 'are responsible for many of the more notorious cases of sexual mal-education that have been highlighted in the last few months'. He said that the family unit is the basis of our civilisation—the sexual subversives do not hide their aim to destroy it. 'So Gay Liberation also gets recommended by the FPA as a source of educational material; that was in June 1974. Surely the most obvious of all ways in which to write off a country is to persuade children to become homosexual—and what better chance of doing this is there than to let Gay Liberation reach a child when he or she is going through that stage?' He believed that the FPA should be abolished forthwith.[14]

The Earl of Lauderdale said that the free availability of contraceptives without regard to marital status was a major blow at the family as a social institution. He questioned whether the FPA 'should be the chosen instrument of sex education on the basis of stark hedonism?' He mentioned, for the record, that the 1972 book list of the FPA included a book called *Sex Education: The Erroneous Zone,* and quoted the following passage: 'We no longer believe in telling the young what to do, but if we were asked for advice on this topic (moral rules) we would say something like this. "Make love if you both feel like it, but first make sure that you are safe."' He then asked the noble Lord Wells-Pestell the direct question: 'Do the Government agree that sex education must be coupled with instruction in right and wrong and in the principle of chastity before marriage?'[15]

Viscount Ingleby said that he believed in the Christian ideals of chastity before marriage and fidelity within marriage. He mentioned the FPA's booklet *Learning to Live with Sex* and said that he could find no mention of marriage in the booklet. He also described a pamphlet produced by the British Pregnancy Advisory Service, 'It is the usual "Boy meets girl" strip cartoon. They go to the cinema and they go home afterwards. He says, "Aren't you going to invite me in?" She says, "M'Mum wouldn't like it, but she's away at me sister's". The strip cartoon goes on, and the girl meets her girlfriend the following day. Talking about the boyfriend she says, "He's great. I would like to sleep with him, but I'm scared of what might happen." The girlfriend answers, "Why don't you go along to the clinic and get fixed up?" If you look inside, it says in capital letters, "You can really enjoy making love if you do not have to worry about getting pregnant."' In concluding, Viscount Ingleby asked the Government why it was giving £26,000 to an organisation which produced the kind of literature he had described, where the words chastity and fidelity are not mentioned, and the subject of marriage is not even seriously discussed.[16]

The Minister of State for Education and Science, Lord Crowther-Hunt, replied to the debate. He said that research showed that only a small minority of children receive adequate sex education from their parents, and a large majority of young people would like to have been taught more at school. 'I am sure that most parents welcome help from the schools, and that many would feel embarrassed, or indeed inadequately informed themselves, if they had to face their children's questions entirely on their own. There are some parents who believe with great sincerity that sex education is wrong in principle and even dangerous, but I am convinced that the case for sex education in the schools, if given in the right perspective, is proven. We are, after all, not faced with the choice between children learning from their parents and teachers or not at all; the alternative is being misinformed by school friends and picking up a selection of sexual folklore in an atmosphere which may do lasting damage.

'Another and more tangible sign of the need for helping young people is the profoundly disturbing number of abortions and illegitimate births among girls of school age... It is profoundly disturbing, since each one is potentially a tragedy for the girl herself and those around her, and since each and every one could have been avoided.' He quoted figures to show that the number of pregnancies in England and Wales in girls aged 15 and under had increased from just over 3,000 in 1970 to 4,800 in 1974. He said that there was some 'comfort to be found in the still very low incidence of sexually transmitted diseases among the population of compulsory school age, suggesting that, despite some prophets of doom, promiscuity is exceedingly rare among children under 16'.[17]

The Earl of Lauderdale interrupted the Minister with a specific question. 'He was talking about health education and health behaviour and these matters being taught covered in breadth and in an integrated way. Could he tell us what those words mean? Does that, or does it not, mean that children are taught that things are right and that things are wrong, and that there is a merit in chastity before marriage? Is the answer yes or no? I am not trying to pillory him; I am just trying to get an answer.'[18]

Lord Crowther-Hunt: 'My Lords, I cannot give the noble Earl a precise "yes" or "no" to that question, because precisely how these things are taught differs in different schools, differs in different local education authority areas, differs in different contexts, and it is not for the Government to prescribe precisely what is taught nor precisely the form of a curriculum at a particular school.'[19] He admitted that when the FPA courses for teachers and others was first announced they included on the reading list the sex education booklet *Sex Education: The Erroneous Zone*, produced by the National Secular Society. It was subsequently removed from the recommended reading list.[20] The Earl of Lauderdale asked if other material explaining the Christian values of right and wrong was also put before the teachers. Lord Crowther-Hunt responded that what is taught in the schools is a matter for the local education authority and for the teachers themselves.[21] The Earl of Lauderdale responded, 'But do they advise them, or do they not advise them; and, if so, in which direction? I am trying to keep my temper, and I know that really the noble Lord is always very kind, and that he is not as angry as he looks; nor am I.'[22] But despite his efforts Lord Lauderdale did not receive a clear answer.

Baroness Elles responded to the speech of Lord Crowther-Hunt, 'I must say that I have never heard a more unsatisfactory answer to the speeches of 25 members of your Lordships' House. Definite and specific questions were put to him, and I do not think he has acquitted himself, on behalf of the Government, as a responsible Government should... The Government has failed to answer the questions put to them by the noble Earl, Lord Lauderdale, about the question

165

of chastity before marriage and about the Government's view on marriage.' She hoped that a 'message could go forth from the Government that they do approve of chastity before marriage for young children and that in the schools of this country sex education will be taught within the context of marriage.'[23] The noble Lord Crowther-Hunt replied, 'I am surprised to note the totalitarian demands for a totalitarian society which are being made by the noble Baroness opposite... What the noble Baroness is talking about is a totalitarian concept of society which, my Lords, is one that I fundamentally reject.'[24]

In her closing remarks Baroness Elles reminded the noble Lord 'that the marriage laws of this country are still in force, and it is surely up to the Government to support the matrimonial and marriage laws of this country'. She hoped that a message would go to all head teachers, staff and parents that 'the vast majority of the members of this House, regardless of totalitarianism, still believe in Christian marriage and still believe that girls should be brought up in chastity, and that there should be fidelity in marriage'. She then addressed herself to Lady Gaitskell. 'I accept that she may not have seen all the recent leaflets which have been published [by the FPA]. They have caused deep concern, as she will have realised from the many examples which have been produced in your Lordships' House today. This has probably been the finest collection of obscene literature which has ever been displayed in this House.' She referred again to the booklet *Learning to Live with Sex* and noted that 92 thousand had been sold in the last year. She asked Lady Gaitskell to use her influence to 'withdraw some of the more obnoxious and vulgar examples that we have seen today. I speak profoundly and with concern regarding the effects this kind of literature is having, and I should be grateful if she would look and see what the FPA is now producing.'

Baroness Gaitskell responded, 'I am not convinced by what the noble Baroness has said. I did not misunderstand her. I still maintain that she has made what was practically a libellous attack on the FPA.' Baroness Elles reminded the Government that it had ratified various United Nations conventions which contained support for the family. 'For that, if for no other reason, they might consider themselves to have an obligation not only to the citizens of this country but to serve as an example to other countries still to support the family. If this Government fails to support the family, we are no longer a progressive society but are going back to the caves.' She said that if the Government did not like the word Christian, or did not like the Christian family ethic, even Aristotle regarded the family as important for the supply of man's essential wants. She demanded from the Government 'strong support for the maintenance of family unity and that this principle of family unity should be taught throughout the whole of sex education which is given in our schools'.[25]

This debate is important for it shows the cosy relationship between the British Government and their agents, the FPA—no matter the serious nature of the criticisms, in the eyes of the Government the FPA could do no wrong and would be defended to the hilt. What was highly significant was the Government's antipathy towards the Christian faith, and its unwillingness to distinguish between right and wrong in matters of sexual conduct. The concepts of chastity and fidelity were an embarrassment, relics from Victorian prudery. Hostility towards marriage, which was central to the ideology of Robert Owen, the father of British socialism, was alive and well among the socialists in modern Britain.

Endnotes

1 Hansard, Lords debate, 14 January 1976, cc134-149
2 Ibid. cc149-156
3 Ibid. cc167-177
4 Ibid. cc177-180
5 Ibid. cc188-189
6 Ibid. c192
7 Ibid. cc191-196
8 Ibid. cc197-200
9 Ibid. cc206-208
10 Ibid. cc215-219
11 Ibid. c220
12 Ibid. cc224-227
13 Ibid. cc229-234
14 Ibid. cc237-238
15 Ibid. cc241-247
16 Ibid. cc247-250
17 Ibid. cc250-255
18 Ibid. c255
19 Ibid. c255
20 Ibid. c262
21 Ibid. c262
22 Ibid. c263
23 Ibid. cc266-267
24 Ibid. c267
25 Ibid. cc269-270

Chapter 12

The FPA sets targets

FPA target to reduce abortions by half within 10 years;

'Make it Happy' promoted by the HEA; 'The State weighs up

what is best for the child' – Lady Helen Brook

In 1976 the Family Planning Association, apparently unmoved by the criticism it received in the House of Lords, officially launched the new, reorganised FPA at a reception attended by 70 guests and members of the press. Lord Wells-Pestell promised continuing Government support to the Association 'because we in our turn need the support of the new FPA, especially – as I have said – in the provision of information to the public and to the staff who provide family planning services.'[1] The new chairman of the FPA, Mr Alastair Service, said that there were still too many unplanned and unwanted pregnancies, illegitimate births and abortions. 'There is far too much unhappiness caused by sexual ignorance. Yet the debate in the House of Lords in January 1976 revealed that many prominent people are out of touch with reality and unaware of the pressures which our society creates and places on young people.'[2]

In launching the 'new' FPA, Alastair Service announced five targets to be achieved in the next 10 years. The targets included establishing suitable programmes for sex education in schools throughout the UK; reducing by half the estimated figure of 200 thousand unwanted pregnancies per annum; and reducing by half the annual number of 100 thousand abortions. And these targets were to be met by improving sex education and the provision of contraceptives.[3] The performance of the FPA in achieving these targets is discussed in chapter 15.

The new FPA was planning to run mobile tutorial teams for schoolteachers, which would provide tailor-made courses on how to teach children about sex. Launching an ambitious programme of sex education courses, the FPA claimed that there was a need for more widespread and thorough sex education in British schools.[4] A conference held at Loughborough University in 1977, sponsored by the FPA, the National Youth Bureau, the Campaign for Homosexual Equality and the Albany Trust, set up a national co-ordinating agency that was dedicated to making sex education an integral part of the school curriculum. The leaflet advertising the conference made the point that 'no one wants to see young people distressed by unwanted pregnancies, venereal disease, or depressed and worried about their sexual orientation'.[5] The conference put pressure on the Government to take sex education more seriously and urged the Health Education Council to spend more on improving sex education.[6]

Meanwhile the BBC had revised its sex education films in the *Merry-go-round* series, which were again broadcast in May 1976. The films contained the birth of a baby with explicit camera shots taken from the foot of the bed. One of the films showed boys and girls bathing together in the nude in a school swimming pool, and another scene showed a naked man and woman side by side. The Director of the Nationwide Festival of Light, Raymond Johnston, stressed the far-reaching effects that this explicit material might have on children. 'In view of this danger, would it not be appropriate for all primary school head teachers who intend to subject children to these programmes to contact all parents by letter beforehand, quoting from the teachers' notes and giving full facilities for alternative activities in the case of those children whose parents do not wish their children to be exposed to such explicit material?' He argued that the BBC was providing sex education material for children of eight or nine, and on school premises, that would undoubtedly have been X rated by the British Board of Film Censors.[7]

The far-reaching effects of sex education were put under the spotlight by a newspaper headline *Storm over 'loveless' school sex*. The article made a link between sex education, with no moral content, and the killing of a 4-year-old girl by a 12-year-old boy.[8] In a sensational court case the boy, accused of sexually assaulting and unlawfully killing the girl in a graveyard, told the police that he met Tracy Mairs during the evening and followed her into the graveyard. He said in his defence that he had been taught about sexual intercourse at school and wanted to find out what it was like. Although the teacher had told him about intercourse, she never mentioned marriage, love and affection. The boy told St Albans Crown Court that 'no one explained the difference between people and animals. The teacher talked about sex, and about reproduction of animals, plants and men and women. We also had flashes on a projector and screen. The teacher never said when these things would happen or about growing up or ages. I wanted to find out what intercourse was like. I thought I could do it with Tracy.' After explaining how Tracy had got hurt he continued, 'Then I went home. I expected her to get up and go home. I climbed back into my bedroom and went to bed. I didn't think I had done anything wrong except I should not have been out of the house. I got the idea from school.'[9] The boy was found guilty of manslaughter and sentenced to be detained for life. The director general of the Health Education Council, Alastair Mackie, commented after the case: 'If sex lessons left out love, then they would be very much at variance with the kind of lessons the Council would recommend.

169

Clearly, any meaningful relationship between two people involving sex must also involve love.'[10]

It was becoming increasingly clear that the FPA and the Health Education Council were setting themselves up as 'sex experts' with a mission to educate the nation's children. Accordingly, in January 1977, the Family Planning Information Service, sponsored by the Government and run jointly by the FPA and the Health Education Council, was established to provide information for those working in family planning and health authorities, and for the general public. In its first two years the information service distributed 12 million leaflets to GPs, clinics, educational establishments and health promotion officers. In addition, the service provided information for 150 radio broadcasts and 60 national TV programmes. Numerous articles were written for publication in various magazines and newspapers.[11] The country was, without any doubt, being flooded with sex education material. Indeed, the sex education resource list prepared by the Health Education Council in 1977 was 23 pages long, including lists of reports, books, pamphlets and leaflets, posters and charts, films and filmstrips, slides, film loops and audiotapes, all providing information and resources for sex educators.

One of the films advertised in the Health Education Council resource list was entitled *'Ave you got a male assistant, Miss?* It is referred to as a light-hearted introduction to the responsibilities involved in sexual relationships amongst young people, and it is indicative of the type of material that was being promoted. In the film the camera roves over a pile of clothes, before settling on a heaving blanket. A background voice cries—'Stop!' Two young people, disturbed in the act, emerge from under the blanket. The voice enquires, 'Do you know that 20 thousand girls get pregnant every year?' The surprised young couple look at each other and shake their heads. The boy then jumps out of bed and, flinging on some clothes, runs down the stairs into the street in search of a chemist shop. He reaches one, only to find it shut. He quickly reads the chemist's rota and then dashes among traffic, scattering a bus queue before jumping on to a bus. When he reaches another chemist shop, a girl assistant at the cosmetic counter serves him. (This, presumably, is where the title fits in.) She calls a male colleague, who solemnly produces a wrapped package, containing condoms no doubt, from under the counter. The boy then runs back through the traffic, pushing past people who stare at him. Entering the building, he flings off his clothes as he rushes upstairs, where he is met with a welcoming look from the girl. They jump back under the blanket, as the voice says, 'This, of course, is ridiculous. You should have forethought and visit a family planning clinic.' I obtained this description of the film from a father who discovered, after the event, that the film had been shown to his child in a mixed sex class of 13-year-olds.

In its report to the Royal Commission on the NHS, the FPA claimed that sex education was most important as a means of preventing unwanted pregnancies. But the FPA felt that the teaching in schools was unsatisfactory because the amount and content of sex education was left to the discretion of school head teachers. The FPA wanted to expand the courses it ran for teachers, youth workers and health educators so that adequate sex education programmes could be started in all schools. It therefore urged the Department of Education to work more closely with the Department of Health and Social Security.[12] The reason was obvious. The FPA was very influential in the health service, which recognised their staff as the experts in sex education, whereas head teachers were more sceptical about their radical approach. Moreover, head teachers knew that they would have to answer to those parents who became aware of the explicit messages that were being imparted to their children.

And head teachers had good reason to be nervous, for they were caught up in the middle of a fierce ideological battle. On one side was the FPA, the Health Education Council and Brook, or what the *Daily Telegraph* columnist, Peter Simple, referred to as 'the horrific empire of the family planning industry'. To take a stand against it, 'head teachers and all others whose duty it is to guide young people need genuine courage. They are opposing one of the most powerful and infamous tendencies of our infamous times.'[13] On the other side, were a number of well-informed people who were highly critical of sex education and ready to publicly expose the excesses of the sex educators. The Responsible Society, formed in 1971 to engage in research and education in matters affecting the family and youth, was particularly well informed about sex education and the activities of the FPA and Brook.

Because parents were largely unaware of what was happening, the Responsible Society produced a pamphlet, entitled *Dear Parents*, which was sent to the Department of Health. Sir John Peel, former president of the British Medical Association, endorsed the pamphlet, saying that the casual approach in teaching about contraception, abortion and venereal disease was totally irresponsible.[14] The Order of Christian Unity produced a handbook, *Sound Sex Education*, which encouraged parents to vet sex education materials, and also the teachers who gave the sex education lessons. Copies were sent to all secondary schools. The booklet said that many parents would rather their children had no specific teaching on contraceptive methods, claiming that the safest contraceptive is the word 'no'.[15]

Mary Whitehouse was concerned that if sex education was made compulsory in schools, parents would not know what their children were being taught, and it would not be possible to withdraw them since the subject would permeate many aspects of education. She emphasised that the influence of the FPA in schools was exerted with the full approval of the Government. 'The function of this organisation has changed. It is now almost entirely involved with the training of sex educators, teachers, youth workers and social workers. Its publication, *Learning to Live with Sex*, is totally amoral in its approach and sows the seeds of confusion about the nature of right and wrong, posing only the choice between using contraceptives and having a baby. The choice of saying 'no' is hardly paid lip service.' The booklet was being freely distributed to youth clubs and schools. She made the point that because successive Governments had funded the FPA, 'we can assume that we are helping to finance the prostitution of our young'. She noted that sex education was a most effective vehicle for the creation of a value-free generation.[16] In her book *Whatever happened to Sex?* (1977) Mary Whitehouse declared that

171

the 'liberators' of the 1960s had become the tyrants of the 1970s. These so-called liberationists 'sneer at fidelity, chastity, commitment to marriage and the family, glamorise and exalt the "one-night stand", and "gay liberation", and in so doing, they destroy the community and emotional stability which is essential to childhood security and social cohesion. A whole generation is being conditioned to accept the "contraceptive society" in which abortion on demand becomes normal, restraint outmoded, and venereal disease presented as no more serious than the common cold – a small price to pay, we are all asked to believe, for the joys of so-called freedom.'[17]

The Responsible Society joined in the attack on *Learning to Live with Sex* in a letter to the *British Medical Journal,* signed by Dr Stanley Ellison, Dr Ambrose King, Sir John Peel, Sir Brian Windeyer and 147 other members of the medical profession. 'We wish to draw the attention of the profession both to the Government funding of organisations which promote juvenile sex and to the environmental health hazards of the behavioural attitudes promoted and encouraged by much of the contents of teenage magazines, many with massive circulations, which reinforce the callous advice of these official bodies. It is our experience that the long-term effects of these influences undermine the role of many responsible parents and, by encouraging irresponsibility in others, leave many children unprotected against sexual exploitation by adults.

'As examples of official organisations undermining the family we will briefly mention some of the promotional/educational activities of the FPA (which handed over almost all its clinics to the NHS in 1974) and of the Family Planning Information Service, together with some of the controversial educational and clinic activities of the Brook Advisory Centres. The FPA is a charity which is in receipt of large sums of public money and which runs its own contraceptive business, Family Planning Sales Ltd. It publishes and promotes a large quantity of aggressively permissive literature for young people—for example, *Learning to Live with Sex*, published in 1972 for children of 13 years upwards. This booklet, which is claimed by the FPA to have a very large circulation, has the following emphasis: (1) it describes sexual intercourse in terms of "boys and girls", which implies an acceptable code of behaviour; (2) there are six full pages on contraceptive methods; (3) there are 10 lines on "responsibility," which is equated almost entirely with the use of contraceptives; (4) there is no section on marriage; (5) it does not mention the positive health and social advantages of self-control, nor does it mention the failure rates of contraceptives, the association of cancer of the cervix with early adolescent intercourse, and the cruel consequences of abortion for many girls who have their first pregnancies terminated.

'The Family Planning Information Service is Government sponsored and funded and administered by the Health Education Council and the FPA. It claims to have sent out millions of copies of a leaflet, *Straight Facts about Sex and Birth Control.* This leaflet describes sexual intercourse in terms of a boy-girl partnership, it advertises the FPA mail order business, and tells of special places where one can get contraceptives where "older relatives and neighbours will not be present." The Brook Advisory Centres specialise in providing contraceptives and (more recently) abortions for young girls and believe that adolescent sexual intercourse is acceptable provided that contraceptives are used. It has long been their policy not necessarily to inform parents of their adolescent children's difficulties. Recently the DHSS has provided £21,000 a year for three years towards their headquarters' administrative costs.'[18]

The FPA defended itself by saying that it was not the intention of the Association to promote irresponsible sexual behaviour among young people. In its view the best form of protection was not ignorance but accurate knowledge.[19]

In an article in *The Times*, Ronald Butt commented on the unofficial agents of the State, paid with State money, who were trying to take over the moral upbringing of children. He made the point that the professional sex educators, who were closely involved with the appropriate pressure groups, never rested in their attempts to use the classroom to instruct children in contraception and abortion. On the grounds that *some* of the children would be 'sexually active' and must not be 'preached at' (or even given moral teaching) these enthusiasts wanted *all* children in every class to be given such instruction. Butt argued that in the process, the assumption was implicitly communicated that there would be nothing intrinsically wrong if those so instructed conducted their lives in such a way as to require the use of these techniques, even if they are under 16, provided they 'know what they are doing'. There was little apparent concern for the permanent emotional scarring likely to result from premature sexual activity. Even the danger of venereal disease was played down by stressing its easy curability. The chief moral imperative was that sexual activity should not lead to pregnancy. If it did, abortion could follow. Butt went on, 'Many sex educators want their kind of instruction to be compulsory so that parents have no right to withdraw their children from it, whatever their views of the moral implications with which it is being taught. Then there is the involvement of the Government and public money with the agencies which propagate this new morality.'[20] Butt's comments are important for he was clearly identifying the Government's support for those who were introducing a 'new morality' into the UK. He was also exposing the dictatorial attitude of the sex educators, who were taking over the moral instruction of children with their permissive views.

The Report of the Committee on Child Health Services, *Fit for the Future* (1976), acknowledged that since the NHS had taken over responsibility for family planning there had been no drop in the proportion of unwanted pregnancies. To reduce the number of unwanted babies the report recommended more extensive and better education on family planning. 'At present information is provided at national level by the FPA and the Health Education Council (both financed from Government funds) and at the local level by the area health education service. At the end of 1975 and the beginning of 1976, the Health Education Council undertook a cinema family planning campaign directed at the young. But more needs to be done. Greater use should be made of informal and formal publicity through the press, TV and other sources of communication. Discussions in school and talks to groups can also be of value.' Another recommendation was that professional groups other than doctors, such as nurses, health visitors, midwives and social workers, needed to be trained in family planning.[21] By this time there were many courses on family planning and the demand for training was enormous. There is no doubt that the Government was putting a great effort into improving family planning services as the 'experts' kept reminding them that the answer to teenage pregnancies lay in easy access to contraception.

The book 'Make it Happy'

In 1978 Virago Press published a sex education manual *Make it Happy* by Jane Cousins. The book is 'written for teenagers, their parents and teachers and for anyone else who wants to know the basic facts'.[22] According to Dr Peter Jackson of the National Council of the FPA, the book 'seeks to dispel much irrationality in current thinking about sex. A book that should be in every teenager's library.' Michael Schofield says that the author 'never lectures or moralises. The moral, if you must have one, is that sex is more fun if the pleasures are shared.' According to Joan Bakewell the book is 'friendly, uncondescending and direct – a good start for teenagers in search of basic facts'.[23] The Health Education Council was so impressed with *Make it Happy* that it was promoted in their list of sex education resources.

While the sex education lobby was raving about *Make it Happy*, others were disturbed by the amoral advice that was being given to young people. George Gardiner (MP) said it was enough to make parents' hair stand on end, and Ronald Butt described it as the filthiest sex education book he had seen. In 1983 the Government told the Health Education Council to withdraw it from their reading list.[24]

An analysis of the sex education manual shows that the message is, in fact, consistent with the ideals of the sexual revolution. First, it provides teenagers with the most wide-ranging factual information about sex that could enter anyone's mind. There are sections on the sex organs, sexual identity, homosexuality, bisexuality, masturbation, orgasms, petting, sex without pregnancy, foreplay, intercourse, sex aids, contraception, pregnancy, having a baby, abortion, sexually transmitted diseases, oral sex, anal sex, incest, bestiality and paedophilia. Consistent with the ideology of Kinsey, the book teaches that bisexuality is the norm; teenagers are informed that, 'Many people if left to their own natural instincts might find they were bisexual and could enjoy relationships with women and men. But society tries to make us hold back these instincts.' Advice on incest is as follows: 'Incest is not particularly uncommon – especially between sisters and brothers, when it can be a loving sexual relationship.' Paedophiles are people who 'get their sexual pleasure from looking at pictures of young children, or from touching a child's sex organs, and they often like a child to touch theirs'.[25]

Second, the language is frank, explicit and coarse. Indeed, the explicit tone of the book can be judged from the fact that it contains a picture of two naked men with erections, with the caption that 'all penises are roughly the same size and shape. The one on the left is circumcised, the one on the right is uncircumcised, but when they are erect it is difficult to tell the difference.'[26] Male and female sex organs and sexual intercourse are all described with coarse four-letter words.[27] Even Wilhelm Reich, the revolutionary who strongly advocated nakedness in sex education, would have been impressed by the explicitness of *Make it Happy*.

Third, the ethic that permeates the book is that teenagers are free to do whatever they want, whatever feels right in their own eyes. 'What we do all need is the basic factual information about sex so that we can make our own decisions about whether we want sex and, if we do, how and who with.'[28] Techniques for a range of sexual activities, including masturbating, are explained. 'Masturbating is usually a very private thing, although some girls and boys sometimes get a kick out of doing it in a group. If that's how you enjoy it, there's nothing wrong in sharing sex in this way.'[29] The reader is reassured, 'you don't have to masturbate if you don't *want* to… Only you will be able to tell whether you *want* it, and when and how you *want* it.'[30] The following quote illustrates the amoral approach: 'Whether you *want* sex and how far you *want* to go doesn't depend on whether you are female or male, but on how you *feel* in yourself as an individual. You may have very good reasons for not wanting a sexual relationship or for wanting to draw the line somewhere. But how other people think you should behave shouldn't be important.'[31] [all italics mine]

Make it Happy is important for it shows the association between sex education and the sexual revolution. Here we have a blatant example of the ideology of the sexual revolution being promoted under the guise of sex education. Like the other sexual revolutionaries, the author demoralises sexual conduct. The underlying objective is to teach teenagers how to achieve sexual gratification free from all restraints imposed by traditional morality. Teenagers are flooded with salacious facts about every sexual activity under the sun, even detestable things that would never normally enter their minds. All the so-called 'facts' are presented in a non-judgemental, morally neutral way, and therefore nothing is wrong, not even bestiality, incest, paedophilia or group masturbation, let alone promiscuity and homosexuality. Everything is as explicit as possible, both in word and image. Having provided teenagers with a mass of sexual facts, *Make it Happy* tells them they should do what they *want*, it is their *own* decision and nobody else should influence the way they behave.

The report *Pregnant at school* (1979), sponsored by the Labour Party and financed by the Department of Education, was produced by a working group for the National Council for One Parent Families, chaired by Dame Margaret Miles, a former London headmistress. The main recommendations of the report were that the age of sexual consent should be abolished and that sex education should start at a younger age – ideally at five or younger. The report argued that 'the law is out of touch with current behaviour because it does not consider consenting sexual relationships among the young. Nor can we be confident that it effectively deters such relationships.' The law on the age of consent did not restrain under-16s from having sex but made it more difficult for them to cope with the consequences. The report urged better and earlier sex education in schools, with lessons in antenatal care. And schoolgirls who became pregnant should have easy and free access to abortion, or if they choose to have their babies they should have proper maternity care and social welfare. Fear of the law prevented young people from coming forward for contraceptive advice. The reason the age of consent should be abolished is that more young women, who were already sexually active, would avail themselves of contraceptive services.[32]

Mary Whitehouse's response was brief and to the point, 'The one message children will receive from this report is that sex is okay. This can only lead to greater promiscuity among the young with consequent rises in VD and cervical cancer.'[33] Mary Kenny, commenting on the report, wrote that the simplest way to judge something is by the results that it produces. 'In 1959, when there was virtually no sex education as we know it now, and when the words "family planning" had only recently been permitted on the BBC, there were 489 illegitimate births to girls under 16 in England; there were no recorded abortions. In 1976, when birth control and sex education were well established, there were 1,338 births to girls under 16 in England; and more than 3,500 abortions. Between 1971 and 1977 alone, there was a 30 per cent rise in "gymslip mothers" and a corresponding rise in teenage abortion, venereal disease, cervical cancer and teenage prostitution.' Mary Kenny quoted research which showed that contraceptive advice was not effective for teenagers and claimed that family planning services would not reduce the incidence of unintended pregnancies among teenagers. Most teenagers seeking abortion had actually used contraception, but had done so erratically, and so had become pregnant.[34]

In early 1980 Mr John Corrie introduced a Private Member's Bill, the Abortion (Amendment) Bill, which proposed to change the criteria for abortion. The purpose of the Bill was to break the financial link between abortion clinics and referral agencies. The Bill aimed to make sure that those who counselled pregnant women had no financial interest in their having an abortion. Opponents of the Bill claimed that it would reduce the number of abortions by three-quarters, and would destroy the abortion charities which carried out a third of abortions.[35] The FPA campaigned against the Bill, sending a letter to all MPs in advance of the third reading, in which it claimed that worries about the health risks of the contraceptive pill and the intrauterine device, coupled with reductions in family planning provision in the NHS, meant that 'there are still many women who through fear, ignorance, misinformation or health reasons are unable to use reliable methods of contraception, or do not use them regularly'. Denied access to safe legal termination, there was no doubt that many couples would be forced to have children which they neither planned nor could afford.[36]

Ronald Butt was incensed by the actions of the FPA, and wrote an article in *The Times*, 'What every parent should know', condemning the activities of the

Association. He argued that it was a scandal that young people who were not fortunate enough to have strong, countervailing principles of their own were being deliberately encouraged to take as a norm standards of behaviour which were bound, in the long run, to turn some of them into customers for the abortion market. Even worse was the fact that the most insidious encouragement came from the active sex educators (who were often closely linked with the family planning lobbies) against whose ministrations neither children nor parents had any real protection. Butt wrote that Parliament had the opportunity to consider what this lobby was up to. Mr George Gardiner, the Conservative MP for Reigate, had put down an amendment to the Government's Education Bill in which he proposed to give parents the right to know what their children were taught, to see the material from which they were taught and to withdraw their children if they disapproved of sex education classes. The amendment was strongly resisted by the sex education missionaries, who had the greatest objections to parents having any control over their children's instruction, and who had the most powerful reasons for wishing to continue their work in secrecy.

Butt went on: 'To the missionaries, there is only one basic principle: don't get pregnant, and don't get anyone else pregnant; and if you do, terminate it quickly. The moral imperative to use contraceptives apart, advice is value-free, and its general burden is: do anything you like as long as you both enjoy it, and we will introduce you to ideas and practices you never dreamed of. Deeper psychological dangers are glossed over, and no effort is spared in instructing in every sort of activity, however perverse. Or, as Mr Gardiner put it to me: the success of sex education seems to be measured by the number of girls on the pill, and the number of boys buying sheaths. Mr Gardiner has particularly cited a sex manual for children and teenagers entitled *Make it Happy* which, he observed, is enough to make parents' hair stand on end—if they ever see it. I have seen it, and it is quite the filthiest book of its kind that I have encountered because, directing itself at the most vulnerable age group, it drains sexual activity of every meaning except what purports to be pleasure, diminishes the subject by its flippancy and vulgarity, and instructs its young readers in degrading concepts that would never naturally occur to them.

'Thus it describes practices of bestiality (the author carefully safeguarding herself and helping her readers by stating those which are, and are not, against the law). The book is such that I cannot quote from much of it without causing the deepest offence—though I am told by Mr Gardiner that the publishers claim that it is used in schools... And meanwhile the FPA continues its indefatigable effort to get into schools, declaring (according to a circular letter sent, unsolicited, to the headmaster of a north London school) that as much time and resources should be spent on teaching sex as on anything else, offering its services and suggesting that it is valuable for classes to have time alone with their FPA sex instructors without the presence of the teacher if they want to ask questions.'[37]

This outspoken article produced an angry response from Lady Helen Brook. In a letter to *The Times* she wrote: 'Ronald Butt's article leads me to say that "what every parent should know" is that there are countless men and women, parents, who are too selfish, too ignorant, too lazy to be bothered about their children's general education. From birth till death it is now the privilege of the parental State to take major decisions—objective, unemotional, *the State weighs up what is best for the child* [my italics]. Innocent ignorance or careful teaching of the facts of life by dedicated teachers in school?'[38] Lady Brook, it appears, was so infuriated by Ronald Butt's article that she let her guard drop and revealed the contempt with which sex educators regard parents. Drusilla Scott replied, 'I am glad of Lady Brook's monstrous letter, for it says plainly what the Brook Clinics and the FPA often conceal, namely that they despise parents and want to remove all responsibility from them in the matter of their children's sex education. She speaks of parents in terms which the most bigoted now hesitate to use about their chosen scapegoat group. Of course there are irresponsible parents: there are also biased teachers. The really ignorant and irresponsible are those who think that 'facts' are truth, irrespective of how they are taught, when, and to whom: who think that 'facts' cannot be used to deceive and corrupt… it should now be clear to parents why they must not let responsibility for their children's sex education slip from them, especially not into the hands of the totalitarian State that Lady Brook envisages.'[39]

The Chairman of the FPA, Mrs Barbara Davis, was more cautious in her reply. 'The FPA has always believed that parents should be the first source of advice and example, and should provide their children with guidance and information. But all too often parents feel that sex is too personal and private an area of life to discuss with their children. They may have no moral or ethical objection to their children learning about sex, indeed they usually see the need—the problem can be embarrassment. The FPA believes that education in human sexuality is essential if young people are to make responsible decisions. We share this view with the World Health Organisation which in its recent survey of sex education in Europe further stated that one of the purposes of sex education is to give "freedom from sentiments of fear, shame, guilt, false beliefs and other psychological factors inhibiting sexual response and sexual relationships".'

She reminded her readers that in 1978 there were over three thousand abortions in girls under 16. 'Many of these young people never received any help or advice about sex or contraception, and might have rushed into sex unsure of both the consequences and whether they really wanted a sexual relationship. Rather than concentrating on negative moral codes like "thou shalt not" we should try to encourage the development of a *positive* morality [my italics]. It is all very well to talk about "moral standards", and to lay down rigid rules about how others, and particularly young people, should behave. However, Ronald Butt and those sharing his opinion would do well to remember the view that has been spelled out again and again in literature, and also in the philosophy of Christianity—that individuals can only reach their full potential if they are able to choose how life is best lived, in freedom and with responsibility, in the basis of full knowledge. We do little service to the young in denying them that information and that choice.'[40]

A director of Virago Press (the publishers) felt obliged to defend *Make it Happy*. 'What was really shocking about Ronald Butt's article on sex education was its witch-hunting tone and his insulting misrepresentation of Jane Cousin's book. *Make it Happy* was written of her experience in the classroom of typical adolescent confusion and anxieties. Since it was published 17 months ago it has been well and widely reviewed and translated into eight languages. And it did indeed win *The Times* Educational Supplement's Information Book Award, as Mr Butt admits. Why we are proud to publish this book, however, is because we believe it achieves precisely the opposite of Mr Butt's imaginings. Its candour and friendliness actually counter the sniggering disinformation of the playground and public school dorm. It also works for loving and responsible relationships... Ronald Butt talks about "sex education missionaries". What he sounds like is a fearful witch doctor, jealously guarding the tribe's taboos and outraged at the thought that control may be slipping from his grasp.'[41]

Dr Stanley Ellison, chairman of the Responsible Society, entered the heated debate. 'The astonishing aspect of the article by Mrs Barbara Davis, Chairman of the FPA, is that she appears to have no knowledge of the content of her Association's sex education publications for boys and girls, or its attitude to parents. The truth of the matter is that all the FPA's persuasive publications for adolescents since the early 1970s share the same characteristics. None of them are directed towards preparing the young for marriage—indeed the word is seldom mentioned—but towards training youngsters to associate sex, not with love and family life, but with the mechanics of contraceptives. No information is given on contraceptive failure rates which are high in adolescents, the side-effects of the pill or abortion, and the hazards of premature sexual intercourse, one of which is the established link with cancer of the cervix... The development of the positive morality, which Mrs Davis says the FPA is trying to evolve, might begin from giving the young the truth: without the truth the young have no basis for responsible choice. As for parents, Mrs Davis' comments cannot be taken at face value. The FPA and its sister organisation, the Brook Advisory Centres, have been the main activists in ensuring that parental duties have been undermined. Both organisations were instrumental in the formulation of Section G of the notorious 1974 DHSS memorandum which effectively removed parental responsibilities with regard to the provision of contraceptives and abortions to their children under the age of consent. As far back as 1972, the FPA's publication *Learning to Live with Sex* for 13 to 16-year-olds, said to be widely used in schools, recommended places where children could go "where no one will tell your parents". In view of all this it is sheer humbug for Mrs Davis to say that the FPA supports the view "that parents have a right to know what their children are being taught".'[42]

In 1980 the Government reviewed its 1974 guidance regarding the prescription of contraceptives to girls under the age of 16. Dr Gerald Vaughan, Minister for Health, said in the House of Commons that a doctor should proceed from the assumption that it would be most unusual to provide advice for individuals about contraception without the consent of the parent or guardian. 'It is, however, widely accepted that consultations between doctors and patients are confidential and I accept the importance doctors attach to this principle. If the principle were abandoned, many young people would not seek advice and would be exposed to the immediate risks of pregnancy and of sexually transmitted disease, as well as of other long-term physical, psychological and emotional consequences. In these circumstances, the aim of supporting stable family life would in no way have been furthered.' Dr Vaughan therefore accepted the occasional possibility that contraception would be provided without parental knowledge or consent. The BMA welcomed the Government's position,[43] and DHSS guidance issued in May 1980 reaffirmed a doctor's right to prescribe contraceptives to girls under 16 without their parents' knowledge or consent.

A journalist of the *Daily Mail* visited a Brook clinic in south London to try and understand why prescribing contraceptives to under-16s was such a delicate issue. In her article she describes the young girls who came to the clinic for their contraceptive supplies. 'Some turned up straight from school, still wearing their uniforms. Others arrived as if they were going out for a night on the town, in high heels, eye make-up and in their trendiest clothes. Almost all of them had lied to their mothers about where they were going. Watertight alibis have to be invented each time they come to this clinic. "Just going to pop over to see Alison" or "I'll be stopping off at Jane's for tea" seemed to work on unsuspecting mothers... And they are literally dead scared their mothers will find out. "If my mum knew I was here she'd kill me" was the most common comment of the under 16-year-olds. Yet once inside the building they feel safe. Especially after they've signed the forms on their first visit stating they don't want their parents to be informed.'[44]

And so the British Government, its agents the FPA and Brook, and the British Medical Association were all agreed that it was in the best interests of children under the age of 16 to be supplied with contraceptives without their father or mother being consulted or even aware of the fact. After all, as Lady Brook reminded us, parents are too selfish, too ignorant, or too lazy to be bothered about their children's sex education. The State claimed to know what is best for children, and the State had decided that children are more likely to use contraceptives if the fact is kept secret from their parents.

Endnotes

1 Family Planning Association, Annual Report 1975-76, p4
2 Ibid. p3
3 Ibid. p8
4 *The Times*, 24 November 1976, Television guidance for parents is suggested
5 *The Times*, 25 March 1977, Pressure groups want serious approach to sex education
6 *The Times*, 18 April 1977, Pressure groups behind sex teaching talks
7 *The Times Educational Supplement*, 23 April 1976, letter, Raymond Johnston
8 *Daily Telegraph*, 27 September 1977, Storm over 'loveless' school sex

9 *Daily Telegraph*, 22 September 1977, Sex lessons left out love, boy tell jury

10 *Daily Telegraph*, 27 September 1977

11 Family Planning Association, Annual Report 1978-79, The Family Planning Information Service, p1

12 *The Times*, 16 December 1977, School sex lessons 'inadequate'

13 *Daily Telegraph*, 12 July 1979, Way of the world, Peter Simple

14 *The Times*, 10 November 1977, Misleading sexual advice given to children

15 *The Times*, 6 May 1977, Check up on the sex teachers

16 *The Times*, 16 March 1978, Compulsory sex education campaign attacked

17 Mary Whitehouse, *Whatever happened to sex?* Hodder and Stoughton, 1978, p25

18 *British Medical Journal*, 29 July 1978, letter, Dr SE Ellison and others, p353

19 *The Times*, 29 July 1978, 'Sick' advice about sex criticised by doctors

20 *The Times*, 8 June 1978, Whose family; yours or the State's? Ronald Butt

21 *Fit for the Future*, The Report of the Committee on Child Health Services vol. 1, Professor SDM Court, 1976, pp129-130

22 Jane Cousins, *Make it Happy*, Virago, 1978, London, p2

23 Ibid. back cover

24 *The Times*, 14 February 1980, What every parent should know, Ronald Butt

25 Ibid. p105

26 Ibid. p12

27 Ibid. pp9-11

28 Ibid. p2

29 Ibid. p31

30 Ibid. p31

31 Ibid. p38

32 Miles M, *Pregnant at school*, Joint working party on pregnant schoolgirls and schoolgirl mothers, National Council for One Parent Families, 1979

33 *Daily Telegraph*, 12 September 1979, Call to scrap law on age of consent

34 *Sunday Telegraph*, 16 September 1979, Miles off the mark, Mary Kenny

35 *The Times*, 29 January 1980, Abortion Bill's full implications

36 *The Times*, 5 February 1980, Corrie Bill 'penalizes those at risk'

37 *The Times*, 14 February 1980, What every parent should know, Ronald Butt

38 *The Times*, 16 February 1980, letter, Helen Brook

39 *The Times*, 22 February 1980, letter, Drusilla Scott

40 *The Times*, 22 February 1980, What every parent should know, Barbara Davis

41 *The Times*, 25 February 1980, letter, Mrs Ursula Owen, director, Virago Press

42 *The Times*, 5 March 1980, letter, SE Ellison, Chairman, The Responsible Society

43 *The Times*, 7 May 1980, New plea to GPs on under-16 pill

44 *Daily Mail*, 21 May 1980, My evening at the clinic where schoolgirls get the Pill, Judy Graham

Chapter 13

Sheer pornography

Controversies of the early 1980s; in Parliament John Stokes

accuses the FPA and Brook of promoting promiscuity

In 1980 the Family Planning Association celebrated its fiftieth anniversary. It had moved a long way since its formation as the National Birth Control Council in 1930, when it campaigned for free birth control for married couples. The FPA, once a highly controversial organisation, was now so much part of the establishment that it received congratulations for its achievements from the Duke of Edinburgh and Patrick Jenkin, Secretary of State for Social Services. In a telegram the Duke saluted the FPA for 50 years of 'most valuable social work' and went on that 'the Association has won the battle for recognition, but as one generation follows another, the campaign of education and enlightenment on birth control is never-ending'. Patrick Jenkin was equally effusive in his praise: 'We owe to its pioneering and persevering work the foundation of the free and comprehensive family planning service, to which, as Secretary of State, I attach great importance. But perhaps an even more significant achievement is seen in the almost universal recognition we find today of the positive contribution which family planning – and the opportunity for choice which it gives – can make to the happiness, harmony and stability of family life. I also welcome the renewed emphasis being placed on responsibility in sexual matters... I am glad that we in Government have been able to reaffirm our support for its work.'[1]

Although the advances of the last fifty years had been striking, and family planning was no longer a taboo subject, the Association claimed that it faced continuing challenges in the 1980s. Surveys had shown a lack of sex education in schools and, although barriers to advertising family planning services had been lifted ten years previously, there were still difficulties over newspaper advertisements. According to the Association there was still a lot of opposition from people who said that knowledge of contraception and sexuality undermined sexual morality.[2] To improve the standards of sex education it was organising a new programme for teachers and other professionals. A team of trained tutors would run courses in London and the regions over the following year.[3]

Opposition to the advertising of contraception in cinemas came from a surprising quarter when the Cinematograph Exhibitors' Association refused to show a commercial about contraception, produced by the Health Education Council and aimed at young people, unless it carried an X certificate. Cinema owners were apparently disturbed at the idea of showing the advertisement to minors, and expressed disbelief that it was in the public interest that the cinema should get involved in an educative role although they conceded it might be all right when no minors were present, hence the suggestion of an X certification.[4]

Dr Adrian Rogers takes a stand

In 1980 the Department of Health and Social Security had renewed its guidance that allowed doctors, in exceptional cases, to give advice and contraceptives to under-age girls without parental consent. A controversy arose in Devon County Council when Dr Adrian Rogers, the doctor for a community home for girls, Farringdon House, refused to prescribe contraceptives for children under 16 who were in council care. Dr Rogers expressed his outspoken views in an article in *Pulse*. 'Incredible though it may seem, the medical profession, in particular the British Medical Association, considers it acceptable and ethical not only to prescribe the contraceptive pill for minors, but also to do so within doctor-patient confidence that excludes this knowledge from the child's legal guardian. Large numbers of GPs, including family planning doctors, actually believe they are being clever, wise and professionally correct in "protecting" such children from pregnancy. In practical terms, they are giving the nod to under-age sex and encouraging its practice. In legal terms, they may be conspiring in an illegal act, in contempt of the law and with no scientific evidence whatsoever that it is for the benefit of society… If doctors continue in prescribing contraception in such a fashion, what protection has the parent from such practice? A parent discovering a child on the pill, prescribed by a doctor, should not only have recourse in a criminal court to the man abusing his child, but also to the doctor for conspiring in the behaviour. The profession should also reprimand such action as unprofessional in the disciplinary courts of the GMC.'[5]

In another article, Dr Rogers made the point that the evidence was clear that contraceptives did not protect children from pregnancy. 'Many children, if they really understood the medical risks, would decline contraception on medical grounds alone. However, even the medical risks do not outweigh the risks of a child becoming pregnant and it has been shown that contraception actually encourages children to have sex. They see the provision of contraception as an assurance that sex is OK—but it removes only the *fear* of pregnancy, not the risk… I remain convinced that children need protection from sex, not from pregnancy, and they can be given that protection by their family. In short, they can find protection in a family where the parent, not the child, is in control. One way parents can make sure that they are in control is to ask their GP for a written assurance that in no circumstances will he give a child of theirs the pill while that child is under 16. Should the parents not be in control, and a child approaches a doctor for contraception, that doctor may be aiding and abetting unlawful sex if he agrees to the request—but he would not be breaking any law by talking with parents and social workers in the child's interest... The thought of a 12-year-old on the pill because some irresponsible doctor considers her parents unresponsive is so totally horrific that limits on the medical profession's autonomy should, and must, be sought.'[6]

The stand of Dr Rogers caused total confusion within Devon County Council. The Social Services department threatened to overrule the doctor's decision and take the girls to a family planning clinic instead. The local MP, Mr Peter Mills, then tabled a parliamentary question asking what advice had been given to local authorities about the provision of contraceptives to girls in council care, and about the state of the law.[7] Devon's Social Services Committee ruled that contraception should be available to girls under 16 in care, but only in exceptional circumstances. In January 1981, when the issue was debated at a meeting of the full Council, Councillor Ronald Sim said that the Council would be condoning promiscuity by allowing under-age girls the pill. Councillor Mary Turner said that in spite of all the sex education and contraception, there had been a rise among children in sexually transmitted diseases, suicides and pregnancies. The chairman of Social Services argued that to deny contraception would not lead to a decrease in intercourse, but would certainly lead to an increase in pregnancy. In a close vote, the council voted by 36 to 34 to prevent under-age girls in council care from receiving the pill.[8]

A spokesperson for the British Medical Association (BMA), Dr Jane Richards, said that the Council was overlooking the fact that a girl had a legal right to make a decision to go on the pill. 'And just because the Council is acting in loco parentis they can't override those rights.'[9] Dr Rogers then received a letter from the Director of Social Services informing him that a complaint that he had abused medical privilege had been passed on to the General Medical Council (GMC). Dr Rogers responded that there was a concerted campaign against the people who opposed the pill for under-age girls. In a letter to *The Times* he made his position clear. 'Contrary to the advice from the British Medical Association and the Department of Health and Social Security, the decision to give a child under 16 contraceptive advice is never the decision of the doctor. A doctor's medical knowledge enables him or her only to judge the type of contraception which might be suitable for an individual, based on medical facts and that individual's medical history. The decision to provide or not to provide contraception for a particular age group is a moral and legal one made by parents and by society as a whole. Legally and morally parents have a right to consent to any medical or surgical procedure recommended by a doctor for their child and for this reason the confidence a doctor has with a child extends to include the child's parents or guardians.' Where the parents were entirely unconcerned 'that is the very worst situation in which to issue contraception... if the nation's teenagers are entitled to run into Brook advisory centres or family planning clinics and obtain contraception, albeit in exceptional circumstances, exceptions will become – and are rapidly becoming – the rule and the whole principle of protecting children within a family will have been thwarted and irreparably damaged.'[10]

The BMA was furious with Dr Rogers' stand, as can be seen from the response of the Chairman of the Central Ethical Committee. 'The BMA has never recommended that doctors provide contraceptives for every girl, or even the majority of girls, under 16. On the contrary, our ethical guidelines demand that every effort is made to involve the parents or guardians in the decision. Most doctors are successful in over 95 per cent of cases, frequently because the girl has approached the doctor so that he can assist her in broaching this delicate matter with her family. The massive publicity Dr Rogers has attracted is not stopping girls under the age of 16 from having sexual intercourse. It is, however, making them afraid to turn to the medical profession for advice. Journalists, responsible for answering questions from young people, are experiencing an unprecedented increase in calls from girls who state that they are now frightened to visit their doctors for fear of their parents being told. Is Dr Rogers happy with this result? Is he satisfied that in undermining the trust of patients in doctors, that he is causing avoidable problems? Does he not realise that there are cases when help and contraception are complementary, rather than alternative?'[11]

The Chairman of Brook commented that Dr Rogers would 'prefer to see a girl under 16 suffer an abortion or childbirth rather than allow her doctor to prescribe contraception to protect her from pregnancy'.[12] Valerie Riches, Secretary of the Responsible Society, replied that Brook was using the old argument 'that children must be supplied with contraception to prevent abortions. Yet the very statistics she quotes show that the policy the Brook has been carrying out over the years is counter-productive. The reason is simple: the more contraception has been made available to under-age children, the more recruits have been drawn in, resulting in more sexual activity. Since the pill and other forms of contraception depend on regular use for effectiveness, they are notoriously unreliable when used by immature and feckless adolescents. So it is that we see more pregnancies, abortions, venereal disease, and cancer of the cervix resulting from premature sexual intercourse.'[13]

Another row broke out when Ronald Butt pointed out that the Mothers' Union had supported the Government's decision to give contraceptives to girls under 16. Betty, Lady Grantchester in a letter to *The Times*, observed that the Mothers' Union had agreed, 'albeit reluctantly, to the prescribing of contraceptives for this age group "in those comparatively few cases where there appeared to be no other way to protect the girl", provided that counselling is always available. One assumes

185

that the Mothers' Union expect the proposed counselling to be given along the lines "that the proper course of behaviour for all is chastity before marriage and fidelity within it". This, if acted upon would prevent illegitimate pregnancies completely. But the point at issue is whether counselling as presently practised is likely to fulfil all that the Mothers' Union, and like-minded organisations, would think adequate. Permissive counselling may accompany contraception and encourage rather than inhibit promiscuity.'[14]

Dr Margaret White was in little doubt about the type of counselling that would be on offer. She wrote, 'I attended a government-funded course on the subject [counselling for girls under 16] and discovered that counselling means helping the "client" to decide what she wants, and when she has done so, to provide it for her. I was told that it is wrong to give her information she needs to know to help her make up her mind, unless she specifically asks. Thus it is quite wrong to tell a girl of 13 the medical and psychological risk of premature sexual intercourse. It is also considered wrong to give any warning to the child of the possible dangers of the pill, even though many doctors consider it should never be given to children because of the additional side effects on the young of the contraceptive steroids. Many counsellors insist that to tell a "client" that sexual intercourse with a girl under 16 is illegal would be moralising, and therefore quite wrong. Not long ago a family planning nurse interviewed on television said, "I've seen a 12-year-old girl put on the pill in 10 minutes flat". I sincerely hope that such a case was exceptional—but I doubt it.'[15] Lady Brook replied to Dr White's letter. 'When a young girl risking pregnancy has the courage and foresight to ask a doctor for contraception the doctor has a grave responsibility to listen and give the information, advice and treatment that will best help this particular patient. In her flurry of indignation Dr White appears to have misunderstood the nature of this crucial counselling which may determine the future life of the young girl and her family. A doctor who moralises and scaremongers instead of listening may simply be writing a prescription for pregnancy.'[16] Another correspondent took umbrage at Lady Brook's definition of courage. 'Surely these qualities are more aptly applied to those girls who risk the mockery of their peers by using the simple device of saying "no" to sex before marriage. Here is true courage and foresight.'[17]

John Stokes denounces the FPA and Brook in Parliament

In May 1980 Mr John Stokes, a Conservative MP, made a fiery attack on the sex education industry in the House of Commons. He said that 'for something like 1,500 years this has been a Christian country where traditional morality has prevailed and where the Christian ethic of chastity before marriage and fidelity afterwards has been held up as an ideal. Now all this has been challenged, and the State itself has not been blameless.' He made the point that there had been an enormous increase in the sex education industry which was forcing its minority views on the public by classroom teaching, conferences, propaganda and numerous pamphlets. 'My prime objection to its view is that it cheapens the sexual act. It treats it as a purely physical thing without any mention of the mental and emotional issues involved.'

He accused the FPA and Brook of being involved in a sinister campaign to undermine the institution of the family with propaganda, delivered in the name of sexual freedom. He urged the Government to withdraw grants from the FPA and Brook, whom he accused of issuing vulgar and tasteless pamphlets. 'The name Family Planning Association suggests stability and respectability, which is far from the case. The Brook Advisory Centres are so revolutionary in their approach to sexual and family morality that there is not even pretence at respectability. The pamphlets of both concerns are written in a vulgar and tasteless way… Their whole theme is not the need for self-control in sexual relationships, but the necessity at once and at the earliest possible age for girls to take precautions against having a baby. This is a positive encouragement to indulge in sexual intercourse at an early age, coupled with the sinister suggestion that everyone is having sexual intercourse with everyone else all the time, and that is the most normal and natural thing in the world. I call that damnable advice. It is based on an entirely false premise, is addressed to young people at a most impressionable age and is tantamount to an encouragement to the widest promiscuity, with the result that fornication and even adultery would appear to be a normal condition of affairs.'

He mentioned the latest pamphlet that had just been sent to MPs, *Safe sex for teenagers*. 'It might just as well be safe bathing for teenagers, for sex is treated as of no more moral concern then bathing or any other harmless physical activity… The introduction has the cheek, in its first sentence to say "The last 20 years has seen a revolution in teenage sexual behaviour", a revolution for which bodies such as the Brook Advisory Centres bear a great responsibility.' Mr Stokes described as particularly sinister the commercial pressure behind this propaganda. The views expressed by the 'new' sexual morality lobby were fully backed by much of the media with newspapers, the wireless and magazines suggesting that young people engage in promiscuous sexual activity. The harm caused to young people's minds by this sort of propaganda was incalculable and made the job of parents, the clergy, teachers and youth leaders much more difficult. 'Most parents still want to bring up their children with traditional standards of morality. It is up to us to help them ward off the challenges from these disagreeable bodies which, if left unchecked, would in a short time build another Dark Age in this land.' Mr Stokes ended his speech by saying that he hoped that the Government would withdraw its funding for the FPA and Brook.[18]

But the Conservative Government, despite the powerful denunciation of John Stokes, was committed to the ideals of the family planning lobby. Sir George Young, junior Minister of Health, announced at a Brook conference that the Government would launch a campaign in the autumn of 1981 to encourage the use of contraception among teenagers. 'I have already stressed my belief that clinic services for young people should not be cut back. I will now go further

and say that we should actively encourage young people at risk to seek professional advice. The FPA by itself and in association with the Health Education
Council already does splendid work here and I am glad to say that the DHSS is
continuing its support for the Association.'[19]

In an article in *The Times* Ronald Butt referred to serious disquiet that had been
growing among many parents who had discovered both the manner and moral
overtones of sex education and the offensive teaching aids that were used. In his
opinion most normal people would regard some of the material as obscene. 'It
uses the language of the gutter, and at least one book widely used in schools
introduces children at a sensitive age even to the details of such perversions as
bestiality.'[20] The Conservative Government was embarrassed when the shocking
nature of some of the material that was being used in schools was brought to its
attention in July 1981. The sex education pack for schools produced by Brook
was described in the House of Commons as pornographic and Lady Young, the
junior Education Minister, criticised some of the material as absolutely appalling.
The main target of criticism was the booklet *A look at safe sex*, which contained
detailed, explicit, close-up, drawings of the sexual organs, including an explicit,
realistic drawing of a condom being fitted to an erect penis. And the message of
the booklet was equally blunt—'if a man and a woman want to have sex but they
do not want to start a baby they can use contraceptives'. A sex word game in the
sex education pack was felt to be frivolous. The Minister of Health wrote to Brook
reminding them of the £30,000 Government grant and suggesting that the pack
should be toned down.[21]

In the annual report of the FPA (1980-81) Patrick Jenkin claimed that there was
still a lot of ignorance and misinformation about birth control and sexual matters.
'The extent of this ignorance has been starkly confirmed once more by the recent
rise in the number of abortions and illegitimate births to women in this country.
These figures, and the personal misery and hardship they represent, are a cause for
the most serious concern. I feel that they make the work of the FPA in providing
accurate and responsible family planning information and education all the more
important... The Family Planning Information Service deals with tens of thousands
of individual inquiries each year from both public and professionals. Though now
only a little over four years old, it has become well established as an authoritative
national information service, as well as supplying very large numbers of leaflets
and other publications requested by health authorities all over the country, on family
planning and related issues.'

The chairman of the FPA, Barbara Davis, was scathing about the small but active
brigade of critics who prevented them from doing their work. 'Their opposition to
our efforts to educate and inform individuals about sex and birth control reminds
us that there exists in certain sections of our society a legacy of fear and prejudice
governing the consideration of these matters.' She was thankful that the grant to
the FPA had been doubled and expressed her gratitude to the Government 'for
its courageous stand on these issues in the face of persistent opposition from

single-minded pressure groups.' And how did she explain the rise in abortions and illegitimate births? She believed one factor could be increasing consumer disillusionment with available family planning methods. 'It could also be that the deteriorating economic climate is adversely affecting the motivation and ability of some people to plan their lives and their families.'[22]

In March 1982 John Stokes asked the Secretary of State for Education, Dr Rhodes Boyson, whether he was satisfied that there were sufficient legal safeguards to enable parents to withdraw their children from sex education if such education was contrary to the parents' philosophy. Dr Boyson replied that there should be fuller consultation between parents and schools in the way sex education was provided. John Stokes asked the Secretary of State if he was 'aware that the sexual propaganda of organisations like the FPA and Brook is considered by many people to be immoral and dangerous'. Dr Boyson agreed that 'some of the material that has gone into schools would be repulsive to everyone in the House. Indeed, we asked for some to be taken away last year, and we are asking for more to be taken away now. Schools must discuss sex education with parents.' Renee Short intervened to ask the Minister to reject the Neanderthal attitude of Mr Stokes. 'Of course it is a matter for parents. No one denies that. However, if they are not willing or able to take on that duty, does not the Minister think that there should be properly structured help from teachers, who are trained to provide help at school?'[23]

In November 1981 the International Planned Parenthood Federation endorsed the use of what it called emergency contraception (also referred to as the morning-after pill) after unprotected intercourse. The Pregnancy Advisory Service used a symposium at the Royal College of Physicians in April 1982 to plead for emergency contraception to be made more widely available from general practitioners and family planning clinics. Their London clinic had been offering emergency contra-ception, and it had already been used by more than 500 women from all over England. This was clear evidence, according to the Pregnancy Advisory Service, of the need for a well-publicised nationwide 'morning-after' service within the NHS. The symposium was informed that although most women using the advisory service were normally conscientious family planners, about half their clients had unprotected intercourse and the rest had contraceptive accidents, primarily broken sheaths.[24] This was a remarkably frank admission of the failure rate associated with contraception, even among those considered to be conscientious family planners. Clearly, the family planners were aware that contraception on its own could not lower the teenage pregnancy numbers—it needed to be backed up by emergency contraception and abortion.

By 1982 the FPA's Education Unit was organising a greater variety and number of courses than ever before. Numerous courses were being held for professional groups such as health visitors, social workers, youth and community workers, teachers and health educators. New groups included pregnancy counsellors, student teachers and scout leaders. A typical course was of three days duration, although some were even longer. The FPA was thrilled that it was being asked to run training courses for health authorities and social service departments.[25]

The FPA had another idea for spreading its message—it would make use of the thousands of pharmacies around the country. In early 1983 more than seven hundred pharmacists were invited to participate in a three month trial to make free family planning literature and advice more widely available. Run jointly by the Pharmaceutical Society of Great Britain and the FPA, the scheme was part of a £100,000 project backed by the Health Education Council. If the trial proved successful, the plan was to introduce the scheme nationally. The idea was to reach an estimated two million people who were either not practising contraception or were doing so ineffectively. The FPA promoted the scheme as one way towards preventing the 200 thousand unwanted pregnancies that were occurring in Great Britain every year.[26] The outcome of the project was the 'Health Care in the High Street' scheme, launched in February 1986, to distribute free family planning information through leaflet stands in 12 thousand pharmacy outlets. Each pharmacy was sent a free leaflet stand headed *Family Health Care – free leaflets – please take one*; the stands contained copies of the leaflet *There are 8 Methods of Birth Control.*[27]

In 1983 sex education literature again caused a stir within Government when the Responsible Society drew attention to the pornographic nature of the literature that was being promoted by the Health Education Council. In response Dr Rhodes Boyson, Education Minister, produced a 16-page document listing what he saw as objectionable quotations from books and pamphlets listed by the Council which was receiving £8.5 million public funding. Two of the most shocking items were *Make it Happy* by Jane Cousins, and *Boy Girl Man Woman* by Bent Claesson. Dr Boyson said that these books could give young people the impression that brother-sister incest, group masturbation and paedophilia were desirable and even socially acceptable. Claesson described paedophiles as being generally 'kindly people who treat the children tenderly and affectionately'.[28] And *Make it Happy* was the book to which George Gardiner (MP) and Ronald Butt had taken such strong exception two years previously. Mrs Valerie Riches, who had alerted Dr Boyson to the explicit content of these books commented, 'Frankly, a lot of this material is sheer pornography.'[29]

As a result of this criticism the Health Education Council promised to undertake a review of its literature. However, the 1985 list of publications and teaching aids was still advertising *Make it Happy*,[30] and the 1990 resource list advertised the revised version, *Make in Happy, Make it Safe*, which explained why 'safer sex' is essential for everyone who is sexually active.[31] It was clear that the Conservative Government did not have the stomach to take on the sex educators. Provided there was no negative publicity they were content to turn a blind eye to the abusive and depraved literature that was being promoted by the sex education industry.

At a press conference in June 1983 the FPA reported on the finding of a survey to ascertain the level of cuts that were being made to family planning services by the newly formed district health authorities. According to the FPA, several health authorities had contacted them since the survey to say that proposed cuts were no longer taking place. It is interesting to observe the power that the FPA exerted over the new health authorities; it did not take them long to realise that family planning services were sacrosanct. The point the FPA wished to get across was contained in the *Guardian* headline – *Family planning clinics shutdown will destroy service, says FPA*. The likely results of closures, the FPA argued, would be more abortions and more unwanted pregnancies.[32] The FPA survey showed that 159 out of 162 district health authorities were using the free Family Planning Information Service.

Endnotes

1 Family Planning Association, Annual Report 1979-80, p1
2 *The Times*, 18 July 1980, Jubilee for family planning group
3 *The Times*, 3 October 1980, Sex lessons still most informal
4 *The Times*, 25 July 1980
5 *Pulse*, 21 June 1980, Is the Pill right for girls under 16?
6 *Daily Mail*, 15 January 1981, Dr Adrian Rogers, The Pill? My answer is No!
7 *Daily Star*, 20 August, 1980
8 *Express & Echo*, 9 January 1981, Pill banned in Devon for the care girls
9 *Social Work Today*, 20 January 1981, vol. 12, no. 20, Doctors to ignore ban on child contraception
10 *The Times*, 12 February 1981, letter, Adrian Rogers
11 *The Times*, 24 February 1981, letter, MJG Thomas, Chairman of BMA Ethical Committee
12 *The Times*, 18 February 1981, letter, Caroline Woodroffe
13 *The Times*, 20 February 1981, letter, Valerie Riches
14 *The Times*, 9 February 1981, letter, Betty, Lady Grantchester
15 *The Times*, 17 February 1981, letter, Dr Margaret White
16 *The Times*, 20 February 1981, letter, Lady Helen Brook
17 *The Times*, 23 February 1981, letter, Anita Beasley
18 Hansard, Commons debate, 14 May 1980, cc1516-19, Mr John Stokes
19 Brook Advisory Centres, Proceedings of one day conference, London, 27 April 1981, pp10-11
20 *The Times*, 22 June 1981, Licence to Corrupt, Ronald Butt
21 *The Times*, 31 July 1981
22 Family Planning Association, Annual Report 1980-81, pp1-2
23 Hansard, Commons debate, 16 March 1982, vol. 20, cc191-92
24 *The Times*, 15 April 1982
25 Family Planning Association, Annual Report 1981-82, p8
26 *The Times*, 22 February 1983, Trial boost for family planning
27 Family Planning Association, Annual Report 1985-86, p1
28 *Daily Telegraph*, 10 January 1983, Schools' sex book list halted after plea by Minister
29 Ibid. *Daily Telegraph*, 10 January 1983
30 *Personal Relationships*, Publications and teaching aids, Health Education Council, revised July 1985, p3
31 *Relationships & Sexuality*, selected resource list for professional educators for 13-18 year olds, Health Education Authority, January 1990, p19
32 *District Health Authority Family Planning Services in England and Wales*, Audrey Leathard, Family Planning Association, 1985, p18

Chapter 14

The Gillick Saga

Law Lords rule on the legality of doctors prescribing contraceptives to under-age children without parental consent

Back in 1978 a young mother, Mrs Victoria Gillick, heard about contraceptive clinics for schoolchildren for the first time. In *A Mother's Tale* she explains her concern when she read in national newspapers about 'special' contraceptive clinics set up in Doncaster and elsewhere by the NHS. Newspaper editors had recognised that there was something decidedly strange about the idea of 'family planning' for schoolchildren and gave the story a great deal of coverage. She wrote: 'The most extraordinary aspect of these clinics, which had amazed journalists as well as local residents, was that the clinic staff had made it widely known throughout schools and youth clubs in the district that schoolgirls of any age could get contraceptive pills from them with an absolute guarantee that nobody – especially not their parents – would be told of their sexual relationships or of the drugs they were being prescribed... Parents in Doncaster were naturally outraged by this deceiving body of medics in their midst, and campaigned vigorously to have the clinics closed, but to no avail.'[1]

A couple of weeks after this press exposé of 'family planning' clinics, the Ipswich Community Health Council (CHC) decided to raise the issue with Suffolk Area Health Authority at a joint public meeting. In October 1978 about a hundred people attended the meeting at which a letter from the Regional Administrator of the FPA, Stephen Dalton, to the secretary of the CHC was read out. Mrs Gillick was startled by what she heard. Stephen Dalton had written: 'May I therefore reinforce my telephone conversation with you... and inform you that the Association would take a very grave view of any variation from the guidelines set down in the DHSS Family Planning Service Memorandum 1974... and we would do anything in our power to see that these guidelines are adhered to in every respect... as the Memorandum states, it is for the doctor to decide whether to provide contraceptive advice and treatment, even if the girl is under the age of sixteen... may I state most emphatically the Association is most anxious that through proper parental guidance and sex education people will be responsible in their sexual activities... It would therefore be most unfortunate if the young people below the age of 16 who reside in Suffolk were deprived of the right to expect confidential advice and help from the doctors at the family planning clinic...'[2]

Parents at the meeting were enraged by this input from the FPA. 'You can imagine what happened to the meeting after that little bombshell was dropped. People began jumping up and down in their seats, calling out and challenging the platform to explain themselves.'[3] Mrs Gillick asked what it had to do with the FPA. 'We are not talking about *family planning*, but about unlawful sex with schoolgirls; so why has the FPA butted in? And what did Mr Dalton mean by saying they would do everything in their power to stop the Health Authority changing its policy? What power does the FPA have over you?'[4] Despite the public's anger at the policy of the Health Authority, the officials were unrelenting, determined not to give way. It appeared that nothing could be done to change Government policy. Parents simply had to accept that the State had the power to give contraceptives to children.

It was then that Mrs Gillick read Dr Adrian Rogers's advice to parents that they should write to their GP seeking written assurance that under no circumstance would the doctor give their child the pill while they were still under 16. Mrs Gillick decided to follow this advice. She explains, 'Right, I thought, that's just what I'll do: and while I'm about it, I shall write to the Health Authority and ask for the same assurances from all their clinics.'[5] As the Gillick family were now living in Wisbech, she wrote to West Norfolk Health Authority to seek an assurance that none of her daughters would be prescribed contraceptives or have an abortion performed while they were under 16 without her consent. Within the week she had received a reply from the Health Authority. Quoting the new DHSS guidelines, the acting chairman of the Health Authority refused to give her this assurance, replying that its doctors would use their clinical judgement in deciding how to treat a patient in their care.

Mrs Gillick described the reply as a crushing body blow. Against everything that she and her husband believed in, the Health Authority, in the guise of its contraceptive clinics, claimed the right to give her girls contraceptives secretly, behind her back, and there was nothing she could do about it. No, she simply could not accept that in a free country the State had such power over her children. Having discussed the issue with a young lawyer Mrs Gillick decided to take legal action. 'How to do it, though? By simply asking a judge to say whether or not the DHSS guidelines were actually lawful. In other words, did Gordon and I, as parents, have ultimate responsibility for the moral and physical welfare of our children – or was it now the role of the State?'[6] Her case against the DHSS was in the hands of the legal profession, and there it was to remain, dormant, for an incredible two and a half years before coming to court in 1983.[7]

No doubt aware of the coming legal challenge, in June 1983 the General Medical Council (GMC) ruled that doctors who broke confidentiality and informed parents that their under-age daughters were using the pill might be guilty of professional misconduct. The ruling reinforced ethical guidance drawn up by the British Medical Association (BMA) to help doctors deal with girls under 16 who wanted contraception. Dr Alexander Macara explained that in future the disciplinary body might ask a doctor to justify a decision to break confidentiality. The general rule was that doctors should always try to persuade a young girl to involve her parents in the decision to use contraceptives. However, if the girl refuses, the doctor must respect confidentiality.[8] In Parliament, Mrs Jill Knight said she hoped the Secretary of State would remonstrate with the BMA over their recent disgraceful ruling that doctors who told parents their daughters were on the pill or had had an abortion would be struck off the register unless the girl agreed to her parents being informed by the doctor.[9]

The actions of the BMA and the GMC stimulated a controversy within the medical profession. Six doctors wrote a furious letter to *The Times*: 'For centuries past, medical practice in civilised countries has respected the unique and irreplaceable role of parents as the primary educators and protectors of their children. Doctors, therefore, have always shared confidentiality with parents. There should be no confusion between confidentiality, which respects privacy, and secrecy, which is unjustifiable silence in the face of danger to an under-age child. Many members of the medical profession view with real foreboding the sinister and incomprehensible ruling from the GMC that all children, if they so wish, have an absolute right to exclude parents, regardless of the nature of the medical condition. We, the undersigned, therefore disassociate ourselves from the GMC's ruling. We know that we speak for many other representatives of the medical profession who have expressed their approval of the contents of this letter.'[10]

High Court Case

In July 1983 Mrs Gillick sought a declaration from the High Court that a Department of Health memorandum, allowing doctors to prescribe contraceptives or perform abortions on under-age girls without the consent of their parents, was illegal.[11] Mr Gerald Wright QC, appearing for Mrs Gillick, said she was asking Mr Justice Woolf for a declaration that none of her five daughters must be given contraceptive advice or treatment without her consent. Mr Wright said that Mrs Gillick found the circular quite intolerable in that it encouraged the secret provision of contraceptives to under-age girls. Mr Wright said a doctor who knowingly gave contraceptives to a girl under 16 could be 'very close' to committing the criminal offence of aiding and abetting unlawful sex. There may be mitigating circumstances, that the doctor considers it to be in the girl's best interest, but neither morally nor legally does the end justify the means – and the end is an illegal act. He informed the court that Mrs Gillick wanted to retain her duty as a mother to the exclusion of any other person, in particular any person who may seek to advise her children on sexual matters or give them any encouragement to have a sexual relationship the law forbids. Mrs Gillick had a fundamental right to concern herself with the moral upbringing of her children and a fundamental right to rebuke interference. Confidentiality cannot cloak illegality. In such cases, the protection given to girls by the law against under-age sex was being completely abandoned.

Mr Simon Brown, for the DHSS, said a girl under 16 can 'give her consent to contraceptive examination, advice and prescription and the role of the parent can properly be set aside. An under-age girl who had sexual intercourse was not guilty of a criminal offence. Therefore, a doctor giving her the pill could not be said to be encouraging or procuring a criminal offence.'[12] Doctors who put under-age girls on the pill are not encouraging them to have unlawful intercourse. Contraceptives are prescribed for their own good, to stop unwanted pregnancies.[13]

Mr Gordon Gillick commented during the court case that it was the intervention into the family by the Department of Health and its agents, like the FPA, that they felt was so wrong. 'They actually go round and sell promiscuity in the schools. They wear different shirts but they are all the same team.'[14]

Mr Justice Woolf said in judgement that prescribing the pill was a palliative against the consequences of a crime, rather than an instrument for crime itself. 'I accept that a doctor who is misguided enough to provide a girl under 16 or a man with advice and assistance with regard to contraception with the intention thereby of encouraging them to have sexual intercourse is an accessory before the fact to an offence. However, I assume this will not usually be the attitude of the doctor. But was a doctor an accessory if he decided to give advice and prescribe contraceptives, although firmly against unlawful intercourse taking place, because intercourse would in any event take place and, in his view, the provision of contraceptives was in the girl's best interests in protecting her from an unwanted pregnancy? There will certainly be some cases, and I hope the majority, where the doctor decides to give advice and prescribe contraceptives despite the fact that he was firmly against unlawful sexual intercourse taking place, but he felt nevertheless that he had to prescribe the contraceptives because, whether or not he did so, intercourse would take place and, in his view, the provision of contraceptives was in the girl's best interests in protecting her from an unwanted pregnancy and the risk of a sexually transmitted disease.'[15]

And so Mrs Gillick had lost her case. The judge had ruled that in a situation where the doctor was convinced that sexual intercourse would take place, he was acting in the girl's best interests by prescribing contraception. Lord Devlin believed that the case might well have been one of the most important to have come before the courts in the last decade. 'I hope that in this case, if it goes further, or in one to come, the argument will not be restricted to speculation as to whether or not a crime may be committed or a trespass to the person. I hope also that the common law will be found still capable of giving an answer to the question of whether it is the parent or the health authority who is to decide whether or not a child under 16 is to be provided with the means of sexual promiscuity.'[16] Another correspondent pointed out the inconsistency in the law. 'Should my daughter, on becoming 16 years of age, wish to enter a stable, loving sexual relationship through marriage, the law will not permit it without my consent. Should she, however, at only 14 wish to enter an unstable, transient sexual relationship, the law will allow her contraceptives to assist the liaison, not only without my consent, but without my knowledge. Where is the logic of that?'[17]

It would be an understatement to say that Victoria Gillick was unpopular with the medical and legal establishments. Who was this ignorant Roman Catholic mother to cause all these problems? The Law Society refused her application for legal aid for an appeal against the High Court's decision, despite Lord Devlin's view that it might well be one of the most important cases to come before the courts in a decade. But when Mrs Gillick expressed her determination to challenge the Law Society's decision,[18] its area committee in Cambridge gave way and granted legal aid.[19] Meanwhile a nationwide petition, organised on a parliamentary constituency basis, had gathered around 500 thousand signatures and received backing from the Salvation Army. Captain Clifton said that it was the Salvation Army in 1885 which had been responsible for the age of consent being raised from 13 to 16.[20] The petition, in which 200 MPs were involved, urged the Home Secretary to recommend to the House of Commons that parents should have a statutory right to consultation in cases where a doctor wished to prescribe contraception to an under-age girl. The Government was clearly worried about the popular support for Mrs Gillick, and promised to review its advice to doctors that contraceptives may be prescribed to girls without their parents' knowledge. Mr Kenneth Clarke said that the promised review would not be carried out until the Court of Appeal had ruled on Victoria Gillick's attempt to have the existing advice declared unlawful.

Mrs Gillick's campaign was now in full swing as she awaited the appeal to the High Court. She appeared on a number of radio and television programmes, and many people saw her as the representative of moral integrity and the defender of parents' rights to control their children. However, to the Department of Health, the medical establishment, and the family planning lobby she was a dangerous, ill-informed campaigner, likely to damage the health and well-being of children. This difference in attitude was brought to a head by a sensational court case involving a girl who had been prescribed the pill when she was only 10 years old. A startling revelation emerged at the Old Bailey when a 48-year-old man pleaded guilty to indecently assaulting the girl. In her statement the girl said she had been taking the pill since she was 10. Incredulously Judge Brian Gibbens exclaimed: 'Taking the Pill at ten! Where did she get it from?' The prosecutor said that the child went to the Brook clinic in Walworth, London, where she claimed she was 14. The Judge remarked, 'It is a pity that some children don't have a period of their life when they can live as children.'[21] He went on, 'The law has to protect precocious children from corrupting themselves.' Naturally the girl's parents were outraged. The father said had he known at the time he would have gone to a solicitor and tried to take action to prevent his daughter from getting the pill. He said the clinic should have told him first and made every possible check to find out how old she was. The mother was disgusted: 'She was only a baby.'[22]

Predictably, the case received a great deal of publicity and led to an increase in support for Mrs Gillick's campaign. However, the chairman of Brook, Mrs Caroline Woodroffe, was very worried about changes to the law. 'People who sign this petition are trying to use doctors as some kind of agents of social control to try to stop young girls having sex. The idea that it is desirable for girls under 16 not to be given contraceptives is based on the spurious premise that this will stop them having sex. All that will happen is that there will instead be an increase in the number of abortions and unwanted pregnancies. We would much prefer to give girls contraceptives than abortions.' Professor John Newton, chairman of the medical committee of the FPA, said at a national conference on contraception, 'The trouble is, I feel she [Mrs Gillick] is not in touch with reality. You have only to work in the inner cities of Birmingham and London as I have and you will realise what you have to do.'[23] The BMA defended their position: 'We don't want to see either the law or the guidelines changed. We are talking about children who have already decided to exclude their parents from their actions. If they can no longer go to their doctor, what is to happen to them?'[24]

Dr Adrian Rogers opposed the BMA's position in the *BMA News Review*. 'We have tried the permissive society and the result has been a huge human disaster. The vast majority of the public disapproves. They see the sexually active children of a permissive society, which has eroded childhood to such a state that no one cares about the behaviour of these children. Children need care and protection and never contraception, and if contraception clinics were prevented from seeing under-age children, this country would begin to produce a healthier environment.' Dr Gerald Vaughan, the former Minister of Health, had now become a supporter of Mrs Gillick's campaign. He said, 'So far there have been 372 petitions to the House of Commons, representing the views of well over half a million people. I am glad to be associated with these petitions.'[25]

Mrs Valerie Riches, in a letter to the press, commented that the no-age-limit policy of the DHSS had not changed and had led to sex education propaganda advising children of clinics which will not check on age. 'In its eagerness to promote children's rights, the DHSS does not require of family planning clinics any accountability of procedure, including irrefutable evidence of age or parental consent. The wants of a child are absolute. In these circumstances, claims made about the number of under-16s who have attended clinics and the percentage who did so with parental consent are not based on evidence but speculation. Furthermore, with monotonous regularity we hear that the provision of the pill is preferable to abortion. Yet, contrary to predictions, there is overwhelming evidence that the free availability of contraceptives to teenagers has been accompanied by an increase in the rate of abortion in all teenage groups.'[26]

Dr John Havard, secretary of the BMA, said that if the appeal succeeded the consequences could be very dangerous, with an increase in unwanted teenage pregnancies and abortions, and possibly illegal abortions. With health ministers promising to review the guidance once the Court of Appeal had passed judgement, the BMA wrote to Norman Fowler, Secretary of State for Social Services, urging that the present position, supported by the BMA, the GMC and the Department of Health, should remain unchanged.

Sir Bernard Braine MP responded to Dr John Havard's statement: 'Over 530 petitions have so far been presented to Parliament drawing attention to the views of the many hundreds of thousands of parents who are not only concerned but outraged at this practice. They are calling in no uncertain terms for the Government to take action immediately to protect their children from both the medical and emotional harm which such drugs and devices may cause. Dr Havard is reported as having said that if doctors were prevented from issuing contraceptives to children then there would be a corresponding increase in the number of unwanted teenage pregnancies. He ought to know that it is an accepted fact that readily available contraception to the young has corresponded with a dramatic increase in the number of abortions performed on young girls. There are two reasons for this—namely, that teenagers do not make good candidates for the regular self-administration of drugs, and that freely available contraceptives leads to an increase in promiscuity amongst the young. Ironically, Dr Havard's statement has coincided with the announcement that both the rates of abortion and illegitimate pregnancy have reached record levels in this country.'[27]

Dr John Havard responded: 'It is tragic that those of us who have children's welfare at heart should be divided by Sir Bernard Braine's narrow arguments... The best way of managing the problem is to place no obstacle in the way of such girls seeking medical advice as the doctor will do his best to persuade the girl to agree to the parents being informed; and only in exceptional cases, and where the doctor is satisfied of the capability of the girl to handle the situation, will treatment be given without the parents being informed... It does not assist the resolution of these serious problems for Sir Bernard to suggest that doctors are encouraging promiscuity.'[28]

Victoria Gillick accused Dr Havard of displaying naivety bordering on culpable ignorance. 'He writes as one 20 years behind the times... before sex and contraceptive propaganda had become the province of the schoolteacher and school broadcasts, and when local authority family planning clinics specifically for the under-16s were unthinkable. He appears not to have equipped himself with recent data and opinion on the results of teenage promiscuity... nor does he even seem to be aware that, unlike himself, those involved in family planning say that there is overwhelming evidence to show that the availability of contraceptives to children, undisciplined to take the drug regularly, leads to an increase in the pregnancy and abortion numbers, not a fall. Equally surprising is the fact that he made no mention of the whole question of whether such long-term hormone therapy on healthy young girls is not in itself a highly questionable practice, as at least three recent medical reports have suggested... For the BMA to allow itself to be led by the nose by those other fringe minority organisations who have for years been advocating sexual liberty for schoolchildren and the abolition of the protective age of consent... is another indication of how wayward a once reputable association can become once the primary ethical declaration to "do no harm" has been abandoned.'[29]

The Chief of Staff of the Salvation Army supported Mrs Gillick. 'One of the landmarks in British social history was the setting of the age of consent at 16 in 1885. One of my predecessors as the Salvation Army's Chief of Staff, Bramwell Booth, supported that ardent journalist, WT Stead, in the campaign. Parliament acted with wisdom and courage and rose to protect young people, not only from themselves, but also from the exploitation of others... One of the lessons from the case of Eliza Armstrong, which led to setting the age of consent at 16, was the focus on the responsibilities of parents in the matter. It is sad that a hundred years later it is precisely this same point that needs re-emphasis. One need hardly cite evidence that parental care and control is, generally speaking, far from satisfactory. We believe that upholding the principles involved in the age of consent will do much to re-emphasise in our own generation the responsibilities of parents and children to each other. The debate that rages nationwide at present over contraception for girls under 16 is but the tip of the iceberg that highlights one of the fundamental problems of our society. Great attention has been given to the potential increase in the abortion rate that might occur in the event of contraception being withheld. That is mere speculation. But even if it did happen we believe that it would be a small, and perhaps even temporary, price to pay for ensuring the greater involvement of parents in the matter. We need to consider the possible consequences, but to concentrate on the negative may deprive us of seeing the positive that could ensue from strengthening the very fabric of society in this way. It is imperative that we recognise that once again we stand at another landmark in the social history of our nation.'[30]

Meanwhile the BMA had written to every MP urging them not to change the contraceptive guidelines. A leaflet explained why doctors should remain free to prescribe contraceptives to girls under 16, in exceptional circumstances, without the consent of their parents. John Havard said: 'Doctors do not prescribe contraceptives in order to encourage girls to have sexual intercourse. However, in nearly all cases girls who see doctors for contraceptives are already having sexual intercourse and have been doing so for some time. Forcing doctors to inform parents will not stop them. It would simply discourage them from obtaining medical help. This would lead to an increase in unwanted pregnancies, the consequences of which can be very serious for young girls.'[31] Professor Michael Adler was concerned that if Mrs Gillick's crusade were to be successful 'a doctor will be unable to treat a minor under 16 years in confidence for anything, including sexually transmitted disease. There is no doubt that the number of infections will increase as a result.'[32]

Some doctors, however, were so upset by the approach of the BMA that they were threatening to resign. Two petitions, signed by two thousand doctors, asked the GMC to change its ruling on confidentiality for under-age children. The petitions, one of which would simply remove the confidentiality clause, while the other would make the doctor's duty to the parents usually outweigh the rule of confidentiality, had been signed by leading doctors including Sir John Peel, the former gynaecologist to the Queen, Dr Derek Stevenson, a former secretary of the BMA and Sir Reginald Murley, a former president of the Royal College of Surgeons.[33]

The Gillick campaign received a blow when Cardinal Basil Hume, Archbishop of Westminster, told her that he could not support her court action. In a letter the Cardinal stated that 'the particular issue which you have brought before the courts has, however, as many have recognised, wider implications for the role of law, medical practice and social welfare in a pluralistic society.'[34] Prime Minister Margaret Thatcher, on the other hand, made public her support for Mrs Gillick.[35]

The Conference of Catholic Bishops of England and Wales, which met in November 1984, stated that parental responsibility must not be undermined. 'Parents have a duty and a right to bring up children to moral and social maturity. Professional people engaged in medical, social, educational and juvenile justice services must respect and promote responsibility and frame their professionals' guidelines accordingly. This emphasis on parental responsibility is required, especially in those delicate moral and emotional situations involving contraception and abortion which, in fact, we hold to be immoral. To envisage such procedures without parental consent is an affront to parental rights and a further undermining of family life.'[36]

The following week in November 1984 the Gillick case was heard in the Court of Appeal. Her counsel, Mr Gerard Wright, QC, explained to the three judges, Lord Justices Eveleigh, Fox and Parker that the essence of the appeal was that if a girl under the age of 16 is involved in sexual relations she is in grave social and moral danger and her physical and mental health is at risk. 'A parent would have a duty to prevent or seek to remove those dangers. Her attitude is not just a question of personal morality founded on her own religious beliefs. It is firmly founded on public policy which protects all girls under the age of 16 from sexual interference.'[37] Having heard the arguments put by counsel the judges reserved judgement.

Appeal of the agony aunts

There was now real concern among the sex education lobby about the outcome of the appeal, and a number of prominent 'agony aunts' wrote to *The Times*. 'Earlier this year we delivered a letter to the Prime Minister signed by 24 "agony aunts" expressing the view that confidential provision by doctors of contraceptive advice to under-16s should be maintained... The pressure for change, organised by an articulate and doubtless well-meaning minority, is based either on remarkable naivety or wishful thinking. We are convinced, not only by our uncomfortably large files of anecdotal evidence, but also by the available statistics, that the premise – the denial of contraception to girls under 16 will stop sexual activity by them – is wholly at variance with the facts. The more probable result would be an increase in pregnancies among 14 and 15-year-olds. The DHSS guidelines, which were brought into effect in 1975, stemmed and reversed rates for 15-year-olds. In a perfect world, children with difficulties would go to their parents with love and trust, but every day we get letters from distressed young women asking for our guidance because there is no other adult to whom they can turn. Where parents find it difficult to communicate, are indifferent, actively hostile, physically brutal or have abandoned the child, then all too often precocious sexual activity may be a search for the approval and tenderness the child has never received... In our view, it would be a cruel experiment to discourage vulnerable and disadvantaged girls from consulting a doctor by the breaching of confidentiality. This does not mean that doctors will always prescribe contraception, but that the advice received should be confidential. If they are mature and sensible enough to make the effort to protect themselves from the hazards of teenage sex, although electing not to involve parents or guardian, then to deny this help does them and any child they may have a grave disservice. We earnestly hope that these arguments will not be ignored and that the present guidelines will be retained.'[38]

Dr Margaret White responded that the heading to the letter from the agony aunts, 'Compassion for the pregnant young' was not well chosen. 'The gist of the letter is a plea by these ladies for doctors to make life easy for males of all ages who choose to have illegal sexual intercourse with children, and refuse to take contraceptive precautions themselves... It is sad that their idea of showing compassion to such children is to give them contraceptive pills. Experience in medical practice and the juvenile courts have convinced me that far from solving an unhappy child's problems such a recipe will compound them.'[39] Another correspondent made the point that while the 'agony aunts' mean well, their view leads to a replacement of parental responsibility by that of individuals or groups who do not have the primary task of bringing up and guiding children and young people.[40]

Victoria Gillick joined the debate: 'It was with a depressing sense of déjà vu that I read the letter by eight women journalists of the Mirror Group of newspapers as they expounded their now well-known solution to the growing social and medical problem of schoolgirl promiscuity. It was in the early sixties, as a college student, that I first became aware that our parents were being publicly vilified in the press, television and films as "squares" and out of touch with the new swinging era of sexual liberation that had begun to mesmerise and engulf the mindless and self-indulgent chorus of "we're all doing our own thing". Now, 20 years on, these same ardent, if ageing, "Lily the pinks" in the world of female journalism are to be seen hard at work again, promoting this dangerous philosophy to schoolchildren. By appealing to their basic appetites, they are training them to become good, unquestioning consumers in this new, lucrative, child-centred sexual market... Everyone must surely know that all under-age girls are "vulnerable" and all will become "disadvantaged" once promiscuity and disease rob them of their youth and their educational chances. Hence the law that protects them from sexual harassment whilst they are still under school-leaving age.'[41]

201

Judgement of the Appeal Court

A few days before Christmas 1984 Mrs Gillick heard that her appeal had succeeded. In a unanimous judgement, the Appeal Court ruled that the Department of Health guidance to doctors, that in exceptional cases they can prescribe contraception without consulting the girls' parents, was unlawful. Lord Justice Parker dealt at some length with the provisions of criminal law intended to protect girls under the age of consent from being seduced. He concluded that it was wholly incongruous, 'when the act of intercourse is criminal, when permitting it to take place on one's premises is criminal and when, if the girl were under 13, failing to report an act of intercourse to the police would up to 1967 have been criminal, that either the Department or the area health authority should provide facilities which would enable girls under 16 the more readily to commit such acts. It seems to me equally incongruous to assert that doctors have the right to accept the young, down, apparently, to any age, as patients, and to provide them with contraceptive advice and treatment without reference to their parents and even against their known wishes.'[42] Lord Justice Eveleigh commented on the question of medical confidentiality. 'A doctor's position is not an easy one. At the same time, in law there is no such right which can justify silence at all times by a doctor, particularly when the welfare of a child is involved.'[43]

The judges ruled that parents have an absolute right to be consulted, and the court granted that none of Mrs Gillick's children be given any contraceptive, abortion advice or treatment without her consent, save in an emergency or after a court order. Naturally, Victoria Gillick was overjoyed at the verdict. 'As we walked down the steps of the magnificent Court buildings, we were almost overwhelmed by cameras, flashlights, microphones and jostling reporters; and it was not difficult to notice that most of them seemed as jubilant as ourselves, particularly the older ones. I suppose it was because a high proportion of them were also the parents of teenage children and had been experiencing the same kind of social pressures as the rest of us.'[44] The family planning organisations were stunned by the ruling and immediately warned that unless the judgement was reversed there would be more unwanted pregnancies and abortions. The BMA responded that under-age sex would not stop because of the ruling and feared an increase in unwanted pregnancies.

The Government, too, was stunned by the judgement and within two weeks the Minister of Health, Kenneth Clarke, decided not to abide by the ruling of the Appeal Court and announced the Government's intention of appealing to the House of Lords.[45] However the Chief Rabbi, Immanuel Jakobovits, was delighted with the outcome. 'Having signed together with other national religious leaders, a statement in support of Mrs Gillick's case against the DHSS guidelines… I naturally applaud the judgement of the Court of Appeal. I welcome this important decision for two quite distinct reasons. The "professional guidance" of the GMC, endorsed by the BMA, had stated: "If the patient (under the age of 16) refuses to allow a parent to be told, the doctor must observe the rule of professional secrecy in his management of the case". In other words, any conflict between parents and doctors in claiming the confidence of children is to be resolved in favour of the doctors. The Appeal Court ruling has restored the supremacy of the Ten Commandments, "Honour your father and your mother" over the medical profession's self-proclaimed guidelines. This is bound to be greeted with immense relief by all who seek to reassert the rights and duties of parents and who see a major cause for the rampant rise of crime and vice in the widespread breakdown of family life, aggravated by officially encouraged challenges to parental control. The BMA has argued that the new judgement will "force doctors into actions that will betray confidences and damage a fundamental principle of medical practice". That may well be so. But surely even doctors will not argue that this principle is more fundamental than the respect owed to parents. Indeed, no other profession – teachers, clergymen, or lawyers – ever made any such claim demanding stronger bonds of trust with themselves than children have with parents.

'The second reason for acclaiming the Court ruling is that it represents a notable reversal of the trend towards an ever more permissive society. The BMA document quite rightly affirms the strong belief that if people under 16 know that their parent will be informed against their wishes, many more will just not seek contraceptive help, and more girls will become pregnant. It is likely that abortion rates would rise in consequence. These consequences are unfortunate and may indeed be inevitable, at least for a while. But what the document does not consider is that an even greater number of girls (and their boyfriends) will now think twice before they irresponsibly embark on sexual adventures, and hold back from the brink of temptation by the very fear that a moment's pleasure may no longer be concealed from parents, or its effect neutralised by the simple expedient of a doctor's prescription.'[46]

The sex education lobby was horrified at the judgement, for it had removed their absolute right to prescribe contraception to children without referring to their parents. Consequently, the power that sex educators had over children had been seriously undermined. The effect of the ruling was immediate, as attendance at contraception clinics around the country fell. Attendance at Brook Centres dropped substantially and Sheffield Health Authority, after a detailed investigation, reported a 30 per cent fall in clinic and GP attendance. But there was no noticeable effect on the number of under-age girls who became pregnant. Nevertheless, the FPA and Brook continued to claim that there would be a rise in teenage pregnancies. One correspondent had heard it all before. 'It's always the same argument: They are going to do it anyhow, so they must be protected from the consequences. But don't doctors believe that prevention is better than cure? If it was *not* possible for an under-age girl to obtain contraceptives or an abortion without informing her parents, might that not deter her from having sexual intercourse? Most girls of that age are naturally chaste. It is the climate of opinion created by the contraception and abortion-on-demand lobby that makes it so difficult for them to remain so without being scoffed at as prudes.'[47]

Despite the vociferous campaign of the BMA, a survey of GPs showed that they were divided on the ruling of the Appeal Court. The survey carried out by *Pulse* showed that 49 per cent believed that doctors should be able to prescribe without consulting parents, and 44 per cent believed that parental consent should be required first. Another 7 per cent were undecided.[48] Ronald Butt, in an article in *The Times*, identified what he believed was the real issue in the Gillick case. It was not simply that, as the Appeal Court had found, the DHSS was breaking the law with its circular which allowed prescription of the pill without parents' knowledge in 'exceptional' cases. Nor was it even that parents' legal rights were infringed, or that the pill had medical side effects, as important as its moral consequences. 'What really lies behind this case is that children are proselytised in sex education, in and outside the classroom, to the belief that they are morally justified in indulging their sexual wishes provided they know the facts and take precautions against conception. If they do this, provided their relationships are reasonably stable, they are told that they are being responsible. Of course the pressure groups that specialise in contraception for the young also offer them counselling, but it is usually of a pretty fatalistic kind. Whoever heard from them an unambiguous declaration that sexual activity at an early age is morally wrong, and carries damaging consequences?'[49]

The BMA was still fuming over what it saw as a public humiliation. Following its high profile campaign, and despite its assertion that contraceptives were essential for preventing teenage pregnancies, it had lost. But it had one more card to play— it could wave the shroud. And so it was that the Central Committee for Community Medicine informed the BMA that two girls had committed suicide since the ruling of the Court of Appeal. In one case a 14-year-old girl, who was being sexually abused by her father, was alleged to have killed herself because she feared her mother would be told of the incestuous relationship if she tried to obtain contraception. In another case a 12-year-old sought contraception from her doctor but her parents objected strongly. And when the family doctor told the girl he could not help, she committed suicide. Family planning doctors on the BMA's committee claimed that the cases showed the terrible dilemma which doctors faced.[50] Predictably, these alleged suicides, apparently because young girls were unable to obtain contraception, received enormous publicity and a couple of tabloids had front-page shock-horror revelations. Was Mrs Gillick responsible for the death of two girls?

The BMA was immediately challenged to substantiate the allegations. Mrs Valerie Riches, secretary of Family and Youth Concern (previously The Responsible Society), challenged the BMA to give details of the deaths or withdraw their claims. Where did these cases occur, when were the inquests held and what were the coroners' verdicts? The BMA confirmed that two cases had been raised at a private meeting of the Association's Central Committee for Community Medicine, but declined to provide any more information. 'Doctors will not comment on any individual cases or reveal the identity of patients or their relatives.'[51] So having waved the shroud, the BMA now played the confidentiality card. But they had not taken account of the determination of Victoria Gillick. When official sources refused to verify the facts surrounding these alleged deaths, she phoned every coroner's court in England and Wales to find the facts, something the Home Office steadfastly refused to do. But none of the coroners had heard of the deaths. Were they an invention of the Central Committee for Community Medicine? Yet Government officials and the BMA were content for Mrs Gillick to be blamed for the alleged suicides. At a meeting at Manchester University a student mob, chanting 'murderess', carried a banner with the words: '2 Suicides – blood on your hands, Gillick.' Mrs Gillick commented: 'I asked the BMA to investigate and MPs asked the Home Office for the facts. We were refused. So I set out to ring all coroner's courts in England and Wales, over 140. I hope I shall now get an apology from those who refused to do anything to stop my life being made a hell over something which turns out to be quite untrue.'[52]

Columnist Bernard Levin had already expressed his disgust at the persecution of the Gillicks. 'Now on the rights and wrongs of such action by doctors I have expressed no public view, and I shall express none now; what interests me is not Mrs Gillick's legal action, but what has happened to her and her family since she began it. She has revealed that they have suffered physical and verbal attacks, that some of her children have been kicked and punched in the street, that gangs have tried to kick down their front door nearly every night, that she has had to take two of her children away from their school because of the bullying they were being subjected to, and that she has received obscene telephone calls and hate mail.'[53] In her book Mrs Gillick argues that much of the abuse that her family suffered was the result of 'the running commentary by women feature writers and those self-appointed humanitarians, the ageing "agony aunts". It was as a direct result of their continuous and carefully orchestrated vilification and personal abuse against myself, my religion, class, clothes, hair, home and children, that incited some of the young men in the town to repeat the abuse, attack the house and bully the children.'[54]

Ronald Butt commented on the way the BBC's *Newsnight* programme dealt with the High Court ruling. 'So the programme told stories of pregnancies risked by the new ruling, and family planning doctors displayed their fury and (in one case at least) an intention to defy it. But the central point of the programme was to convey the message that the Gillick case was no more than the tip of a dangerous iceberg. The programme's presenter, Ms Joan Bakewell, spelt it out: "The forces of the moral Right are on the move… For them Mrs Gillick is only the start".' But argued that one of the achievements of the kind of people enraged by the Gillick ruling had been to reduce the status of 'moral' to that of a non-respectable word. 'They take it as axiomatic that it is wrong to "preach" or "moralise" in talking to children about sex; indeed, it is as though sex is the one part of life to which it is almost indecent to apply the word morality.'[55] A letter to the press was scathing about the attitude of the BMA: 'The medical profession's media spokesmen (and women) are doing harm by spreading the attitude that the age of consent is irrelevant. What this has led to is increasing child prostitution and sexual abuse, among other things.'[56]

A determined opponent of the Gillick campaign and prominent member of the Mothers' Union, Mrs Menel Oliver, wrote a well-publicised letter to her doctor giving hypothetical written consent for him to prescribe contraceptives to her 13-year-old daughter should the occasion arise and should he see fit. She explained her actions as trying to do the best for her daughter by loosening control, 'if my daughter could not discuss the subject with me, I would rather she had medical advice than that her boyfriend go to a slot machine in the gents'. The Royal College of Nursing declared that the ruling undermined its members' judgement and ability to care.[57] A mother, Mrs Serena Allen, responded: 'I find it ironic that the Royal College of Nursing should object to the ruling on the grounds that it undermines its members' judgement and ability to care, since those are the grounds on which I base my support for it. My husband and I chose to have children and until they are legally adult, our judgement and ability to care will guide them; for good or ill, they remain our responsibility. I strongly object to that responsibility being removed before time.'[58] Another letter made the point that those people who worked closely with children could only be sad at the attitude that sought to portray Mrs Gillick as a misguided eccentric who had taken on a campaign to frustrate those who sought to protect the young from harm.[59]

Meanwhile a number of professional women in London, including Patsy Jorgensen, chair of the Church of England Children's Society, convened a group under the name Mothers United to gather a thousand signatures from mothers opposed to the Gillick ruling.[60] The chairman of the FPA, Dr John Dunwoody, expressed his horror at the thought that the Gillick ruling might go the wrong way. 'If the House of Lords' ruling upholds the decision of the Appeal Court, there could be disastrous consequences as far as teenage pregnancies and abortions are concerned and equally disastrous emotional and family problems as a result... The FPA believes that the challenges in the coming years will centre very much on the need to stand firm in the face of those who would seek to perpetuate ignorance. It is only by such determination in the past that we have the services that people benefit from today.'[61]

Appeal to the Law Lords

In June 1985 the Law Lords began hearing an appeal by the DHSS against the Appeal Court's judgement. Mr John Laws appeared for the DHSS and opened the challenge. He told Lord Fraser of Tullybelton, sitting with Lord Scarman, Lord Bridge of Harwich, Lord Templeman and Lord Oakbrook Brandon that the Court of Appeal ruling raised a grave question of difficulty.[62] Legal arguments were presented and the hearing lasted for nine days, the longest in the House of Lords for forty years, before their Lordships retired to consider their judgement. On the opening day of the BMA conference, only days before the Law Lords were expected to give their judgement, Dr Havard made the following statement: 'We wish to make it clear to worried parents that we believe it is medically undesirable for such girls to be having sex because of the increased risks to them of cervical cancer.' He added, 'We must place the interests of the girls first. It is their rights, more than the rights of their parents that must be protected.'[63] Apparently, the BMA saw itself as the knight in shining armour defending the 'rights' of children against their parents.

The Law Lords delivered their judgement in October 1985, and by a majority of three to two ruled against Victoria Gillick. At the final hurdle she had lost the legal battle to protect her daughters, as doctors won back the right to prescribe contraceptives to her under-age daughters without her knowledge or consent. The Department of Health was ecstatic at the ruling and immediately announced that it was reinstating its guidance, although the Minister for Health, Mr Barney Hayhoe, promised that it would be fully reviewed. Cardinal Basil Hume, Archbishop of Westminster, said: 'This judgement of the House of Lords, while clarifying the present state of the law, does not, and cannot, decide what is morally right and wrong.' The decision was welcomed by the BMA, the FPA, the Church of England Children's Society and the Royal College of Nursing.

Judgement of the Law Lords

Lord Fraser argued that it seemed to be verging on the absurd to suggest that a girl or boy aged 15 could not effectively consent to a medical examination of some trivial injury to his body, or even have a broken arm set. Provided the girl was capable of understanding what is proposed, and of expressing her own wishes, he could see no good reason for holding that she lacked the capacity to express her own wishes. Accordingly, he could not agree that a girl aged less than 16 lacked the power to give valid consent to receiving contraceptive treatment, merely on account of her age.

In his view it was contrary to the ordinary experience of mankind, at least in Western Europe in the present century, to say that a child remained, in fact, under the complete control of his parents until he attained the definite age of majority, and that on attaining that age he suddenly acquired independence. Once the rule of the parents' absolute authority over minor children is abandoned, the solution to the appeal could no longer be found by referring to rigid parental rights at any particular age. It depended upon a judgement of what was best for the welfare of the particular child. The only practical course was to entrust the doctor with discretion to act in accordance with his view of what was best in the interests of the girl who was his patient. In Lord Fraser's opinion a doctor would be justified in proceeding without the parents' consent provided he is satisfied on the following matters: (1) That the girl (although under 16) will understand his advice; (2) that he cannot persuade her to inform her parents, or allow him to inform the parents that she is seeking contraceptive advice; (3) that she is very likely to begin or to continue having sexual intercourse, with or without contraceptive treatment; (4) that unless she receives contraceptive advice or treatment her physical or mental health or both are likely to suffer; (5) that her best interests require him to give her contraceptive advice, treatment or both, without the parental consent.[64]

Lord Scarman agreed with the judgement of Lord Fraser. He said that the law had to be found by a search in the judge-made law for the true principle. The difficulty was that they found themselves in the field of medical practice where parents' rights and a doctor's duty may point in different directions. Three features had emerged in today's society—contraception, the increasing independence of young people and the changed status of women. The availability of the pill had given women a choice of lifestyle with a degree of independence greater than any law of equal opportunity could by itself effect. The law ignored those developments at its peril.

Parental rights related to both the person and the property of the child – custody, care and control of the person, and guardianship of the property of the child. But the common law had never treated such rights as sovereign or beyond review and control. Nor had our law ever treated the child as other than a person with capacities and rights recognised by law. Parental rights were derived from parental duty and existed only so long as they were needed for the protection of the person and property of the child. Parental right must be exercised in accordance with the welfare principle and can be challenged, even overridden, if not. Parental right yields to the child's right to make his own decision when he reaches a sufficient understanding to be capable of making up his own mind.[65]

Lord Brandon's dissenting judgement said that the inescapable inference from the Criminal Law Amendment Act 1885, and the Sexual Offences Act 1956, was that Parliament had for the past century regarded sexual intercourse between a man and a girl under 16 as a serious criminal offence so far as the man was concerned. Parliament enacted these laws for the purpose of protecting the girl from herself. It followed that for any person to promote, encourage or facilitate the commission of such an act might itself be a criminal offence, and must be contrary to public policy. That applied equally to a parent, doctor or social worker.

To give a girl contraceptive treatment was largely to remove the inhibition against unlawful sexual intercourse arising from the risk of an unwanted pregnancy. He rejected the argument that some girls under 16 would have sexual intercourse, whether contraceptives were made available to them or not, for two reasons. First, because the mere fact a girl under 16 sought contraceptive advice indicated that she, and probably also the man with whom she was having sexual intercourse, were conscious of the inhibition arising from the risk of an unwanted pregnancy and were more likely to indulge their desires if it could be removed. Second, if all a girl under 16 needed to do in order to obtain contraceptives was to threaten that she would go ahead with unlawful sexual intercourse unless she was given contraceptives, a situation tantamount to blackmail would arise which no legal system ought to tolerate. The only answer the law should give to such a threat was 'wait till you are 16'. He did not consider it right for their Lordships' House, by holding that girls under 16 can lawfully be provided with contraceptives, to undermine the criminal law which Parliament had enacted.[66]

Lord Templeman said that, in his opinion, an unmarried girl under 16 did not possess the power in law to decide for herself to practise contraception. It was submitted that a doctor may lawfully make a decision on behalf of the girl, and in doing so may ignore the parent who has custody of the girl. The Judge raised several objections to this approach. First, the doctor, acting without parental views, cannot form a reliable judgement that the best interest of the girl is served by contraception. The doctor at the family planning clinic only knows that which the girl chooses to tell him. The second objection is that a parent will sooner or later find out the truth, and may do so in circumstances which bring about a complete rupture of good relations between family members. The third and main objection is that the secret provision of contraceptive facilities for a girl under 16 would encourage participation by the girl in sexual intercourse, and this practice offends basic principles of morality and religion which ought not to be sabotaged in stealth, by kind permission of the NHS. The interest of a girl under 16 requires her to be protected against sexual intercourse. Such a girl is not sufficiently mature to be allowed to flout the accepted morality of society.

The Judge referred to controversial arguments which were not legal in character. Those who favoured doctors' power asserted that the failure to provide contraceptives in confidence led to an increase in pregnancies amongst girls under 16. As a general proposition this assertion was not supported by evidence, was not susceptible to proof and was of doubtful validity. The confidential availability of contraceptives may increase the demand. Contraceptives for females usually required daily discipline in order to be effective and girls under 16 frequently lacked that discipline. The total number of pregnancies among girls under 16 might therefore be increased, and not decreased, by the availability of contraceptives.

Those who favoured parental power asserted that the availability of confidential contraceptives would increase sexual activity by girls under 16. This argument was not supported by evidence and is not susceptible to proof. But it was clear that contraception removed, or gave the illusion of removing, the possibility of pregnancy and therefore removed restraint on sexual intercourse. Some girls would come under pressure if contraceptives were known to be available, and some girls under 16 were susceptible to male domination.

A doctor was not entitled to decide whether an under-age girl should be provided with contraceptives if a parent in charge of the girl was ready and willing to make that decision in exercise of parental rights. In the present state of the law the DHSS memorandum was defective. The practical effect of the memorandum, which was couched in opaque language, was to enable an inexperienced doctor in a family planning clinic, exuding sympathy and veiled in ignorance of the girl's personality and history, to provide contraceptives as if they were sweets withheld from a deprived child by an unfeeling parent. As the memorandum now stood a clinical judgement by the doctor may amount to no more than a belief that a parent will not consent to contraception and a fear that the girl may practise sex without contraception.[67]

An editorial in *The Times* summarised the views of the judges. 'Lord Templeman held that a girl under 16 is not sufficiently mature to be allowed by the law to decide for herself that she will practise contraception for the purposes of sexual intercourse. Lord Brandon of Oakwood argued that to provide a girl under 16 with contraceptive treatment is to promote what the Sexual Offences Act of 1956 prohibits, which is contrary to public policy. He held that such treatment is in no circumstances lawful, with or without parental approval. Lord Fraser of Tullybelton, Lord Scarman and Lord Bridge of Harwich held that a legal capacity to consent to medical treatment does belong to persons under 16 provided certain conditions are fulfilled. That view prevails, although the crude score over 27 months is five judges to four the other way. The DHSS wins its appeal. Mrs Gillick is refused relief. Pre-Gillick practice is sustained as lawful.'[68]

One correspondent drew attention to an apparent inconsistency in the law. 'Perhaps someone could explain to this struggling mother why my daughters will be unable to buy cigarettes, alcohol or fireworks under the age of 16 (presumably because they are not yet considered mature enough to make decisions about such health hazards) yet at the same time they will be regarded as mentally and physically mature enough to make decisions about the health hazards resulting from sexual intercourse; and that, while I will have redress in law against those who sell my children harmful substances, I will not against doctors who prescribe possibly damaging chemicals, thereby encouraging them to risk their health and break the law?'[69]

The Brook was overjoyed at the ruling of the Law Lords. Their practice of giving contraception to under-age girls without the knowledge of their parents was now completely vindicated. Their press officer, Alison Frater, wrote an article reminding people that in spite of the Gillick ruling girls still needed help to get their supplies of contraceptives. 'Some people seem to think that the House of Lords' ruling in the Gillick case has solved the problem of advice to teenagers about sex and contraception. It has not.' She advised local clinics to advertise their opening hours, which should preferably be outside school and work hours. 'Time in each session should be reserved for young people who turn up at the last minute—for post-coital contraception, a pregnancy test or because it was their first appointment and they are late, or lost their pills or arrived on the wrong day... Despite an undoubted rise in sexual activity the teenage conception rate has been declining since 1974... yet too many sexually active teenagers are not using contraception... only the same proportion of teenagers attend family planning clinics as 10 years ago. It is not the motivation of teenagers that is responsible for this disappointing trend, it is the lack of appropriate services.'[70] Valerie Riches responded, 'The article on the need for young people to receive every encouragement and assistance to engage in sexual relationships, which was written by the press officer of the Brook Advisory Centres, was more remarkable for what it left out than for what it included. In her obsession to provide youngsters with cosy, convenient clinics, staffed by warm and sympathetic professionals willing to dance attendance on the adolescent clients' every whim, Ms Frater ignores the central issue. Sexual relationships are known to have serious medical and emotional consequences for children and young people. Most parents, if they learned that their children were engaging in them, would take steps to remedy the situation. A multi-million pound chain of birth control drop-in centres, or contraceptive takeaways would not address this problem. For Ms Frater and her colleagues, keeping parents in the dark is the means to an end; for those who are concerned about the effects on young people of premature sexual relationships it is the vital link in a chain of undesirable influences on their children.'[71]

Another letter commented that Alison Frater described as a 'disappointing trend' the fact that the same proportion of teenagers attended 'family planning' clinics as did 10 years ago, whilst there had been an undoubted rise in sexual activity amongst that age group. 'Which does Alison Frater find more disappointing; the increase in potential child customers for the clinics, or the failure to attract them inside?'[72]

The GMC issued new guidance which followed the Law Lords ruling that doctors could, under certain conditions, prescribe contraceptives to girls under 16 without telling their parents, provided the girl was sufficiently mature, in the doctor's judgement, to understand what was involved. According to the guidance, where a doctor believes the patient to understand fully what is involved, he may, after seeking to persuade her to tell her parents, prescribe treatment without informing them. But if the doctor does not believe the girl is sufficiently mature he may decide to disclose the information learned from the consultation. The aim of the new guidance was to take account of Lord Fraser's ruling, which overturned the position the GMC held prior to Gillick—the pre-Gillick guidance was that any doctor who breached confidentiality in matters of contraception would have laid himself open to disciplinary action by the GMC.

But the BMA had no qualms about even paying lip service to the Lords' ruling and was furious with the position of the GMC. Dr John Dawson, head of the BMA's professional committee commented, 'It turns going to the doctor over contraception and abortion into a lottery for a girl under 16. She will not know until the end of the consultation whether the doctor will respect her confidence.'[73] Sir John Walton, president of the GMC, said he hoped that in the great majority of cases doctors would still preserve confidentiality. John Havard responded on behalf of BMA. 'The result of the GMC's revised guidance is that an under-age girl may feel she can no longer consult a doctor without her parents being informed, both of the fact that she has consulted the doctor and of the information which she disclosed. A girl can no longer be sure that her consultation will be kept secret unless she is certain that she can convince the doctor that she is mature within the GMC's new guidance and few under-age girls are likely to take this risk… The GMC's guidance on this issue is not, of course, mandatory and the clinics, fearful of the public health consequences, have announced that under-age girls can consult them in confidence.

The result is that girls at risk will now be even less likely to consult their own family doctors…'[74]

The BMA's central ethical committee called on the GMC to reconsider and 'make it absolutely clear that the right to consult a doctor in complete confidence has not been changed in any way'. The BMA had taken legal advice and claimed that the GMC's advice was wrong in law and likely to harm patients.[75] The BMA argued that the guidance meant, in effect, that an under-age girl must prove to the doctor she is mature enough to understand all the issues involved before she could be sure the consultation would be kept confidential. Despite strong pressure from the BMA, which claimed that the guidance made going to the doctor for contraception a lottery for under-age girls, the GMC decided that the guidance should stand.[76] In a way the BMA was right in its argument, for it knew that Lord Fraser's so-called competencies would be unworkable in practice; a doctor would first have to complete a consultation before he would be in a position to decide if the girl was sufficiently mature to understand his advice. This meant that a young girl could not be given an assurance that her parents would not be informed prior to the consultation. The BMA knew that, in practice, most doctors who prescribed contraceptives for under-age girls would simply ignore the Fraser competencies. Did the GMC really believe that a doctor working in a Brook or NHS contraceptive clinic would phone the parents of an under-age girl to inform them that their daughter was too immature to understand their advice? The BMA, of course, knew that it would be impossible to prove that a doctor had not abided by the competencies, so the GMC's guidance was pointless.

And so ended one of the most amazing ideological battles in British history. The Government, using all the powers of the mass media, the machinery of officialdom, the propaganda of the sex education lobby and the influence of the medical profession, had won the legal battle to provide contraceptives to children without the knowledge or consent of their parents.

During 1985, the year during which the ruling of the Appeal Court supported Mrs Gillick, the number of girls under 16 visiting family planning clinics fell by one-third, from 18 thousand in 1984 to 12 thousand in 1985. Despite the doomsday predictions of the sex education lobby, the abortion rate in under-age girls also fell, from 5.6 per 1000 in 1984, to 5.4 per 1000 in both 1985 and 1986. In other words, the increase in abortions threatened by Mrs Gillick's opponents did not occur. As usual, the sex educators were wrong in their predictions.

Endnotes

1 Victoria Gillick, *A Mother's Tale*, Hodder and Stoughton, London, 1989, p150
2 Ibid. pp155-56
3 Ibid. p156
4 Ibid. p157
5 Ibid. p209

6 Ibid. pp211-12
7 Ibid. p214
8 *The Times*, 23 June 1983, Doctors must keep sex secrets
9 *The Times*, 28 June 1983, Parliament 27 June 1983
10 *The Times*, 30 June 1983, letter, JH Scotson, NC Brown, BG Gretton Watson, C Metcalfe Brown, R St John Lyburn, LB Scott
11 *The Times*, 16 July 1983, Mother to challenge ruling on the pill
12 *The Times*, 19 July 1983, Giving the pill to under-age girls nearly a crime says QC
13 *The Times*, 20 July 1983, Judgement deferred
14 Ibid.
15 *The Times*, 27 July 1983, Mother loses action on pill for children
16 *The Times*, 29 July 1983, letter, Lord Devlin
17 *The Times*, 5 August 1983, letter, Carole Chapman
18 *The Times*, 26 August 1983
19 *The Times*, 8 September 1983, Legal aid for pill challenge
20 *The Times*, 14 October 1983, Salvation Army back petition
21 *Daily Mail*, 5 November 1983, 'The girl of 10 they put on the pill', Tim Miles
22 Ibid. *Daily Mail*, 5 November 1983
23 *The Times*, 19 November 1983, Proposal to ban pill for young girls 'unrealistic'
24 *The Times*, 11 November 1983, Hectic day in pill campaign
25 *The Times*, 12 November 1983, Rebel GP opposes pill for youngsters
26 *The Times*, 1 December 1983, letter, Mrs Valerie Riches
27 *The Times*, 15 December 1983, letter, Sir Bernard Braine, MP
28 *The Times*, 22 December 1983, letter, Dr John Havard, Secretary BMA
29 *The Times*, 13 January 1984, letter, Victoria Gillick
30 *The Times*, 4 January 1984, letter, Caughey Gauntlett, Chief of Staff , The Salvation Army
31 *The Times*, 19 March 1984, MPs urged not to change pill guidelines
32 *The Times*, 13 February 1984, letter, Professor MW Adler
33 *The Times*, 15 November 1984, Doctors ask for change of rule on the pill
34 *The Times*, 5 April 1984, Hume will not back Gillick over pill action
35 Ibid.
36 *The Times*, 16 November 1984, Catholic bishops support doctors' petition on pill
37 *The Times*, 20 November 1984, Mother's appeal against pill for girls based on public policy, QC says
38 *The Times*, 10 December 1984, letter, Marjorie Proops (Daily Mirror), Katie Boyle (TV Times), Gill Cox (Woman's Realm), Virginia Ironside (Woman), Alix Palmer (Daily Star), Claire Rayner (Sunday Mirror), Deidre Sanders (Sun), Angela Williams (Woman's Own)
39 *The Times*, 14 December 1984, letter, Dr Margaret White
40 *The Times*, 17 December 1984, letter, RJ McNair
41 *The Times*, 18 December 1984, letter, Victoria Gillick
42 Butterworths LexisNexis Direct, House of Lords, 17 October 1985, p12
43 Cited from Victoria Gillick, *A Mother's Tale*, Hodder and Stoughton, p248
44 Ibid. *A Mother's Tale*, p249
45 Ibid. p250
46 *The Times*, 31 December 1984, letter, Immanuel Jakobovits, Chief Rabbi
47 *The Times*, 3 January 1985, letter, George Martelli
48 *The Times*, 4 January 1985, GPs split on Court's ruling
49 *The Times*, 10 January 1985, When want is just indulgence, Ronald Butt
50 *The Times*, 8 February 1985, Pill ruling linked with suicides
51 *The Times*, 9 February 1985, Pill deaths challenge to doctors
52 *The Times*, 2 May 1985, Pill suicides 'an invention'
53 *The Times*, 31 December 1984, Bernard Levin: the way we live
54 Ibid. *A Mother's Tale*, p232
55 *The Times*, 7 March 1985, Not only moral but right, Ronald Butt
56 *The Times*, 14 March 1985, letter, Elizabeth Elliot
57 *The Times*, 19 June 1985, Gillick: the anxiety and opposition grow
58 *The Times*, 26 June 1985, letter, Mrs Serena Allen

59 *The Times*, 26 June 1985, letter, Michael Lawlor
60 *The Times*, 19 June 1985
61 Family Planning Association, Annual Report 1984-85, p2
62 *The Times*, 25 June 1985, Lords hear appeal on Gillick judgment
63 *The Times*, 15 October 1985, BMA wants legislation if Gillick wins appeal
64 Butterworths LexisNexis Direct, House of Lords, 17 October 1985, Lord Fraser, pp4-12
65 Ibid. Lord Scarman, pp12-23
66 Ibid. Lord Brandon, pp25-28
67 Ibid. Lord Templeman, pp28-33
68 *The Times*, 18 October 1985, editorial, Gillick's law
69 *The Times*, 22 October 1985, letter, Diana McKinley
70 *The Times*, 22 January 1986, After Gillick, why girls still need help, Alison Frater
71 *The Times*, 1 February 1986, letter, Valerie Riches
72 *The Times*, 3 February 1986, letter, Rev Jeremy Hummerstone
73 *The Times*, 12 February 1986, Doctors overturn ruling on pill
74 *The Times*, 26 February 1986, letter, Dr John Havard, BMA
75 *The Times*, 5 March 1986, BMA red-faced over advice on pill
76 *The Times*, 24 May 1986, GMC rejects plea to change guidelines on pill for under 16s

Chapter 15

AIDS moves on to the political agenda

The AIDS threat; positive images of homosexuality;

Section 28; the Sex Education Forum established

Shortly after the landmark Gillick judgement the House of Lords again debated the increase in teenage abortions. Lord Winstanley, one of the sponsors of the Abortion Act of 1967, asked the Government what steps were being taken to improve counselling and other services for young people in order to combat the rise in abortions performed on teenagers.[1] Lord Buckmaster made the point that during the period between the ruling of the Court of Appeal and the judgement of the Law Lords, in other words while the law was supporting Mrs Gillick, the number of abortions performed on under-age girls fell for the first time from 2,040 for the March and June quarters of 1984, to 1,910 for the same period of 1985, a fall of 6.4 per cent. After expressing his admiration for Mrs Gillick, he said that he believed the judgement of Lord Scarman was misguided. The Gillick ruling had created in the minds of many teenagers the erroneous impression that they can misbehave as much as they like and the doctor will help them by providing contraceptives. He said that many people accepted that the general standard of sex education was highly unsatisfactory and often morally harmful. 'It is harmful because, for the most part, it concentrates on the purely physical aspect of sex—often in the most explicit and provocative way, with no trace of moral guidance. Allied to that is the attitude of the Brook Advisory clinics whose declared policy is that the customer is always right and that sex is fine provided one takes proper precautions... And what of the Churches, my Lords? What indeed! How sad we all see the spiritual benches empty.'[2]

Baroness Trumpington, responding on behalf of the Government, was also concerned that so many abortions were necessary among young people. She believed that family planning advice was infinitely more desirable than abortion.

'The Government recognises the importance of health education in the matter of avoiding unwanted pregnancies. The Health Education Council (HEC) recognises this too, and this year over a quarter of a million pounds is being spent from HEC monies on the Family Planning Information Service which is jointly run by the HEC and the FPA, and provides a comprehensive information system for all age groups on matters relating to contraception... I firmly believe that a free family planning service is an essential preventative measure which contributes to the avoidance of unwanted pregnancies.' She said that the Brook clinics, run on behalf of health authorities, had done a great deal to develop a model service sensitive to young people's needs. 'We give grant support to specialist organisations such as the FPA and the Brook Advisory Centres... and I certainly recognise the valuable work that the Brook Advisory Centres do generally.' She welcomed the FPA's 'Men Too' campaign, which aimed to encourage men, particularly young men, to increase their sense of responsibility in sexual relationships.[3]

Lord Buckmaster in a letter to *The Times* wrote: 'The prevailing ethos in this country seems to be far more permissive than most parents would wish; and it has been the concern of such parents whose complaints to head teachers have all too often proved unavailing that has impelled me to pursue this difficult matter. One important aspect of their complaints not mentioned in your columns is the all too frequent coupling of sex education with the provision of contraception, in the mistaken belief that the wider availability of contraceptives reduces unwanted teenage pregnancies. In fact, it would seem to encourage experimentation. Furthermore, a young girl makes a poor candidate for the regular, daily administration of the pill, which, incidentally, causes 150 different hormone changes in her body. During the decade up to 1984 the number of illegitimate births to girls under 20 increased by almost 60 per cent – and this at a time when organisations like the Brook Advisory Centres and the Family Planning Association were peddling the pill as never before, with substantial support from public funds.'[4]

The FPA's 'Men Too' campaign, launched in October 1984, was aimed at civilising men's sexual behaviour. Much of the campaign was directed towards teenage boys, who, according to the FPA, were growing up expecting their girlfriends to take the contraceptive pill. As part of the campaign the FPA produced a sex education video, entitled *Danny's Big Night*. The plan was to distribute the video, probably the first sex education video made specifically for boys, to schools and youth clubs.[5] Family and Youth Concern provided the following review: 'Perhaps the most unpleasant manifestation of the FPA's condom campaign so far has been their own videocassette *Danny's Big Night*, which is supposed to encourage "responsible" attitudes in boys towards contraception. This tells the story of Danny, an unpleasant and foul-mouthed youth, who takes his girlfriend Lorraine back to his house one night when his parents are away intending to "go all the way". Whilst she is out of the room he rummages through her handbag looking for a cigarette and discovers a packet of Durex (the brand name is mentioned four times). When she returns he asks her who else she is seeing. She says no one; he disbelieves her and calls her a slag. She walks out.

'She is seen discussing the episode with her girlfriends. She explains that she had to come off the pill, and took to carrying Durex as the next best thing. They commend her sensible approach. Danny is then seen discussing it the next day with his mate at work who tells him he has handled it badly and that Lorraine behaved responsibly. The video fades out as Danny apologises to Lorraine over the phone for misjudging her, and suggests that they get together again. We are left with the happy thought that this condom-based relationship is now back on course.

'Apart from the indescribably bad language, which includes every four-letter word many times over, the most unpleasant and damaging aspect of *Danny's Big Night* is its underlying assumption that it is normal for youngsters to have sex on a casual basis, and that the only important issue is avoiding conception. No mention is made of the medical, social and emotional hazards of early sex; nor is there any suggestion that boys and girls might be able to enjoy each other's company, and actually get interested in each other, for any other reason. Surprisingly, perhaps, for the relentlessly trendy FPA, the video is rabidly sexist in its attitudes. As far as the boys are concerned, girls exist to satisfy their appetites and for no other reason. Girls are referred to throughout as birds, slags and cows.'[6]

In March 1985 the FPA issued a statement asserting its belief that sex education should be taught as part of the school curriculum, with the aims of providing information and increasing understanding, promoting responsible behaviour, combating exploitation, and promoting the ability to make informed decisions. According to the statement, while ignorance about sexuality and sexual behaviour can be humiliating and harmful, 'there is no evidence that sex education increases sexual activity or is in any way damaging to children'. Moreover, as 'research has shown that the vast majority of parents are in favour of their children having sex education in schools', schools should seek the co-operation of parents. 'Speakers from outside organisations can have a place in planned sex education programmes, but the FPA sees its role as offering a training and consultancy service to teachers.'[7] The next FPA annual report (1985-86) commented that sex education needed to acknowledge the wide diversity of cultures and family structures in society. 'Those who talk of a threat to the family often do so in complete ignorance of the facts. The greatest threat is the lack of recognition that there are so many different kinds of family, that all are valid and that family stability depends not on rigid family structures but on enabling all members of families to develop and grow in caring and supportive personal and sexual relationships.'[8]

The 1986 annual report of the FPA claimed that its information service had distributed over 50 million items of literature in the past 10 years, but the report did not mention the FPA's targets to reduce the number of abortions and illegitimate births by half within the decade, launched with such fanfare 10 years before. By 1986 the FPA had conveniently forgotten these targets. So how successful was the FPA in achieving its abortion target? The number of abortions in England and Wales in 1976 was 130 thousand; by 1986 the number of abortions had increased to 172 thousand. Moreover, illegitimate births among teenagers had more than doubled, from 19.6 thousand in 1976, to 39.6 thousand a decade later. Clearly, the FPA had not achieved its targets. What had the 50 million items of literature achieved? Why was an organisation that was receiving large amounts of public money not held to account?

The AIDS threat

By 1986 the threat of AIDS was becoming a major issue. The draft circular implementing the Education Act of 1986 made it clear that schools should use sex education to warn pupils of the health risks of promiscuous sexual behaviour and provide them with factual information about AIDS. The circular reminded schools that it was important for all children to receive sex education as an essential element in the curriculum, which should be taught in a moral framework supportive of family life. This was the philosophy of the Conservative Government of Margaret Thatcher. But did they really believe that sex educators trained by the FPA would promote a moral framework that supported traditional family life?

In 1987 the newly constituted Health Education Authority (previously the Health Education Council) was made responsible for the prevention of HIV/AIDS through public education.[9] One of its first actions was to set up a national AIDS helpline which provided 24-hour confidential sexual advice. Another action was to produce a variety of leaflets, including *AIDS: What Everyone Needs to Know*, (6 million distributed within three years) *AIDS and You*, and *Safer Sex and the Condom* (3 million of each distributed within 2 years). These leaflets were made available through health education units to a range of audiences, including local libraries, schools and colleges, GP surgeries, youth clubs, social service departments and hospitals.[10] In addition, there were major educational initiatives on radio and TV. Thames TV produced an AIDS update series of 10 minute programmes, broadcast in July 1988, while BBC Radio One broadcast a series of four 45-minute documentaries *What's love got to do with it?* at weekly intervals. Briefings were offered to sections of the media and fifty agony aunts from national newspapers were circulated with a briefing pack.[11] Another initiative was an AIDS 'Speakout' in London, which consisted of a discussion with members of the general public. About a thousand young people attended four sessions hosted by a celebrity, when various sensitive issues, for example, HIV testing, homosexuality, and openness in relationships were discussed, and the national AIDS helpline advertised.[12]

In response to the AIDS threat the Government launched a nationwide 'safe sex' condom campaign in 1986-87. A television campaign, *AIDS – Don't Die of Ignorance*, used an iceberg to suggest that AIDS was a major public health threat. Joining in the fight against AIDS, Richard Branson, chairman of the Virgin Group, launched his own campaign costing in the region of £8 million, promoting condoms everywhere from supermarkets to youth clubs. Television advertisements for the group's brand, Mates, appeared on Independent Television, while the BBC put on what it called 'public information films' without mentioning the name of the product. All profits from the campaign went to the Virgin Healthcare Foundation, set up by Richard Branson to raise £5 million for AIDS projects.[13] In order to cope with the expected demand, Branson ordered 700 million condoms, five times more than the annual British market, to be sold at half price in record shops and cafes. 'His advertising and marketing emphasised eroticism, sexual playfulness and cheerfulness (women are only interested in men who are well-equipped).'[14] *Cosmopolitan* magazine joined the 'safe sex' campaign with the slogan 'Safe Girls Carry Condoms'. Schools, the media and teenage magazines were all involved in the nationwide drive to promote the 'safe sex' message.

Ronald Butt was angry that the BBC was being used as a vehicle to promote Branson's condom campaign. He argued that the advertisements were socially irresponsible and breached the BBC's obligation not to advertise. 'Still that evidently does not worry Mr Grade, who is a trustee of the foundation which will distribute to AIDS charities the profits of the latest Branson venture. At its launch he denied the BBC was advertising. He said, "The BBC is not in the business of selling (trade name omitted) condoms. We are in the business of changing attitudes to condoms and trying to get more people to use condoms, whichever make." But who appointed the BBC to "change attitudes to condoms"? Who sanctioned a quasi-advertisement which by its style is liable to encourage teenagers to assume that promiscuity is an acceptable and safe norm?' Ronald Butt concluded that young people, the targets of the campaign, were being offered a dangerous hope of security in terms which, by suggesting that sleeping around (with a condom) was perfectly all right, implicitly encouraged promiscuity. 'The BBC has been irresponsibly screening a public disservice film, and ITV too should think again about advertisements which cash in on the fear of AIDS while self-interestedly avoiding the hard truth about promiscuity.'[15]

Local Authorities promote homosexuality

Meanwhile the Greater London Council (GLC), under Ken Livingstone, had been actively campaigning for greater rights for lesbians and gay men. The document *Changing the World – A London Charter for Gay and Lesbian Rights*, published by the GLC in 1985, became the standard for left wing councils. The charter defined heterosexism as similar to racism and sexism, and encouraged positive attitudes towards homosexuality.[16] It declared that 'lesbian and gay pupils and students should see reflected in the curriculum the richness and diversity of homosexual experience not just negative images... sex education... should not attempt to pretend that homosexuality, bisexuality and lesbianism do not exist, or to present a negative description of them'.[17] The document *Tackling Heterosexism – a handbook of Lesbian Rights*, produced by the women's committee of the GLC in 1986, stated that schools should make information available on 'the variety of possible relationships, e.g. celibate, bisexual, homosexual, and it should not be inferred that these are inferior choices'. Secondary school education should not imply that one sexuality is preferable or superior to another. 'Lesbian-gay sex does not lead to pregnancy, and is therefore a very acceptable option...'[18]

The Hackney Teachers' Association endorsed a policy on anti-heterosexism, which was defined as a belief that heterosexuality is the only natural and normal kind of sexuality. Expressing heterosexist views would lead to a verbal warning from the head teacher.[19] Haringey Council decided to run a positive images campaign, and in June 1986 sent a letter to all secondary school heads informing them that it was establishing a fund for curriculum projects from nursery, through primary and secondary education, to further education which was specifically designed to promote positive images of gays and lesbians. Parents in the borough had not been consulted and were outraged at the idea. This led to the formation of a Parents Action Group to oppose the Council's initiative. When parents tried to put their case in a public meeting of the Council's Education Committee they were prevented from speaking, and punched and spat upon by gay rights activists bussed into the meeting from all over London.[20]

As a response to the excesses of the radical inner London boroughs, in November 1986 the Earl of Halsbury introduced a Bill in the House of Lords (Local Authority Act 1986 Amendment Bill) with the objective of preventing local authorities promoting homosexuality in schools. Lord Halsbury said that the purpose of his Bill was to prevent a local authority from giving financial or other assistance to any person for the purpose of publishing or promoting homosexuality as an acceptable family relationship. He said that he had had overwhelming support for the Bill from all over the country. 'Only two dissenting voices have been raised against the Bill. One is (surprise, surprise) that of the most reverend Primate the Archbishop of York.'[21]

Lord Campbell said that the presentation of positive images of homosexuality involved a direct attack on heterosexual family life. The attack came in two ways. 'One is that they attack the paternalistic discipline of an ordinary family as being totally wrong because children should be totally free. Another is to teach children that in some way the reproductive potential of the heterosexual relationship constitutes a positive social mischief in an overpopulated world. In this age of tolerance, have we not really reached the intolerable where parents seeking to protect their children from moral corruption are exposed to abuse, ridicule, threats of violence and even visitations of violence? Parental rights are virtually denied and challenged; and what is more, the traditional ethos of local government has been traduced.' He reminded the House that the Inner London Education Authority (ILEA) had set up a project on relationships and sexuality in 1984, which included as one of its stated aims the development of materials that presented positive images of lesbians and gay men. 'It is common ground that children are exposed at this moment to corruptive influences as a matter of local government policy.'[22]

Lady Saltoun was horrified by what was going on in certain schools. She quoted from the GLC's charter for gay and lesbian rights, *Changing the World*. Under

220

the heading 'Tell it in the Classroom' the charter said 'there should be openly understood procedures for complaints by college students and school pupils and students about heterosexism as about racism and sexism. Parents of lesbian and gay students should be allowed to complain about heterosexism.' She had looked through *The Playbook for Kids about Sex.* 'I cannot bring myself to quote from it. As a mother and grandmother, I was more than appalled, I was horrified. I have said before in this House that I believe corrupting children in this way is one of the worst crimes that anyone can commit, and I make no apology for repeating it. I believe that we in Parliament have a duty to protect young people from this kind of pernicious and harmful indoctrination.'[23] Lord Bellwin wondered whether 'everyone knows that in the London boroughs of Islington and Lambeth the word "family" is proscribed. It is not permitted to be used. The term to be used is "social unit". One might ask: have we all gone mad?'[24]

Baroness Cox supported the Bill for two reasons. 'The first is an urgent need to put a stop to the use of public money to promote teaching and other policies in our schools which are causing such grave offence to many parents and members of the public; and, secondly, because of the harassment and intimidation meted out to those parents who have tried to protect their children's interests.' She said that the balance had swung to the active promotion of positive images of homosexuality and outright attacks on the concept of the normality of heterosexuality. These developments were taking place not only in Haringey but also in other parts of London and other parts of the country. A book called *Tackling Heterosexism*, which had been brought out by nine London boroughs, recommended that the Inner London Education Authority and other local education authorities should 'put resources into developing materials and changing curricula in order effectively to challenge heterosexism in lessons at all stages in the education system from primary school up to colleges of further education, and that a variety of materials be developed, for example videos for use in lessons which would raise the issues of heterosexism and present lesbians in a positive light'. She referred to the publication *The Milkman's on his Way*, which described in very explicit detail intercourse between a 16-year-old boy and his adult, male, homosexual lover. She mentioned that parents had been subjected to gross intimidation in ways that were totally unacceptable. 'When parents have attended council meetings they have been harassed, spat upon, had eggs thrown at them and have even been urinated upon. They have been denied the right to put their views. After one meeting they were followed home and during the night their cars were vandalised. They have received numerous abusive phone calls including death threats.'[25]

Lord Denning wholeheartedly supported the Bill. 'If this Bill passes, it will give an immediate remedy to stop local authorities using their funds, if I may say so, for homosexual purposes.' He then quoted from the Bible. 'I looked up the book of Genesis again. "But the men of Sodom were wicked and sinners before the Lord exceedingly." And the Lord destroyed Sodom and Gomorrah. When I read the article in *The Times* this morning, I thought of altering those words and saying:

"But the councillors of the borough of Haringey were gay, and corrupted the children of the borough exceedingly." And, I should like to add, after this Bill, "The Lords destroyed those councillors".'[26]

Lord Skelmersdale spoke on behalf of the Government. He said that it was extremely disturbing to see some of the material made available by local authorities. 'The Government believes unequivocally that to promote homosexuality as a normal way of life – to anyone, let alone children – is to go too far and to create the serious risk of undermining those normal family relationships which are the very fabric of our society... The Banquo's ghost haunting this debate has been the connection with AIDS.' He said the Government was firmly committed to the provision of appropriate sex education in schools, and equally to the need for effective action to prevent irresponsible and inappropriate teaching in this field. Full control over the content and organisation of sex education was to be placed in the hands of the new-style school governing bodies. 'The Government's policy is that schools should be prepared to address the issue of homosexuality, provided they approach it in a balanced and factual manner, appropriate to the maturity of the pupils concerned... As the Government's public education campaign about AIDS makes clear, ignorance is the greatest ally of this terrible disease.' But it was because the distinction between proper teaching about homosexuality, and the improper advocacy of homosexuality could not be drawn sufficiently clearly in legislation, in the Government's view the Bill was unnecessary.[27] The Bill was read a second time and then sidelined by being sent to a Committee of the whole House.

Early in 1987 a number of Labour-controlled councils, in the name of sexual equality, were planning to ensure as a matter of policy that schools taught children positive images about homosexuality. Many parents in Haringey were extremely worried that the Council's sex education policies in schools were promoting homosexuality. Mrs Pat Headd, chairman of Haringey Parents Rights Group, told more than 150 parents that it had engaged a law firm and was seeking more than £50,000.[28] Meanwhile in Ealing Council a report on sexual equality, presented to the education committee, recommended that provision should be made for lessons about homosexuality in high schools and colleges.[29] Mr Harry Greenway, MP for Ealing North, was alarmed by the actions of the Council and urged the Government to ensure that the Council did not pressurise teachers into asserting that homosexuality and lesbianism were as normal as heterosexuality.[30]

Mrs Doreen Smith, a teacher from the ILEA, told the Professional Association of Teachers conference at Exeter University that teachers at an inner London primary school had drawn up a policy which suggested punishing children and staff who revealed heterosexist attitudes. Schools in some areas were inundated with books, videos and other resources advocating homosexuality as a viable, alternative way of life for children to consider. She mentioned a recent issue of *Gen*, a women's rights magazine, published by the GLC, that was devoted to challenging heterosexism. Although the ILEA had withdrawn the magazine it was still circulating in outer

London boroughs.[31] An example of the type of material being used was the book *Jenny Lives with Eric and Martin* which contained an illustration of a five-year-old girl sitting in bed with her homosexual father and his lover.[32]

Section 28

The Government of Margaret Thatcher was now deeply concerned about the activities of many left wing Labour councils, and decided to take action to prevent local authorities from promoting homosexuality. Mr David Wilshire, a Conservative backbencher, tabled a new clause into the Local Government Bill, clause 28, during the committee stage. The purpose of the clause was to prohibit local authorities from the promotion of homosexuality by teaching or by publishing material. It also prohibited local authorities from funding bodies that promoted homosexuality. Dame Jill Knight, one of the sponsors of the new clause, said that the major concern was that small children as young as five when they start school had actually had homosexuality thrust at them. 'There has been a promotional exercise on very young children and this worries us.'[33] In Parliament the Labour Party, aware of genuine public concern around the issue, decided to approve the clause without a vote. Mr Michael Howard cited books recommended by Haringey Council which called for teachers to be barred from wearing wedding rings and which were 'glorying in detailed descriptions of the homosexual act'.[34] And so clause 28, which prevents local authorities from promoting homosexuality, became law. Section 28 was repealed by the Scottish Parliament in 2000 and the UK Parliament voted for repeal in England and Wales in 2003.

There was, of course, an enormous irony in the Government's action aimed at preventing local authorities funding the promotion of homosexuality, when it was itself funding the Health Education Council and the FPA that were doing exactly the same thing. The Health Education Council, which claimed to be the largest school curriculum and development agency in Britain, was promoting a philosophy of sexuality that was sympathetic towards a homosexual lifestyle. Its list of publications in 1985 contained numerous books and teaching aids that presented homosexuality in a positive light.[35] Examples include, *Prejudice and Pride: Discrimination against Gay people in Modern Britain,* published by Routledge; *Attacks on Gay People:* a report of the Commission on Discrimination of the Campaign for Homosexual Equality; *We Speak for ourselves – experiences in Homosexual Counselling,* produced by SPCK; *Homosexuality, Facts and Fallacies,* a leaflet about lesbians, and *Framed Youth – Revenge of the Teenage Perverts,* a video made by the Lesbian and Gay Youth Video Project, published by the Campaign for Homosexual Equality; *Breaking the Silence: Gay Teenagers Speak for Themselves* by the Joint Council for Gay Teenagers; *Homosexuality: Time to Tell the Truth* by Leonard Barnet; *Society and the Healthy Homosexual* by George Weinberg; *Understanding Homosexuality,* a leaflet produced by the Mothers' Union; *About Men... and Men,* a video distributed by Concord Films Council; and of course, *Make it Happy,* by Jane Cousins.

Sex Education Forum

In 1987 another pressure group, The Sex Education Forum, based in the National Children's Bureau, was established. It acted as an umbrella body to bring together 40 national organisations involved in sex and relationships education. The Forum claims to have three functions. First, it aims to set the climate for sex education through national and local policy development. Second, it disseminates information on sex education by means of its newsletter, *Sex education matters*, and also by its website and regular publications. Thirdly, it develops models of good practice. The Forum believes that sex education should be an entitlement for all children, young people and adults. Sex education should meet the needs of boys as well as girls, and of those who are heterosexual, and those who are lesbian, gay or bisexual. In 2001 the Forum published *Just Say No! to Abstinence Education*, which is based on a sex education study tour of the USA, and purports to show the ineffectiveness of abstinence sex education. Included among the membership of the Forum are the following organisations: AIDS Care and Education Training (ACET), Barnado's, Brook Advisory Centres, Church of England Board of Education, FPA, Families and Friends of Lesbians and Gays, Health Education Authority, Lesbian and Gay Christian Movement, National Children's Bureau, National Society for the Prevention of Cruelty to Children (NSPCC), One plus One, RELATE, Royal College of Nursing, Society for Health Promotion Officers and Education Specialists, Terrence Higgins Trust, The Children's Society and the Methodist Church. The Forum's website provides children who need an urgent answer to a sexual problem with a list of helpful organisations, including Brook, the FPA, the Lesbian and Gay Switchboard, Childline, the National AIDS helpline and Sexwise.

AIDS was now firmly on the political agenda. A Government working party calculated that 'at the end of 1987 there were probably between 20,000 and 50,000 persons infected with HIV in England and Wales', and estimated that there would be between 10,000 and 30,000 AIDS cases diagnosed by the end of 1992.[36]

The Minister of Health, David Mellor, during a visit to seriously ill patients in a leading London hospital, was warned that Britain faced an AIDS epidemic of massive proportions. The co-ordinator of AIDS services, Dr Brian Gazzard, told Mr Mellor: 'We are still seeing a doubling in the number of cases every year, and the figures will become horrific as the years go by. There will be a huge explosion in the number of cases.' Experts estimated that the true number of people infected with the HIV virus in the UK was between 50 and 100 thousand.[37] Adding to the panic was a prediction by the Office of Population, Censuses and Surveys that by the year 2000 AIDS would have killed 100 thousand men in England and Wales.[38]

The first World AIDS Day was held on 1 December 1988. The Minister of Health declared, 'Apathy must not rule, many people who should know better still refuse to accept the implications that the HIV epidemic has for everyone who is sexually active.' To fight what he called 'the greatest threat to public health this century' the Minister announced that £14 million was being made available for health education campaigns.[39]

A symposium in London in November 1989 considered the current and future spread of HIV and AIDS in the UK. The Chief Medical Officer, Sir Donald Acheson, estimated that 'in total we have between 3,000 and 4,000 people we know of in this country who have either been infected as a result of heterosexual intercourse, or by other means but who are of heterosexual habit, and are probably infectious throughout their lifetime. Those are the ones we know about, but we can only guess what figure we should multiply by to get the real figure. Perhaps it is twice, perhaps it is three times, perhaps it is as much as five times.' He concluded: 'I believe few will leave this hall today unconvinced that HIV and AIDS are indeed a serious public health problem. AIDS is indeed unprejudiced, and can kill anyone whatever their sexual orientation or their age. And let us make certain that neither we nor our children die of ignorance or indeed as a result of blind prejudice.'[40]

The Minister of Health, Virginia Bottomley, said that 'we have to ensure that there is more enlightenment and less prejudice and that together we can work to tackle this major threat to modern life... If unchecked, AIDS has the potential not this year or next year perhaps, but in the longer term to touch every family in the country... Some claim that AIDS is not a problem for heterosexuals, and that money spent educating the general population and finding out more about the spread of infection within it, is money wasted. In the light of today's Symposium no respectable policy-maker can accept this narrow view... We must establish the facts, we must plan and we must educate.' The Minister announced £43 million for AIDS research and £44 million for the development of a major education campaign. 'This year we have allocated over £10 million for AIDS public education to the Health Education Authority.' In addition to the resources for research and public education, a further £130 million was provided to the NHS for AIDS treatment and £7 million for social services departments.[41]

The Government's anxiety about AIDS was inspired by the official estimates that by the mid-1990s there would be at least 10 thousand new HIV infections every year. But these were wild overestimates, encouraged by a vociferous AIDS lobby, and it is no surprise that the predicted AIDS epidemic in the UK has never materialised. (In 1992, the actual number of diagnosed HIV infections was 2,741, of which 780 were acquired through heterosexual intercourse. However, of the 780 cases acquired heterosexually, only 143 were exposed to the infection in the UK, while 627 were exposed abroad, mainly in Africa.[42] In other words, 80 per cent of heterosexually acquired cases were imported into the UK, mostly from Africa.) Although the risk of acquiring AIDS through heterosexual intercourse in the UK was remote, the slogan 'Anyone can get AIDS' was a powerful propaganda weapon in the hands of those who were intent on promoting a condom culture under the guise of the 'safer sex' message.

In August 1990 the British Safety Council launched 'national condom week' with a rallying cry to women that they should buy and carry condoms instead of relying on their partner. The director of the Council, James Tye, said that if women wanted to reduce the risk of infection from sexually transmitted diseases they should make sure their partner always used a condom during intercourse, irrespective of any other method of contraception being used. The aim of 'national condom week' was not only to increase the personal and social acceptance of the condom, but also to educate people into modifying high-risk behaviour and to become part of the condom-friendly generation. He explained that casual sex is risky and until a vaccine was available using a condom could be a life-saver. In its enthusiasm the Council published a ten-point condom safety code, warning of the pitfalls of failing to use contraceptives correctly. The safety code encouraged both partners to learn how to put on and take off a condom properly, and warned that only condoms bearing the British Standards Institution kite mark should be bought.[43]

A new manual on sex education *Knowing me, knowing you*, which gave teachers advice on telling primary children about contraception, sexual penetration, mastur- bation, homosexuality and the transmission of AIDS was published in 1990. However, the general secretary of the Professional Association of Teachers, Peter Dawson, was not impressed with the new sex education tool. He said that it was a corrupting influence: 'Children of that age cannot challenge these propositions – it is a form of indoctrination.' However the authors, Pete Sanders and Liz Swinden, defended their sex manual as a counterblast against the ill-informed and haphazard way very young children find out about sex. Liz Swinden, a health education adviser in inner London, denied that the manual could encourage sexual activity among very young pupils.[44]

Concern about the growing number of abortions persuaded the Royal College of Obstetricians and Gynaecologists (RCOG) to set up a working party 'to review the education and services related to contraception in view of the continuing high rate of unplanned and unwanted pregnancy'. The Royal College was particularly concerned because a previous working party (page 137), which considered the same topic in 1972, had recommended that the provision of a comprehensive contraception service in the NHS was the answer to the problem of unplanned teenage pregnancies. Yet the recommendation had not worked. The numbers and rates of teenage abortions had continued to rise for more than 20 years. The report of the Royal College, *Unplanned Pregnancy* (1991) commented, 'We are particu- larly concerned about unplanned pregnancy in the teenager, which points directly to the lack of education in schools on the importance of family planning and related matters.' The first recommendation of the new working party was to improve sex education. The report said that sex education should concentrate on teaching children to discuss sexual matters openly without embarrassment, so that they would later be able to talk about contraception and their sexual needs more easily. 'Young people may know about the biology of sex but have rarely been given the vocabulary and skills they need to communicate with each other about this aspect of their lives.'

The report continues, 'We believe that this would lead to a more open and less guilt-ridden attitude to sexuality that, in turn, would result in the better use of contraception and reduction in both unplanned and unwanted pregnancies. Easy access to effective contraception is an essential factor in preventing unwanted pregnancy, but, to use contraception, couples have to feel that their sexual behaviour is legitimate and have to be able to communicate about sexual matters so that contraception can be planned.'[45] The report recommended that all schools needed one or more teachers with special training in sex education. 'Sex education would improve if a specialist teacher in each school co-ordinated the teaching of health education, including education about relationships, sexuality and contraception.'[46]

Dr James le Fanu, medical correspondent of the *Daily Telegraph*, responded to the report of the Royal College. He argued that the liberal sexual attitudes promoted by the RCOG, and organisations like it, might be part of the problem rather than its solution. An analysis of the statistics found in the RCOG's report revealed a curious paradox in the rising incidence of teenage abortion over the past 20 years. 'In the first year of the Abortion Act of 1968, there were 4,000 abortions among the under-20s, a figure which, two years later, had risen to 15,000. In an attempt to combat this rising trend, the RCOG in 1972 called for more sex education and universal free access to contraceptive services for all women to be provided by a network of nationally funded family planning clinics. These were set up in the following years, but by 1977 the number of teenage abortions had reached 28,000. Since then the numbers have continued to rise and the most recent statistics reveal there are now 40,000 teenage abortions a year. It thus appears that sex education and universal access to contraception, far from reducing the numbers of abortions, has actually increased them.'[47]

In a letter to *The Times*, John Kelly also challenged the recommendations of the Royal College report. 'For over 20 years explicit sex education and freely available contraception, irrespective of age or parental consent, have played a huge part in pushing up the rate of teenage abortions. As Dr Judith Bury of the Brook stated in 1981, "There is overwhelming evidence, that contrary to what you might expect, the availability of contraception leads to an increase in the abortion rate." Yet Dr Bury is one of the authors of this latest report. Surely the kind of sex education advocated has had a lengthy trial and has proved not only ineffective but also harmful; certainly it is time that sex education was improved in schools. But not with more of the same. Real responsibility for ourselves and others is not achieved by treating youngsters as "units of reproduction". Now is the time to promote chastity before marriage as a healthy, rewarding lifestyle.'[48]

The FPA's *Manifesto for Sexual Health and Family Planning* outlined its strategy for the 1990s. According to the manifesto the FPA had built up a respected information service which each year produced four million leaflets on family planning methods and dealt with tens of thousands of enquiries. 'It is now widely recognised that family planning will only be fully effective if people have adequate information and knowledge about reproductive health and are comfortable with

227

their sexuality. They will then be better equipped to make *informed choices* about their fertility and to enjoy safer sex… The FPA seeks to promote *informed choice* not only by ensuring people have accurate information, awareness and knowledge of sexual health, but also by encouraging appropriate social measures, policies and legislation…[49] Sex education for all must be a priority. If people are to enjoy *positive* sexual health, they need knowledge and awareness from which to make *informed choices*, and the confidence to express their sexuality. They also need to know how to avoid unplanned pregnancy…[50] Many teenagers are poorly informed about sex and contraception and are frequently bombarded with dubious messages from the media… Sex education is vital if young people are to be enabled to deal with issues of relationships and sexuality, sexual orientation, safer sex and contraception. Lack of early sex education allows myths and ignorance to persist'[51] [all italics mine]. In the strategy the FPA committed itself to campaigning for improved accessibility and availability of services in sexual health and family planning, to raising awareness and knowledge by means of public education and information programmes, to encouraging the development of sex education for young people, and to developing resources and training for parents, among other things.[52]

The FPA had developed strong links with teenage magazines such as *Just 17* and was using these channels to educate young people about contraceptive methods. In 1990 the FPA was actively campaigning in the media 'to raise awareness of emergency contraception and to emphasise that women can start taking the emergency pill up to 72 hours after unprotected intercourse, not just on the morning after. If more couples knew about this very effective method, and how to get it, there would be fewer unwanted pregnancies and abortions.'[53]

The Brook helpline for teenagers was launched in February 1991 with funding from the Department of Health. Widely publicised in the media, youth clubs, schools and colleges, in its first year it received nearly nine thousand calls. In the following year Brook teamed up with the magazine *Just 17* to run four separate helplines in order to provide a service streamlined to the specific information needs of teenagers. Advertised every week in *Just 17*, the helplines had proved popular, taking some five thousand calls over a three-month period. The greatest proportion of calls were about missed periods (34 per cent), followed by emergency contraception (25 per cent), general contraceptive advice (23 per cent) and abortion (18 per cent).[54] Brook was delighted with the response, and in the following year teamed up with *Just 17* and *More* to launch two new lines, namely, 'Are you ready for sex?' and 'The condom line'. According to Brook the new lines were proving to be enormously popular. 'Separate lines under specific headings appear on the problem pages of each issue and attracted around 35 thousand calls during 1992-93. A breakdown of the calls shows the greatest interest to be in information about emergency contraception, although the younger readers of *Just 17* appear more concerned about missed periods… An increase in calls to Brook's central office from young teenagers wanting to talk about starting a relationship suggests the helpline is a useful way of referring them to an appropriate service.'[55]

The Health Minister, Virginia Bottomley, announced a review of NHS family planning services in July 1991. The NHS executive expected to see specific progress on family planning. In a press release the Health Minister commented, 'We are also funding development work in a number of family planning areas, such as teenage pregnancy counselling, consumer surveys and the assessment of local needs for family planning. Family planning services are – and continue to be – a valuable part of our health service. They play a key role in helping to prevent the distress of unwanted pregnancies.' A priority was to ensure that GPs and family planning clinics were more effectively integrated. The public needed reliable information about family planning and sexual health. 'We are working with the FPA, Brook and others about ways of achieving this. The NHS also has a role in helping to inform and educate people about family planning. Health authorities should consider, in consultation with local educational interests, how they might help with sex education programmes – particularly in school.'

The Government was spending nearly £100 million a year on family planning in England – an estimated 33 per cent increase in real terms since 1979. In addition, over £500 thousand from Government funds was being provided to voluntary organisations such as the FPA and Brook.[56] The Conservative Government of Margaret Thatcher was totally committed to family planning and sex education.

Endnotes

1 Hansard, Lords debate, 10 March 1986, cc473-476, Lord Winstanley
2 Ibid. cc482-486, Viscount Buckmaster
3 Ibid. cc492-497, Baroness Trumpington
4 *The Times*, 16 June 1986, letter, Lord Buckmaster
5 *The Times*, 30 March 1985
6 Family and Youth Concern, Family Bulletin no 45, Autumn 1985
7 Family Planning Association, Annual Report 1984-85, p9
8 Family Planning Association, Annual Report 1985-86, p3
9 Health Education Authority, AIDS Programme, First Annual Report: October 1987 to September 1988, p5
10 Ibid. pp10-11
11 Ibid. p15
12 Ibid. p11
13 *The Times*, 11 November 1987, Condom campaign
14 Cate Haste, *Rules of Desire*, Chatto & Windus, London, 1992, p279
15 *The Times*, 19 November 1987, A BBC public disservice, Ronald Butt
16 *Changing the World – A London Charter for Gay and Lesbian Rights*, Greater London Council, 1985, p7
17 Ibid. p18
18 *Tackling Heterosexism – a handbook of Lesbian Rights*, Greater London Council, 1986, cited from *Sexuality and the Church*, Action for Biblical Witness to Our Nation, 1987, 'The present context of the debate', Tony Higton, p14
19 *Sexuality and the Church*, Action for Biblical Witness to Our Nation, 1987, 'The present context of the debate', Tony Higton, p14
20 *The Times*, 18 December 1986, A grass-roots rebellion, leading article
21 Hansard, Lords debate, 18 December 1986, cc310-311
22 Ibid. cc311-314

23 Ibid. cc316-317
24 Ibid. c318
25 Ibid. cc320-323
26 Ibid. cc324-325
27 Ibid. cc332-337
28 *The Times*, 23 January 1987, Parents take action
29 *The Times*, 25 February 1987, Council's gay move
30 *The Times*, 24 February 1987
31 *The Times*, 29 July 1987, Schools to punish sexists
32 *The Times*, 12 August 1987, Gay book is recalled
33 *The Times*, 8 December 1987, Government to ban schools' promotion of homosexuality
34 *The Times*, 9 December 1987, Homosexual Bill wins Labour vote
35 Health Education Council, Personal Relationships, publications and teaching aids, revised 1985
36 *Short-term prediction of HIV Infection and AIDS in England and Wales*, Report of a working group chaired by David Cox, HMSO, 1988, p41
37 *The Times*, 27 October 1988, Mellor is warned of huge AIDS explosion, Thomas Prentice
38 *The Times*, 11 October 1989, 200,000 men 'will die of AIDS within 30 years', David Walker
39 *The Sunday Telegraph*, 29 November 1992, Nationalised sex. The AIDS epidemic has not materialised but a huge industry has, James Le Fanu
40 *HIV & AIDS, an assessment of current and future spread in the UK*, Proceedings of symposium held on 24th November 1989, Health Education Authority, 1990, p37
41 Ibid. p39
42 *HIV and AIDS in the UK in 2001*, Communicable Disease Surveillance Centre, Autumn 2002
43 *The Times*, 14 August 1990, National condom week opens with rallying cry to women
44 *The Times*, 31 October 1990, School sex manual under fire from union
45 *Unplanned Pregnancy*, Report of the RCOG Working Party, The Royal College of Obstetricians and Gynaecologists, September 1991, p57
46 Ibid. p58
47 *Sunday Telegraph*, 6 October 1991, Review: Abortion and the plight of teenagers, James le Fanu
48 *The Times*, 11 September 1991, letter, Mr John Kelly
49 *Family Planning Association Manifesto for Sexual Health & Family Planning*, 1990, p3
50 Ibid. p4
51 Ibid. p5
52 *Family Planning Association Manifesto for Sexual Health & Family Planning*, 1990
53 Family Planning Association, Annual Report 1990, p6
54 Brook Advisory Centre, Annual Report 1991/92, p3
55 Brook Advisory Centre, Annual Report 1992/93, p7
56 Press release, Virginia Bottomley announces review of NHS family planning services, Department of Health, H91/359, July 1991

Chapter 16

'Safer sex' campaign

Promoting a condom culture; teaching parents
to talk about sex with their children

In 1991 the Department of Health claimed that AIDS was increasing at a faster
rate among women and heterosexuals than among any other group. The statistics
showed that the number contracting AIDS by heterosexual intercourse rose from
92 to 150, an increase of 63 per cent, during the twelve months to June. Cases
among homosexuals continued to dominate the figures, but the rate of rise was smaller,
numbers increasing from 815 to 956 (17 per cent). According to the Department of
Health, 'These figures underline the importance of the Government's campaign
to educate the general population, particularly the young and sexually active, about
the continuing danger of HIV infection.'[1] What the Department of Health did not
say was that the vast majority of new heterosexual cases of AIDS were actually
imported into the UK by new immigrants from sub-Saharan Africa. Yet such was
the AIDS hysteria that Barnardo's, the childcare charity, produced a leaflet for
children aged eleven and older – *What Can I Do About AIDS?* – which explained
the disease in simple terms, how it spread and where to go for further advice.[2]

The death from AIDS of rock star Freddie Mercury raised a great deal of public
comment. Dr Patrick Dixon, the director of AIDS Care Education and Training
(ACET), a charity which runs a campaign of AIDS education in schools, said that
the admission by Mercury that he had the disease would save more lives than all the
statistics about the epidemic. 'We may be able to protect a generation by convincing
children in the classroom that AIDS is for real. It is often said that a million deaths
is a statistic, but one death is a tragedy.'[3] A huge crowd of young people, an
estimated 72 thousand, attended a rock concert in Wembley Stadium in memory
of Freddie to raise money to fight AIDS. Elizabeth Taylor gave the crowd
straightforward advice on the value of condoms, 'Look at yourself, look at how

many you are. In just two short weeks, there will be as many new infections as there are people here tonight. Protect yourselves. Every time you have sex, use a condom. Every single time. Straight sex, gay sex, bisexual sex, use a condom whoever you are. And if you use drugs, don't share a needle.'[4]

The Health Education Authority's campaign slogan 'AIDS does not discriminate' was aimed at convincing the public that all were at equal risk of the dreaded disease. The sex education lobby, claiming that AIDS was the largest public health threat of the twentieth century, was being provided with large amounts of money for its 'safer sex' propaganda. The threat was portrayed as so serious that it was necessary to educate all secondary schoolchildren about the dangers of HIV/AIDS and the techniques of 'safer sex', lest they 'die from ignorance'.

On World AIDS Day 1991 Dr Patrick Dixon said that although an epidemic had not yet started in Britain, 'it is very worrying that there has been a reversion to high-risk behaviour in heterosexuals and young homosexuals in the past 12 months which has resulted in soaring rates of sexually transmitted diseases such as gonorrhoea. Will there be a heterosexual epidemic? Yes. I find it unbelievable that anyone can possibly still think that we are going to be immune from a spread among heterosexuals'. But Dr Susil Gupta, a lecturer in sociology at the City of London Polytechnic, disagreed. He explained that AIDS was restricted to certain specific social and geographic communities and did not present a threat to the general population. He observed that in 1987 the Government had estimated that AIDS deaths and new infections would be running at 100 thousand each year by the mid-1990s. In 1988 the estimate was reduced to 30 thousand and in 1989 the Government was predicting a figure of 13 thousand. A more recent report reduced the estimate to 6,500 deaths per year.[5] A decade later, the national strategy for sexual health and HIV showed that in the year 2000 there were around 3 thousand newly reported cases, and that three-quarters of the infections that were acquired through heterosexual contact were from abroad, in other words, imported into the UK. The epidemic predicted by the Department of Health had proved to be a gross exaggeration.

In February 1992 the Secretary of State for Education and Science, Kenneth Clarke, laid before parliament a statutory order for a revised national curriculum for science which made it compulsory for 11 to 14-year-olds to be taught about HIV/AIDS. A booklet, *HIV and AIDS: a guide for the Education Service*, was sent to all schools. It explained that pupils should be taught that HIV could be caught through drug misuse and infected blood products and through risky sexual activities. Teachers were instructed to avoid giving the impression that the disease was confined to high-risk groups such as homosexual men.[6] The guide described casual sex, multiple sexual partners, sexual experimentation and various unusual sex practices in explicit detail, saying that they were activities which children should avoid.

In a debate in the Lords, the Earl of Liverpool asked whether 11-year-olds were ready for such compulsory and explicit education. The Government spokesman, Baroness Denton of Wakefield, responded that, 'Given that HIV constitutes probably the most serious threat to public health this century, it is our view that children should learn about it at an age when the majority are sufficiently mature to understand.' Baroness Phillips asked whether the Government seriously wanted to defend a pamphlet 'which explicitly describes oral sex, which cannot be of any assistance in the subject, and may be totally misunderstood'. Lord Elton said the information was being put forward in an amoral context. However, Lord Ennals informed the House that the position taken by the Minister 'is warmly supported by the Family Planning Association, the National AIDS Trust and Health Education Authority'.[7] Family and Youth Concern was highly critical of the Department of Education's advice, which it believed would alert children to perverted practices of which they might not be aware. The advice contained in the booklet was described as crude, inaccurate and condom-based by Valerie Riches.[8] In the House of Lords, Baroness Cox criticised the teacher's guide for its complete lack of moral content.

As part of the AIDS sex education initiative the BBC Open University team produced the video, *Your Choice for Life*, for the Department of Education and Science. The video, aimed at children aged 14 to 16, was publicised by the Health Education Authority, and distributed free to all secondary schools. The video followed the usual ideology of the sex education movement, suggesting a 'positive' and 'healthy' approach. The assumption that ran through the video was that its viewers were promiscuous, and that it was only by using condoms that AIDS could be controlled. The video exhorted children to 'be prepared for the time when you find someone you want to make love with'. The words marriage, husband and wife did not feature. Instead young people were treated to the mechanics of erection and the unrolling of the condom. It was, in fact, a 24-minute advert for condoms.

It was not surprising that the first national strategy for health, the *Health of the Nation*, published in 1992, identified sexual health as one of the key priority areas for action. The strategy included two national targets for improving sexual health. The first was to reduce the incidence of gonorrhoea by at least 20 per cent by 1995, and the second was to reduce the rate of conceptions among the under-16s by at least 50 per cent by the year 2000. The full weight of the NHS, working with local authorities and voluntary organisations, was directed towards achieving these targets. All health authorities were required to produce a sexual health strategy, and Brook reported that the number of its branches, funded by health authorities, had almost doubled. 'This expansion has been accompanied by a proliferation of other birth control services specifically designed for young people, as health authorities develop their strategies to meet the *Health of the Nation* targets.'[9]

The Health Education Authority's report, *Sexual Health* (1994), announced that sex education would play an important role in helping to reach these targets.[10] Sex education would persuade teenagers to practise 'safer sex' by using condoms. And this was particularly good news for the producers of condoms, who, in 1992, were already selling 150 million condoms per year, a 110 per cent increase since 1980. *Sexual Health* made the point that 'the condom market has a highly developed retail distribution network and one that has been expanded in recent years by the growth in the condom market and by efforts to make condoms more accessible to consumers'.[11] Condoms were available from chemist shops, super-markets, vending machines in pubs, family planning clinics, drugstores, garages, by mail order, and from convenience stores. And there was no shortage of money when it came to advertising contraceptives, with most of the effort directed towards the promotion of condoms. In 1986 the expenditure on promoting condoms was £173,000, rising to over £1.5 million in 1987 and 1988. Moreover, since 1987 the Health Education Authority had been allocated about £10 million per year by the Government for the promotion of sexual health. In the financial year 1992/93 nearly £4 million was spent on the mass media promoting the 'safer sex' message.[12] The Health Education Authority believed that 'a sexual culture which encourages teenagers to ask for, and use, contraception is as important as issues of access and quality of services'.[13]

Clearly, the Health Education Authority saw itself engaged in a mission to change the sexual culture of the country, and it had the full backing of the Government and a vast amount of public money to achieve this end. Needless to say, neither of the *Health of the Nation* targets were met. Indeed, despite the massive 'safer sex' campaign, the second half of the 1990s was characterised by an epidemic of sexually transmitted diseases among young people, and still no reduction in the teenage pregnancy or abortion rate.

The Education Act of 1993 made it clear that 'sex education must be provided in such a manner as to encourage young people to have regard to moral consider-ations and the value of family life'.[14] It became a legal requirement for state schools to provide sex education, including information on HIV/AIDS and other sexually transmitted diseases, from September 1994. In primary schools the basic biology of sex was to be covered in science in the national curriculum. Any further sex education was optional, and it was up to school governors to decide whether or not to provide any more. If they decided to provide more sex education, 'they must publish a written policy on the content and organisation of the sex education, including information about the right of withdrawal'. Middle schools deemed to be secondary were legally required to provide sex education for all pupils and to publish a policy. There were no legal requirements regarding independent schools.

Encouraging parents to talk about sex

In March 1993 the junior Minister of Health, Tom Sackville, announced on BBC radio that Britain was a nation in which parents were reluctant to talk to teenage children about sex. He said that parental failure meant that many young people were entirely unprepared for adulthood, and this was reflected in the high rate of teenage pregnancies. 'Mr Sackville's solution – announced yesterday on Radio 4's *World at One*, is to face up to these figures, learn from them, and take a positive step. This step, given the consent of school governors and parent-teacher associa-tions, would be to hand out free condoms to pupils over the age of 16.'[15]

Addressing Brook's national conference, Tom Sackville again identified the British reluctance to talk about sex as a key factor responsible for the country's high teenage pregnancy rate. He said that one of the results of the 'great silence' on sexual and moral issues was that messages simply did not reach young people. 'Everyone is too embarrassed about the propriety of talking to young people about sexual health. The under-16s are a particular problem.'[16] But not everybody was convinced by the junior Minister, and a leading article in the *Daily Telegraph* responded that all the evidence showed a relentless rise in unwanted pregnancies, illegitimate births and abortions, at the same time as there had been more sex education in schools and more use of contraception and contraceptive services. 'In 1976, for example, 23 in every thousand girls under 16 visited clinics for contraceptive services, 7.9 got pregnant and 4.2 had abortions. In 1990, 67 took the advice, 10.1 got pregnant and 5.1 had abortions. The trend is so persistent that one wonders if the contraceptive propagandists really believe their own argument that more condoms will reduce unwanted pregnancies, or whether they are just in favour of contraception for other reasons... The current idea of sex education in schools would be laughable if it were not so sad.'[17]

In November 1993 William Oddie wrote a powerful denunciation of what he called 'the real child abusers'. He related a story about the experience of an 11-year-old girl. The parents had received a circular asking if they had any objection to their daughter receiving sex education at school. In response the father wrote and asked whether the sex instruction would discourage promiscuous sex, and received a reassuring answer. The parents then forgot about the whole matter. About a year later the father noticed a piece of paper on his daughter's bedroom floor. 'He discovered that on it was a series of drawings, under a large, carefully printed heading: "How to get a boy into bed". The first drawing showed a boy and girl looking at each other with sickly expressions. Over their heads was a large red heart. The second drawing made him gasp: it was of the same boy and girl, now naked; the boy was effecting sexual penetration. Hearts and small birds circled above. The third drawing was of a small disembodied hand negotiating (one of the terms beloved to sex educationists) a condom on to a massively erect male organ. The child was now 12. The headline was undoubtedly her own: it was what she had concluded the lessons were about. She had formerly supposed that sex was something for parents; now she had been told, in effect, that it was something for children of her own age.'[18]

The Director of the FPA responded to William Oddie's article. 'The FPA was founded to alleviate the misery caused by unplanned pregnancy. The FPA runs a respected nationwide information service helping over 7,000 individuals a month and distributes over 4.5 million free leaflets each year. We aim to give people the knowledge and skills to use contraception effectively, to plan pregnancies and to be able to enjoy rewarding sexual relationships, free of the fear of unwanted pregnancy... Sex education has a clear place in Government policy. The Department for Education has recently made sex education compulsory in all secondary schools.'[19]

The policy of the sex education lobby was now to recruit parents as sex educators. In March 1994 the FPA launched its 'Parents Project' with an advertising campaign which encouraged parents to talk to their children about sex. The Director of the FPA explained: 'Our first ever radio advertising campaign in Spring 1994 was designed to encourage parents to talk to their children about sex. Funded by the Department of Health as a *Health of the Nation* initiative, the adverts were broadcast in London and the north west of England and offered a free copy of the FPA booklet *Answering your child's questions* to parents ringing a freephone number. The campaign was a tremendous success, generating over 7,500 responses, an all-time high. We hope to build on this success and take the campaign UK-wide in the forthcoming year.'[20] The FPA's national conference made a call for more support to help parents become better sex educators. Doreen Massey said that talking about sex was still a national taboo, especially where parents and children are concerned. 'Our UK-wide work with parents shows that these barriers can, and must, be broken down if we are to have an impact on teenage pregnancy rates.'[21]

A survey designed to gauge parents' views of sex education, commissioned by the Health Education Authority, which reported in October 1994, was used to boost the 'Parents Project'. The aim of the survey was to find out how parents perceived their own and the school's role regarding sex education. Key findings showed that 94 per cent of parents thought that schools should play a part in educating their children about human sexuality and sexual development. With regard to the question on sexual preferences, 56 per cent thought it should be covered in secondary schools, and nearly 25 per cent thought that it should only be taught after the age of 16. The majority of parents (81 per cent) said they felt confident about providing sex education for their children, although one in four identified specific topics, such as HIV, homosexuality and contraception, about which they would like expert guidance. Only 26 per cent of parents reported that the school had consulted them about sex education, although all of the schools claimed to have done so. Many parents wanted to know more about the content of sex education in schools and how it was taught.[22]

Sex education receives a bad press

There was a furore when the Health Education Authority published its latest sex education booklet, *Your Pocket Guide to Sex*, which showed an angel astride a condom on the cover. The booklet, written by Nick Fisher the agony aunt for *Just 17*, was aimed at 16 to 24-year-olds. It contained information on the use of vibrators, oral sex and masturbation. Lord Stallard believed the booklet promoted promiscuity and was insulting to women. He quoted from the booklet: 'The number of people you have sex with is much less important than how you have sex. If it's safer sex and you use a condom, you could screw hundreds of people and never come in contact with HIV.' The Earl of Lauderdale called it 'a glossy but degrading incitement to anti-family behaviour'.[23] In a letter Valerie Riches wrote, 'Since it was established in 1968 the Health Education Authority has been surrounded by controversy over its approach to sexual matters. The "smutty" sex handbook for youngsters is just another example of its explicit and amoral liberalism. Last month the Authority, in association with a glossy magazine, *Company*, published 20 pages of completely uncensored facts, "69 Bravest Sex Questions: Bold, spicy, frank – they're the ones you've always wanted to ask". Readers were treated to an orgy of information about every orifice of the human body which the Authority deems suitable for sexual pleasure, provided, of course, that pregnancy does not result. Government departments have previously responded to public concern about the Authority's activities with evasion and prevarication. The Authority itself, which exists on public money, has hidden under the cloak of respectability of being an agent of the Government.'[24]

The Government was clearly embarrassed by the booklet and the Minister of Health, Brian Mawhinney, said that he found it distasteful, inappropriate and smutty and advised that the 12 thousand copies be withdrawn and pulped. The HEA responded that the booklet contained passages on celibacy and saying 'no' to sex. The booklet also referred to sexually transmitted disease and contraception – information which would help to curb HIV and reduce teenage pregnancies.[25] The director of the FPA defended the booklet as one attempt to fill a gap, and a spokesman for Brook said the controversy showed that people did not understand the truth about sex education, and quoted the number of teenage pregnancies that occurred each year.[26] This controversy is important for it shows that even the most explicit, amoral sex education material usually contains a section on saying 'no' to sex, as we saw in chapter 2.

Sex education received more bad press when it was revealed that 10 and 11-year-olds had been taught about extramarital affairs and how chocolate bars could be used as oral sex aids in a sex education lesson. Parents of children attending Highfield Primary School, Leeds, complained when their children came home and told their parents that they had been involved in a role-play scene which included mummy, daddy and mummy's lover.[27] The Minister of Education, Chris Patten, expressed concern that primary schoolchildren might have been subjected to what he called completely value-free education. In the ensuing row the school admitted an error of judgement, while the Royal College of Nursing supported the nurse who gave the class, urging the Minister of Education to give better guidance on the role of school nurses in sex education.[28]

Early in 1996 the junior Home Office minister, Tom Sackville, who a few years previously had suggested that schools should make condoms available to children, met the publishers of teenage magazines to discuss concern over the explicit nature of their contents. This meeting was as a result of a campaign by Peter Luff, MP for Worcester, to persuade publishers to show a greater responsibility towards their young readers. Mr Luff became concerned about the contents of teenage magazines when his wife bought one for their 10-year-old daughter. Although the cover looked harmless enough, Mr Luff and his wife were shocked when they glanced through its pages. He asked other parents about the magazines read by their daughters, and those who knew the contents were all profoundly unhappy, but felt powerless to do anything. They felt that their young daughters of 10, 11 or 12 did not need to learn about the intricacies of oral sex, about masturbating their boyfriends or about the finer points of lesbianism. The parents resented what these magazines were doing—any girl approaching her teens was being encouraged to believe that sexual activity, although illegal, was the norm.[29]

As a consequence of his experience Peter Luff started a campaign to encourage publishers to show greater responsibility towards their young readers. Letters he received from parents showed either that they did not know what was in the magazines, or that they thought their reservations were not widely shared and were afraid of embarrassing their children by forbidding the magazines. He believed that these magazines were an important part of a culture which debased childhood and sex. Motivated by greed and cynicism, they preached that promiscuous sex was the norm.

A self-regulatory group, the Teenage Magazine Arbitration Panel, was set up as a result of Tom Sackville's meeting with the publishers. Its first report said that teenage magazines were misleading their readers and pressurising them into having early sexual relationships. The impression was being created that sexual intercourse in the early teenage years was nearly universal, but this was not the case. The report also claimed that teenage magazines had a major part to play in sex education.[30]

In 1996 the FPA was awarded a three-year contract for a 'contraceptive education service' funded by the Department of Health. The chairman of the FPA, Dr David Robertson, thanked the Department for their consistent and unfailing support.[31] The 'contraceptive education service' would supply a comprehensive range of leaflets on all the different methods of contraception and had a dedicated helpline and postal enquiry service for the public and health professionals. It had run a six-month campaign to improve knowledge about emergency contraception, including adverts in the national press, women's magazines and on radio. Information packs were sent to all primary health care teams, family planning clinics and pharmacists. The booklets *Is everybody doing it?* and *4 Boys: a below-the-belt guide to the male body*, aimed at 13 to 17-year-olds, had been launched. The booklet *4 Girls*, published in 1997, received the following review in *The Observer*: 'It is full of naked women and explicit descriptions of the female body. Pubic hair, breasts and masturbation are discussed in detail. But, if it is successful, a copy will be owned by every young girl in the country.'[32]

By the end of 1997 it was becoming clear that the threatened AIDS epidemic had fizzled out. The apocalyptic forecasts of a decade ago had proved false. We had been told that AIDS was the greatest public health threat of the century, that it was not exclusively a 'gay plague' but would afflict thousands of heterosexuals each year. It had been predicted that AIDS would claim up to 15 thousand lives a year by the late 1990s.[33] Yet in 1998 there were only 508 AIDS related deaths in the UK. Moreover, in the 16 years between 1982 and the end of 1997 there had been just fewer than 16 thousand AIDS cases, of which the vast majority were homosexuals (10,672).

In the 16 years of the so-called epidemic, only 291 people were diagnosed with AIDS who had been exposed within the UK to presumed heterosexually infected partner(s).[34] In other words, on average, there had been about 20 new cases of AIDS per year acquired by way of heterosexual intercourse within the UK. So the risk of children acquiring AIDS through sexual intercourse was so remote as to be almost non-existent. And yet the Government had made it compulsory for all secondary schoolchildren in the country to be taught how to use condoms in order to protect themselves against AIDS. Moreover, the NHS planned to spend over £52 million on AIDS prevention in 1997, including making generous grants to organisations which distributed condoms and promoted 'safer sex'.

During the summer of 1997 a 'love bus' toured the beaches of Cornwall offering free contraceptives to teenagers as young as 13. The red double-decker bus was staffed by young women volunteers who handed out 'safer sex' leaflets. Teenagers were told about local family planning clinics and provided with information on the morning-after pill. Every teenager took part in a lucky dip which offered CDs and massage oil as prizes, and all left the bus with a condom and a 'choose safer sex' sticker. The aim of the project was to take sexual advice to young people rather than waiting for them to seek help. The 'love bus' was held up as an example of best practice at a conference of public health directors in London.[35]

The foreword of the 1996-97 annual report of the FPA claimed that sexual health was the Cinderella service. 'Seldom thought of, seldom discussed, seldom prioritised. It makes us angry that a service which is so fundamental to the lives of people in the UK is neglected and disregarded.' This claim was, of course, total nonsense—during the last two decades most Ministers of Health had made family planning services a priority, and the FPA had been highly skilful in making sure that the subject was never off the political agenda. The foreword concluded with a missionary appeal. 'We urge you to do what you can to help us. Support our campaigns. Lobby MPs. Talk to school governors. Speak out for sex education being included in the curriculum. And please consider a financial contribution. At a personal level, be brave and seek advice for your sexual health if you need to, be open with your friends and particularly your children, so that future generations can enjoy the health and quality of life to which they have a right.'[36]

The FPA's Annual Review 2000 commented on newspaper headlines which agonised over the poor sexual health of Britain's 'promiscuous' and 'feckless' young people. 'But beneath the inevitable media hype and unhelpful moralising, there is a real problem. Despite the popular misconception that young people in the UK have never known more about sex, much of the information available to young people, from an early age right the way through puberty and teenage years, is inaccurate, misleading and poor quality.'[37] So the real problem, according to the FPA, was the poor quality of information. Over the last two decades the Family Planning Education Service had distributed over 50 million leaflets at enormous cost to the public purse, yet the FPA was claiming that young people had been provided with misleading and poor quality information!

From January 2001, as a result of a Ministerial Order, emergency contraception, which had been available from GPs since 1985, was made available over the counter from a pharmacist for women aged 16 and over. This Ministerial Order must be viewed in the context of the existing use of emergency contraception. In the year 2000, GPs in England issued 550 thousand prescriptions for emergency contraception, while another 240 thousand prescriptions were issued by family planning clinics. Of the clinic prescriptions, about 25 thousand were for children under 16.[38] (The number of under-age children receiving emergency contraception from GPs is not known.) Despite the current massive use of emergency contraception the Government's intention is to increase its use still further in the hope of achieving the teenage pregnancy target. Accordingly, pharmacists have been advised to develop links into existing networks for family planning services so that under-16s can be referred on quickly. The clear implication of this initiative is that simply providing children with free contraceptives is not preventing unintended pregnancies, hence the emphasis on emergency contraception. As we saw in chapter 1, the Government has now recruited supermarkets and school nurses to assist with the distribution of emergency contraception to under-age children.

The National Strategy for Sexual Health and HIV was issued in July 2001 as a consultation document. In the foreword, the parliamentary Under Secretary of State for Public Health, Yvette Cooper, claimed that 'there have been success stories in the way new and emerging threats to sexual health have been tackled'. In her mind the successes included the open access clinics which treat sexually transmitted diseases, needle exchange schemes for drug addicts, and the availability of a broad range of contraceptives provided free by the NHS. Despite these 'advances' serious challenges remained, including the increase in sexually transmitted diseases and the high rate of unintended pregnancies. After three decades of Government sponsored sex education the evidence 'suggests that many people lack the information they want and need to make informed choices that will affect their sexual health'.[39] The strategy aimed to improve England's sexual health by fostering 'a culture of positive sexual health by making sure that everyone gets the information they need – without stigma, fear or embarrassment – so that they can make informed decisions to prevent sexually transmitted diseases, including HIV, and about services.'[40] Improving abortion services is a key aspect of the strategy. 'The earlier in pregnancy an abortion is performed, the lower the risk of complication. NHS funded abortion should be more readily available, ensuring that women who meet the legal requirements for an abortion are referred without delay.'[41]

Sex education – the propaganda arm of the sexual revolution

Throughout this book we have heard that the purpose of sex education is to reduce teenage pregnancies, abortions and sexually transmitted infections. Yet the evidence of the last three decades demonstrates that sex education has been spectacularly unsuccessful in achieving its publicly stated aims, and it is doubtful that even the most ideologically blind can still believe that contraceptive based sex education provides the answer to teenage sexual tragedies. Indeed, it seems doubtful that the sex educators actually believe their own rhetoric. So the mantra – sex education reduces teenage pregnancies, abortions and sexually transmitted infections – appears to have been no more than a smoke screen to obscure the real objective of sex education. So what is the *real* objective?

It is my contention that sex education has evolved out of the ideas of the sexual revolutionaries. When we grasp this essential point, the real objective of sex education becomes clear. Our examination of the history of sex education has shown its close ideological link with the sexual revolutionaries. We have seen that Marie Stopes, one of the original revolutionaries, was the motivating force behind the FPA, the organisation that sets the sex education agenda for the UK and that 'educates' sex educators. We have seen that the IPPF, the organisation set up to promote the ideology of Margaret Sanger, advocates that sex education, family planning and legal abortion should be accepted as human rights. The IPPF aims to make sex education for children compulsory, and its Youth Manifesto declares that society must recognise the right of all young people to enjoy sex and to express their sexuality in the way they choose.

The revolutionaries – Marie Stopes, Wilhelm Reich, Alfred Kinsey and Wardell Pomeroy – all understood that sex education could be a powerful vehicle for promoting their ideas among children. Wardell Pomeroy's two sex education books, *Girls and Sex* and *Boys and Sex*, which taught an amoral view of sexual conduct and presented positive images of homosexuality (pages 24 and 136), have been enthusiastically promoted by the FPA. We have seen that the messages of sex education literature, discussed in chapter 2, are consistent with the amoral ideology of the sexual revolution. Moreover, there is a clear link between SIECUS, the main organisation promoting sex education in the USA, and Kinsey's idea that human sexuality is a continuum, ranging between heterosexuality, bisexuality and homosexuality. We saw that the booklet *Sex Education: The Erroneous Zone*, which openly supported the objectives of the sexual revolution (page 124–27), has been endorsed by the FPA. We saw that the amoral ideology behind the sex education manual *Make it Happy* (page 174), which was lauded and promoted by the sex educators, was consistent with that of the sexual revolution.

The evidence considered above leaves no doubt that sex education is, in reality, no more than the propaganda arm of the sexual revolution. In my opinion, the real objective of sex education is, and always has been, to promote the amoral ideology of the sexual revolution. In this, it has been remarkably successful.

Endnotes

1 *Daily Telegraph*, 8 August 1991, AIDS warning for women as cases double, David Fletcher
2 *Daily Telegraph*, 27 November 1991, Comic-strip advice for children of AIDS victims, David Fletcher

3 *Daily Telegraph*, 26 November 1991, Freddie Mercury's AIDS frankness will save lives, David Fletcher

4 *Daily Telegraph*, 21 April 1992, Keep yourselves alive, Liz Taylor tells Mercury fans

5 *Daily Telegraph*, 1 December 1991, AIDS expert lured away by rival hospital

6 *Daily Telegraph*, 26 April 1992, Patten faces challenge on AIDS lessons, Fran Abrams

7 *Daily Telegraph*, 6 March 1992, Parliament and Politics, Anthony Looch

8 *Daily Telegraph*, 14 February 1992, letter, Valerie Riches

9 Brook Advisory Centres, Annual Report, 1992/93, p1

10 Health Education Authority, *Health Update, 4 Sexual Health*, Joanna Goodrich, Henrietta Lang and Mary Sayers, 1994, p35

11 Ibid. p16

12 Ibid. p17

13 Ibid. p26

14 Department of Education, Education Act 1993: *Sex Education in Schools*, circular no. 5/94

15 *Daily Telegraph*, 25 March 1993, Commentary: How not to, as well as how to, Kirsty McLeod

16 Brook Advisory Centres, Annual Report, 1992-93, p4

17 *Daily Telegraph*, Leading article, Sex mad, 28 March 1993

18 *Sunday Telegraph*, 14 November 1993, Sunday comment, The real abusers – our children are being taught that anything goes provided that it's 'safe', William Oddie

19 *Sunday Telegraph*, 21 November 1993, letter, Doreen Massey

20 Family Planning Association, Annual Report 1993-94, p4

21 Family Planning Association, press release, 4 November 1994

22 Health Education Authority, *Parents, schools and sex education survey*, conducted by National Foundation for Educational Research, October 1994

23 Hansard, Lords debate, 9 March 1994, cc1423-1426

24 *Daily Telegraph*, 26 March 1994, letter, Smut posing as sex education, Valerie Riches

25 *Daily Telegraph*, 25 March 1994, Smutty guide casts cloud over future of sex education authority, Philip Johnson and Peter Pallot

26 *Daily Telegraph*, 30 March 1994, Sex advisers back booklet that Minister banned, Peter Pallot

27 *Daily Telegraph*, 23 March 1994, Primary class has explicit lesson in sex and adultery, Colin Wright

28 *Daily Telegraph*, 24 March 1994, Patten orders inquiry into explicit lesson, Paul Marston

29 *Daily Telegraph*, 26 February 1996, Sex between the magazine covers, Peter Luff

30 *Daily Telegraph*, 20 December 1996, Teen magazine surveys 'put pressure on girls to have sex', Alison Boshoff

31 Family Planning Association, Annual Report 1995-96, p1

32 *The Observer*, 7 December 1997, Martin Wroe, cited from Family Planning Association, Annual Report 1996-97, p3

33 *The Times*, February 1989, AIDS deaths could be 100,000 by year 2000, Thomson Prentice

34 AIDS/HIV quarterly surveillance tables, no 58, May 2003, Health Protection Agency

35 *Daily Telegraph*, 29 July 1997, Love Bus offers condoms to 13-year-old girls on holiday, Sean O'Neill

36 Family Planning Association, Annual Report 1996-97, p1

37 FPA Annual Review 2000, p2

38 *NHS Contraceptive Services, England: 2001-02*, bulletin 2002/20, Department of Health, ed. Lesz Lancucki, October 2002

39 Department of Health, *The National Strategy for Sexual Health and HIV*, July 2001, p2

40 Ibid. p12

41 Ibid. p28

Chapter 17

Explicit education in the light of sexual purity

Talking about sex and explicit images contrasted with the
virtues of modesty and chivalry

The idea that children are ignorant about sex has been a key message of sex education over the last three decades or more. In 1968 the television documentary *What shall we tell the children?* (Thames) described how British parents neglected to tell their children the facts of life. A review of the programme reached the conclusion that 'the ignorance of the children interviewed was matched by the embarrassment of their parents. Schools were only slightly free from this dreadful prudery.'[1] Two and a half decades later, despite the massive efforts of the sex education industry, including national campaigns promoting 'safer sex' and the distribution of tens of millions of sex education leaflets, children in the 1990s were apparently still sexually ignorant. To help overcome this ignorance the junior Minister of Health, Tom Sackville, launched a campaign in 1994 encouraging parents to talk to their children about sex. According to the director of the FPA, Doreen Massey, the campaign was designed to give parents the support they need to talk confidently to their children.[2]

Talking about sex

In chapter 1 we saw the Government's *Teenage Pregnancy* report put foward the idea that the reluctance of parents to talk to their children about sex is a major reason for the high incidence of teenage sexual tragedies. To overcome this deficiency the Department of Health has commissioned a national campaign to help parents talk to their sons and daughters about sex.[3] According to the Government, it is essential that schools also help children and young people develop confidence in talking, listening and thinking about sex and relationships.[4] The leaflet

SRE & Parents (2001) has been written to persuade parents to take a more active role in the sex education of their children. It suggests 'some useful values statements' for parents to think about when talking with their children. For example, a parent may say to their child, 'Have sex with someone you really care about and who will share responsibility for contraception and safer sex.' Or a parent may say, 'It would be better to wait to have sex until you are old enough to take responsibility.'[5] The clear message is that parents should persuade their children that responsible behaviour means using contraception when they decide to 'have sex'. In other words, parents, when they talk to their children about sex, should encourage them to practise 'safer sex'.

The feature article 'Never too young for the facts of life' presents the argument of those who believe that 'sex talk' is an important aspect of sex education. Mary Ann Sieghart, a *Times* columnist, explains that one of the best favours a parent or teacher can do for a child is to talk openly about sex. She advises that the easiest way to avoid inhibitions and anxieties about sex in later life is to learn about it early, to talk about it as freely as any other natural part of life, and to think about it rationally. She believes that ignorance of or guilty feelings about sex are far more likely to lead to difficulties in adult life. And when should sex education start? 'There is an advantage in talking about sex before children start experiencing sexual feelings, so that discussion can be freer from the embarrassment brought on by confronting adolescents with their own secret urges... The puritan lobby seems to be terrified that learning about sex encourages schoolchildren to be promiscuous – as if sex were not a natural human urge, as if not knowing about it would stem all sexual desire... Those parents who are most likely not to want their children to learn about sex at school are also those who are least likely to talk openly about sex at home. Why should parents foist their own sexual repressions on their children?'[6]

An essay on sex education in *Sexuality Today – and tomorrow* by Sol Gordon explains the importance of talking about sex. Parents should recognise that 'before they can communicate freely with their children they must be able to talk freely about sexuality with each other and to develop sensitivity to their own feelings... Parents must be willing to talk about sex. Those who are uncomfortable hearing or speaking sexual words can practise them – alone, with their spouse, or in conversation with a friend. This step is important because children are sensitive to the emotional value parents give to certain words and can pick up what their parents feel rather than what their parents say.'[7]

A key presumption of sex education ideology is that parents should learn to discuss sex with their children in an open and frank way, always stressing the importance of 'safe sex'. The FPA booklet *Talking to your children about sex* (1998) explains that 'children need to learn about the positive side of sex as well as being aware of risks and dangers. Showing children that it's alright to talk about sex gives them a positive message.' And to overcome embarrassment parents are told to 'introduce the topic when your child is very young... if you show your

244

child that you are happy to talk about sex, relationships and feelings, they will know they can ask questions about anything they don't understand'.[8] If parents don't talk to their children about sex, they pick up the message that sex is scary and shouldn't be talked about.[9] But it's embarrassing to talk to children about sex. All parents know that. 'It's OK to go red and tell your child you're embarrassed. You can help your child learn about sex even if you don't feel very comfortable talking about it.' And the earlier parents start the better.

The FPA booklet points out that the real problem arises with older children because teenagers often find it much harder to talk to their parents about sex. 'If your children say they know all about sex, just ask them what they know – and fill in the gaps.' And then comes the difficult bit, explaining sexual responsibility to children. 'You will need to explain that being responsible about sexual behaviour means considering the needs and feelings of the partner, and discussing the kind of relationship both partners want. It means not having sex if one's partner isn't ready. If both partners decide to make love, it means being able to talk about safer sex to avoid sexually transmitted infections, and using contraception unless they both want a baby.'[10]

The booklet, however, does not advise parents to talk to their children about marriage, nor does it advise them to explain the dangers of sexual promiscuity; it does not even mention the great value of teaching children the discipline of self-control. Instead, parents are exhorted to teach their children that sexual responsibility means using contraception. Parents are expected to be supportive when their daughter and her partner 'decide to make love'.

In his book, *The Parentalk Guide to Your Child and Sex*, Steve Chalke follows the line of the FPA, explaining the importance of talking to children about sex. His message is that the sooner parents start talking to their child about sex the better. 'The more they get used to talking about sex with you, the more they'll feel able to open up and discuss intimate and personal things.'[11] Chalke points out that 'sooner or later, your son or daughter will make their own choices about when, where and with whom to have sex. If you want these choices to be informed and responsible, you'll need to talk to them about sex in a positive, natural and guilt-free way.'[12] Moreover, as parents we 'all want the first time our child has sex to be special. We want them to be able to look back and think, "I'm really glad I did that!" Many people's ongoing attitude to sex is coloured by their first time. For some, this will have been planned and prepared for – even long-hoped for – with the moment, partner, location and atmosphere chosen with care... So the harder you work at helping your child appreciate their real value and understand the truth about sex and their own sexuality, the more in control they'll be in terms of when, where, why and with whom they first do it, and the more you'll have contributed to their enjoyment not just of the first time, but every time. By talking to them about it on a regular basis, you can help ensure that when they do have sex, it's for the right reasons, with the right person, at the right time, and because both they and their partner genuinely want to.'[13] Chalke tells parents 'that most unintentional pregnancies happen because people are uninformed or ill-prepared, so it's vital for you to teach your child the facts about contraception and pregnancy.'[14]

A SIECUS booklet *Now What Do I Do?* aims to help parents of children aged 10-12 years answer questions about sex. The booklet suggests that children of this age might ask questions about their parents' sexual behaviour. For example, a 12-year-old might ask one of his parents, 'How old were you when you first had sexual intercourse?' Parents must decide on a response that gets their message across, and teaches their children what they want them to learn. A suggested response to the above question is, 'I'll be happy to talk about what choices I made; I gave it a lot of thought and they were right for me at the time. My choice may not be the right one for you when you get older. But first, tell me why you want to know.' The message this response delivers is that 'this is an okay topic for parents and children to discuss. Some decisions are right for some people at certain times and wise choices require thought. A parent's job is to help children learn to choose wisely.'[15]

Sex word games

Sex education aims to help children overcome any feelings of embarrassment, shame or guilt that may occur as a result of talking or thinking about sex. And so the earlier children start learning sexual words the better. The sex education manual, *Knowing me, knowing you*, has devised a sex word game for primary schoolchildren. The purpose is to help children think about the language they use. Working in pairs children are asked to think of polite and impolite words for wanting to go to the toilet, for describing the sexual body parts of a man and a woman, and for describing a sexual activity. They are asked to think of the impolite word, but to write down only the polite word. The author suggests that it may be necessary 'to use anatomical drawings to help the children to be aware of the medical words for body parts'.[16]

An FPA training manual, *The weird and wonderful world of Billy Ballgreedy*, acknowledges that 'talking about issues relating to sex is often unfamiliar and uncomfortable for young people, invariably causing much embarrassment and laughter – although this can be true for adults'. But the FPA has a technique for overcoming this embarrassment – the sex words brainstorm. The sex educator allocates children into a number of small groups with a sheet of flip chart paper divided into four sections. They are asked to write the word 'penis' in one section, and then to think of as many alternative words as possible. They are told to think of all the times and settings in which the word has been mentioned. The children are asked to repeat the process, writing the words 'vagina', 'having sex' and 'masturbation' on the flip chart. The groups are then asked to call out all their words, and the group with the highest number is declared the winner of the sex word brainstorm.[17] In another word game children are given a jumbled set of display cards with half a sex word on each. They are set the task of matching the cards to complete the sex words.

The purpose behind these techniques is to empower both adults and children to use sex language without any sense of embarrassment. According to the sex educators, even young children need a sexual vocabulary; the larger the vocabulary the more they will feel able to talk about sex. All words used to describe the sexual organs should be mentioned openly, and discussed by groups of children. Nothing is taboo, and nothing should be too embarrassing. The effect of these games is to desensitise children against sexual embarrassment; to overcome their sense of shame and extinguish their natural inhibitions. If they become used to using sex words, and if they repeat the words often enough then gradually, over time, they become less embarrassed. Eventually, when they are fully desensitised, they are able to talk freely and openly about sex. An interesting aside is to notice the words that sex education does not include in the sexual vocabulary of children—marriage, modesty, chastity, self-control and fidelity.

Explicit sexual images

Another dimension of sex education is to teach children about the genitals in a way that is blatant and explicit. Many sex education films, books and pamphlets provide children with graphic visual images of the sex organs, and it is now widely accepted that displaying the genitalia is simply a part of a child's education. The central feature of the board game *Contraception*, discussed in chapter 1, is the life size model of an erect penis. The Brook booklet *A look at safe sex*, contains detailed, explicit, close-up, drawings of the sexual organs, including an explicit, realistic drawing of a condom being fitted to an erect penis. The sex education manual *Make it Happy* provides a photograph of two naked men with erections. In the minds of the sex educators, the genitalia are just like any other part of the body. After all, what is the difference between a penis and a knee? Are both not simply anatomical structures? One sex education game gives children a large, detailed, explicit diagram of the male and female genitalia, with 20 body part labels. Children are required to arrange the labels so as to identify, in careful detail, the anatomy of the male and female organs. The level of detail would test the ability of a medical student. A condom demonstrator (an object shaped like an erect penis) is a common tool of the sex educator. Children are encouraged to unroll condoms on a realistic model of an erect penis. And all this must be done with no sense of shame, for children are only truly liberated when all things sexual are in the open. The sexual organs must be uncovered and exposed; nothing is to be hidden, nothing is private, nothing is sacred—all is exposed in the name of sex education. So as the sex educators go about their work, they leave behind children who have images of the sex organs imprinted in their impressionable minds.

SIECUS believes that sexually explicit materials are an important aspect of sex education. According to a position statement on sexually explicit materials: 'When sensitively used in a manner appropriate to the viewer's age and developmental level, sexually explicit visual, printed, or on-line materials can be valuable educational or personal aids helping to reduce ignorance and confusion and contributing to a wholesome concept of sexuality.'[18] A SIECUS pamphlet, *Talk about Sex* (1992), encourages children to use sexual messages in the media as an aid to stimulate sexual talk between young people. 'When talking to a friend or a possible sex partner, speak clearly… Movies, music and TV… often have a message about sexuality and can help possible sexual partners express their affection and sexual interest… Use entertainment to help talk about sexuality.'[19]

The above illustrates the enormous contrast between the Victorian approach to human sexuality, which did all it could to discourage sex talk, and the modern sex education movement, which does all it can to encourage it. The explicit approach of sex education would have been unthinkable to the Victorians, who believed that modesty was an essential virtue. And as true modesty meant purity of thought and language, it was unthinkable to Victorians that contraception would be a topic of discussion among anybody, let alone among children. The Victorians would have been deeply shocked at the practice of exposing children to visual images of the sex organs—they would have regarded modern sex educators as the promoters of lewdness and obscenity. In the last 40 years, since the advent of sex education, there has been a radical change in what society accepts as sexual decency. In the last four decades of sex education, we have moved from a society that believed in sexual modesty to a society that glorifies sexual explicitness. This transformation raises a number of questions. Are we sure that the sex talk promoted by sex education is good for children? Are we content to allow children to participate in sex word games? Is it good for children to be desensitised against their natural sense of embarrassment? Do we want children to grow up with no sense of shame?

Biblical teaching on sexual purity

Biblical teaching on sexual purity flows from the holiness that is central to the character of God. In his book, *The Beauty of God's Holiness*, Thomas Trevethan shows that holiness is the fundamental attribute of God that conditions and qualifies all other attributes. 'The true God is distinct, set apart, from all that he has made as the only truly self-sufficient Being. All his creatures depend on him; he alone exists from within himself. And the true God is distinct, set apart, from all that is evil. His moral perfection is absolute. His character as expressed in his will, forms the absolute standard of moral excellence. God is holy, the absolute point of reference for all that exists and is good.'[20] In a vision of heaven, the prophet Isaiah sees the Lord seated on his throne and is overwhelmed by the holiness of God, as the seraphim call to one another: 'Holy, holy, holy is the Lord Almighty; the whole world is full of his glory' (Isaiah 6:2-3). The Lord God of the Bible lives in unapproachable light (1 Timothy 6:16); his eyes are too pure to look on evil and he cannot tolerate wrong (Habakkuk 1:13).

The Bible makes it clear that holiness must be exhibited in the sexual realm. 'It is God's will that you should be holy; that you should avoid sexual immorality; that each of you should learn to control his own body in a way that is holy and honourable, not in passionate lust like the heathen, who do not know God… (1 Thessalonians 4:3-5).

It is God's will that his people should be holy and pure in their relationships with members of the opposite sex. Christians should learn to control their passions

248

and desires in a way that is honourable and that does not take advantage of other people. This means avoiding sexual immorality through practising self-control. In *Possessed by God*, David Peterson explains that if our bodies belong to the Lord, we are no longer free to use them selfishly or in accordance with the accepted values of the time. 'Gaining control over one's body and refusing to use it for self-indulgence expresses a true knowledge of God and his will for human life... God's initial calling of us "in holiness" is to be the ground and motivation for holy living. God did not call us "for impurity" but, by setting us apart for himself, he indicated his desire for us to live differently, as those who belong to him... Those who teach a more permissive policy or disregard Paul's words by their actions are setting aside the explicit will of God. Indeed, the Spirit he gives to Christians is the Spirit of holiness, and nothing unholy can be tolerated in the lives of individuals or communities where the Holy Spirit dwells.'[21]

The standard that God has set for his people is that we should be pure in body and spirit. Jesus said, 'Blessed are the pure in heart for they will see God' (Matthew 5:8). The apostle John teaches that when Christ appears 'we shall be like him... everyone who has this hope in him purifies himself, just as he is pure' (1 John 3:3). The message of the apostle Paul is 'keep yourself pure', and Timothy is instructed to relate to young women 'with absolute purity' (1 Timothy 5:22, 2). Those who seek to live a Christian life, therefore, purify themselves from 'everything that contaminates body and spirit' (2 Corinthians 7:1). Sexual purity is a quintessential characteristic of the Christian life, an attitude of mind and desire of the heart that comes from an understanding of God's holy character. Because God is holy, those who would obey his moral law, as an act of spiritual worship, offer their bodies as living sacrifices, holy and pleasing to God (Romans 12:1). Sexual purity is manifest in our thoughts and speech and the way we behave. The Christian, who strives to conform to the image of Christ, longs for sexual purity that brings honour to God.

One of the essential marks of Christian conduct is purity of speech. We are to rid ourselves of 'filthy language' (Colossians 3:8). We should 'not let any unwholesome talk' come out of our mouths, and there must not be 'obscenity, foolish talk or coarse joking, which are out of place...' The Bible warns that no immoral or impure person 'has any inheritance in the kingdom of Christ and of God' (Ephesians 4:29 and 5:3-5). Christian believers do not indulge in lewd and indecent language. The sex talk promoted by sex education is completely unacceptable.

Jesus condemns the impurity that comes through the sense of sight. He said that anyone who looks at a woman lustfully has already committed adultery with her in his heart. 'If your right eye causes you to sin, gouge it out' (Matthew 5:28, 29). He said that the eye is the lamp of the body. 'If your eyes are good, your whole body will be full of light. But if your eyes are bad, your whole body will be full of darkness.' (Matthew 6:22, 23). Here Jesus is warning of the inner darkness that comes from using the eyes for impure purposes. The apostle John warns that the lust of the eyes is not of God, but of the world (1 John 2:16). The explicit images of the sex educators are a source of moral pollution and anathema to the Christian faith.

So we see that an attitude of mind that seeks after sexual purity is at the heart of biblical teaching. Implicit within the idea of purity is an undivided heart which renounces sensual and sexual pollution, and a spirit of obedience to God's moral law. A pure heart inculcates a duty of self-restraint and self-denial. The people of God desire purity in all areas of their lives, and especially in sexual relationships. Moreover, we know that the impure person has no part in God's kingdom.

The virtue of modesty

Christian sexual conduct is expressed in the four virtues—modesty, chivalry, chastity and fidelity. Sexual purity is the foundation on which these virtues are built. While each virtue applies to an aspect of sexual behaviour, together they form a coherent inner belief system that witnesses to God's holiness, and sets a standard for sexual conduct that gives meaning to marriage and the family.

Modesty is the virtue that recognises the rightful purpose of sex as something private, mysterious, and meant for the relationship between husband and wife. Modesty discourages lust and encourages faithful love. Chivalry is the virtue that teaches men to relate to women with honour and respect. It gives men the inner motivation to practise self-control, honesty and decency in relationships. Chastity is based in the desire for sexual purity, both before and after marriage. It welcomes the discipline of self-control and self-denial. Fidelity is based in faithfulness that rejoices in the lifelong nature of the marriage union, and so provides security for all members of the family. Modesty and chivalry are the roots from which the virtues of chastity and fidelity grow, flourish and bear the fruits of marital faithfulness and family security. Without the desire for purity there is no inner moral foundation and so the virtues of modesty, chivalry, chastity and fidelity when faced with sexual temptation lose their cohesion and gradually decay. Marriage and the family flourish when all four virtues are practised. And most important of all, these are the Christian virtues that guard children from danger and abuse— they provide children with God-given security, protecting them from the ravages that result from sexual immorality. In his great wisdom, God has instituted moral laws around human sexual conduct that preserve marriage, secure the family and protect children. These virtues are based in the holy, righteous character of God, and are reflected in his moral law.

Modesty in the Garden of Eden

The first indication of sexual modesty occurs in the Garden of Eden. After creation and prior to the Fall, 'the man and woman were both naked and they felt no shame' (Genesis 2:25). But then sin entered into the picture. When Eve 'saw that the fruit of the tree was good for food and pleasing to the eye, and also desirable for gaining wisdom, she took some and ate it. She also gave some to her husband, who was with her, and he ate it. Then the eyes of both of them were opened, and they realised that they were naked; so they sewed fig leaves together and made coverings for themselves' (Genesis 3:6-7).

One of the first consequences of the original sin is the disappearance of sexual innocence. The first man and woman looked at each other and became aware of their nakedness. As they gazed at each other's naked bodies they were overwhelmed by a sense of shame and embarrassment. Claus Westermann makes the point in his commentary on Genesis, 'Being ashamed is rather a reaction to being discovered unmasked.'[22] Aware of their nakedness they are embarrassed and feel an instinctive need to cover their sexual organs, and so use fig leaves as a cover. Following God's judgement for their disobedience, 'the Lord God made garments of skin for Adam and his wife and clothed them' (Genesis 3:21). By this action God confirms the need for sinful men and women to cover their nakedness with clothing. And wrapped up in the idea of covering is the virtue of modesty, which implies sexual reserve, and the avoidance of displaying the sexual organs. Gordon Wenham comments: 'It therefore follows that in Eden, the garden of God, man and woman must be decently clad, so God clothes them himself... Just as man may not enjoy a direct vision of God, so God should not be approached by man unclothed.'[23] It was God's will that sinful mankind, both men and women, should be clothed—it is indecent for them to expose their private parts.

The nakedness of Noah

The biblical story then moves on to Noah after the great flood. 'Noah, a man of the soil, proceeded to plant a vineyard. When he drank some of its wine, he became drunk and lay uncovered inside his tent. Ham, the father of Canaan, saw his father's nakedness and told his two brothers outside. But Shem and Japheth took a garment and laid it across their shoulders; then they walked in backwards and covered their father's nakedness. Their faces were turned the other way so that they would not see their father's nakedness. When Noah awoke from his wine and found out what his youngest son had done to him, he said, "Cursed be Canaan! The lowest of slaves will he be to his brothers"' (Genesis 9:20-25).

The incident of Noah and his son Ham emphasises the importance of sexual decency—to be uncovered is a disgrace. Nakedness in the Old Testament usually refers to the loss of human and social dignity.[24] His son Ham enters his father's tent, sees his father's nakedness, and, it seems, takes sensual delight in what he has seen. He does not cover his father's nakedness and this was an outrage against his father's dignity and modesty.[25] And Ham compounds his offence by going outside and telling his brothers. They instantly grasp the seriousness of the sin that Ham has committed. The brothers, appalled by what the younger brother has done, enter the tent backwards to avoid looking at their naked father. They cover his nakedness, so protecting their father's dignity. Notice how 'their faces were turned the other way' to ensure that their eyes do not see their father's nakedness.

According to Calvin this incident commends the modesty of the two brothers. 'They gave proof of the regard they paid to their father's honour, in supposing that their own eyes would be polluted, if they voluntarily looked upon the nakedness by which he was disgraced. At the same time they also consulted their own modesty.

For there is something so unaccountably shameful in the nakedness of man…'[26] When Noah awakes and discovers what has happened he is appalled by the depravity of the son who has looked on his naked body. So serious is the offence that Noah curses Canaan, Ham's son. Henceforth the Canaanites, the descendants of Ham, became notorious throughout the Old Testament for their sexual depravity. This incident shows the sin of the indecent look, and illustrates the principle of sexual modesty.

Marriage of Isaac and Rebekah

We have the example of Rebekah and Isaac. Abraham, the father of the faithful, instructs his loyal servant to ensure that Isaac, his only son, does not take a wife from among the Canaanites, who were known for their sexual immorality. Instead, the servant is to go to Abraham's family and there find a wife for his son. When the servant sees Rebekah, he observes that 'the girl was very beautiful, a virgin; no man had ever lain with her' (Genesis 24:16). Note the biblical emphasis on the chastity of Rebekah. After the servant explains to her family the purpose of his journey, and the way that God has answered his prayer for guidance, she agrees to travel back with the servant and his men. Accompanied by her maids, Rebekah sets out on the journey to meet her future husband. As they approach the home of Abraham, Rebekah looks up and sees a man coming to meet them. When told that it is Isaac, she gets down from her camel and 'she took her veil and covered herself' (Genesis 24:65). The clear inference is that chaste Rebekah is behaving with modesty in the presence of her future husband.

Canaanite depravity and God's holiness

After giving the Israelites his holy law, God commanded them to take possession of Canaan, the Promised Land. When they take possession of the land they are instructed by God to destroy the Canaanites totally. 'When the Lord your God has delivered them over to you and you have defeated them, then you must destroy them totally. Make no treaty with them, and show them no mercy… This is what you are to do to them: Break down their altars, smash their sacred stones, cut down their Asherah poles and burn their idols in the fire. For you are a people holy to the Lord your God' (Deuteronomy 7:2, 5-6). The people of God were commanded to wipe out the Canaanite people, their religion and culture. 'Otherwise, they will teach you to follow all the detestable things they do in worshipping their gods, and you will sin against the Lord your God' (Deuteronomy 20:18). It was in order to prevent the idolatry of the Canaanites, their detestable practices and sexual depravity from corrupting the people of God, that God commanded their total destruction.

But what was it about the Canaanites that was so detestable in the eyes of God? Canaanite worship elevated sex to the realm of the divine.[27] The Canaanite gods were sexual in nature and were worshipped in sexual rites. The chief god El and his son Baal were complete moral degenerates. According to Canaanite epic poetry a symbolic re-enactment of the incest between Baal and his mother Asherah formed an essential part of Canaanite fertility rites. Horrible sexual perversions are associated with El. He is represented as practising vile sex acts and influencing others to do likewise. It is little wonder that the evidence indicates that the Canaanites followed their gods in such abominations. In Canaanite religion, homosexuals and prostitutes were employed to raise money for the support of temples. It is not an exaggeration to say that these pagans elevated sex to the status of a god.[28] According to GE Wright, 'The amazing thing about the gods, as they were conceived in Canaan, is that they had no moral character whatsoever. In fact, their conduct was on a much lower level than that of society as a whole, if we can judge from ancient codes of law. Certainly the brutality of the mythology is far worse than anything else in the Near East at that time. Worship of these gods carried with it some of the most demoralising practices then in existence.'[29]

In worshipping their gods the Canaanites did 'all kinds of detestable things the Lord hates' (Deuteronomy 12:31). In *The Enigma of Evil*, John Wenham shows how the Old Testament directs its bitterest venom against Baalism and the cult of Molech. 'Baalism was a fertility cult, in which sexual licence was glorified as something religious and meritorious. There were "holy" prostitutes, male and female, for the gratification of the worshippers.'[30] The detestable things included human sacrifice, demonism, homosexuality, lesbianism and incest. Sexual orgies and promiscuity were commonplace among the phallic cults that permeated Canaanite religion. And the priests of the phallic cults performed their functions naked. And this exposure was prevalent throughout the ancient cults.[31] The Asherah, originally a symbol of the tree of life, was corrupted and debased into the organ of procreation. 'These symbols, in turn, became the incentive to all forms of impurity which were part of its libidinous worship, with the swarms of "devotees" involved in its obscene orgies… There can be no doubt about it being, in its essence, phallic worship pure and simple, whatever may have been its origin. This abomination was common to all the ancient nations; and relics of it are found today in various forms, in India and elsewhere.'[32]

The sexual debauchery of the Canaanites was an affront to the moral perfection of God. Moreover, God knew that the depravity of the Canaanites would prove to be a snare to his people, who were called to be holy. But the Israelites were disobedient and did not drive out the Canaanites as God commanded. It was not long before the Israelites learnt the detestable practices of the Canaanites, and did evil in the eyes of the Lord. 'They followed and worshipped various gods of the peoples around them. They provoked the Lord to anger because they forsook him and served Baal and the Ashtoreths' (Judges 2:12-13). Clifford Hill, in *Prophecy Past and Present*, shows that the great harvest festivals of Israel became associated with the fertility cults of the Asherah poles. 'They were predominantly sex cults and included both male and female shrine prostitution. These practices all became incorporated into the religion of Israel and Judah. Manasseh, for example, even introduced these practices into the Temple... These idolatrous practices included child sacrifice as part of the fertility rites which were roundly condemned by the prophets... It was not simply that the prophets disliked the disgusting practices of animal sacrifice, the detestable practices of ritual fornication or even the unthinkable horror of human sacrifice; their opposition to the whole sacrificial system was because their thinking about God was on an entirely different plane. To the ordinary Israelites sin was the neglect of ritual, but to the prophets it was the *violation of moral law*.'[33]

The purpose of God in his dealings with the Canaanites is to show that there can be no compromise with evil. The people of God are taught to detest utterly, and abhor, the abominations of the Canaanites. It is not difficult to see the similarity between the Canaanites and the modern day sex educators. Both are amoral, both have deified sex and both are devotees of depraved sexual practices. The uncovering of the sex organs is common to both. Indeed, phallic worship played an important part in Canaanite ritual, just as the condom demonstrator plays an important part in the work of the sex educator. Is the condom demonstrator not another phallic symbol?

Covering nakedness

It was because God is holy that only priests could enter into his presence in the temple. Moses was commanded to consecrate Aaron and his sons so that they could minister as priests, and they needed to be suitably covered before approaching the altar. 'Make linen undergarments as a covering for the body, reaching from the waist to the thigh. Aaron and his sons must wear them whenever they enter the Tent of Meeting or approach the altar to minister in the Holy Place, so that they will not incur guilt and die' (Exodus 28:42,43). As a witness to the holiness and purity of God, Aaron, the high priest, and his sons wore a plain linen undergarment to cover their genitals. This command for the priests of Israel to cover their genitals was in contradistinction to the priests of Baal. It was a heinous sin for the priests of Israel to appear before God with uncovered genitals, whereas in Canaanite worship exposing the genitalia was common practice.

In Leviticus the Bible gives a list of unlawful sexual relationships. The people of God were warned not to follow the detestable sexual practices of Egypt or Canaan. 'None of you shall approach to any that is near of kin to him to uncover their nakedness' (Leviticus 18:6). Incest, homosexuality and bestiality are forbidden. In the Old Testament, human nakedness and gross sexual immorality are linked in the mind of God. The principle of modesty, as expressed by the Aramaic word *tze'niut*, rejects the very idea of nakedness, both in public and at home. The opposite of modesty is 'abandon, looseness, and the absence of self-control' (*helkerut*). Extreme sexual immorality is described in the Bible as 'the uncovering of nakedness' (*gilui arayot*).

From the Old Testament texts considered above we have discovered a profound biblical truth—modesty is associated with the covering of sexual nakedness, while gross, shameless sexual immorality and idolatry is associated with the uncovering of nakedness.

Inner beauty, outward conduct

The apostle Paul emphasises the importance of modesty as a Christian virtue. 'I also want women to dress modestly, with decency and propriety, not with braided hair or gold or pearls or expensive clothes' (1 Timothy 2:9). A modest woman does not make an outward show of her female attributes and does not dress in a way that is sexually provocative or that attracts attention. The Greek word *aidos*, translated 'modestly' in this verse, signifies an appropriate reserve or sense of shame which preserves a woman from unbecoming behaviour. To dress modestly and decently implies that clothing must provide sufficient covering for the body so that others are not embarrassed or tempted. The purpose of modesty is not only to prevent lustful desires, but also to preserve the marital relationship. Modesty helps husband and wife to maintain a deep, intimate relationship. A modesty of spirit expresses itself in outward conduct, and influences the way a woman dresses and speaks, her general demeanour, and especially the way she behaves in the presence of men. Based on this great biblical principle, a modest woman is careful to avoid any outward sexual display; she does not use revealing clothes, or make up, or jewellery in order to attract the opposite sex.

The apostle Peter also explains the importance of modesty as a virtue that enhances the inner beauty of women. The wife of an unbelieving husband should let him see the purity and reverence of her life, for her beauty 'should not come from outward adornment, such as braided hair and the wearing of gold jewellery and fine clothes. Instead, it should be that of your inner self, the unfading beauty of a gentle and quiet spirit, which is of great worth in God's sight' (1 Peter 3:3-4). A quintessential characteristic of modesty is a quiet and gentle spirit, which shows an underlying desire for sexual purity. It demonstrates a woman's true worth as a person. By its very nature, because of its sexual connotation, modesty is primarily directed towards men, and makes a clear statement of a woman's intention to preserve her sexuality for the one man who will be her husband and the father of her children. And there is a mystery about the modest woman, for although she does not strive to be overtly sexual, she radiates true feminine attributes. Because modesty reveals a woman's inner beauty, it is attractive to the man who loves her and chooses her to be his wife. So a woman who follows the moral standards of the Bible is careful not to parade her sexuality in a way that encourages lust.

New Testament teaching reinforces the idea that God's moral law requires sexual purity. Jesus set the standard of sexual purity when he warned men not to look at women with lustful thoughts—to do so is tantamount to adultery (Matthew 5:28). Notice that it is men who are warned, not women, as men are especially prone to the temptation of sexual lust. The woman's body attracts men, and our Lord recognised this fact when he set a new standard of sexual purity. Because of their relative sexual freedom in that they do not have the responsibility of bearing children, men are able to satisfy their sexual cravings without the consequences that women face, and are especially prone to the sin of lust in a way that women are not. So a man must not look at women with evil cravings; he must learn the virtue of self-control for it helps him deal with sexual temptation.

Jesus' command that men should not look with lust at women places an onus on women to dress, speak and behave with decency and propriety, and not in a way that is sexually enticing. The woman who displays herself is foolish for she is attracting men for all the wrong reasons. There is the grave danger that men show interest in her not because of her worth as a person, but because they think that they may gain her sexual favours. The immodest woman, who appears to attract many men, finds that the respect she longs for is not there, and the more men she has, the less she is respected and the more she devalues her womanhood. Even in our sexually liberated society men lose respect for the 'easy' woman, although they don't always say so. Immodesty has its price.

Mother of all the living

By her nature, woman was created to be 'mother of all the living' (Genesis 3:20). By design of the Creator a woman's sexuality is inextricably bound up with bearing children, and so it is natural for women to desire motherhood. In this regard there is a fundamental difference between the sexual nature of a man and that of a woman. For women one of the potential consequences of sexual activity is pregnancy, and all women instinctively understand this, and this is why most are repelled by the idea of casual sex. They know that sexual sin, unlike most other sins, has consequences that may be lifelong and may affect many other people, especially members of their family. It is the height of immorality for a woman to become pregnant by a man who is not her husband, for she is disregarding God's moral law, showing that she does not really care that her children may grow up without a father, and outside a legitimate family structure. Such a woman has put her own selfish desires before the welfare of her children. Because motherhood is the ultimate purpose of female sexuality, a prudent woman will only have sexual intercourse with her husband, so that her children have a father who shares in their upbringing.

Men, on the other hand, can escape the consequences of nurturing children in a way in which women cannot. Women are pregnant for nine months and always physically present at the birth of their children. Not so men—they are only present if they choose to be present, and we all know that some men desert the women they have impregnated. Women therefore must be on their guard against predatory men who seek only to gratify their sexual desires, caring nothing for the consequences of their actions. The man who persuades a single woman to 'have sex' on the pretext that he loves her is a deceiver—what he really wants is to satisfy his lust. The man who truly loves a woman will not place her in the position where she may become the mother of a child he does not want.

The book 'Return to Modesty'

In her book *Return to Modesty*, Wendy Shalit, a young Jewish woman, testifies to the importance of sexual modesty. She explains how she became aware of the Jewish modesty law which meant not touching boyfriends before marriage. She argues that many of the problems facing modern young women, such as sexual harassment, stalking and rape are all expressions of a society which has lost its respect for female modesty.[34] She relates the story of her experience of sex education as an innocent nine-year-old girl. She tells how the sex educator confronted the class with the question: 'What is 69?' Wendy Shalit realised that there was more to the question when some of the boys started giggling. The sex educator responded by telling the children that there was absolutely nothing to giggle about. Wendy explains her embarrassment at the proceedings and how she excused herself and escaped to the toilet. She related the incident to her mother who was so upset by the whole episode that she arranged for Wendy to be withdrawn from future sex education lessons.

Shalit believes that young girls are still experts on embarrassment. 'Everyone tells us not to be self-conscious, but we always are. It's as if the world's embarrassment passed through us, from generation to generation.' Why do young girls get so embarrassed? 'It's a very important question in the life of a girl. Today, embarrassment is something to "overcome", but maybe if so many girls are still embarrassed, even in an age when we're not supposed to be, maybe we have our embarrassment for a reason. The natural embarrassment sex education seeks so prissily to erode—"Now remember, boys and girls, there is absolutely nothing to giggle about!"—may point to a far richer understanding of sex than do our most explicit sex manuals. Children now are urged to overcome their "inhibitions" before they have a clue what an inhibition means. Yet embarrassment is actually a wonderful thing, signalling that something very strange or very significant is going on, that some boundary is being threatened—either by you or by others. Without embarrassment, kids are weaker; more vulnerable to pregnancy, disease and heartbreak.'[35]

Shalit believes that most women do not want a whole series of sexual partners, but really want 'one enduring love', one man who will stick by them, for better or for worse. She concludes that 'modesty is a reflex, arising naturally to help a woman protect her hopes and guide their fulfillment—specifically, this hope is for one man'.[36] When a man lets a woman down, her hopes are dashed. This is where modesty comes in. 'For modesty armed this special vulnerability—not to oppress women, but with the aim of putting them on an equal footing with men. The delay modesty created not only made it more likely that women could select men who would stick by them, but in turning lust into love, it changed men from uncivilised males who ran after as many sexual partners as they can get to men who really wanted to stick by one woman.'[37] Shalit believes that women who dress and act modestly conduct themselves in a way that shrouds their sexuality in mystery. They live in a way that makes womanliness more a transcendent, implicit quality than a crude, explicit quality.[38]

While Shalit's argument that most women want a sexual relationship with only one man is intuitively correct, a large survey of teenage sexual behaviour undertaken in the UK in the early 1960s confirms it to be true. In response to the question 'would you like to be a virgin when you marry?' 85 per cent of the girls, aged 15 to 19 years, responded yes.[39] According to *The Sexual Behaviour of Young People*, when young girls were asked why they had not become sexually active, many took it for granted that their first experience of sexual intercourse would occur after they had married. Among sexually experienced young women, the vast majority (88 per cent) admitted that they had thought about pregnancy when they had sex with their boyfriends, and 70 per cent had feared pregnancy. Among the sexually experienced boys, on the other hand, only 51 per cent said that they had been afraid of a possible pregnancy on one or more occasions. 'An important inhibiting influence on teenage sexual behaviour was fear of pregnancy, just as it was the most usual reason for restraint given by the sexually active girls.'[40]

Girls mentioned moral reasons and reputation as important restraining factors. Those 'who permit premarital intercourse are disparaged by some boys, even by the boys who are seeking to have intercourse with them'.[41] In response to the question 'would you like to have sex with your fiancé before you marry?' only 22 per cent of girls responded yes, compared to 40 per cent of boys. Furthermore, 61 per cent of girls agreed that sexual intercourse before marriage is wrong, compared with 35 per cent of boys. 'Most girls do not want to have sex before they marry, and they believe that their boyfriends want to marry a virgin. They also believe, more often than the boys, that a girl who has sex before marriage gets a bad reputation.'[42]

The findings of this survey, conducted in the early 1960s when the permissive era had already begun, shows beyond any doubt that the vast majority of young women wanted to be chaste, and did not want to have sex before marriage. And the large majority of those who were sexually active were afraid of pregnancy, which is recognised as a restraining influence on female behaviour. The young men tended to have different views, and were more liberal in their attitude to premarital sex. It is clear that all teenagers expected girls to be much more circumspect than boys. The majority of girls accepted the view 'that girls who have sex before marriage get a bad reputation. They also want to be virgins when they marry and realise that this is what the boys expect; more girls than boys believe that most boys want to marry virgins.'[43] Young women know that if they sleep around they get a bad reputation. In their heart of hearts they want to keep themselves pure for their husband.

The virtue of chivalry

Chivalry is the virtue that flows from Peter's instruction to husbands to treat their wives with respect 'as the weaker partner and heirs with you of the gracious gift of life' (1 Peter 3:7). It is a male virtue based in the respect that men have towards women. It is founded on biblical truth, and provides the moral framework in which worthy men relate to women; it teaches a man to become a gentleman, committed to honour and principle. It reveals itself in a man's courteous behaviour towards women. Like modesty it comes from the inner self and is a reflection of God's moral law; men, as created in the image of God, have an innate potential for defending, serving and honouring women. In 1878 the United States Court declared, 'Man is, or ought to be, woman's protector and defender... it is the law of the Creator'. Two weeks after the sinking of the Titanic in 1912, Second Officer Lightoller told a United States Senate panel that 'women and children first' was more than just the law of the sea—'It is the law of human nature.' It is God who ordained man as the head of the family, charged him with the protection of his family, and instructed him to treat his wife deferentially as the weaker partner. It is because men are called to lead that they must be the first to give their lives.[44]

Bound up in the virtue of chivalry is a recognition that women are the weaker sex, for they do not have the same physical strength or aggressive nature as men. Chivalry recognises a woman's sexual vulnerability in that she is prone to pregnancy, childbirth and motherhood. This leads to a general respect for womanhood, which results in men treating women with special esteem and honour. A chivalrous man understands that for a woman there is no such thing as casual sex, for she bears the awful responsibility of conceiving a new life and all that that involves. A chivalrous man does not take sexual advantage and does not place a woman in a compromising position. He is careful to do nothing that will impinge on her sexual propriety or tarnish her reputation. Chivalry and honour inspire genuine relationships between the sexes, such as courtship, love, and marriage—they reveal a man's true worth, and are the essential masculine virtues that capture a woman's heart.

It is natural for the chivalrous man to protect a woman from physical danger; he defends a woman against the designs of brutish men. For centuries a distinguishing mark of the western maritime tradition was that, in times of crisis, women and children received preferential treatment. A chivalrous man also protects the dignity and modesty of a woman. He behaves with respect, politeness and decorum in the presence of a woman; he does not use foul language or behave in a loutish way; he does not tell smutty jokes in her presence and he does not make sexual innuendoes that are offensive to her modesty; he always stands up when a woman enters the room and he holds the door for her. So we see that chivalry modifies men's conduct towards women just as modesty modifies women's conduct towards men.

In Victorian England the idea of the gentleman was taken seriously. The worth of the true English gentleman depended upon moral character. According to Gertrude Himmelfarb the gentleman was identified by his moral virtues of integrity, honesty, generosity, courage, graciousness, politeness and consideration for others. 'By moralising the idea of the gentleman, the Victorians democratized it as well, extending it to the middle classes and even, on occasions, to the working class.'[45]

In his essay on chivalry Mitchell Kalpakgian explains that, unlike the Christian ideals of manhood as described in Louisa May Alcott's novel, *Little Men*, and the heroism exalted in Victorian England, the postmodern world fails to teach that maleness is essentially noble and chivalrous. 'Chivalry can flourish only when a culture clearly defines the meaning of masculinity and femininity. A gentleman knows that a woman deserves to be treated in special, considerate, sensitive ways that are reflected in manners, speech and courtesy. If men and women look alike, dress alike, talk alike and act alike, then the mysterious, idealistic or romantic relationship between men and women disappears... Chivalry also flourishes when women hold men to high standards, expecting them to be magnanimous, gallant, civilised and chaste. The ideals that women instil in boys, and that they expect of men, determine the moral climate of a society. Do sex education courses, coeducational dormitories, and condom distribution in schools promote the chivalrous treatment of women, or do they encourage the lustful exploitation of women for selfish pleasure? Without the virtue of chastity governing the relationship between men and women, the respect due to a woman's honour is absent.'[46]

He argues that contraception undermines chivalry. Instead of being treated, by men and herself, as worthy of courtship, respect, dignity, and devotion, woman has become a mere instrument of selfish enjoyment, rather than a man's respected and beloved companion. A woman intuitively senses when she is loved for her own sake and responds with gratitude, beauty, and generosity. 'This kind of love is dynamic and surprising, not perfunctory; a mutual giving and receiving in self-donation, not a hidden form of selfishness; a priceless gift, not a calculated risk. This is the mystery of love that is lost in the sexual revolution that substitutes "safe sex" for the adventure of romance. When women are taught to resent masculinity, chivalry is stifled. When chastity is not the norm, men and women cannot idealise or respect each other. When educators assume that boys and girls must be sexually active rather than gentlemen and ladies, ideals such as honour evaporate. Instead of romance, which leads to the wonderful vision of the true, the good, and the beautiful incarnate in the beloved, we are left with only the various forms of lust advertised as sexual liberation. Without chivalry, love loses its heart, and men and women become less than human.'

Kalpakgian concludes that chivalry trains the male heart to put the woman first, while sexual liberation puts self-gratification first and women last. 'While chivalry evokes the princess or lady in a woman, the contraceptive mentality treats her as an object. While chivalry glories in the femininity of women and in the idealism of love, unisex thinking reduces sexuality to mere orgasm. Without chivalry informing the characters of men and shaping the education of boys, preparation for marriage suffers.'[47]

Embarrassment

We have already seen that an important aim of the sexual revolution is to undermine the Christian virtue of modesty. In *The Sexual Revolution*, discussed in chapter 7, Reich made the point that nakedness and exposure of the sexual organs was a crucial element of sex education's attack on conventional morality. He believed that society could only become 'sex-affirming' when people lost the shyness to expose their genitals. A key question was 'whether one should accustom them [children] to the sight of the naked human body, more specifically, to the human genitals'.[48] Reich propagated the idea that parents should appear naked before their children. David Mace, in his vision of a world in which the sexual revolution had already taken place, saw sexual language as part of a child's means of communication as soon as he began to speak.

A problem for the sexual revolutionaries is the innate, God-given, emotional response of embarrassment that has the function of protecting against sexual indecency. We become embarrassed when sexual matters are dealt with in a manner that offends our inner spirit. As we know, virtually all children and parents are highly embarrassed at the mention of sexual matters and the sight of sexual images. Our sense of embarrassment inhibits us from talking openly about sex or exposing our sexual organs. This innate sense warns that we are overstepping a boundary; that we are intruding into territory that is not open to us; that we are entering into the forbidden area of sexual indecency.

Sex educators know that to teach explicit messages they need unembarrassed, receptive children. This is why sex education has developed techniques for over-coming embarrassment. Children are coerced into using words and looking at images from which they would naturally recoil. But in a group situation children are under subtle pressure to conform. They are expected to appear cool, adult, unconcerned, and at all costs, to avoid showing their embarrassment. In these circumstances it takes enormous courage for a young child to object. The sex educator hopes that if children are exposed for long enough their sense of embar-rassment and shame will diminish and eventually disappear. And when children are no longer embarrassed, they become receptive to explicit sexual images and feel no shame. Everything becomes permissible, and nothing, no image, no suggestion, no conduct is shameful. Sex educators, with their desensitised children, can plummet the depths of depravity in the name of 'safer sex'.

The promotion of sexually explicit images among mixed groups of children undermines modesty in girls and chivalry in boys. Teaching girls to use sexual words, to view sexual images and to unroll condoms on to a condom demonstrator, is to demean their modesty and dishonours them in front of other children. The assumption that girls need to know about contraception creates the impression in the fertile imagination of young boys that girls cannot wait to become sexually active. Girls are placed in a situation where they appear to be interested in sex, and in the minds of boys they become sex objects. What excuse can any girl have for not agreeing to have sex with her boyfriend when she knows all about 'safe sex'? And what girl who has practised unrolling condoms can pretend to be modest? These girls are trapped—they are being prepared for a life of promiscuous sex.

It is not difficult to see the link between sexual explicitness and sexual temp-tation. Boys are introduced to explicit images that arouse unnatural thoughts and inflame sexual lust. Suddenly the idea that they can have sex with a schoolgirl is not a distant fantasy, but a distinct possibility. In the minds of boys, girls become potential sexual partners, for they know about sex and they know about the mechanics of contraception. Boys, in their fantasy life, imagine that girls really do want to have sex. Any chivalrous thoughts towards girls are blown away, and the gateway to promiscuity is opened wide.

When modesty is destroyed, girls lose their innate protection against sexual lust. They lose their sexual innocence and appear to be sexually available; they become objects of pleasure, to be used and discarded. Casual sex becomes the norm and there are no restraints. Sex is no longer an intensely private matter between husband and wife, but a trivialised game, a plaything, something to give pleasure to lustful males. When boys lose their God-given chivalry, they lose respect for the female sex and themselves, and become sexual predators, who feel entitled to satisfy their lusts on the objects of their sexual desire.

To appreciate the value of modesty and chivalry we need to grasp the universal truth that all mankind struggles against the 'lusts of the flesh which war against the soul' (1 Peter 2:11). The acts of our sinful nature include sexual immorality, impurity and debauchery (Galatians 5:19). The first chapter of Romans warns that those who reject the truth of God are susceptible to sexual impurity (Romans 1:24). Fallen human nature is liable to seek ways of gratifying the desires of the flesh (Romans 13:12). Yielding to these desires leads to impurity and sexual immorality.

For this reason it is vitally important for men, women and children to avoid anything that may arouse sexual lust. In particular, young men should avoid sexual images and suggestions, for they are especially prone to sexual cravings. One of the reasons why sex education is so wrong is that it encourages impure thoughts and inflames sexual desires that lead to sexual temptation. The Bible protects young people from sexual sin by teaching the fundamental importance of sexual purity, thereby promoting modesty among women and self-control among men. The modest young woman avoids any sexual display that may arouse lust, while the chivalrous young man practises self-control, carefully avoiding sexual talk and images that may inflame the lusts of the flesh. He relates to young women with absolute purity (1 Timothy 5:2), which helps to avoid sexual temptation .

Contrasting the sexual revolutionaries with the Victorians

Here we need to pause for a moment to recognise the vast gulf between the moral teaching of the Bible and the teaching of sex education. What we have uncovered is a conflict between two world-views—the biblical view, founded on God's standard of sexual purity and the virtues of modesty and chivalry, and the sex education view, founded on sexual explicitness. This conflict is vividly illustrated by comparing the behaviour of the Victorian Christians and the sex educators. We have already seen, in chapter 3, the enormous emphasis that Victorians placed on the virtue of modesty. In their conduct and dress code Victorian women were models of modesty. We have also seen the Victorian's determination that language and literature should be pure and free from sexual innuendo and indecency.

262

Now look at the sex educators. We have seen how Marie Stopes used explicit language in her books. We have seen Reich's strong approval of nakedness, and his claim that explicit sex education would remove one stone after the other from the edifice of Christian morality. He understood that sexual explicitness constituted an attack on the ideals of purity, modesty and chastity. Look at the shameful sexual images that are presented to children in sex education materials. The sexual revolutionaries have correctly identified sexual purity and modesty as the greatest obstacles to their revolution. And this is an important truth; purity and modesty form a powerful bulkhead against the sexual revolution, for they teach young people to recoil from the explicit images of sex education and discourage children from talking about sex. The revolutionaries knew that for their ideology to gain acceptance, they needed to destroy the virtues of modesty and chivalry that were such characteristic features of Victorian England. The revolutionaries skilfully transformed the virtue of modesty into the vice of Victorian prudery. And Victorian prudery, of course, was an easy object for ridicule.

It is arguable that the explicit images of sex education are, in reality, part of a modern phallic cult that worships at the shrine of sexual gratification. The explicit images are designed to inflame the imagination, and make young men and women burn with lust. Inevitably some children will be tempted into promiscuous sexual activity by the action of the sex educators. They have a lot to answer for.

Endnotes

1 *The Times*, 7 August 1968, Facts about life, Julian Critchley
2 *Daily Telegraph*, 3 March 1994, Drive to cut teenage pregnancy, David Fletcher
3 *Teenage Pregnancy*, HMSO, London, June 1999, p95
4 *Sex and Relationship Education Guidance*, DfEE, July 2000, p22
5 *SRE & Parents*, DfES publications, 0706/2001
6 *The Times*, 31 October 1990, Never too young for the facts of life, Mary Ann Sieghart
7 Sol Gordon, 'Freedom for Sex Education and Sexual Expression', in *Sexuality Today – and Tomorrow*, ed. Sol Gordon and Roger Libby, Duxbury, California, 1976, pp333-34
8 Family Planning Association, *Talking to your child about sex*, 7/98
9 Ibid.
10 Ibid.
11 Steve Chalke, *The Parentalk Guide to your Child and Sex*, Hodder & Stoughton, 2000, p17
12 Ibid. p39
13 Ibid. pp31-32
14 Ibid. p43
15 SIECUS, website, *Now What Do I Do?*
16 Pete Sanders and Liz Swinden, *Knowing me, knowing you*, LDA, 1990, pp111-12
17 FPA, *The weird and wonderful world of Billy Ballgreedy*, Matthew Crozier, p8
18 Cited from Judith Reisman, *Kinsey: Crimes & Consequences*, The Institute for Media Education, 1998, 2nd edition, p177
19 SIECUS, *Guidelines for Comprehensive Sexuality Education*, the National Guidelines Task Force, 1991, p9, cited from *Kinsey: Crimes & Consequences*, p179
20 Thomas Trevethan, *The Beauty of God's Holiness*, InterVarsity Press, 1995, p13
21 David Peterson, *Possessed by God; A New Testament theology of sanctification and holiness*, InterVarsity Press, 1995, pp82-84

22 Claus Westermann, *Genesis 1-11*, translated John Scullion, Augsburg Publishing House, 1984, p236

23 Gordon Wenham, Word Biblical Commentary, *Genesis 1-15*, Word Books, Texas, 1987, p84

24 Ibid. Claus Westermann, *Genesis 1-11*, p488

25 Ibid. p488

26 John Calvin, *The Book of Genesis*, translated by John King, The Banner of Truth, reprinted 1979, p303

27 Bernhard Anderson, *Understanding the Old Testament*, 4th edition, 1986, pp14-92

28 Wayne Jackson, *Old Testament events and the goodness of God*, Christian Courier: Archives

29 GE Wright, cited from John Wenham, *The Enigma of Evil*, Eagle, 1994, pp140-41

30 John Wenham, *The Enigma of Evil*, Eagle, 1994, p140

31 *Idolatry and the Phallic Cult*, Malachi, 2:9-12, www.realtime.net

32 The Companion Bible, *The Asherah*, appendix 42, written by EW Bullinger

33 Clifford Hill, *Prophecy Past and Present*, Highland Books, Crowborough, 1989, pp151-52

34 Wendy Shalit, *Return to Modesty*, The Free Press, New York, 1999, p10

35 Ibid. pp21-22

36 Ibid. p94

37 Ibid. p95

38 Ibid. p97

39 Michael Schofield, *The Sexual Behaviour of Young People*, Penguin Books, 1969, p111

40 Ibid. p107

41 Ibid. p107

42 Ibid. p110

43 Ibid. p110

44 Doug Phillips, 'Titanic Chivalry', *Living*, Lutherans for Life, vol. 11, no. 4, winter 1998

45 Gertrude Himmelfarb, *The De-moralization of Society*, The Institute of Economic Affairs, London, 1995, p46

46 Mitchell Kalpakgian, *Chivalry Scorned is Love Denatured*, New Oxford Review, October 2000, pp29-32

47 Ibid.

48 *The Sexual Revolution*, Wilhelm Reich, translated by Theodore Wolfe, Vision Press, 1969, p61

Chapter 18

Sex education, marriage and the family

The biblical view of human sexuality;
marriage and the traditional family traduced

For centuries Western society believed that the marriage of one man and one woman for life is the basis of a good society. Consistent with this belief is the idea that procreation should take place only in marriage. It was widely believed in society that for women to give birth outside marriage is immoral and, as a consequence, children born to unmarried women used to be referred to as illegitimate. Christianity has always believed that cohabitation, a relationship in which a man and woman live together and engage in sexual intercourse without being married, is against the moral standards of the Bible. The sexual revolutionaries, on the other hand, have always seen marriage as a bulwark against their permissive ideas.

The early British socialists, under the leadership of Robert Owen, attacked marriage as a source of oppression. Their assault was based mainly on economic and political arguments, as they believed that marriage denied women equality, and was a cause of economic dependency. But these arguments had little popular support. Early revolutionaries, such as Edward Carpenter and Wilhelm Reich, attacked marriage on moral grounds. Carpenter opposed marriage of the 'common prayer book type' that made a woman subservient to her husband.[1] He argued for a marriage relationship that was freer, more companionable and less exclusive. He asserted that the odious marriage law, which bound people together for life, needed to be abolished or at least modified.[2] Reich's argument was that the institution of marriage acted as the brake on sexual reform. He believed that the sexual repression inherent in marriage helped to maintain chastity and marital fidelity. To Reich the family was 'the foremost breeding ground of traditional morality'. It deprived women and children of their sexual rights and educated people in the ideals of lifelong, monogamous marriage; and the patriarchal family demanded sexual abstinence of youth as the logical measure. The links between chastity, lifelong marriage and the family meant that there was a 'contradiction between the desire for sexual reform and conservative marriage ideology'.[3] There is no doubt that in the mindset of the sexual revolutionaries, marriage and the traditional family were regarded as major barriers to a sexually free society. For the revolution to succeed the obstacle created by marriage needed to be overcome.

According to the revolutionaries society needed a 'new morality' that was not based on oppressive moral laws; a 'new morality' that allowed people the freedom to express their natural sexual desires without the restraints imposed by marriage. Their slogan was 'free love', and they sought social acceptance for men and women to live together, in a sexual relationship, without being married.

The biblical view of human sexuality

The sexual nature of mankind is central to the biblical message and is explained in the very first chapter of the Bible. 'God created man in his own image, in the image of God he created him; male and female he created them. God blessed them and said to them, "Be fruitful and increase in number; fill the earth and subdue it"' (Genesis 1:27, 28). God created mankind as sexual beings with the God-given gift of reproduction, and instituted marriage immediately after he had created the first man and woman, while Adam and Eve were still in the Garden of Eden. It is God's will that men and women should be united in marriage—thereby creating the families that will propagate the human race.

At the time of creation the Lord God emphasised the need that mankind has for companionship, and this companionship is central to the sexual relationship between male and female. Men and women are not created to live in isolation, but to live in relationship with each other. 'The Lord God said, "It is not good for the man to be alone. I will make a helper suitable for him." ...Then the Lord God made a woman from the rib he had taken out of the man, and he brought her to the man' (Genesis 2:18, 22). God created a woman from the rib of man, thereby highlighting the closeness of the relationship between the sexes and providing a symbol of the one flesh union created at marriage. The words 'a helper suitable for him' refer to the personal community of man and woman in the broadest sense – both a bodily and a spiritual community, with mutual help, understanding and contentment as the main characteristics. Creation reached its goal in the complementary society of man and woman.[4] Men and women are created in such a way that it is natural for them to be joined to each other in a sexual relationship.

So we see that the sexual nature of mankind is fundamental to God's creation plan. In the original purpose of God, humanity is complete in man and woman. The human race is divided into two sexes and both are required for procreation. Neither male nor female is complete on his or her own—men and women need each other. The sexuality of mankind is both integral and indispensable in the structure of human society. According to Philip Hughes, writing in *Christian Ethics in Secular Society*, biblical teaching concerning the purpose of sexuality is clear and consistent. Hughes makes the point that 'the primary function served by the creation of two sexes is the procreation of children and the propagation of the race. The design of the sexual organs is obviously for this purpose, enabling the man to contribute and the woman to receive the male sperm for the impregnation of the ova in her womb, where during gestation the new human being is formed and grows; her breasts are intended for the suckling of the newborn child. The difference between male and female physical and anatomical structures plainly points to procreation as the primary purpose of sexuality. Erotic stimulation is meant to serve this end, not to be an end in itself.'[5]

God's command to be fruitful and multiply and fill the earth is to be fulfilled by man and woman joining together in sexual intercourse. And God has placed within human nature a strong natural sexual attraction between men and women, as is clear from Adam's response when he first sees the female form. In delight he sings out, 'this woman is now bone of my bones and flesh of my flesh' (Genesis 2:23). We are endowed with sexual desires that make it natural for us to be attracted to the opposite sex and to enter a sexual relationship. But we are not free to indulge our sexual appetites as we wish, for God has given us moral laws to control our behaviour. These moral laws are not only right, they are also for our good. At the heart of God's moral law on sexuality is the command that sexual intercourse should take place within the marriage union. God's command to be fruitful and increase in number is fulfilled by the marriage of a man to his wife. Human sexuality, therefore, finds its true meaning in the marriage relationship and the procreation of the human race.

The marriage ordinance (Genesis 2:24)

Following the introduction of Eve to Adam, God lays down the principle that is to govern the sexual relationship between men and women. 'For this reason a man will leave his father and mother and be united to his wife, and they will become one flesh' (Genesis 2:24). Here we have the explanation for the universal instinct which impels a man to separate from his parents and cling to his wife.[6] The scripture explains the reason for marriage—it is because of the fundamental unity between man and woman. By joining together in sexual intercourse, husband and wife have the potential to create a new life which is the natural fruit of their marriage union. Husband and wife, through the fruitfulness of their marriage union, become father and mother to children born as a consequence of their 'one flesh' union. Both Jesus, in the gospels of Matthew and Mark, and the apostle Paul, in Ephesians 5:25-33, referred to Genesis 2:24 to explain the mystery of the 'one flesh' union created by marriage.

The sinfulness of men and women (Genesis 3)

The inherent sinfulness of mankind is widely acknowledged, and the pathway of history is strewn with evidence of mankind's sinful nature. The Bible provides a clear explanation of mankind's tendency to sin. The third chapter of Genesis tells how Adam and Eve disobeyed God's command not to eat from the tree of the knowledge of good and evil. By this act of rebellion against God, sin entered the human race and all became sinners. The Bible tells us, 'There is no one righteous, not even one... All have turned away, they have together become worthless; there is no one who does good, not even one' (Romans 3: 10, 12). This truth, that all people are sinful, is one of the most profound truths of the Bible, for it demonstrates that all mankind are in need of salvation from sin. It also explains why we live in an imperfect world, with imperfect human relationships. The corollary of this is that relationships between men and women are affected by the tendency to sin. It follows that all marriages will have problems, for both husbands and wives are imperfect sinful human beings.

The maternal instinct

Marriage is the God-given way in which the mandate to be fruitful is to be fulfilled. After the Fall, when Adam and Eve rebelled against the law of God, the Lord God addressed the woman and the man in turn, telling each the consequences of their sin. To the woman God said, 'I will greatly increase your pains in childbearing; with pain you will give birth to children. Your desire will be for your husband, and he will rule over you.' To the man God said, 'Cursed is the ground because of you; through painful toil you will eat of it all the days of your life' (Genesis 3:16,17). The main role of the man in the marriage union is 'painful toil' as he works to provide for his family, and the main role of the woman is to 'give birth to children'. Adam showed that he understood the role of women when he 'named his wife Eve, because she would become the mother of all the living' (Genesis 3:20). In God's plan for mankind, it is the role of women to bear children and become mothers. There is no more universal truth than the fact that every living person has a mother. And God has created women in such a way that it is natural for them to become pregnant and bear children. And more, it is natural for a woman to desire to become pregnant by her husband, the man who will be the father of her children. This natural desire is sometimes referred to as the maternal instinct.

Because woman is created in the image of God, she has an inborn, innate understanding of the maternal role. This is seen in her desire to have children and also in an understanding that she should have children only within the marriage relationship. Biblical wisdom teaches that the 'special sphere of the wife's authority is seen as the home, where she is in charge of all the domestic arrangements and, as the homemaker, makes provision for the care and well-being of the whole family'.[7] It is God's will that children should be born into a family created by marriage. God has placed within the conscience of womankind strong natural inhibitions to restrain them from abusing their gift of motherhood by giving birth outside marriage. A woman feels a natural restraint against a sexual relationship with a man who is not her husband. Her conscience warns that sex outside marriage is wrong, and she fears the consequences of an unintended pregnancy. This is why most young women are afraid of having sexual intercourse with a man who is not their husband; most women do not relish casual sex. The stakes are simply too high—momentary pleasure followed by the unmitigated disaster of a pregnancy with no prospect of marriage. And what of the child that is born as a result of a casual sexual relationship? The following testimony of a young woman born in such circumstances demonstrates the long-term consequences of sexual immorality: 'I feel guilt—horrid, deep, dirty feelings of guilt—guilt at being a mishap, a mistake, an unwanted inconvenience—guilt at only feeling half a person, anger with my mother for allowing this to happen to her, anger with my father, whoever he is, for indulging himself and then avoiding all responsibility for his actions...'[8] Few women want their child to suffer the wretchedness associated with being born outside wedlock. This is why women instinctively want to wait until after marriage before they engage in a sexual relationship with their husband.

According to the Bible, marriage has two main purposes. The first is to create a lifelong, secure, personal, intimate relationship between a man and woman. Having set up home together, sexual intercourse is the physical bond that unites husband and wife; they enjoy a sexual relationship, which expresses their love and commitment to each other, without guilt, fear or shame. A husband loves his wife for she is his one flesh partner, a part of his body. A wife respects her husband and submits to him, for he is the head of the family, and the father of her children. The second purpose of marriage, inexplicably intertwined with the first, is to produce children. By joining together in a sexual relationship, husband and wife accept with joy the possibility that children may be born into their family. Children are a gift from God, the ultimate expression of the one flesh union created by marriage. Husband and wife are now also father and mother, and together they provide a home in which their children are nurtured as they grow into adulthood. A marriage blessed with many children is blessed indeed, for blessed is the man whose quiver is full of children (Psalm 127:5). And there is no greater joy than for a married couple to see their children, as they grow into adulthood, marry and start families of their own and, in time, produce grandchildren.

The marriage rates in England and Wales have declined dramatically over the last three decades, to reach their lowest point since statistics were first collected in 1838. Behind this decline is a serious and ongoing ideological challenge to the relevance and meaning of marriage. The institution of marriage has come under a sustained attack from the intelligentsia and opinion formers in Britain as a growing body of literature has challenged the relevance of marriage in the modern world. Many social commentators claim that marriage is a cause of women's oppression, an institution that inhibits psychological growth. Marriage has been portrayed as the foundation of the patriarchal society, an institution based on sexual inequality. It has become fashionable for articles in women's magazines, feature articles in newspapers and comments on radio and television to adopt a position that is cynical about marriage. Many celebrities now openly express their opposition to marriage, and many choose to live with their partners without being married.

In today's world the distinction between legal marriage and informal cohabitation has become blurred as many people claim that there is no essential difference. Language is used in a way that encourages the idea that marriage and cohabitation are morally equivalent relationships. The word 'partner' is now used to refer to couples living together, whether they are married or not, while the words 'husband' and 'wife' are falling into disuse, no longer used in polite conversation for fear of causing offence to unmarried couples. Official Government publications now routinely use the word 'partner' in place of 'husband' or 'wife'.

Sex education and marriage

We saw in chapter 1 that the Government's guidance on sex education makes it clear that children should be taught 'that there are strong and mutually supportive relationships outside marriage. Therefore pupils should learn the significance of marriage and stable relationships as key building blocks of community and society.'[9] The problem with this approach is that it suggests that so-called 'other stable relationships' are morally equivalent to marriage. Implicit within the term 'other stable relationships' are cohabiting and same-sex relationships. It follows that Government sponsored sex education is teaching children that it is morally acceptable to live in so-called 'stable' sexual relationships without being married. The impression created in the minds of children is that marriage is simply one lifestyle choice and cohabitation another, and young people are free to choose whichever option suits them.

In its response to the Government's guidance on sex and relationships education, the FPA explains that 'emphasising marriage in a hierarchy of relationships excludes or stigmatises sections of the population that other Government policies are seeking to include. These include those from single parent families, unmarried mothers, young gay men and lesbians. To emphasise marriage is also to promote hetero-sexuality, although the document states on numerous occasions that to promote sexual orientation would be inappropriate. Rather than emphasise the importance of one type of relationship over another, we recommend that relationships are described in terms of the positive qualities that are necessary.'[10] Clearly then, both the Government and the FPA are agreed that sex education should not emphasise the importance of marriage. Instead, marriage should be presented as simply one type of relationship among a number of others, so that children, when they grow up, are free to choose the type of sexual relationship with which they feel comfort-able. A significant objection to marriage, in the mind of the FPA, is that it promotes heterosexuality, and this flies in the face of sex education's position that homo-sexuality, bisexuality and heterosexuality are moral equivalents.

While sex education is profoundly anti-marriage in its underlying ideology, its usual technique is simply to ignore marriage. In other words, sex education usually teaches young people about sex without mentioning marriage. This point is illustrated in an article written by a teacher, Susan Elkin, who is brave enough to report what is actually happening in sex education. She explains how the head of

270

science asked her to teach a sex education module to a class of 14 and 15-year-olds. She was provided with a pile of worksheets and a box of contraceptive samples, and given the task of teaching the children the mechanics of contraception, with the clear instruction, 'We don't, as a matter of policy, mention marriage or use the terms "husband" or "wife".'[11]

The unwritten text for much of what passes as sex education therefore is to give young people the impression that it is the norm to 'have sex' without being married. Sex education invites young people into a world of sexual pleasure in which marriage is irrelevant. Indeed, in a survey of sex education literature we will be hard pressed to find the word marriage, and where it is mentioned, it will always be in a negative light, and always with the caveat that 'other stable relationships' are the moral equivalent. Take as an example the first edition of the FPA booklet *Learning to Live with Sex* (1972) aimed at teenagers. The booklet contains details of the mechanics of sexual intercourse, advice on contraception and a defence of homosexuality, but does not explain marriage. In the discussion on homosexuality, the teenager is informed that 'because a man or woman is a homosexual does not mean that he or she is perverted or carries out strange practices. For homosexuals, lovemaking is as natural as it is for anyone else... Many homosexuals set up homes with one another as a husband and wife might.'[12] But marriage is not even discussed.

Following severe criticism in the House of Lords of the fact that the booklet did not mention marriage, a second edition published in 1974 felt obliged to respond. It described marriage as a 'formal commitment by two people to live together, share their responsibilities, care for one another "for better, for worse, in sickness, in health", and if they decide to be parents to bring up children together.' But the booklet goes on, 'many marriages do not work out like that. More people are now choosing to live together without formalising their vows because they may wish to separate later on, and some people are more tolerant of unfaithfulness or other close sexual relationships outside marriage.'[13] This is the view of marriage which sex education has been presenting to children for the last 30 years. There is no suggestion that sexual intercourse should be reserved for marriage. Indeed, *Learning to Live with Sex* advises teenagers that 'people's needs are different, and everyone has to make up his or her own mind about the value of chastity'.[14]

Learning to Live with Sex goes on to reassure those girls who 'may be worried about having sex if they are not married'. The reassurance is particularly aimed at young people who belong to a church and have definite religious beliefs and so will probably be upset by doing things which are against their conscience. The booklet informs teenagers that 'many people don't go along with those beliefs any more, but if your parents still believe them and think you should too, you may have a rather difficult time trying to sort out what is the right thing for you to do. If possible try and talk these things over with someone outside your family.'[15] Here we see the FPA actually persuading young people that the moral teachings of the Christian faith are out of date and so sex before marriage is perfectly acceptable. And those young people who attend church should not listen to the warning of their conscience, or the advice of their parents, that sex before marriage is wrong. The implication is that the virtue of chastity is based on the old-fashioned and discredited religious beliefs of their parents, which no sensible person believes any more. To salve their conscience young people are encouraged to discuss their sexual beliefs with someone outside their family. This is an open invitation to rebel against the old-fashioned (Christian) moral beliefs of their parents, and shows contempt for the role of the family. Parents are portrayed as out of touch and out to spoil their children's sexual fun. Indeed, 'adolescence is a time for trying out new ideas and rejecting the old, but it is a bit hard on parents to be told they are old-fashioned and stupid. It is better to give them a chance to explain why they think the way they do—and then get your own point of view across... Sometimes, the things *they* think you want are not the things *you* think you want, and you let them know it.'[16] Notice the invitation for children to rebel against their parents. It is disgraceful for the FPA to advise children to turn away from their families for advice on issues that can have the most profound long-term implications for their future. And to whom should they turn? The FPA provides young people with a list of organisations that are ideologically committed to the sexual revolution. Young people are assured that 'all these places will treat your problems sympathetically and not tell your parents unless you want them to know'.[17] This advice is openly defiant of the biblical view that parents are responsible for the moral instruction of their children. It encourages children to break the Fifth Commandment to honour their parents and constitutes a blatant attack on the family.

The pamphlet *Lovelife* (HEA) provides young people with the greatest possible information on contraception, answers a question on the safety of oral sex, and yet does not mention the word marriage. Even when discussing the issue of an unwanted pregnancy, marriage is not presented as an option. Instead, the pregnant young woman is advised to 'take time to think about what you want to do. You will have to decide if you are going to carry on with the pregnancy or not. This is a big decision and you can get information and advice on what you can do from: your doctor, Brook Helpline, British Pregnancy Advisory Service, Marie Stopes Clinics or your local young people's service. If you choose to have the baby, be prepared for mixed reactions from your friends and family. Having a baby is a big responsibility. It can limit your chances for education and training, as well as making it harder to have a social life. If you choose to keep your baby, there are different things you can do. Social services or special agencies arrange adoptions. You can't formally agree to an adoption until your baby is six weeks old – in case you change your mind.'[18] And for the young single woman who chooses to have the baby, the important things for her to know about are folic acid (to prevent congenital abnormalities) and that the baby can be adopted.

Notice the options that the pregnant young woman is presented with; abortion, and if she decides to go ahead with the pregnancy, folic acid and adoption. The option of marrying the father of her child is not even mentioned, although she may love him and desire to get married. But this booklet does not advise a pregnant young woman that marriage is an option—in the world of sex education marriage no longer matters. Even in the scenario where a young woman is pregnant and wants to have the baby, the sex educator, in the shape of the Health Education Authority, does not advise a young couple to consider the option of getting married and providing a home for their child. Such is sex education's implacable opposition to marriage.

Notice also that the pregnant young woman is not advised to seek the support of her family, those who love her the most, those who are truly committed to her best interests and those who will be the most affected by her decision. Instead, her family is presented as a problem, and she is advised to go for help to impersonal agencies that will almost definitely persuade her to have an abortion. Moreover, we are left with no doubt that in the event of a young woman becoming pregnant the Health Education Authority would rather that she become a single mother than marry the father of her child. It cares nothing for the moral well-being of the pregnant young woman or her baby, or for her parents who will inevitably be involved as their daughter becomes a single mother.

The pamphlet *Sexual health for men* (HEA) provides the following advice to a young man and his 'partner' who are *planning* to have a baby. 'If you and your partner want to have a baby, your partner should' give up smoking, cut down on alcohol and take folic acid.[19] So even in a situation where a young couple plans to have a child, the sex educator does not mention marriage. The advice is that the woman should give up smoking and take folic acid and become a single mother. The problems associated with single motherhood are completely disregarded. Sex education literature simply ignores the overwhelming evidence that marriage is the safest and most secure environment in which to bring up children. Because of its ideological opposition to marriage, sex education does not advise young people, whatever the circumstances, that marriage is an option.

What sex educators think of parents

Sex education identifies parents as a large part of the problem. William Oddie made the point that 'parents need to understand that, so far as the experts are concerned, parents are the enemy. As one family planning activist put it in the seventies: "If we do not get into sex education, children will simply follow the mores of their parents." Or, in the immortal words of Lady Brook, founder of the Brook Advisory Centres (an offshoot of the FPA): "It is now the privilege of the Parental State to take major decisions – objective, unemotional, the State weighs up what is best for the child".'[20] We have seen that the Government has made it legal for family planning doctors to prescribe contraceptives for under-age children without the knowledge of their parents. Clearly the Government believes that it is the family planning doctors, and not their parents, who act in the best interests of children.

Sex educators often claim that parents are incapable of teaching their own children about sexual behaviour. According to Gill Mullinar in *Developing sex education in schools: a practical guide*, young people frequently reflect the discomfort and uncertainty of their parents where sex education is concerned.

273

'Schools which offer sex education provide access to reliable adults who are outside the immediate family and a secure environment within which the child or young person can check if what is happening to her or him is 'normal' and acceptable. It can also feel 'safer' because it is less 'personal' than discussing sex with parents.'[21] The chief officer of the National Marriage Guidance Council asserted that the reason why sex education could not be left in the hands of parents was that 'many parents lack not only the factual information, but also the verbal capacity or the confidence in their relationship with their children to enable them to do so'. The sex educators believe that parents are simply not up to the task. It follows that parents must step aside for the sex educators, for they have a special esoteric knowledge about sex which parents apparently lack. So we see that in the mind of the sex educator even married parents, who are living together in a permanent sexual relationship, who have conceived, borne and nurtured their children, do not have the ability to instruct their children in the matter of sexual behaviour. The clear inference is that sex educators have a special, hidden body of sexual knowledge about which parents are ignorant. In a way this is true, for most parents are not going to instruct their children in a manner that meets with the approval of the sex educators.

The Government's sex education guidance makes it clear that 'teachers are not legally bound to inform parents or the head teacher of any disclosure unless the head teacher has specifically requested them to do so'.[22] And so the FPA reminds schoolteachers that 'they are not legally obliged to inform parents about subjects discussed with pupils, if they believe it is not in the best interests of the young people to do so. However, by contract, teachers must follow the instruction of head teachers in these situations. In a survey carried out for the FPA, most 13 to 15-year-olds said that they would find it useful to talk to a teacher about matters such as contraception, but two-thirds would not do so if the teacher was likely to tell their parents.'[23] This policy has the potential for promoting a secret liaison between teacher and child, to the exclusion of the parents. Why do two-thirds of children not want their parents to be told that they have spoken to the teacher about contraception? The answer, I suggest, is that a child knows that her parents would be saddened at the thought that their daughter was receiving advice on how to use contraceptives from a teacher. Most children would be deeply ashamed if their father and mother knew that they were contemplating sexual intercourse. So the contraceptive talk between the sex educator, who is aiding and abetting the young girl into a life of sexual promiscuity, and the girl, who is ashamed of her conduct, must be kept secret from her parents.

Anguished parents wrote the following account of a sex education lesson given in a large Sheffield comprehensive school to their 13-year-old daughter. 'We enclose a pamphlet which was given to our daughter... We were appalled at the way sexual intercourse was presented as "the norm", as much a part of life to the reader as catching a cold or playing a hockey match. As you can see, not only is there not one shred of moral guidance but there is no encouragement given to turn to one's parents for advice—rather the opposite, an encouragement to deceive their

274

parents. The lectures were given to mixed classes who were then almost pressurised into asking questions. Although our daughter has already learned the facts from us, gradually, as she was able to absorb them, this experience at school was little short of traumatic. We had difficulty in getting her to attend. She begged us not to, as she put it, "make the situation even more awful" by contacting the headmistress, and we rightly or wrongly, respected this request. We did, however, complain to the Chief Education Officer in Sheffield who wrote assuring us that the subject was dealt with at this particular school by "qualified people".'[24]

Sex education and the family

Another aspect of sex education is to teach schoolchildren about families. According to the FPA, there were two problems with the Government's legislation passed in 1986, that sex education should 'encourage pupils to have due regard to the value of family life'.[25] 'The first is that schools need to interpret the word "family" in a way which includes everyone and avoids damaging any pupil's sense of self-worth. The second is that teachers, governors, parents and pupils need to identify exactly what they think the value of family life is.' The FPA suggested that schools should take account of the World Health Organisation definition of the family: 'Our concept of family is not limited to relationships of blood, marriage, sex partnerships or adoption. It extends to a broad range of groups whose bonds are based on feelings of trust, mutual support and a shared destiny.'[26] What is clear from this definition is that the biblical understanding of the family as being grounded in marriage is being rejected.

In March 1994 the FPA issued a two-page position statement on the family. According to this statement the FPA believes that the family has evolved over time and 'welcomes the development and diversity of family life, and regards all family structures which respect the human rights and freedoms of children, young people, women and men as equally valid, and equally deserving of societal support'. The FPA makes it clear that, in its understanding, there is no universally applicable means of defining 'the family' or of determining membership of a family. 'While it may be possible broadly to categorise a number of apparently similar family patterns, experiences of family life are unique to the individual; family membership and relationships can only be defined by the individual for themselves… The FPA believes that the value of family life is dependent on the quality of the relationships between family members; the strength of the family is not determined by characteristics such as family structure/size or the age, gender or marital status of family members… The FPA believes that it is advantageous both to children and parents for more than one adult to take responsibility for the practical and emotional aspects of childcare, and to share the demands of parenting. However there is no proven basis for insisting that any one childcare system, or number/gender combination of parents, carers and educators is inherently superior or inferior to any other. Meeting the developmental and social needs of children includes offering opportunities for them to interact safely with a diversity of trustworthy adults, and to experience different roles and relationships; this may be successfully achieved within different family groups and also through wider community networks and organisations.'[27]

What is significant is that the words marriage, husband, wife and father are not mentioned. The word 'mother' is mentioned only for the FPA to say that it believes that mothers who wish to enter paid employment should be encouraged to do so. According to the FPA's vision there is no connection between marriage and the family. A family is composed of any assortment of two or more people who choose to live together. In fact, the statement goes so far as to say that the strength of the family has nothing to do with marital status. The traditional (and biblical) belief that the family created by marriage is best for children is anathema to the sex educators.

To help primary school teachers with their sex education lessons, and to educate children about families, *Healthwise*, a Liverpool based voluntary organisation, has produced *The Primary School Sex and Relationships Education Pack*. The introduction explains that, 'In the past some people have suggested narrow, moralistic aims for sex education. This has included suggestions such as promoting marriage in the family, dissuading children from having sex before marriage, telling children what is right and wrong etc in a manner which has more to do with propaganda than with education.'[28] Under the heading 'families and parenting', the resource pack explains that teachers should tell children aged 7 to 11 that families come in many different forms. Children are shown a picture of six different types of 'family'—two children with their mother and father, two children with mother and stepfather, one child with her single mother, one child with her grandparents, one child living with a foster family, and two children living with their mum and her lesbian partner. Children are invited to choose one of the families and to write a story about it. The class is then asked to discuss the advantages and disadvantages of being married in a non-judgemental way. The message that is being imparted to children is that there are many types of family and the traditional family of father, mother and children is simply one arrangement, no better or worse than any other 'family' arrangement.

The idea that sex education is trying to get across to schoolchildren is that there are many different forms of family, *all of which have equal moral validity*, including a same-sex family, stepfamily and single parent family. According to Sarah Gammage, in the essay *The Teaching of Sexuality*, 'Teachers cannot, and should not, teach children that the only acceptable form of family is that of mother, father and children. This would be to deny that the experience of love, care and responsibility are possible without this configuration of people. It would be gross insensitivity toward the backgrounds of pupils.'[29]

The above analysis leaves no doubt that the message of sex education, like the ideology of the sexual revolution, is profoundly hostile to marriage and the traditional family. In *The Triumph of the Therapeutic: uses of Faith after Freud*, Philip Reiff concluded that sex education is the main weapon in an ideological war against the family; its aim is to divest the parents of their moral authority. 'Sex education is meant to replace the moral authority of the family with that of the State, acting through its primary agent, the public [State] school system.'[30] What is deeply disturbing is that the British Government is content to use the national curriculum as an ideological weapon to indoctrinate children against the Bible's teaching on marriage, a teaching that has been accepted by the vast majority of the population for centuries. It seems likely that the negative view of marriage generated by sex education has contributed to the decline in marriage rates (figure 6, page 319) that is now such a feature of the social landscape of modern Britain.

Endnotes

1 Edward Carpenter, *Love's Coming-of-Age*, First edition 1896, reprinted 1948, George Allen & Unwin Ltd, London, 1948, pp103-104

2 Ibid. p118

3 *The Sexual Revolution*, Wilhelm Reich, translated by Theodore Wolfe, Vision Press, 1969, p32

4 Claus Westermann, *Genesis 1-11*, translated John Scullion, Augsburg Publishing House, 1984, p232

5 Philip Hughes, *Christian Ethics in Secular Society*, Baker Book House, Grand Rapids, 1983, p151

6 John Skinner, *Genesis*, T & T Clark, 2nd edition, Edinburgh, 1930, p70

7 Ibid. p156

8 Hansard, Lords debate, 22 February 1967, c741

9 *Sex and Relationship Education Guidance*, DfEE, July 2000, p4

10 *FPA response to DfEE Guidance on Sex and Relationships Education*, Family Planning Association, website, FPA.org.uk, January 2001

11 *Daily Telegraph*, 12 January 1994, Education: In my view – the moral side of sex, Susan Elkin

12 *Learning to Live with Sex*, Family Planning Association, 1972, p27

13 *Learning to Live with Sex*, Family Planning Association, 1974, p29

14 Ibid. p15

15 Ibid. pp23-24

16 Ibid. *Learning to Live with Sex*, 1972, p37

17 Ibid. p59

18 *Lovelife*, Health Education Authority, 1999, p17

19 *Sexual health for men*, Health Education Authority, 1999, p20

20 *Sunday Telegraph*, 14 November 1993, 'The real sex abusers', William Oddie

21 Gill Mullinar, *Developing sex education in schools: a practical guide*, FPA, 1994, pp14-15

22 *Sex and Relationship Education Guidance*, DfEE, July 2000, p33

23 FPA website, Sex education in schools, confidentiality, January 2002

24 Hansard, Lords debate, 14 January 1976, c243

25 Education (No. 2) Act 1986, section 46

26 Ibid. *Developing sex education in schools: a practical guide*, p40

27 Family Planning Association, FPA position statement on the family, March 1994

28 *The Primary School Sex & Relationships Education Pack*, Healthwise publications, 1999 edition

29 Sarah Gammage, *The Teaching of Sexuality*, in Children and controversial issues, ed Bruce Carrington and Barry Troyna, The Falmer Press, p200

30 Philip Reiff, *The Triumph of the Therapeutic: uses of Faith after Freud*, Harper & Row, 1966, cited from 'The Sex Education Fraud', Chuck Morse, website chuckmorse.com

Chapter 19

The 'Christian' version of sex education

Reluctance of Christians to use the Bible in opposing sex education; CARE's approach to sex education

Our examination of biblical standards have revealed an unbridgeable chasm between God's moral law and the ideology behind the sex education that is being promoted by the Government, and its agent organisations like the FPA and Brook. In chapter 17 we saw that sexual purity, which flows from the holiness of God, is undermined by explicit sex education, and in chapter 18 we saw that the underlying ideology of sex education is profoundly hostile to marriage and the traditional family. Christians can no longer avoid the uncomfortable truth that sex education imposes serious moral dangers, and many people are now starting to realise that something needs to be done to protect children from the worst excesses of the sex educators. Parents cannot, with a clear conscience, simply abandon their children to the amoral teaching of the sex educators. But what should be done? How should Christians counter the false teachings of sex education?

In my view, the Christian witness is ineffective because of a widespread reluctance to use biblical truth to counter the amoral ideology that lies behind sex education. Many Christians believe that it is futile to use the Bible because nobody takes it seriously any more. I attended a meeting of people deeply concerned about sex education where the plea was for doctors to produce evidence to show the harmful health effects of contraceptives on children. The hope was that if convincing evidence could be produced, then maybe the Government could be persuaded to modify its policy. Christians are being encouraged to enter the debate on sociological and health grounds, demonstrating the negative health effects of contraception, arguing that sex education is not effective in preventing teenage pregnancies.

Those who promote this point of view fail to understand that the moment Christians enter into a debate about the 'evidence', they are, in fact, condoning the demoralisation of sexual behaviour, and their arguments soon become indistinguishable from those of the sex educators. This is because the real issues are moral in nature, and cannot be decided on the basis of 'evidence' or expert opinion. Indeed, it is axiomatic that God's revealed moral law alone can answer moral questions. All the evidence in the world does not affect God's moral truth. Moreover, as sex education is ideologically based it is impervious to facts or reasoned argument; the sex educators only accept those facts that support their ideological position. So the appeal to evidence is not only futile – for the evidence is always open to dispute – but unwise, for it denies the moral imperative that lies behind sexual conduct.

The Bible teaches that the concept of moral obligation flows from the truth that human beings, created in the image of God, have moral responsibility. All morality is grounded in the character of the Lord God who made the world and everything in it; all moral distinctions flow from God's moral law. Moreover, the whole world is held accountable to God for their actions, and all will appear before the judgement seat of God. According to David Jones, writing in *Biblical Christian Ethics*, 'The moral law is that which is universally and perpetually binding on human beings by virtue of their creation in the image of God. The substance of the moral law is the same whether revealed in human nature or in the Scripture.'[1] The Bible makes it plain that God's law is for all people, and especially for the irreligious and unbeliever. The unbelieving world needs to hear the moral law of God just as much as the Christian world does. 'We also know that the law is made not for the righteous but for lawbreakers and rebels, the ungodly and sinful, the unholy and irreligious' (1 Timothy 1:9). Furthermore, the moral law of God serves the purpose of restraining evil and promoting righteousness. It brings people under conviction of sin, pointing them to their need of salvation through faith. For believers it is a rule of life, reminding us of how we ought to live.[2]

In my view, it is unwise for Christians to discuss sexual conduct without reference to God's word, for it alone has the authority to distinguish right from wrong. As sex education deals with moral issues, it must be approached from within the moral framework of biblical revelation. If Christians ignore this truth, our position is compromised, for we have fallen into the trap of demoralising sexual conduct. We have moved into the mindset of the sexual revolutionaries, and now the argument is about who can produce the best 'evidence'. Moreover, because God's moral law is based in righteousness and goodness, it has an enormous appeal to the hearts of men, women and children. And in our postmodern society there is a growing hunger for truth, for many people know in their consciences that the Bible provides the standard by which they ought to live. Most parents want their children to be taught the difference between right and wrong, and are delighted when the Church gives a clear moral lead, and pronounces unequivocally, with all the authority of God's word, that promiscuity and homosexuality are wrong.

Christians therefore must have the courage to engage in the issues raised by sex education with their Bibles open. Of course, our opponents will claim that nobody will listen, that the Bible is irrelevant, judgemental, patriarchal, out of date and all the rest. Of course, our opponents will say that young people don't listen to the Bible any more, that it puts them off. Of course, those who promote the amoral messages of sex education do not want children to hear what the Bible has to say. But how can Christians take a stand against one of the greatest moral evils of our time without the word of God, which is the sword of the Spirit? God has promised that the word that goes out from his mouth will not return to him empty, 'but will accomplish what I desire and achieve the purpose for which I sent it' (Isaiah 55:11). In moral warfare, in our struggle against spiritual forces in high places, the Christian must enter the battle with the full armour of God, including the sword of the Spirit, which is the word of God (Ephesians 6:17). 'For the word of God is living and active. Sharper than any double-edged sword, it penetrates even to dividing soul and spirit, joints and marrow; it judges the thoughts and attitudes of the heart' (Hebrews 4:12). The message of the Bible is powerful because it appeals to the heart of man; the Holy Spirit convicts 'the world of guilt in regard to sin, righteousness and judgement' (John 16:8).

Unfortunately we now have the situation in the UK where few Christians are prepared to tackle, without compromise, the moral evils associated with sex education. Like the children of Israel, we prefer to come to an accommodation with the detestable practices of the Canaanites. So there is virtually no Christian opposition to the claim of the sexual revolutionaries that children need to receive sex education in school. Most Christians accept, without any biblical justification, the view that children need sex education—and so the challenge is to find a sensitive 'Christian' version. Those who support this view argue that it is not good enough for Christians simply to criticise the sex education that is being delivered by the Government, we need to come forward with a positive alternative. While acknowledging the shortcomings of secular sex education, and accepting that some resource materials are too explicit, most Christians believe that the basic aims of sex education are, in fact, good. Many feel that children should be taught the 'facts of life' and argue that children need to understand their sexuality in order to have successful relationships. So the issue is to develop a 'Christian' version of sex education that avoids the excesses of secular sex education. What is surprising about this approach is that it seems oblivious to the amorality that is such a feature of the sex education propagated by the State. The purpose of this chapter is to examine the sex education that is being promoted in the name of Christianity.

Christian views on sex education

The leading Christian organisation involved in sex education is Christian Action, Research and Education (CARE). It claims that although there is a debate in society as to the best methods of reducing teenage pregnancies, as well as ways to reduce under-age sexual activity, 'there is no doubt that schools are recognised as having a part to play. Sex education is not an issue that can be ignored!'[3] It appears that CARE accepts, without question, the need for children to be taught about sex in the school classroom. The only question is what they should be taught, and how it should be taught. They are seeking a Christian version of sex education. The Christian Institute, in its *Manifesto for Marriage in Sex Education*, is against what it calls explicit, extreme sex education and proposes five principles that should guide the way sex education is delivered in the classroom.[4] The Maranatha Community is strongly opposed to current trends in sex education and believes that children should be taught about marriage and self-control. While it believes that 'the presentation of factual information should be carefully balanced with modesty and self-respect and always within the context of a moral framework,'[5] it is becoming increasingly sceptical about the value of much sex education in the school classroom. In a submission to the Health Committee of the House of Commons, Maranatha expressed the view that 'in some sex education programmes children are cruelly introduced to adult sexual practices some of which are utterly grotesque. At a sensitive and impressionable time in their lives they are often given misleading information...Educational material should be produced warning of the huge dangers of promiscuity, and should be intensely promoted throughout the country, particularly amongst young people.'[6]

CARE's approach to sex education

CARE has been involved with sex education since the early 1990s, and in 1994 produced the video *Make Love Last*, with the message that it's okay to say 'no' to sex. The project was partly funded by the Department of Health and the video has been widely bought and used by secondary schools. In 1995, CARE produced a training package *Parents First – Sex Education within the Home*, which focuses on the importance of parents having the first responsibility for their children's sex education, and encourages parents to talk to their children about sex. In 1997, CARE for Education launched two CD-ROMs, *Growing Up Together*, for primary schools, which address sex education at Key Stages 1 and 2. CARE for Education also works with head teachers, teachers and school governors and the document *Your School and Sex Education* (1996) provides detailed guidance on how to produce a school sex education policy. It has since been revised and updated and published as *Sex and Relationship Education* (2001).[7]

The video 'Make Love Last'

CARE's video, *Make Love Last*, is done in a contemporary, vox pop style; the main sources of advice are a health education consultant, Angela Flux, the agony aunt from the magazine *Just 17*, Annabel G, and a youth worker, Paul Francis. The ostensible message of the video is that virginity is a sensible choice, and a number of teenagers express their desire to remain virgins until marriage.

However, the video contains many smutty sexual innuendoes. One character, Randy Factor, asks a group of young people whether they are 'putting it around a bit, you know, dipping your wick'. Randy promotes an exercise programme to make people 'bonking' fit. He uses phrases like, 'You need to get bonking fit'; 'pumping for humping'; 'leg-over time'; 'the more I score the better I score' and 'the sponsored bonk'. A dictionary defines most of these phrases as 'coarse slang' for having sexual intercourse. In a 'stud of the month' competition, Randy gets a young man to admit that, in his dreams, he had impregnated the entire female staff of a nightclub between two and four in the morning. In a skit on the TV programme Blind Date, Randy has his game show called Find a Mate. The young male contestant explains to the first female that strip poker is his favourite game and asks her: 'Will you go all the way when I let you play with me?' He asks the second young woman: 'Will you let me touch you up, or should I use a stripper?' His question to the third woman is even more direct: 'Will you have sex with me?' The prize is a dirty weekend in Paris, staying at Bonking Motel. It's surprising that CARE thinks it is necessary to use this type of language to deliver a message to young people.

Another character in the video, Uncle Roger, shown in black and white, is presented as a rather ridiculous fuddy-duddy who is supposed to represent traditional old-fashioned views on sexual behaviour. While traditional views are parodied and ridiculed, the views of the modern sex educator and the journalist from *Just 17* are presented as authoritative voices that young people should take seriously. They are presented as experts who know about sex and young people are encouraged to follow their advice.

Annabel G of *Just 17* tells teenagers: 'I think saying no if you don't *want* sex is the most crucial word, and I don't think it is used often enough [my italics].' Angela Flux advises: 'There's no need to be apologetic, everybody has got the right to say I don't *want* to have sex with you *now*, and I think young people need to have the confidence to say that, and I think young people need to feel good about saying it, because it can be a very *positive* choice for young people [my italics]'. In other words, young people are being advised that their decision to have sex or not, depends on what they want at that moment in time, and not on any objective standard of right and wrong. The message of the video is similar to that of the Health Education Authority: 'It's your right to say "no" if you don't want to go all the way. It doesn't mean you don't like or want your partner – just that you're not ready. So don't be pushed into doing something you'd rather not.'[8] *Lovelife* puts it this way: 'Remember, it's your body, your choice and your right to say no. Only have sex because you want to.'[9]

This video bends over backwards to appear trendy. But what is the moral message? Does it teach sexual purity? Certainly not! Young people are left with the impression that coarse sexual talk is okay. Does it teach chastity? Clearly not! Young people are advised to say no if they don't want sex now. The corollary is that young people who do want sex now should say 'yes'. So while ostensibly promoting virginity, young people are left with the impression that abstaining until they are ready for a sexual experience is a positive choice. The advice offered by *Make Love Last* is consistent with the morality of desire discussed in chapter 2.

Moreover, CARE is apparently content for its message on sexual behaviour to be associated with the magazine *Just 17*, widely known for its salacious sexual outlook, despite the biblical injunction: 'Do not be yoked together with unbelievers. For what do righteousness and wickedness have in common? Or what fellowship can light have with darkness?' (2 Corinthians 6:14).

The course leader's manual 'Parents First'

Parents First – Sex Education within the Home (1995) is a resource that is supposed to help parents tackle sex education confidently and appropriately with their children. It is of such importance that CARE is encouraging all church leaders to consider incorporating *Parents First* into their church teaching programme. The booklet starts by providing a list of biblical references that describe God's blueprint for sex and sexuality, although there is no discussion of the texts. The resource provides a broad range of activities that will guide parents on how to talk to their children about sex. CARE warns that while 'the material is firmly based on Christian teaching', the course leader 'may encounter embarrassment, even hostility at first and this needs to be anticipated and worked through'.[10] According to CARE ground rules for the teaching session should include respect, non-judgementalism, openness, trust and confidentiality.

CARE claims that discussions around sexual language are very important. The purpose is for parents to be aware of the sexual language that their children confront; to feel more comfortable dealing with sexual language, and to work out what sort of language they want their children to use. An activity sheet is handed out which requires parents to categorise a list of sexual words into polite, neutral, clinical and rude/offensive. For example, the words for sex are: sleep with, making love, sexual intercourse, and screwing. Other words on the activity sheet are penis, female genitalia, and oral sex. It is stressed that the parents will not have to show their completed activity sheet to anyone else or share their words with the group. If the 'group is quite comfortable with sexual language, the words can be anonymously collated on to a flip chart and used to illustrate the discussion on appropriate sexual language'. The discussion that follows focuses on how the rude words make them feel, 'the importance of working out what type of language children should use' and 'the importance of parents and children being familiar with sexual language other than the "proper" word, to avoid innocent mistakes'.[11] Apparently CARE feels that it is 'important' for Christians to have a vocabulary of lewd words. But why do these words need to be collated anonymously? Is it because the offensive words that are generated by this activity might arouse a sense of shame?

Another activity is designed to help parents gain confidence in talking to their children about sex and sexuality. Parents are divided into small groups and given a starter card with a topic for discussion. One starter card, for example, contains the statement: Your daughter of 12 asks you: 'What's oral sex?' Responses parents are asked to think about include the following, with an invitation to select the one they favour:

- Ask your father/mother (ie. the other parent)
- Who told you about it?
- Why do you want to know?
- It's a very personal sexual activity which some people enjoy; it can be done by a person, male or female, to their sexual partner.
- It's the name given to kissing/licking a man's penis or a woman's vagina. Some people like it, others don't.
- It's disgusting; who told you about it?[12]

What is so disturbing about the activities described above is that, in the name of sex education, Christian people are being persuaded to use lewd words and discuss oral sex in a group situation. CARE would do well to note Christ's warning to the Church in Thyatira: 'I have this against you: You tolerate that woman Jezebel... by her teaching she misleads my servants into sexual immorality' (Revelation 2:20).

Another starter card poses the problem: 'Your daughter of 15 says she wants to go on the pill.' Parents are asked how they would feel. Disappointed, in that their daughter had let them down, or pleased that she had come to talk about it? And what would parents want to talk to their daughter about – the legal situation, their views, her feelings, the side effects, or her future? Yet another discussion starter suggests: 'Your 18-year-old wants his/her partner to be able to share his/her room at the weekends?' Parents are asked how they would feel about this. 'What would you want to discuss: their sexual relationship; their intentions; contraception; nothing – it wouldn't happen; levels of trust; temptation?'[13] The emphasis is on parents' feelings; there is no advice that they should give their children moral guidance.

And what is CARE's advice about same-sex friendships? 'Close same-sex relationships during early adolescence can be a time for teenagers to develop the confidence to approach the other sex; sometimes a relationship or feelings of attraction may develop with a friend of the same sex and parents need to keep the channels of communication open if this is the case. Strong messages of disapproval or concern will not help the situation. How would you feel if a son/daughter of yours told you they were attracted to people of the same sex? How do you feel about adults who make different sexual choices from you? Do you have any needs which are not met by people of the other sex?'[14] Note that parents are warned not to show disapproval of same-sex relationships. Apparently CARE believes that parents should not warn their children of the moral danger of a homosexual relationship, and its spiritual consequences as taught in the Bible (1 Corinthians 6: 9-10).

Another activity uses the technique of the values continuum (see page 14 in chapter 2) to help 'parents clarify what they actually believe and value about sex and sexuality'. The purpose is to help 'parents realise that within the Christian Church there may be a range of beliefs and values held about particular issues'.[15] A specimen pair of value statements is placed at the opposite ends of the room with a clear space between them. For example, 'homosexuality is part of God's created order' is placed at one end of the room, and 'homosexuality is against God's created order' at the other end. Parents are then invited to read the statements and decide where they stand on the continuum between these two statements. The purpose is to help Christians clarify what they believe. After each pair of statements there must be some discussion. The objective is 'not necessarily to get to a definitive RIGHT answer, but to help parents realise they do hold certain beliefs that they will transmit to their youngsters and that all issues are not easily resolved'.[16] As we saw in chapter 2, the underlying aim of this technique is to demonstrate that there are no absolute, right answers to moral questions, that there is no absolute moral truth. Parents, therefore, must clarify their position on a moral continuum— this is usually referred to as relative morality, and is diametrically opposed to the absolute moral truth taught in the Bible.

CARE's response to the Social Exclusion Unit's consultation

CARE's sex education philosophy can be gleaned from its submission to the Government's Social Exclusion Unit in response to a questionnaire on the issue of teenage parenthood. CARE draws attention to a moral ambivalence about the sex education message that is being communicated to young people. CARE is concerned that 'sex education has not been good at getting the message across about the appropriate context for sexual relationships or pregnancy. Concentrating on preventing conception is treating a symptom rather than a cause – it does not address the issue of why young people are having early and unprotected sex. Indeed, there is moral ambivalence about what we want to say to young people – we are not communicating clear messages. The message of this consultation is "teenagers should not get pregnant". Yet, there appears to be few who are asking the question "Whether it is *healthy* [my italics] for teenagers to be having sex"?'[17]

By suggesting that the issue surrounding teenage sex is *health*, CARE is avoiding the moral dimension. But this is a false analysis, for it is obvious that sexual inter-course among married teenagers is perfectly healthy and right—it is teenage sex outside marriage, what used to be called fornication, that is the problem. And while it is reasonable to warn teenagers of the health dangers associated with sex outside marriage, the really important message for teenagers is that promiscuity is immoral. By promoting the idea that teenage sex is a *health* issue, and not that fornication is *wrong*, CARE sidesteps the moral issue. It appears to be content to suggest that teenagers should delay the onset of sexual activity for *health* reasons, and reluctant to state, unequivocally, that sexual promiscuity is wrong. The obvious weakness in CARE's pragmatic position is this: if the *health* problems can be overcome, then the objection to promiscuous teenage sex would have disappeared. The moral teaching of the Bible, however, is clear and unequivocal: 'Flee from sexual immorality. All other sins a man commits are outside his body, but he who sins sexually sins against his own body' (1 Corinthians 6:18).

CARE believes that a partnership with parents is key to the successful delivery of sex education. It urges that all sex education should be placed within a clear moral and values framework, that affirms the place of marriage.[18] CARE also urges 'that accurate factual information is given to young people about sex, unplanned pregnancy, STIs, contraception, abortion, and its effects, both physical and emotional. We also support programmes that include self-awareness, self-image, decision-making, and promote emotional literacy.'[19]

According to CARE, 'appropriate sex education can take place at school from age 5'.[20] 'Clear, unembarrassed appropriate early sex education provides a good foundation for more detail at secondary school age... Older children can learn more explicit details about sex in the context of loving relationships, with as much emphasis placed on the emotional aspects of teenage sex, pregnancy and abortion, as well as the physical.'[21]

CARE acknowledges that 'there may be some aspects of sex education where pupils will appreciate being able to talk to adults who are not their teachers.'[22] While emphasising that the information provided must fall within the school sex education policy as set out by the governors, CARE believes that 'teaching staff can be helped with the task of sex education by networking them with outside agencies and by providing a directory of local and national organisations who can provide resources, support or speakers.'[23] What outside national organisations does CARE have in mind? And who does CARE have in mind when they suggest that 'sex education needs to be taught by those who want to do it, and are properly trained to do so'?[24] We know that the FPA and Brook 'want to do it', and we know that a major activity of the FPA is to train 'sex educators'. Is CARE supporting the idea that the sex educators 'properly' trained by the FPA should teach children sex education?

The booklet 'Your School and Sex Education' (1996)

CARE's booklet *Your School and Sex Education* (1996) has been written 'to help teachers, parents and governors who are involved in discussions about sex education or are concerned with the task of producing, revising or reviewing a school sex education policy'.[25] The document makes it clear that its intention is not to discuss the pros and cons of the Government's guidance, only to clarify what schools are required to do. CARE believes that an important aspect of any school sex education programme is to make young people aware of the implications of early sexual intercourse. 'They need to be equipped with the skills required to make informed choices... For the medical and social well-being of the students, abstinence must be presented in a favourable light. Those students who are already sexually active, should be given the opportunity to consider changing their behaviour and choosing abstinence.'[26] Sex education lessons should provide 'the opportunities for pupils to consider abstinence from sexual activities in a positive way, as well as 'safer sex' options'.[27] So CARE's philosophy appears to be similar to that of SIECUS, discussed on page 108. Young people are offered the choice between sexual abstinence, presented in a favourable light, and 'safer sex', and invited to make an informed choice.

In *Your School and Sex Education*, CARE provides a list of sex education resources used in schools, with the qualification that those working in the area of sexual health should evaluate the value base of the resources which they intend to use. 'For the guidance of Christian parents and governors, the resources listed below are some which are used selectively by Christians working in a wide spectrum of schools and groups.' With this qualification, CARE provides a detailed list of sex education resources. Some are marked with an asterisk to indicate that the author is working in a specifically Christian moral framework. Useful websites provided include the Health Education Authority and the Sex Education Forum. In order to gain an understanding of the type of material that CARE has brought to the attention of school governors and teachers, I have analysed three examples from their list.

The resource manual 'Body of Knowledge'

The first, entitled *Body of Knowledge*, is described by CARE as a resource which provides material for training teachers about sex education in primary schools within a specifically Christian moral framework.[28] What should primary school-children be taught about condoms? 'It would be a natural progression from discussion about reproduction and lessons in sexual intercourse to teach that some people use condoms to prevent a pregnancy. Some simple discussion of other forms of contraception could also be introduced...'[29] Contraception should be taught to 9 to 11-year-olds in a context of preventing pregnancy and reducing infection.[30] And what should children be taught about homosexuality? 'A homosexual relationship is understood to be a partnership between two consenting adults of the same gender who may share sexual attraction and pleasure. It is acknowledged that men and women can find friendship and fulfilment with those of the same and opposite gender. Children should be encouraged to see same-gender relationships as part of a natural friendship and not necessarily homosexual.'[31]

If a child specifically asks for a teacher's moral view on a particular controversial subject, such as, 'Is abortion wrong?' the teacher can say, 'People have very different beliefs about this and everyone needs to think about it carefully' or 'It is not important what I think about it, people have different opinions and *have to decide what is right for themselves* [my italics].'[32] And if teachers are unclear about policy they should direct questions to the headteacher, the Family Planning Association or the Sex Education Forum.[33]

Body of Knowledge provides a long list of recommended resources, including many publications from the FPA, Brook and the HEA. In particular, the FPA's *Primary School Workbook* (1993) written by Gill Lenderyou is listed as a resource which can be used in promoting good practice.[34] Background reading for teachers, governors and parents includes Doreen Massey's *School sex education, Why, What and How* (1991) produced by the FPA. Useful addresses provided for teachers, parents and school governors include the FPA, Brook, the HEA and the Sex Education Forum.[35] It recommends *Knowing me, knowing you* as a book of practical ideas and workshops for primary school sex education.

The book 'Knowing me, knowing you'

The second example, taken from CARE's list of resources, is the book *Knowing me, knowing you*, which is referred to as containing 'useful material with some excellent activities and worksheets'.[36] The book claims that there is a need for sex education in the primary school, and sets out an agenda and list of activities to help teachers.[37] The role of the teacher is: not giving 'rights and wrongs'; allowing exploration of personal values by providing a non-threatening, open climate; enabling the child by sharing rather than directing and imposing; being non-judgemental and as neutral as possible.[38] Teachers are advised that to teach about the traditional family 'might well be downright offensive to some' children, and are encouraged to teach about homosexuality and to 'challenge prejudice and discrimination when it rears its head in the classroom'.[39]

What are the excellent exercises and activities endorsed by CARE? One exercise helps children to understand polite and impolite words for the sexual parts of men and women and for sexual activity. Working in pairs, primary schoolchildren are invited to think about impolite sexual words,[40] and brainstorm on the reasons why people have sex.[41]

Another activity assesses primary schoolchildren's understanding of sexual penetration—working in pairs the children are invited to put a circle around statements such as, 'for sexual penetration to take place, a man's penis has to be hard' or 'for sexual penetration to take place, a man has to lie on top of the other person' [implies either male or female], if they think they are true. The children are then asked to compare answers with their partner. Yet another activity offers children a worksheet with information on masturbation: 'some people enjoy rubbing these areas in a certain way. If they do this for a while, they may reach a moment when it is very exciting.' Children are asked to respond to questions such as, 'To my knowledge I have never masturbated. Is this okay?' and 'Can it hurt me?' and 'Does everybody do it?'[42] Children are provided with a list of the advantages and disadvantages of contraceptives. The advantages of the condom are that it is easy to obtain from a chemist or family planning clinic and easy to use. It can also protect against sexually transmitted diseases. Against the condom is the fact that it is important to put one on before penetration, it must be taken off carefully and it needs gentle handling.[43]

The whole class continuum encourages children to explore issues and attitudes together. 'The teacher displays the sheet of paper entitled 'True' at one end of the room, and the sheet entitled 'False' at the other end of the room, and indicates these to the children. The teacher also points out an imaginary line joining one to the other. The teacher then reads out a statement which relates to a forthcoming subject to be covered. The children are asked to stand at some point on the line, according to whether they think the statement is true or false. They can be somewhere in the middle.'[44] It is helpful if the teacher points out that they do not have to go to one extremity or the other. Suggested continuum statements include the following: 'It is embarrassing for a girl to carry a condom', 'one in every ten people is sexually attracted to someone of the same sex', 'masturbation is bad for you', 'people always have sex in bed' and 'for sexual activity, the man has to lie on top of the woman'. The teacher asks different children why they are standing in a particular place on the continuum.

It is not difficult to see the similarity between this activity and that recommended by CARE in *Parents First*. The underlying purpose is to promote the idea that truth and morality are relative concepts. *Knowing me, knowing you* is teaching children that there is no absolute right or wrong, no absolute truth. Significantly, *Knowing me, knowing you* is advertised by Brook in its 1991 and 2001 catalogues. This suggests a level of agreement between Brook and CARE about the type of sex education that is suitable for primary schoolchildren.

The book 'Sexuality'

The third example from CARE's resource list is the book *Sexuality* that is endorsed as covering some good ground: 'body image, stereotyping, type of relationships, decision-making, feeling good'.[45] The book recommends word games to help people feel comfortable talking about sexuality. An exercise on decision-making has the caption: 'Don't let anyone push you into doing something which doesn't feel right. You must do what's right for you.' The section on safer sex and contraception reminds young people that: 'if you decide to have sexual intercourse with someone, you will need to think about contraception, and making sex safer'. *Sexuality* provides the addresses of the FPA, Brook and Health Education Authority and advises young people to collect some of their leaflets. 'If possible, obtain samples of contraceptives. Your family planning clinic, or health promotion resource library, will have a contraceptive kit which they might lend your college or school.'[46] Once again CARE is content to guide teachers to a sex education book that promotes the FPA and Brook.

CARE and contraception

We have seen that *Body of Knowledge* teaches that it would be natural, following discussion about sexual intercourse, to teach primary schoolchildren aged 9 to 11 that condoms are used to prevent a pregnancy[47] and to reduce infections.[48] In *Your School and Sex Education*, CARE reminds teachers that they 'are recommended not to provide individual advice on contraception to those under 16 but there is nothing in the guidance or legislation to prevent teaching about contraception within the whole class situation… teachers can provide young people with information about where confidential advice can be obtained, and as this information is not regarded as sex education *per se*, it can be freely available to all students irrespective of parental wishes regarding sex education. Doctors and school nurses may be free to give contraceptive advice to individual pupils if requested by the pupil to do so. This is irrespective of parental wishes regarding sex education.'[49] CARE is simply reminding teachers of the Government's policy on contraceptives for under-age children, without any guidance on whether it is consistent with biblical teaching on sexual behaviour. Indeed, teachers and school governors are left in the dark as to whether CARE actually supports this policy or not.

CARE's response to the Government's Social Exclusion Unit makes clear its view that there is a role for centres which offer contraception to young people faced with the possibility of an unplanned pregnancy. 'When a young person visits a centre, communication and discussion with parents either directly or by encouraging the girl to speak to her parents, is seen as an important part of supporting the girl as she considers the options open to her. In addition, young people's advice centres and specifically dedicated family planning facilities can be effective especially if young people are given an opportunity to discuss their situation and decision-making as well as being provided with contraception, if appropriate.'[50] CARE believes 'that it is not appropriate to make contraception available to young people in the absence of discussion and advice, so casual distribution of condoms for example at youth clubs or schools is not acceptable.'[51] However, CARE registers no objection to contraceptive clinics for young people, which provide advice on decision making and how to use contraception, such as those run by Brook and the NHS.

The case against CARE

So we must ask the question: In what way does CARE's version of sex education differ from that of the secular sex educators? CARE, like the FPA and Brook, believes that children should be taught about sex in primary school, starting at the age of five. CARE, like Brook, recommends *Knowing me, knowing you* as a sex education resource for primary schoolchildren. CARE, like the FPA and Brook, believes that schoolchildren should be taught a sexual vocabulary. CARE, like the FPA and Brook, believes that parents should be encouraged to talk to their children about sex. CARE, like the FPA and Brook, believes that children should be taught the facts about sexual intercourse, STDs, abortion and contraception. CARE, like the FPA and Brook, believes that dedicated family planning clinics, which give young people advice on decision making and how to use contraception, can be effective. CARE, like Brook and the FPA, has used the teenage magazine *Just 17* to promote its sex education messages. CARE, like the FPA and Brook, promotes moral relativism.

CARE will undoubtedly protest that it is different because it promotes sexual abstinence. Indeed it does promote abstinence, as does the FPA, Brook, the HEA and SIECUS, but it does not teach chastity. CARE's video, *Make Love Last*, tells teenagers to learn how to say, 'I don't want to have sex *now* [my italics]'. But the FPA, Brook, the HEA and SIECUS all teach the same message—they all advise young people to abstain until they are ready to have sex. The comprehensive sex education promoted by SIECUS teaches that 'helping adolescents to *postpone sexual intercourse until they are ready* for mature relationships is a key goal of comprehensive sexuality education [my italics]'. Effective sex education pro-grammes 'include a strong abstinence message *as well as* information about contraception and safer sex [my italics]'.[52] So what is different about the abstinence message promoted by SIECUS, and the abstinence message delivered by CARE?

While CARE promotes the idea of abstinence, the reason it gives for doing so is because of the potential health dangers associated with premature sexual activity, not because promiscuity is wrong. CARE teaches that children ought to make sexual decisions on the basis of feelings generated by self-esteem, rather than the certainties taught by biblical morality. Children are advised to make 'positive' or 'healthy' choices and to avoid 'unhealthy' or 'inappropriate' relationships. Parents are advised to consult their 'feelings' to understand moral issues, such as when their daughter wants to go on the pill.

One of the most concerning aspects of CARE's approach is its moral relativism—in CARE's version of sex education there are no moral absolutes and there is no moral instruction. In *Parents First*, CARE's aim is not to bring parents' beliefs into line with biblical teaching, but rather to 'clarify' their beliefs. In *Body of Knowledge*, teachers are advised to respond to moral questions by telling children that 'people have different opinions and have to decide *what is right for themselves*'. CARE, like the FPA and Brook, has demoralised sexual behaviour. Indeed, CARE is promoting an ideology that is indistinguishable from that of the FPA and Brook. CARE makes no attempt to teach young people about God's standard of sexual purity, or the Christian virtues of modesty, chivalry and chastity.

Christian Institute

The Christian Institute has outlined some of its principles in *A Manifesto for Marriage in Sex Education*. It believes that sex education, 'if it is done badly, has the potential to provoke a great deal of parental concern'.[53] The Institute sets out 'five positive principles for sex education which we would like to see adopted by all Scottish schools'. The crux of their position is that the problem with sex education is its insensitive and extreme nature, but, fortunately, such insensitive sex education is relatively rare. 'Sex education in most Scottish schools is not extreme. Let's keep it that way. The problem comes from outside: outside groups which take lessons in schools, overzealous health board officials or politically correct education authorities. It is essential that teachers and parents retain control over sex education.'[54] According to the manifesto, sex education should upgrade the importance of marriage and support family values and not undermine the home.[55] Children should be taught that sex is for adults. 'Sex is special. It involves a degree of commitment and intimacy which is entirely wrong for children to engage in. It may result in damaging sexually transmitted diseases, or pregnancy. Children cannot cope with these things. They should be taught what the real risks are... When it comes to deciding how to teach about sex in schools, we must be prepared to look at what works... Schools should promote sexual abstinence. They should teach young people to say no to sex.'[56] The Institute believes that children's innocence should be protected. 'It's time for modesty in sex education. Parents fear that certain approaches to sex education take away children's innocence. Children do not have to be presented with a smorgasbord of sexual activities in order to be prepared for adulthood. They need to be taught modesty, morality and self-restraint.'[57]

Another publication by the Institute, *Sex Lessons for Kids*, has drawn attention to the appalling nature of the materials being used for sex education in Scottish schools. The main thrust of this booklet is that sex education should use more appropriate materials. The Institute also sees the need in the UK for programmes that teach the message of sexual abstinence, emphasising that sex is meant for marriage, such as are currently being used in the USA. Short of that, the Institute will continue to oppose any attempts to liberalise the sex education that is being taught in schools.

The Institute is right in its campaign to expose the excesses of sex education. It is also right in pointing out the importance of modesty, and that children do not need to be taught about sexual activity. However, the it needs to be aware that the 'abstinence' message is open to interpretation. As we have seen, those who promote comprehensive sex education teach abstinence as a pragmatic choice, motivated by what's best for me. Furthermore, many abstinence programmes uses self-esteem techniques to help young people make positive, healthy sexual choices.

Chastity is completely different—it's a choice based on obedience to God's moral law, motivated by a desire to do what is right in God's eyes and a desire for sexual purity. There is a world of difference between the pragmatic, amoral advice offered by abstinence education and the Bible's teaching on chastity.

The failure of Christian sex education

We have seen that the so-called 'Christian' version of sex education delivered by CARE is inconsistent with biblical morality. So can sex education be improved? The answer must be a resounding no! And this is because the concept of sex education, which has flowed from the ideology of the sexual revolution, is fundamentally hostile to biblical morality. It follows that all attempts to find the elusive, sensitive 'Christian' version are doomed to failure, for there is no such thing. Sex education is an ideological weapon of the sexual revolutionaries and should be exposed for the moral evil that it is. In my view it is imperative for Christians to oppose sex education on moral grounds—the reason sex education is so wrong is that it is contrary to the moral teaching of the Bible. The Christian position is for parents to teach their children about sexual conduct within the framework of God's moral law, and this includes the virtues of modesty, chivalry and chastity.

Endnotes

1 David Clyde Jones, *Biblical Christian Ethics*, Baker Books, Grand Rapids, p109
2 Louis Berkhof, *Systematic Theology*, The Banner of Truth Trust, 1979, pp614-15
3 *Your School and Sex Education*, CARE, 1996, p3
4 *A Manifesto for Marriage in Sex Education*, Christian Institute, Scotland, March 2001

5 *Teenage Parenthood Response*, Maranatha, 12 November 1998, question 9
6 Maranatha submission to the Health Committee at the House of Commons, *The National Strategy for Sexual Health and HIV*, 3 June 2002, (personal communication)
7 *Sex and Relationship Education*, CARE for Education, 2001.
8 *One love*, Health Education Authority, 1998
9 *Lovelife*, Health Education Authority, 1999, p4
10 *Parents First – Sex Education within the Home*, CARE, 1995, p5
11 Ibid. p35
12 Ibid. pp63-64
13 Ibid. pp 63-64
14 Ibid. p64
15 Ibid. p46
16 Ibid. p48
17 *Teenage parenthood*, A submission to the Social Exclusion Unit, CARE, November 1998, p5
18 Ibid. p6
19 Ibid. p7
20 Ibid. p9
21 Ibid. p9
22 Ibid. p10
23 Ibid. p15
24 Ibid. p8
25 Ibid. *Your School and Sex Education*, CARE, p3
26 Ibid. p26
27 Ibid. p28
28 Ibid. p43
29 Angela Flux, *Body of Knowledge*, A report of Sex Education Workshop 1994, p10
30 Ibid. Appendix 9
31 Ibid. p10
32 Ibid. p12
33 Ibid. p12
34 Ibid. Resource 15, resources
35 Ibid. Resource 16, useful addresses
36 Ibid. *Your School and Sex Education*, CARE, p43
37 Pete Sanders and Liz Swinden, *Knowing me, knowing you*, LDA, 1990, p4
38 Ibid. p26
39 Ibid. p154
40 Ibid. p111
41 Ibid. p152
42 Ibid. pp168-69
43 Ibid. p182
44 Ibid. p191
45 Ibid. *Your School and Sex Education*, CARE, p41
46 Gay Gray, Heather Hyde, *Sexuality*, Oxford University Press, p22
47 Ibid. *Body of Knowledge*, p10
48 Ibid. Appendix 9
49 Ibid. *Your School and Sex Education*, CARE, p12
50 Ibid. *Teenage parenthood*, A submission to the Social Exclusion Unit, CARE, pp15-16
51 Ibid. p16
52 SIECUS, Adolescence and Abstinence Fact Sheet, published in SIECUS Report, vol. 26, no.1, November 1997
53 *A Manifesto for Marriage in Sex Education*, The Christian Institute, March 2001, p2
54 Ibid. p6
55 Ibid. p8
56 Ibid. pp10-11
57 Ibid. p12

Chapter 20

A great moral evil

The demoralisation of sexual conduct; the fallacies behind sex education; parental responsibility

The story of sex education is a story that must put fear into the hearts of most parents. From the evidence that we have uncovered in this book it is clear that sex education is being used as a medium for communicating the amoral ideology of the sexual revolution. Slowly but surely the idea is taking root among children and young people that they can do whatever appears to be right in their own eyes—that they can even set their own standards of sexual behaviour. Many are being persuaded that they are entitled to make informed decisions to have sex when they want to, when they feel ready, provided they practise 'safer sex'. According to Melanie Phillips, children are being treated as mini-adults. 'Not only parents but the State now refuses to treat children as the immature, uninformed individuals they are, requiring the effort of protection and guidance. Instead, through sex education in schools it [the State] equips them for the sexual marketplace—and congratulates itself for its "responsibility" as it dishes out condoms to under-age youngsters. The result is that sex has become a recreational sport for children just as it is for adults, with shocking and shameful results.'[1] As a consequence, many children are experiencing all the physical, emotional and spiritual problems associated with sexual promiscuity. Teenage sexual tragedies are now common-place, and many young lives are being shattered by the dreadful consequences associated with sexual immorality. Indeed, a national screening pilot for chlamydia (a sexually transmitted disease associated with infertility) has found that 13.8 per cent of under-16s who attend contraceptive services for young people are infected with this unpleasant disease.[2]

In view of these dangers, no parent can stand back and leave the moral education of their children in the hands of the sex educators; to do so is tantamount to child neglect. Parents must take the lead in the moral instruction of their children. In this chapter I summarise the case against sex education and offer a Christian alternative.

The demoralisation of sexual behaviour

A theme that runs through this book is that the underlying objective of the sexual revolution is the demoralisation of sexual behaviour. The anti-Christian position of the revolutionaries is obvious, and they do not try to hide their hatred of traditional Christian morality, which in their minds is the major factor responsible for sexual repression. The sex educators, on the other hand, as the propagandists of the revolution, have been careful about revealing their hostility, for they realise that the population at large is still sympathetic to traditional morality. Nevertheless, the ultimate aim of the sex educators and the sexual revolutionaries is the same—to create a world free from moral restraint; a world liberated from the sexual repression of the Victorians; a world in which all people are free to indulge their sexual desires. In his book *How Now Shall we Live?* Charles Colson explains that 'the founders of sex education never did seek simply to transmit a collection of facts about how our bodies work. Rather, they were evangelists for a utopian worldview, a religion, in which a "scientific" understanding of sexuality is the means for transforming human nature, freeing it from the constraints of morality and ushering in an ideal society.'[3]

While the sex educators are careful not to appear to be openly hostile to Christian morality, they have used a number of subtle ploys to undermine it. The first was to promote the idea that sex education should be value-free and non-judgemental. The underlying agenda was to exclude 'judgemental' teachings that condemned certain sexual practices as immoral. But when it dawned that value-free sex education meant, in fact, amoral sex education, most people did not want that for their children.

The next approach was to say that sex education should be taught in a 'positive' moral framework, without specifying what that moral framework should be. This deceived many people, for they automatically assumed that in Great Britain this would mean a Christian moral framework. But the sex educators had other ideas. They had no intention of promoting biblical morality; instead, they used the technique of values clarification to disparage traditional morality. This technique is subtle in that it encourages children to challenge the fundamentals of the moral framework that they have been taught by their parents. Everything a child has been taught about sexual conduct, family and parents is taken apart and 'clarified'. In this way doubt is cast on traditional moral teaching, and children are left with the clear impression that, as there is no absolute moral law, they are free to develop their *own* system of values and beliefs. And because values clarification is done in a classroom situation there is peer pressure on a child to conform to the ideas of the group. The fundamental assumption underlying values clarification is not a neutral point of view but rather a view that actively supports moral relativism.

Another method of demoralising sexual conduct is the appeal to self-esteem. Children are invited to make 'positive' (not moral) decisions about their sexual relationships on the basis of their feelings. Sex educators claim that the subjective feelings of children are the source of 'healthy' sexual decisions. The appeal to self-esteem discourages the use of judgemental messages that condemn certain behaviours, such as promiscuity. Many New Age techniques are used to engender feelings of positive self-esteem.

The final amoral approach has been to develop a so-called 'Christian' version of sex education that promotes abstinence as a 'healthy' and 'positive' choice. In the previous chapter we saw that while the 'Christian' version of sex education aims to present abstinence in a favourable light, and so delay the onset of sexual intercourse, its reasons for doing so are pragmatic, and it does not teach the importance of sexual purity, the virtue of chastity, or the discipline of self-control. Although the teaching of abstinence has the appearance of being Christian, its basic message is amoral.

What all these approaches have in common is the absence of any sense of distinguishing right from wrong. Instead of a moral decision to remain chaste, children are encouraged to make a 'positive', 'appropriate' or 'healthy' choice not to have sex until they are ready. Children are encouraged to develop their *own* standards of sexual conduct using the techniques of values clarification and self-esteem. Young people are free to decide for themselves what they want, free to make an 'informed' decision to 'have sex' or not, free from the influence of 'moralisers', free from the teachings of the Bible, and free from the traditions of their family and community.

The document produced by the Social Exclusion Unit, *Teenage Pregnancy*, while encouraging values clarification and self-esteem, warns against the serious error of 'moralising'. It claims that preaching at children 'makes it less likely they'll make the right decision'.[4] Any attempt to introduce a moral dimension into sex education is portrayed as unhelpful. It is interesting to note the negative connotation the Government attaches to the 'moralisers'. They are simply dismissed as bigots who threaten children by their strict, judgemental and unreasonable rules. Consequently, the model of sex education that is being promoted in our schools takes no account of the moral teaching of the Bible. What is so disturbing about the Government's advice is that it coincides exactly with the policy of the International Planned Parenthood Federation, namely, that all moral discussions of sexual behaviour should be avoided. The British Government, the IPPF, the FPA, Brook and CARE all teach sex education in a framework that is either indifferent to, or ignores, biblical morality.

The effect of demoralising sex is that no conduct is, of itself, wrong. It follows that sex education does not teach that promiscuous sex, homosexuality, abortion, cohabitation or adultery is wrong. In the view of sex education, the only problem with promiscuity is that it may result in an unintended pregnancy or sexually transmitted disease, and provided that these problems can be avoided by contraception, there is nothing intrinsically wrong with teenagers having sex before marriage. So the promiscuous young girl, who manages to avoid becoming pregnant by using contraception, is considered to be acting 'responsibly'. Demoralising sexual conduct allows children to be taught anything—there are no boundaries. Consequently, explicit sexual images and lewd language, which would usually be regarded as obscene and pornographic, are justified in the name of sex education.

The amorality of pro-choice dogma – making 'informed' choices

Having demoralised sexual conduct, sex education is now in a position to invite children to make an 'informed' decision about whether they should have sex or not. An example of 'pro-choice' sex education is the Northern Ireland programme, *Love for Life*, which encourages teenagers to make 'informed choices' with regard to their sexual conduct on the basis of factual information and positive self-esteem.[5] Two options are set before children—to delay the onset of sexual intercourse or to practise 'safer sex'. Because this is seen as a difficult choice, sex education helps by providing teenagers with the information they need to make an 'informed' decision. In support of the one option, children are given information about sexual intercourse, the importance of being in a stable relationship and the ability to access contraception. In support of the other option, children are provided with information about the failure rates of contraceptives and the incidence of sexually transmitted diseases. On the basis of the factual information provided, children are in a position to weigh up the pros and cons, and then to make an 'informed' decision about which option appeals to them most.

We have seen that sex education offers those young women who become pregnant the option of an abortion. For example, *Lovelife* (HEA) says: 'If you or your partner are pregnant, take time to think about what you want to do. You will have to decide if you are going to carry on with the pregnancy or not.'[6] CARE's pamphlet, *Making a Decision*, which helps a woman make an 'informed' choice whether or not to have an abortion, provides a good example of pro-choice dogma. The pamphlet explains to a pregnant woman that 'when you're ready, you and your husband or partner will need to consider the options available: parenting, adoption or abortion... Although the decision ahead of you may be one of the most difficult you'll ever have to make, it must be your decision and no-one else's. This leaflet is designed to help you through the decision making process... Make sure you have read all the factual information about each option before you make a final decision. Having looked at all the facts and explored thoroughly how you feel about each option, you may be ready to make your decision. It's important that you feel able to live with the decision you have made.'[7] Note the elements of 'pro-choice' dogma. First, the issue is demoralised; as there is no right or wrong, abortion and parenting are presented as moral equivalents. Pro-choice propaganda encourages a woman to believe that her informed decision is a morally neutral action—she is not warned of the moral consequences. Second, as abortion and parenting are moral equivalents, a woman is invited to make an informed decision on the basis of factual information and how she feels. She is persuaded to do what she believes to be right in her own eyes—it is her own decision, she decides for herself what is right.

So we see that 'pro-choice' dogma is an essential element of sex education. It sets before children the proposition that delaying the onset of sexual intercourse, and making an 'informed' choice to have sex, are moral equivalents. Both options are open to a girl, and the choice she makes is not really important—as the HEA puts it: 'If you've decided you're not ready for sex, then fine.'[8] What is important is that a girl makes her *own* decision, not influenced by anybody else, and especially not by the negative 'thou shalt nots' of the Bible or the traditional views of her parents. The girl who chooses to 'have sex' is described as having made a 'responsible choice' provided she uses contraception. Sex education even offers to help those who choose to 'have sex' by teaching them how to negotiate 'safer sex' with a partner. And those who choose not to have sex are reassured that they can always change their mind when they meet the right person or when they feel ready for sex. And if they become pregnant, sex education offers to help them make an informed decision whether or not to have an abortion.

To offer children the option of having sex, without warning that promiscuity is against the moral law of God, is leading them into the path of temptation. To place before children the choice of sexual intercourse, and suggest that it is for them to make an 'informed' decision on the basis of the facts, guided by how they feel, is damnable advice. Those who provide this type of advice should take heed of the biblical warning. Jesus said, 'Temptations to sin are sure to come, but woe to the one through whom they come! It would be better for him if a millstone were hung around his neck and he were cast into the sea than that he should cause one of these little ones to sin' (Luke 17:1-2).

Christian teaching about sexual conduct is completely different. The Bible makes it abundantly clear that human sexual behaviour is subject to the moral law of God. And God's law demands sexual purity, decency and self-control. Sexual conduct is so inextricably linked to inner beliefs that the physical aspect of sex can never be divorced from the moral dimension. Jesus taught that the outward, physical manifestations of sexual behaviour are always a manifestation of the inner self. 'For from within, out of men's hearts, come evil thoughts, sexual immorality...' (Mark 7:21). Any attempt to teach about sexual conduct in a moral vacuum is to promote amorality, which always leads to sexual immorality. The God of the Bible demands that his people control their bodies 'in a way that is holy and honourable, not in passionate lust like the heathen, who do not know God' (1 Thessalonians 4:4-5). The New Testament warns that we should 'flee from sexual immorality' (1 Corinthians 6:18).

Propaganda of sex education

The Family Planning Association and Brook were the first organisations to use propaganda techniques to promote the messages of the sexual revolution.

Although these organisations are ideologically committed to the revolution they do not openly declare their intentions. Instead, they achieve their objective by means of a propaganda war—the main vehicle for their indoctrination is 'sex education'.

One of the most common of propaganda devices is the use of virtuous words. By this device the propagandist identifies his programme with favourable words such as 'family' and 'education'. It is instructive to note that the Birth Control Council changed its name to the 'Family' Planning Association. It was a propaganda masterstroke for an organisation promoting the ideals of the sexual revolution to associate itself with the word 'family', a word that has favourable connotations for most people. Notice the incredible irony that the unmarried teenager who uses contraceptives to avoid becoming pregnant is said to be practising 'family' planning. What she is doing is trying to *avoid* becoming a mother. Anyone who has read Orwell's *Nineteen eighty-four* will recall the term 'newspeak'. Orwell shows how in 'newspeak' words are subtly manipulated to mean whatever the movement wants them to mean, so that the usual meaning no longer applies. The word 'family' as used by the FPA is an example of 'newspeak'. Who would suspect that the ideology of the 'Family' Planning Association is intent on undermining the traditional family?

The phrase 'sex education' also has real propaganda value in that the majority of people accept that education must be a good thing. Linking the words 'sex' and 'education' was another brilliant move by the sexual revolutionaries, for by making sex an academic subject to be taught in schools it legitimised the agenda of the sexual revolution. The open and explicit discussion of sex became acceptable when it was done under the umbrella of sex education.

Notice the subtle use of words. Most sex education literature refers to 'sex' in a way that makes no distinction between the legitimate sexual expression of husband and wife and immoral sexual activity based on lust. The inference is that 'having sex' is a morally neutral activity. Now turn to the word 'education'. In propaganda terms, 'education', like 'motherhood' is a virtuous word. The psychological effect of the word is irresistible. So with little thought or understanding everybody is in favour of sex 'education'. When the sexual revolutionaries coined the term 'sex education' they had virtually won the propaganda war at a stroke. So powerful is the propaganda effect of the term 'sex education' that there is almost no defence and most people are seduced. Consequently, most parents want their children to gain the benefits of 'sex education'. For anyone to argue that 'sex education' is not necessary, or even harmful, is regarded as ridiculous. And so the term 'sex education' has been used to legitimise the mass indoctrination of children with the ideas of the sexual revolution.

Another favourable word which permeates sex education is 'safe'. Having sex using condoms is referred to as 'safer' sex. Of course, the propagandist seldom mentions that condoms fail, nor that the only really safe sex takes place in a faithful marriage. For a young woman to carry condoms in her handbag is referred to as 'being prepared', and those who use contraceptives are said to be 'responsible', for they are promoting their sexual 'health'.

Conversely, sex educators attach pejorative words to the ideals that they want us to condemn and reject. Therefore traditional Christian moral teaching is referred to as 'repressive' and 'old-fashioned'. Those who teach sexual restraint are called 'moralisers'; those who promote biblical morality are 'preachers' and those who teach that the Bible condemns promiscuity are 'judgemental'. The moral law of God is parodied as a list of 'thou shalt nots'. Those who practise sexual restraint are 'prudes'. In this way the propagandist labels biblical morality with pejorative words, persuading people to reject it without further thought.

In her article 'Bonking for beginners' Patricia Morgan argues that sex education is not intellectual or academic, but ideological, in that it corrupts children and makes them ungovernable. She writes that 'never before have children been exposed to so much sex so soon... Sex education exponents and practitioners are not social and medical researchers, or child development specialists. They are lobbyists or public and private entrepreneurs, out to sell and extend the freedom of the sexual revolution and promote "alternatives" to the much despised family. Ads, clothes and pin-ups aside, what goes on in the sex education manuals and the glossy "puberty press" is identical.'[9] Patricia Morgan is developing the argument that sex education is simply another branch of the sexual revolution that is hiding behind the euphemism 'sex education'.

The false presuppositions of sex education

Sex education propaganda is based on three false assumptions. The first is that it is natural for children to be sexually promiscuous; the second is that children are sexually ignorant. The third assumption, which follows on from the first two, is that promiscuous, ignorant children need to be educated in the skills of 'safer sex' to avoid sexual tragedies.

The fallacy that sexual promiscuity is natural

Sex education makes the assumption that it is natural for children to be sexually promiscuous. Because 'having sex' is so much fun, such a source of physical pleasure, it is ridiculous to think that children will deny themselves. It's common sense that most children will indulge in sex the moment they pass through puberty, and anybody who thinks otherwise is not living in the real world. Consistent with their amoral approach, sex educators promote the idea that children, like rabbits, are likely to copulate the moment they become sexually mature, and so the issue is simply to prevent them from becoming pregnant. According to one social commentator, 'Sex has become a pastime like skiing, with children being told how to improve their technique while making sure they avoid any nasty accidents. So Boots is opening a drop-in clinic where children and others can get free contraceptives. It is so easy: just remember to add condoms to lip salve and Elastoplast.'[10] Because the message of sex education is 'non-judgemental', promiscuity is not to be condemned.

But the assumption that children are basically amoral is false, for human beings, created in the image of God, have a conscience that writes the law of God in their hearts. Those children who have been taught the basics of biblical morality have a tender conscience that warns them against promiscuity—they know in their inner being that it is wrong to 'have sex' outside of marriage. Young girls, in particular, have a natural aversion to promiscuity, for they have an innate fear of becoming pregnant. They know that sex may result in pregnancy, and they fear the consequences of becoming an unmarried mother, or, worse, of having an abortion. This innate fear acts as a natural restraint against promiscuous sex. However, it is not only the fear of pregnancy that acts as a restraint, but also the knowledge that to 'have sex' is a huge life-changing step, from which there is no returning. Such a decision cannot be taken lightly and in their hearts most women want to remain chaste until they are married.

Even those who do not know the basics of biblical morality know in their inner self that there is a right way of behaving, since the requirements of the law are written on their hearts, and their consciences bear witness to God's moral law (Romans 2:15). They know in their heart of hearts that promiscuity is wrong, and those who ignore the warnings of their consciences feel shame and guilt. This is why children are too ashamed to let their parents know that they are getting a supply of condoms from the local clinic. This is why clinics that treat sexually transmitted infections are clouded in secrecy. Most children know that sexual immorality is wrong and that it has serious consequences. Despite the propaganda of sex education, most children remain chaste and do not quickly give way to their sexual desires.

The fallacy of sexual ignorance

Throughout this book we have seen the claim that ignorance is a major cause of sexual tragedies. According to the Government, one of the main reasons for the high teenage pregnancy rate is ignorance—'young people lack accurate knowledge about contraception, sexually transmitted diseases, what to expect in relationships and what it means to be a parent'.[11] The *Teenage Pregnancy* report asserts that 'young people are frequently ignorant or misinformed about sex... certainly the huge number of calls to helplines like Sexwise and the enduring popularity of problem pages in teen magazines points to a great unmet need among teenagers for basic, factual information about sex'.[12] Steve Chalke, the author of *The Parentalk Guide to Your Child and Sex*, agrees: 'The truth is, your child's *innocence* is far more likely to be protected if the time bomb of their *ignorance* is removed.'[13] The sex educators use this assumption of ignorance as a pretext for teaching children a large number of sexual *facts*, with the assertion that children must be taught the 'truth'. According to a SIECUS sex education guide, the acceptance of 'truth' as a core value implies that all sex practices should 'be described as objectively and scientifically as possible, whether or not the results conformed to the official mores or to a particular social code'.[14]

So the sex educators have taken to themselves the right to teach children a catalogue of sexual facts. The booklet *Sex Education: The Erroneous Zone* contends that children should be taught a vast range of *facts* about sex. The sex manual, *Make it Happy*, provides teenagers with an encyclopaedic knowledge of sex, including facts about the sexual organs, masturbation and incest. CARE promotes the idea that young people should be given accurate *factual* information about sex, unplanned pregnancy, STIs, contraception, abortion and its effects, both physical and emotional.[15]

Here it is necessary to make a distinction between facts and truth, for facts are not truth. Whereas facts can be used to corrupt and deprave, truth always has a moral dimension and never corrupts. Truth is based in God's word: 'I, the Lord, speak the truth; I declare what is right' (Isaiah 45:19). And Jesus, in his high priestly prayer to his Father, declared: 'Your word is truth' (John 17:17). God's truth always promotes sexual morality and that which is decent, pure and right; facts, on the other hand, contain no moral dimension and may be used, and are used, to promote sexual immorality. So facts about sex, without the moral implications that flow from those facts, do not constitute truth, and may be a pathway to sexual temptation. The Bible encourages Christians to think about whatever is true, noble, right, pure, lovely, admirable, excellent and praiseworthy (Philippians 4:8).

So why do innocent children need to be taught sexual facts that would not ordinarily enter their minds? The *facts* that children are being taught about contraception do not represent truth—the truth is that children who remain chaste do not need contraception. The *facts* that children are being taught about sexually transmitted diseases are not truth—the truth is that these unpleasant diseases are the consequence of sexual immorality. Chaste children gain no benefit from having the *facts* about pubic lice, gonorrhoea and genital warts forced on them. The *facts* that children are taught about sexual orientation are not truth—the truth is that homosexuality is a perversion, and children gain no benefit whatsoever from being taught the *facts* about sexual perversions.

While sex education gives children *facts* about sex, it does not tell them the truth about God's standard of sexual behaviour and the consequences that flow from rejecting God's moral law. The sexual *facts* imparted by sex education are designed to undermine sexual purity and invite lustful thoughts. The *facts* compel children to turn their innocent minds to sexual matters, to focus on sex, to think about that which is immoral, unclean, depraved and perverted. The real purpose of the *facts*, so beloved by the sex educators, is to promote pornographic ideas and images, gradually introducing children into the perverted, sex-obsessed mindset of the sexual revolutionaries. The unsolicited *facts* of the sex educator invade the innocence of childhood, and what is so shocking is that schoolchildren are a captive audience who have no way of escaping the deluge of facts thrust on them in the name of sex education.

Sex education claims that another major cause of sexual ignorance is the failure of parents to educate their children about sex. According to sex educators, 'many parents cannot, will not, or simply do not educate their children explicitly about sex',[16] and research shows that the majority of parents find it difficult to give sex education to their teenage children.[17] Because the vast majority of parents do not discuss sex with their children, they are seen as a part of the problem—they are simply too ignorant, too embarrassed or too lazy to teach their children about sex.

The usual explanation for this failure is that parents and children find it embarrassing to discuss sex with each other. Even those parents who have cared for their children in the most intimate way, who read the Bible to their children, who talk to their children about every subject under the sun, including moral issues, find it embarrassing to discuss sex with their children. The experience of Anthony Clare, the well-known psychiatrist, is probably typical of most parents. He explains the reserve felt by both parents and children when it comes to sexual matters. 'My adolescent offspring, and I do not believe that they are in this regard atypical, value their privacy. They do not want uninvited information to be thrust upon them. While they are not adults, they are not children either, and didactic, heart-to-heart exchanges are more the stuff of rather po-faced educational material than the real life cut and thrust of parent-adolescent relationships.'[18] And this is a psychiatrist, trained in medicine, who knows the details of sexual anatomy and is an expert in the behavioural sciences, who feels that it is unnatural to speak to his children about sexual matters. The reason is an instinctive reluctance to intrude into the private life of his children.

If children really benefit from sex education, as the sex educators tell us, and if parents do not give children this type of education, then it follows that others need to take on the task. Because parents are failing in their duty, sex educators have taken on the responsibility of providing children with the knowledge they need to practise 'safer sex'. On the pretext of overcoming sexual ignorance, sex educators teach children a vocabulary of sexual words, show them explicit images, educate them about sexually transmitted diseases and techniques for unrolling condoms, and train them to make 'positive', 'healthy', 'informed' sexual decisions. But there is something wrong here. We know that the Bible teaches that parents are responsible for the moral instruction and discipline of their children. God commands his people to teach their children about his laws. It is the responsibility of parents to 'train a child in the way he should go, and when he is old he will not turn from it' (Proverbs 22:6), and fathers are to bring up their children 'in the training and instruction of the Lord' (Ephesians 6:4). It follows that it must be wrong for parents to hand the moral instruction of their children over to the sex educators. Does this mean that parents should overcome their innate embarrassment in order to teach their children the large body of factual knowledge suggested by the sex educators? Or is the assumption that children need a large body of factual knowledge to make informed sexual choices fundamentally wrong?

Yes indeed! The reason that parents find it so embarrassing to talk about sexual matters with their children is that it is unnatural and wrong for them to do such a thing. How many good parents do you know who talk to their children about sex?

What seems remarkable is that among the finest, most devoted parents almost none discuss sex with their children in the way suggested by the sex educators. Even among Christian parents who pray daily for their children's spiritual welfare, who take the keenest interest in teaching their children the Christian gospel and are willing to make considerable personal sacrifices for their moral well-being, there is no sex education of the kind advocated by the sex education movement. Why is this so? Why do the most devoted, good parents, who really love and nurture their children, not spend time teaching them about sex? Are these parents, as suggested by sex education, failing their children? Does this mean that Christian parents who do not talk to their children about sex are failing in their duty? And are children being deprived because their parents are not educating them about condoms?

Of course not! The incessant clamour that children must be 'educated' about sex comes from the sexual revolution, not from the Bible. It was the Bloomsbury Set who talked incessantly about sex; it was Sigmund Freud, Marie Stopes, Margaret Sanger and Alfred Kinsey who were obsessed with sex. And the sex education movement, as the propaganda arm of the sexual revolution, has been enormously successful in persuading society of the benefits of 'educating' children about sex. So we see that the idea that children need to be 'educated' about sex flows from the sexual revolution—and nobody it appears, not even the Christian Church, has challenged this proposition.

The fallacy of 'safer sex'

A major assumption of sex education is that contraception prevents sexual tragedies. We have repeatedly heard the mantra—contraception reduces the rate of unwanted pregnancies, abortions and sexually transmitted diseases. Remember the Government's guidance to schools, discussed in chapter 1. 'Knowledge of the different types of contraception, and of access to, and availability of contraception is a major part of the Government's strategy to reduce teenage pregnancy.' The Government emphasises that 'trained staff in secondary schools should be able to give young people full information about different types of contraception, including emergency contraception and their effectiveness'.[19] Steve Chalke is a keen supporter of the Government's policy on contraception. He writes that a wise parent presents 'the facts about the various different types of contraception available – and why they could be a real lifesaver – alongside moral, social and emotional arguments as to where, when, how, why and with whom sex can best be enjoyed. This way your child will begin to understand how contraception fits into the overall picture of their sexuality before making their own informed – and hopefully wise – decisions.'[20]

Current orthodoxy holds that a comprehensive programme of sex education, sensitively and well taught, and backed up by a well-organised family planning service, which makes contraceptives freely available to children, will reduce the frequency of untoward accidents among sexually active teenagers. Three decades ago Lord Avebury argued in the House of Lords (1973) that if there was an efficient and comprehensive family planning service, the abortion figures would decline and sexual tragedies would no longer take place.[21] In a letter to *The Times* the chairman of Brook argued that under-age children must be supplied with contraception to prevent unwanted pregnancies.[22] It was on the strength of such arguments that in 1974 contraceptives were made freely available to children on the NHS. Access to contraception was considered to be so important for protecting children that the Government made it lawful for doctors to prescribe contraceptives to under-age children without the knowledge or consent of their parents. One result of this policy is that more and more children are using contraceptives, and in the year 2001, 80 thousand under-age children attended family planning clinics for the first time.

It is not widely known that contraceptives are associated with significant failure rates—so the more sexually active teenagers there are, the more who will experience a sexual tragedy. Few people realise that most children who become pregnant have been using contraception. For example, a study of 147 teenagers with unplanned pregnancies found that 80 per cent claimed to have been using contraception at the time of conception.[23] As we saw in chapter 1, recent research of teenage pregnancies in general practice shows that most teenagers who became pregnant had discussed contraception (71 per cent) in the year before conception. Moreover, as this research was based solely on GP records and did not take account of contraception provided by family planning clinics, it certainly underestimates the total provision of contraception to teenagers who become pregnant.[24]

When I was Director of Public Health for Croydon Health Authority, all the evidence I came across convinced me of the inability of contraception to prevent pregnancies among teenagers. To demonstrate this point I examined the relationship between the use of condoms at first sexual intercourse, and the conception rate among under 16-year-olds, for the period 1975 to 1991. My letter, published in the *British Medical Journal*, showed a remarkably powerful correlation between the two trends, with pregnancies *increasing* (not decreasing) with increasing condom use.[25] While it is not possible to say that there is a causal link, a feasible explanation is that the promotion of contraception among the young has contributed to an increase in promiscuous sexual behaviour, which in turn has inevitably contributed to the increase in teenage pregnancies. The letter concludes, 'Sex education and the national campaign to promote contraception through safer sex campaigns have undoubtedly been successful in increasing the proportion of teenagers who use condoms. Most people assume that increasing the use of contraception leads to a reduction in unplanned pregnancies. Yet my analysis shows that this has not happened. A plausible explanation is that the main factor in unplanned teenage pregnancy is contraceptive failure, not the lack of contraceptive knowledge and availability.'[26]

An epidemiological assessment of family planning, sponsored by the Department of Health, provides information on the percentage of women who become pregnant in the year of using different contraceptive methods. The failure rate for condoms is estimated to be between 10 and 19 per cent, and for oral contraceptives between 4 and 9 per cent. And failure rates among teenagers are considerably higher.[27] This means that one in five young women who depend upon condoms for contraception are at risk of pregnancy during each year of sexual activity. Clearly, contraception does not provide foolproof protection against pregnancy. This means that the Government's policy of promoting contraception among children, discussed in chapter 1, will inevitably result in a high teenage pregnancy rate, such as we have at present in the UK.

So children are being misled into believing that they can become sexually active without any adverse consequences provided they practise 'safer sex'. We now have a remarkable paradox—despite a massive nationwide campaign promoting contraceptives over the last three decades, the problems that sex education claimed it would solve have actually got worse. The claim that contraception prevents sexual tragedies is false and the reason is not difficult to understand. Providing children with contraception is an open invitation to engage in sexual intercourse without any apparent danger, an invitation to enjoy 'safer sex'. By removing the fear of pregnancy, one of the natural factors that inhibit sexual intercourse is also removed. Consequently, many young women, believing themselves to be safe from pregnancy, are recruited into a life of sexual promiscuity. Moreover, the fact that the Government provides contraception for children, creates an impression in their young minds that it cannot be wrong for them to use contraceptives.

Hundreds of thousands of children who have suffered the emotional trauma and moral guilt associated with sexual promiscuity can testify to the fact that the 'safer sex' message is dishonest, misleading and cruel, for it hurts young people, especially young girls, who often feel that they have been used as a sex object. Those girls enticed into promiscuity by the 'safer sex' message find that they have entered not into a world of sexual fun, as promised by the sex educators, but into the dark world of sexual immorality, characterised by anxiety, insecurity, and fear. Amoral sex education, of course, does not acknowledge the existence of sexual immorality and glosses over the moral devastation that results from its teaching. The Bible, however, warns that sexual immorality has serious spiritual consequences. While 'safer sex' may prevent some of the physical consequences, some of the time, it cannot protect against the spiritual and moral harm that flows from disobeying God's moral law. The terrible truth is that sexual immorality has consequences. 'Do not be deceived: God cannot be mocked. A man reaps what he sows. The one who sows to please his sinful nature, from that nature will reap destruction…' (Galatians 6:7,8). Sadly, sex outside marriage has serious consequences—the worry of resorting to emergency contraception, the pain and guilt of abortion, the shame of sexually transmitted disease, the deception of parents, the sadness of broken promises, children without fathers, to mention some of the more obvious.

Parental responsibility

We have seen the overwhelming case against sex education. We have seen that it has demoralised sexual conduct. We have seen that the whole edifice is based on false assumptions. How then should parents respond?

It is the responsibility of all parents, Christian and non-Christian alike, to teach their children a moral framework on which to base their lives, and this is especially true when it comes to sexual conduct. God reminded his people that his laws were righteous and good. 'These commandments that I give you today are to be upon your hearts. Impress them on your children. Talk about them when you sit at home and when you walk along the road, when you lie down and when you get up... Teach them to your children and to their children after them' (Deuteronomy 6: 6-7, 4:9). Children need both formal instruction and to learn from the example of their parents. The home environment becomes a means of bringing children up in the training and instruction of the Lord.

Parents, therefore, should make a definite decision to teach their children the moral law of God contained in the Bible. (Even among parents who are not practising Christians, many still want their children to be taught the basics of biblical morality.) Parents should teach Jesus' standard of sexual purity and the importance of the biblical virtues of modesty and chivalry. Children should be taught the value of self-control, chastity and fidelity, and about the meaning and purpose of marriage and the family. The first nine chapters of Proverbs can be used to teach children the value of wisdom and discipline, and to warn young people of the dangers of sexual immorality. The book of Titus can be used to teach children the great value of self-control and the importance of saying no to ungodliness and worldly passions (Titus 2). Parents can show their children that the Bible condemns sexual impurity, fornication, adultery, incest, homosexuality, filthy language and coarse joking. Those children who have been taught about chastity and self-control gain no benefit from being told about contraceptive techniques and how to 'be prepared' for sex. Those children who understand Jesus' standard of sexual purity will regard the explicit sexual images of sex education as pornographic, and will object to being taught a vocabulary of indecent words. Having learned the biblical principles of sexual morality, children do not need to know the facts about 'safer sex' or the details of sexually transmitted diseases.

When it comes to sexual behaviour, a wise parent recognises that God has given children a time of innocence during which they should be taught the difference between right and wrong. Slowly, as they mature, children learn to understand the mystery of their sexual nature. They absorb the differences between male and female by living with their parents and siblings in a family. As they observe the different roles of their father and mother in everyday family life, they slowly discern the differences in behaviour and dress, and the way their father and mother relate to each other. They see that their father and mother love each other, share a bed together, and sleep together. The family situation with parents, brothers and sisters feels secure, natural and right and gives a great sense of belonging. As children slowly mature into adolescence they have the model of their parents and family as an example. They hear the way members of the family speak to each other and soon realise that explicit, foul, obscene language has no place in the family situation. And children that grow up in a home where their father and mother love and respect each other, see a model of what marriage and family relationships should be and come to understand the importance of faithfulness in a sexual relationship.

Because sexuality is a part of human nature, as children grow older and pass through puberty it is natural for them gradually to understand how their body functions. As they become aware of their sexual nature, they should do so in accordance with the moral standards that they have learned from their parents. They develop moral beliefs about sexual conduct in the context of their parents' marriage, the standards implicit within their family, and from the message of the Bible. As they grow into adolescence they do not need to be taught about sexual techniques and condoms, for they have already learnt that certain forms of behaviour, such as sexual promiscuity, are plainly wrong. They also know that such behaviour would cause deep distress to their parents and family.

It is natural for a mother to prepare her daughter for womanhood and menstruation. It is also natural for parents to answer the questions that their children ask about sex in an honest and thoughtful way, taking account of the child's age. Wise parents stress the importance of sexual purity and advise their children to behave with decency in their friendships with members of the opposite sex. But just as parents do not need to teach children how to walk or talk, for they learn these skills naturally as they grow older, so they do not need to teach children the details of sexual physiology, for children come to understand their sexual nature as they mature into adulthood. By observing their parents, children learn the cardinal sexual virtues of modesty and chivalry. Daughters learn from their mothers to dress and behave with modesty, and not to encourage sexual advances from boys. They see how their mother behaves and learn from her example. Sons learn to respect their mother and to behave with decency and honour towards women. They are taught to treat all women as they treat their mother, and most young men are very protective of their mother's honour. A well brought up young man knows that he should not take advantage of a young woman.

The assertion of the sex education movement that parents should talk to their children about sex is contrary to biblical teaching. In biblical times it was the Canaanites who were obsessed with sex and used children in sexual rituals. The people of God, on the other hand, talked to their children about the law of God and instructed them in the moral standards by which they ought to live. Exposing children to sex talk is unnatural, an assault on the innocence of childhood and a subtle form of child abuse. Moreover, because of the moral imperative that surrounds sexual behaviour, because children know in their conscience that certain forms of behaviour are wrong, they can only be confused and embarrassed by the crass attempts of their parents to talk about sex. Indeed, most children are deeply embarrassed by the thought of discussing the details of sex, condoms and sexually transmitted diseases with their mother or father.

There is, of course, the issue of those children who grow up in single parent homes, who do not have the model of a family as a guide for their behaviour. One reason children from single parent homes are especially prone to sexual tragedies, is that they do not have the same degree of moral teaching that is implicit in the family situation. It is, therefore, especially important that those children who grow up in such situations should to be taught the moral framework of the Bible. Those who claim that such children are offended by being taught the importance of marriage and the family are wrong. Children from broken homes (like the author) and single parent homes know of the joys of a proper family, and desperately want something better for themselves. It is completely wrong to withhold the Christian teaching of marriage on the pretext of upsetting children whose parents are not married.

A great moral evil

Our study of the sex education movement has exposed one of the great moral evils of our time. We have seen that it teaches children to follow the pagan ethic of 'do as you want'. We have uncovered a modern phallic cult, like the Canaanites of the Old Testament, who worship sex and take pleasure in spreading their amoral lessons of depravity among children. We have exposed the lessons of depravity that implant unnatural and indecent sexual thoughts into the minds of children. We have seen the graphic sexual images that introduce children to lewd ideas and arouse sexual lust. We know that children of 12 and 13 are being given contraceptives without the knowledge of their parents. We know that children are being given condoms at school. We also know that the delights of sexual pleasure are explained to children, with the assurance that being 'prepared with condoms doesn't mean taking the fun out of sex'.[28] We know that children are told that 'safer sex' allows them to have sexual fun whenever they like, with as many partners as they like, free from any worry or problem. The message of the sex educators sounds so plausible, for the hollow words of the sex propagandist are as sweet as honey, smooth, reassuring, and persuasive. But the Bible warns of the deceptiveness of sexual temptation—'let no one deceive you with empty words' (Ephesians 5:6).

The God of the Bible hates evil, and in Deuteronomy six times commands his people to purge the evil from among them. According to Thomas Trevethan, 'God's perfect goodness, his moral holiness, demands that he stand opposed to evil and sin just as light stands opposed to darkness. The two are incompatible. And because this holiness, this light, is divine goodness, his opposition is not the passive resistance of a mere spectator. His holiness rises up in active resistance to all evil, to all that cheapens and distorts and destroys his creatures. The Holy One, in his perfect goodness, is actively and intensely set against evil. He judges it as the only holy Judge of all his creatures.'[29] In view of God's holiness, the Christian has a responsibility – more, the Christian has an obligation – to expose the fruitless deeds of darkness and to oppose their wicked practices. 'Have nothing to do with the fruitless deeds of darkness, but rather expose them. For it is shameful even to mention what the disobedient do in secret' (Ephesians 5:11,12).

There can be no compromise with the detestable teachings of sex education. The struggle is not against flesh and blood, but against the spiritual forces of evil in the heavenly realms. Sex education is one of the devil's cunning schemes we are warned about in the sixth chapter of Ephesians. To take a stand against this evil we need the full armour of God—the belt of truth, the breastplate of righteousness, the shield of faith and the helmet of salvation. The weapon with which to attack the forces of evil is the sword of the Spirit, which is the word of God. I invite those who are reluctant to use the Bible in the struggle against the evil of sex education, on the pretext that it puts people off, to think again. We know that the sexual revolutionaries at all costs want to avoid having their depraved messages exposed to the light of God's word. 'This is the verdict: Light has come into the world, but men loved darkness instead of light because their deeds were evil. Everyone who does evil hates the light, and will not come into the light for fear that his deeds will be exposed' (John 3:19-20). Without the sword of the Spirit we are going into battle against the spiritual forces of evil without our main weapon. With the full armour of God the Christian Church should take a stand against the evil of sex education.

———————

The moral condition of Great Britain at the beginning of the twenty-first century is similar to what it was before the great evangelical awakening of the eighteenth century. In the present state of moral degeneracy the only hope for Great Britain is to turn to the same Christian gospel that transformed the nation under the ministry of George Whitefield and John Wesley. As the light of the world, the Christian Church must bear witness to the truth that God's moral law, as it relates to sexual behaviour, is for all people and brings great blessing to those who hear and obey it. The depraved messages of the sex educators should be rejected for what they are— lessons in depravity.

There is a better way, there is a message of hope. Without compromise the Church must take every opportunity to teach the biblical virtues of modesty, chivalry, chastity and fidelity. These virtues must be preached from pulpits across the land and parents must teach them at home. And this is the message: 'It is God's will that you should be holy; that you should avoid sexual immorality; that each of you should learn to control his own body in a way that is holy and honourable, not in passionate lust like the heathen, who do not know God; and that in this matter no one should wrong his brother or take advantage of him. The Lord will punish men for all such sins, as we have already told you and warned you. For God did not call us to be impure, but to live a holy life. Therefore, he who rejects this instruction does not reject man but God, who gives you his Holy Spirit' (1 Thessalonians 4:3-8).

310

Endnotes

1 *Daily Mail*, 14 December 2002, Sex and the selfish society, Melanie Phillips

2 V Moens, G Baruch, P Fearon, Opportunistic screening for Chlamydia, *British Medical Journal*, vol. 326, 7 June 2003, p1252

3 Charles Colson and Nancy Pearcey, *How Now Shall We Live?*, Marshall Pickering, 1999, p242

4 *Teenage Pregnancy*, Report of the Social Exclusion Unit, HMSO, London, June 1999, p90

5 *Love for Life*, cited from website, www.loveforlife.org.uk

6 *Lovelife*, Health Education Authority, p17

7 *Making a Decision*, CARE confidential leaflet, CARE

8 *Sexual health matters for young women*, Health Education Authority, inside front cover

9 *Sunday Telegraph*, 30 October 1994, Bonking for beginners – sex education corrupts children and makes them ungovernable, Patricia Morgan

10 Melanie Phillips, *The Sex-Change Society*, Social Market Foundation, 1999

11 Ibid. *Teenage Pregnancy*, p7

12 Ibid. p37

13 Steve Chalke, *The Parentalk Guide to Your Child and Sex*, Hodder & Stoughton, p23

14 Isadore Rubin, 'The Sex Educator and Moral Values', SIECUS Study Guide 10, 1969, pp6-9, cited from *The SIECUS Circle*, Claire Chambers, Western Islands, 1977, p4

15 *Teenage Parenthood*, a submission to the Social Exclusion Unit from CARE, 1998, p7

16 Sarah Gammage, *The Teaching of Sexuality*, in Children and controversial issues, ed Bruce Carrington and Barry Troyna, The Falmer Press, 1988

17 Allen I, *Education in sex and personal relationships*, London, Policy Study Institute, 1987, p203

18 Anthony Clare, Sex and the confused parent, *The Listener*, 2 October 1986, p21

19 *Sex and Relationship Education Guidance*, DfEE, 2000, p15

20 Ibid. *The Parentalk Guide to Your Child and Sex*, pp60-61

21 Hansard, House of Lords, 1973, Lord Avebury, c1338

22 *The Times*, 18 February 1981

23 Pearson VAH, et al. Pregnant teenagers' knowledge and use of emergency contraception. *British Medical Journal*, 1995; 310: p1644 (24th June)

24 Dick Churchill et al, Consultation patterns and provision of contraception in general practice before teenage pregnancy: case control study, *British Medical Journal*, 321, pp486-89

25 Williams ES, Pregnant teenagers and contraception. Contraceptive failure may be a major factor in teenage pregnancy, *British Medical Journal*, 1995; 311: pp806-7 (letter, 23 September)

26 Ibid.

27 Ashton JR, Marchbank A, Mawle P, Hotchkiss J. *Family Planning, Abortion and Fertility Services Health Care Needs Assessment* vol. 2. Radcliffe Medical Press, 1994, p588

28 Ibid. *Lovelife*, p6

29 Thomas Trevethan, *The Beauty of God's Holiness*, InterVarsity Press, 1995, p101

Appendix

Statistics of the sex education era

The sex education movement has always been insistent about its aims—to reduce the number of teenage pregnancies and abortions, and to protect young people from the dangers of sexually transmitted diseases. In December 1972, in a statement to the House of Commons, Sir Keith Joseph said that 'with modern contraceptive methods available there should be fewer abortions and much less unhappiness and ill health which results from unplanned pregnancies'. Here we have a clear example of the ideology that believes that contraceptive services will reduce the need for abortions. In 1976 the FPA set a target to halve the number of abortions and unwanted children within the decade as its information service helped young people overcome their sexual ignorance. In 1992 the Conservative Government set a target to reduce the rate of conceptions among under-16s by at least 50 per cent by the year 2000. In 1999 the Social Exclusion Unit of the Labour Government claimed that young people lack accurate knowledge about contraception. To overcome this lack of knowledge, enormous sums of public money have been spent on educating children about contraception. The Government is so confident of its approach that it has set a target to reduce the rate of teenage pregnancies by 50 per cent by the year 2010.

Since 1974 the NHS has funded a comprehensive family planning service; and to make it as easy as possible for children to gain access to contraception, in the same year the Government issued guidance which allows doctors to prescribe contraception to under-age children without the knowledge or consent of their parents. Sex education has become compulsory in secondary schools, where teachers are trained to give children confidential advice on contraception and some secondary schools now provide contraceptives on site. As a consequence of Government policy the distribution of condoms has reached record levels, and the proportion of young people who use a condom at first intercourse has risen from around 30 per cent two decades ago to 82.5 per cent in 1999.[1]

Opponents of sex education, such as Valerie Riches, Victoria Gillick and Dr Adrian Rogers, have argued consistently that promoting contraception among children is part of the problem, that it leads not only to an increase in sexual activity among young people, but also, because of contraceptive failure, to an increase in sexual tragedies. And so the question arises, how effective has sex education been in achieving its stated aims of reducing teenage conceptions, abortions and sexually transmitted diseases? In this section we examine some of the evidence that relates to the sexual behaviour of young people during the decades of sex education.

Sexual behaviour

The national survey of sexual behaviour, which collected data from a random sample of nearly 19,000 representatives of British society, is the largest survey of sexual behaviour conducted in the UK and provides a large amount of information on young people. First, we look at the age at which young people become sexually active. Here we need to remember the claim of sex educators that there is no evidence to show that sex education increases promiscuity. One measure of the level of teenage sexual activity is the proportion of children who have sexual intercourse before the age of 16, the age of sexual consent (**figure 2**). The dividing line in the figure broadly divides women between those who received little or no sex education in school, and those who were increasingly likely to be exposed to sex education in school.

Since school sex education really started in earnest in the early 1970s, we can assume that those in the 35-39 age group, born between 1952-56, and therefore aged 15 between the period 1967-1971, were the first group liable to be exposed to sex education. At the time of the survey, which was carried out in 1991, fewer than 1% of women aged 55-59 reported intercourse by the age of 16, compared

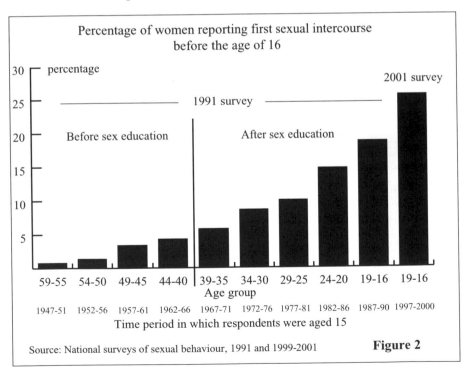

Percentage of women reporting first sexual intercourse before the age of 16

Source: National surveys of sexual behaviour, 1991 and 1999-2001

Figure 2

with 18.7% of those aged 16-19 in 1991.[2] The second national survey conducted in 1999-2001 found that among women then aged 16-19, 25.6% reported first intercourse below the age of 16.[3] It seems clear that under-age sexual intercourse has increased substantially following the introduction of sex education. This finding suggests that there may be a link between sexual promiscuity and sex education, as claimed by opponents of sex education.

What is particularly disturbing about the increasing number of under-age children becoming sexually active is the finding of the national survey that 'for men and women of all age groups, those reporting first intercourse before the age of 16 are consistently more likely to report two or more partners in the last year.'[4] In other words, the survey findings show that early sexual experience is associated with a higher number of sexual partners later in life (**figure 3**).[5] And, of course, the relationship between multiple sexual partners and sexually transmitted diseases, and especially cancer of the cervix, is well known. Therefore, those who become sexually active before 16 are embarking upon a lifestyle with many dangers.

The second national survey showed that a large proportion of young women regretted their first experience of sexual intercourse. Among those aged 13 or 14 at first intercourse, over 80 per cent wished that they had waited longer, as did half of those aged 15 and a third of those aged 16 and 17. Moreover, young women were overwhelmingly more likely than men to report that they were not equally as willing to have sex as their partner was. For example, among girls aged 13 or 14, one-third reported that the decision to have sex was not equal; their male partner was more willing to have sex than they were.[6] This data suggests that many girls are being pressurised into sexual intercourse by their boyfriends against their will.

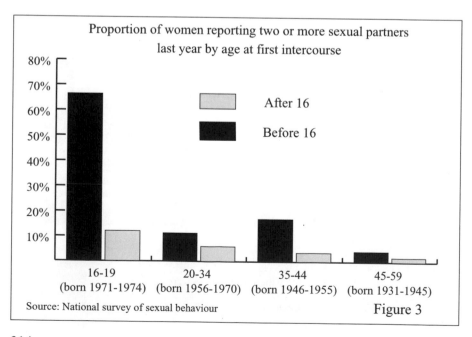

Proportion of women reporting two or more sexual partners last year by age at first intercourse

After 16
Before 16

16-19 (born 1971-1974)   20-34 (born 1956-1970)   35-44 (born 1946-1955)   45-59 (born 1931-1945)

Source: National survey of sexual behaviour

Figure 3

314

Contraception usage among young women

The best measure of contraceptive use among young women is attendance at family planning clinics. Some young women, of course, obtain their contraceptive supplies from GPs, but there is no readily available data on this source. In 1975, among girls under 16, just as sex education was beginning to take off, 8 thousand attended a family planning clinic for contraceptive supplies. The numbers attending increased steadily to 18 thousand by 1984. During the Gillick challenge to the legality of supplying contraceptives to under-age girls without the knowledge of their parents, the number of under-16s attending declined to 12 thousand. The 1990s saw an alarming increase, from 20 thousand in 1990 to 80 thousand in 2001—a tenfold increase since 1975 (**figure 1**, page 8). In 2002, it is estimated that about 16 per cent of 15-year-old girls (that is, 48 thousand), and 5 per cent of girls aged 13 and 14, attended family planning clinics.[7] Clearly, during the sex education era there has been a massive increase in the use of contraception among under-age girls. This increase has coincided with an *increase* in the number of pregnancies in this age group. Among young women in the 16-19 age group, numbers attending family planning clinics for contraceptives have increased more gradually, from 207 thousand in 1975 to 256 thousand in 1997, an increase of around 20 per cent.

The second national survey of sexual behaviour provides important data on the link between contraception at first intercourse and pregnancy. In 1972, when sex education was still in its infancy, among women aged 16-19, 37.2 per cent reported using a condom at first intercourse (31.8 per cent used nothing). By 1997, after three decades of intensive sex education, the use of contraception had increased significantly, and among women aged 16-19, 80.3 per cent were now using a condom at first intercourse (9.8 per cent used no contraception).[8] These figures suggest that sex education has been remarkably effective in increasing the use of contraception among young women. But what happened to the pregnancy rate? In 1972, among the women in the 16-19 age group, 7.7 per cent became pregnant before the age of 18, while in 1997, despite the enormous increase in the use of contraception, 10.7 per cent became pregnant before the age of 18. This data shows that increasing the use of contraception at first intercourse has not led to a reduction in the rate of teenage pregnancy.

Emergency contraception

Emergency contraception is a key weapon in the Government's strategy to reduce the rate of teenage pregnancies. When a young woman has sexual intercourse and has not used contraception effectively, or when a condom has split, she has the option of taking a high dose of female hormone to prevent the fertilised ovum from implanting itself in her womb. Emergency contraception became available during the 1980s, and in 1988, the first year for which figures are available in England, 80 thousand women were prescribed this form of contraception by their GP. In 1989, GPs issued 120 thousand prescriptions and family planning clinics

315

37 thousand. By 1994, the total number of prescriptions increased to 460 thousand, by 1997 to 770 thousand, and numbers peaked in 2000 at 790 thousand.[9] Numbers declined marginally in 2001 due to the fact that emergency contraception became available over the counter from pharmacies and supermarkets without a doctor's prescription. While the number of over the counter prescriptions are not known, there has almost certainly been a further increase as a result of the ease with which emergency contraception is now available.

The age of the girls receiving emergency contraception is only available from contraceptive clinics. In 2001, almost 26 thousand girls aged under 16, and 78 thousand aged 16-19, were given emergency contraception in clinics.[10] The number of under-age girls prescribed emergency contraception by GPs is not known.

How many under-age girls who end up using emergency contraception to avoid becoming pregnant have already attended family planning clinics for a supply of contraceptives?

Abortion

The promoters of sex education have consistently claimed that free access to contraception for young people would reduce the abortion rate. So how successful has sex education been in reducing the number of abortions? National figures show that the rate for girls under 16 increased from 1.2 per 1000 in 1969, to 3.8 in 2000 (**figure 4**); over the same period, the rate for those in the 16-19 year group increased from 6.1 to 26.7 per 1000. So the abortion rate for teenagers has increased during the sex education era.

The first national survey of sexual behaviour (1991) showed that recent abortion, that is, abortion in the last five years, was most common amongst those in the

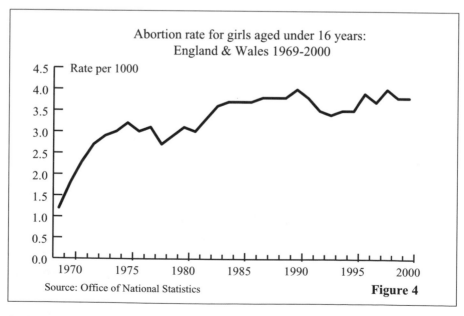

Abortion rate for girls aged under 16 years:
England & Wales 1969-2000

Source: Office of National Statistics

Figure 4

16-24 age group, 'possibly reflecting poor use of contraception, greater numbers of sexual partners and a higher prevalence of uncommitted relationships resulting in unwanted pregnancy in this group'.[11] The likelihood of abortion was strongly related to the number of sexual partners. For instance, 'women reporting 10 or more partners in their lifetime were more than five times more likely to have an abortion than those who had one partner (34.4% and 6.0%).' After adjusting for other risk factors, such as age and marital status, the results showed that the likelihood of abortion among women with between five and nine partners in the last five years was four times greater than those who had one partner; those with 10 or more sexual partners were 10 times more likely to have an abortion. The authors conclude that sexual lifestyle exerts a strong influence over the likelihood of an abortion. 'Such a relationship is not unexpected, in terms of both increased exposure to risk and less commitment to partners, and is supported by the increased rates of sexually acquired infections observed in women attending abortion clinics.'[12]

This evidence provides little comfort for the sex education movement. It has patently been unsuccessful in *reducing* abortion rates among young women, as it set out to do. Indeed, if it has contributed to the increase in sexual activity among children and young women, as seems highly probable, then it has contributed to the increase in abortion rates.

Sexually transmitted disease

Attendance at special disease clinics is used as a proxy measure for the incidence of sexually transmitted disease (STD), since open-access clinics, free at the time of use, are available throughout the UK. Most people with a sexually transmitted disease are treated in these clinics. A report by the Public Health Laboratory (1989) of sexually transmitted disease in Britain showed that between 1951 and 1986 the new cases seen at special disease clinics increased sixfold after the decline in the early 1950s which followed the post-war peak. Most of the increase took place in the 15 years after the 1970s,[13] during the era of sex education. A more recent report from the Public Health Laboratory (2001) shows that between 1990 and 2001, new episodes seen in special disease clinics in the UK rose from 624,000 to over 1.3 million (**figure 5**). In other words, the number of cases has doubled in the last decade. The most consistent trend has been an increase in acute diseases diagnosed since 1995. Between 1995 and 1999 the diagnosis of genital chlamydial infection rose by 76%, gonorrhoea by 55%, infectious syphilis by 54%, and genital warts by 20%. The greatest rise in sexually transmitted infections has occurred among teenagers,[14] the group targeted by sex education.

The national survey of sexual behaviour shows a strong association between the number of sexual partners and attendance at special disease clinics. For example, among women who had one sexual partner during the last 5 years, 1.2% attended a special disease clinic compared with 15.7% of those who had five or more sexual partners.[15] In other words, women who have multiple sexual partners are 13 times

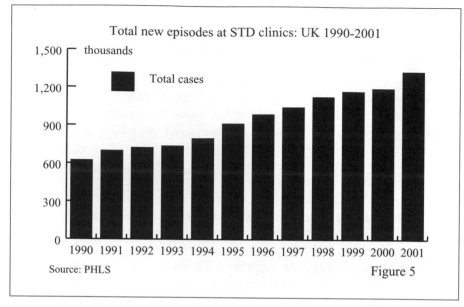

Total new episodes at STD clinics: UK 1990-2001

Source: PHLS

Figure 5

more likely to get a sexually transmitted infection. The authors of the survey comment, 'the high proportion of individuals with multiple partnerships who attend STD clinics confirms the relationship between sexual lifestyle and the probability of STD acquisition'.[16]

The claim of sex education that those who follow its 'safer sex' message will be protected from sexually transmitted infections has proved to be false. Indeed, the incidence of sexually transmitted infections has increased dramatically during the era of sex education. And those most likely to be infected are the young and those who have many sexual partners. The promise of the 'safer sex' campaign – that condoms provide an all-in-one protection – is not borne out by the facts.

Marriage and cohabitation

During the last three decades the proportion of cohabiting couples has increased dramatically. Information from the General Household Survey, a continuous survey of private households in Great Britain, showed that in the early 1960s around 5 per cent of single women lived with their future husbands before marriage. By the 1990s about 70 per cent were doing so, and among women marrying for the second time around 90 per cent cohabited before their second marriage.

During the 1960s the first marriage rate was fairly stable, before peaking in 1972 at 100 per 1000 eligible population for spinsters and 86 per 1000 for bachelors. The following years have been characterised by a steady decline in rates, as shown in **figure 6**. Among bachelors, for example, the rate fell by 69 per cent in the 25 years after 1971, and in 1999 the rate of 27 per 1000 was the lowest since records have been kept. Among women, the first marriage rate declined by 66 per cent over the same period, to a rate of 34 per 1000 in 1999. The decline in remarriage

318

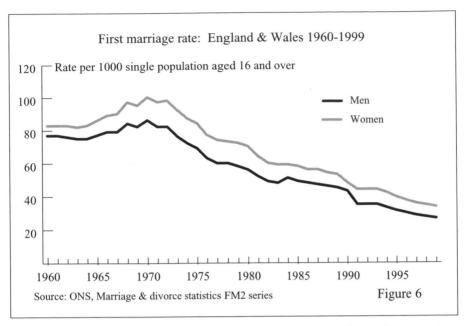

First marriage rate: England & Wales 1960-1999

Rate per 1000 single population aged 16 and over

— Men
— Women

Source: ONS, Marriage & divorce statistics FM2 series

Figure 6

rates has been even more dramatic, rates for divorced men declining from a peak in the early 1970s of 284 per 1000 to 42 per 1000 in 1999, a decline of over 80 per cent in just 25 years. It seems likely that sex education's hostility to marriage has contributed to the decline in marriage rates.

Births outside marriage

During the sex education era there has been a remorseless increase in the proportion of babies born to unmarried women. In the early 1960s, around 6 per cent of children were born outside marriage. The proportion of babies born outside marriage increased gradually during the 1960s, doubled during the 1970s, doubled again during the 1980s, and by the 1990s over one-third of all births were to unmarried mothers. By 2000 the rate had increased to around 39 per cent—a sixfold increase in the three decades of the sex education era. The annual number of births outside marriage reached 200 thousand for the first time in 1990, increased to 220 thousand in 1995, and 241 thousand in 1999. The greatest increase in the proportion of births outside marriage has occurred among teenage women. In 1960, around 20 per cent of teenage births were outside marriage; by 1991, almost 83 per cent were outside marriage.

One of the most important factors contributing to this increase is the change in society's attitude towards the single-parent family. For centuries Western society believed that procreation should take place only in marriage. Illegitimacy, therefore, was frowned upon as immoral and universally condemned. According to *Encyclopaedia Britannica* 'not to condemn illegitimacy would be to attach no special significance to marriage'.[17] Whereas births outside marriage were once condemned as illegitimate, sex education teaches that single-parent families are an equally legitimate lifestyle, and births outside marriage are regarded as a personal choice.

A profile of child abuse

The sexual revolution has been associated with a sea change in sexual mores as young people become sexually active at increasingly younger ages. Even among children there has been a large increase in sexual activity; the latest national survey of sexual behaviour found that over 25 per cent of young women reported first intercourse before their 16th birthday, compared with about 4 per cent before the advent of sex education. This increase in sexual activity has been characterised by a massive increase in the use of contraception by children, and also by an increase in the use of emergency contraception. Yet the abortion rate has increased, and there is an epidemic of sexually transmitted diseases among young people. The idea that children benefit from sex education, contraception and emergency contraception is not supported by the evidence. On the contrary, it could be argued that these figures represent a catalogue of cynical child abuse by the British Government and its agents, the FPA, Brook and HEA.

The above statistics leave no doubt that if the purpose of sex education has been to protect young people against the damaging consequences of sexual activity, then it has been a spectacular failure. However, if the real purpose of sex education has been to promote the sexual revolution, as I have argued in this book, then it has been remarkably successful.

Endnotes

1 Kaye Wellings et al, Sexual behaviour in Britain: early heterosexual experience, *Lancet*, vol. 358, p1844 (table 1)
2 Kaye Wellings, Sally Bradshaw, 'First Intercourse between Men and Women', in *Sexual Attitudes and Lifestyles*, Blackwell Scientific Publications, 1994, p74
3 Ibid. Sexual behaviour in Britain: early heterosexual experience, *Lancet*, p1844
4 Ibid. *Sexual Attitudes and Lifestyles*, p126
5 Ibid. *Sexual Attitudes and Lifestyles*, p126
6 Ibid. Sexual behaviour in Britain: early heterosexual experience, *Lancet*, p1847 (table 3)
7 NHS Contraceptive Services, England: 1997-98, published February 1999, and NHS Contraceptive Services, England: 2001-02, published October 2002, ed. Lesz Lancucki
8 Ibid. Sexual behaviour in Britain: early heterosexual experience, *Lancet*, p1844, (table 1)
9 Ibid. NHS Contraceptive Services, England: 1997-98, and England: 2001-02
10 Ibid.
11 Jane Wadsworth, Anne Johnson, 'Physical Health and Sexual Behaviour', in *Sexual Attitudes and Lifestyles*, Blackwell Scientific Publications, 1994, p288
12 Ibid. p292
13 Sexually transmitted disease in Britain: 1985-6, Public Health Laboratory, Genitourin Med, 1989; 65, pp117-121
14 Trends in sexually transmitted infections in the United Kingdom 1990-1999, PHLS, 2001, p iv
15 Ibid. *Sexual Attitudes and Lifestyles*, p277, table 9.7
16 Ibid. *Sexual Attitudes and Lifestyles*, p276
17 Meyer F. Nimkoff, 'Illegitimacy', in *Encyclopaedia Britannica*, London, William Benton, 1963, vol. 12 p83

Index

A

abortion 112, 113, 141, 197, 240
  numbers 114, 145, 158, 212, 218, 227, 316–317
  Private Member's Bill (1980) 176
Abortion Act of 1967 111–112
abstinence 53, 286. *See also* sexual abstinence
Acheson, Sir Donald
  Chief Medical Officer 225
Adam and Eve 266, 268
age of sexual consent 8–10, 142, 147, 152, 175, 196, 199, 208
AIDS 218–219
  epidemic exaggerated 232
  epidemic had fizzled out 238
  increasing among heterosexuals 231
  no threat to general population 232
AIDS Care Education and Training (ACET) 19, 231, 232
Altick, Richard
  Victorian People and Ideas 41
amoral sex education 20, 171, 175, 233, 237, 300, 306, 309
amorality 16, 23, 90, 120, 122, 126, 297

B

Bakewell, Joan 174, 205
Baroness Cox 222, 233
Baroness Denton of Wakefield 232
Baroness Elles 139, 157, 165
Baroness Gaitskell 29, 138, 140, 143, 159, 166
Baroness Phillips 233
Baroness Summerskill 113, 140, 141, 162
Baroness Trumpington 215
BBC 103, 118, 131
  defends sex education films 121
  Merry-go-round series 120, 121, 169
  Where do babies come from? 118, 120
Bedborough trial 66
Besant, Annie 55
bestiality 90, 137, 174
Betty, Lady Grantchester 185
Bevan, Dr Peter 118
Bible reading 41, 42
bisexuality 24, 25, 137
Bishop JC Ryle 33, 34
Bishop of Bath and Wells 142
Bishop of Norwich, Maurice Wood 149
Bloomsbury Set, 70, 71, 304
Bottomley, Virginia (MP) 225, 229
Boyson, Dr Rhodes (MP) 150, 189, 190
Bradlaugh, Charles 55

Braine, Sir Bernard (MP) 198
Branson, Sir Richard
  condom campaign 219
Bready, Wesley J
  England: Before and After Wesley 32, 35, 37
British Medical Association 19, 144, 180, 183, 184
  contraception a lottery for girls 212
  doctor must respect confidentiality 194
  fuming over public humiliation 204
  furious with Dr Rogers 185
  furious with position of GMC 211
  Private & Confidential booklet 19
  two alleged suicides 204
British Pregnancy Advisory Service 164, 189
Brook Advisory Centres 12, 105-106, 127, 173
  customer always right 105, 215
  helpline for teenagers 228
  immoral and dangerous 189
  overjoyed at ruling of Law Lords 210
Brook Advisory Centres literature
  A look at safe sex 12, 188, 247
  Cool lovers guide to slick condom use 26
  Making sex education easier 106
  Play safe on holiday 23
  Say yes? Say no? Say maybe? 25
Brook Advisory Centres manifesto
  Safe Sex for Teenagers 105
Brook, Caspar 135
Brooks, Edwin (MP) 110
Browne, Dr Robert 127
  Brook statement 128
  trial before the GMC 127
Butt, Ronald 153, 173, 176, 177, 178, 179, 185, 188.
  See also Ronald Butt

C

Cambridge Social History of Britain 40
Campaign for Homosexual Equality 169, 223
Canaanite depravity 252–254
Cardinal Basil Hume 200, 207
Cardinal Heenan 149
CARE 281–291, 297
  Body of Knowledge 287
  contraception 287, 289, 290
  Family Planning Association 287
  homosexuality 284, 287
  indistinguishable from FPA and Brook 290, 291
  Knowing me, knowing you 288
  Make Love Last 281–283, 290
  Making a Decision 297
  moral relativism 285, 291
  non-judgementalism 283, 288
  oral sex 283
  Parents First (1995) 283–285

response to Social Exclusion Unit 285–286
'safer sex' options 286
sex education from age five 286
sexual abstinence 290
sexual language 283
useful addresses 287
values continuum 284, 288
Your School and Sex Education (1996) 286
Carlile, Richard 53
Carpenter, Edward 65, 96, 265
Castle, Barbara (MP) 148
Chalke, Steve 245, 301
contraception 303
talking about sex 245
The Parentalk Guide to Your Child and Sex
245, 301
Changing the World
Charter for Gay and Lesbian rights 219, 220
chastity 21, 23, 99, 102, 105, 158, 164,
186, 282
chivalry 258–260
Christian Action, Research and Education
(CARE). *See* CARE
Christian Ethics in Secular Society
by Philip Hughes 266
Christian faith 10, 47, 48, 51, 76, 86, 98,
167, 272
Christian Institute 12, 281, 291–292
Manifesto for Marriage in Sex Education 291
Sex Lessons for Kids 12, 292
Christian morality 98, 163, 295
'Christian' version of sex education 292, 296
Christian virtues 29, 105, 124, 250, 310
Christianity 36, 47, 48, 52, 56, 61, 68,
163, 265
Claesson, Bent
Boy Girl Man Woman 190
Clare, Anthony 303
Clarke, Kenneth (MP) 196, 202, 232
cohabitation 270, 318
Cole, Dr Martin 122
Comfort, Alex 102, 125
Sex in Society 102
The Joys of Sex 102
comprehensive sex education 6, 107
abstinence message 108
condoms
all colours, textures and flavours 26
card scheme 2
children playing party games 26
free in schools 1, 234
free supplies 26
girls buying condoms 26
growth in condom market 234
on holiday 27
confidentiality 106, 128, 193, 194, 202, 211

consent of parents 194, 199, 204
Conservative Government 13, 187, 188, 218,
223, 229
contraception 77
importance of using 5
information about 6, 78,
success in preventing pregnancy 8
teaching children about 2, 7, 158
trend in under-age girls 7–8, 315
without knowledge or consent of parents
147, 151, 156, 180, 193
Contraception, board game 2, 247
contraceptive clinics 117, 135
contraceptive failure 27, 163, 305, 306
contraceptives for children 7–8, 106, 147,
148, 149, 150, 151, 180, 183
Cooper, Yvette (MP) 240
Corrie, John (MP) 176
Cosgrave, Patrick 152
Cossey, Dilys 111
Criminal Law Amendment Act 1885; 8, 208
cross-generational sex 90
Crossman, Richard (MP) 112
Curtis, Sarah 132

D

Danny's Big Night 216
Davis, Barbara 178, 179, 188
Dawson, Dr John 211
decision-making 17, 107, 286, 296–297
delaying onset of sexual activity 7, 17, 21, 285
demoralisation of sex 91, 175, 279, 295–298
Devon County Council 184–185
DHSS Memorandum of Guidance
prescribing contraception to under-16s
147, 150, 179, 192
Dickens, Charles 42
Dixon, Dr Patrick
director of ACET 231, 232
Drysdale, George 54, 96
Duke of Edinburgh 182
Duke of Norfolk 162
Dunwoody, Dr John 206

E

Ealing Council 222
Earl Ferrers 158
Earl of Halsbury 220
Earl of Lauderdale 140, 158, 164, 165, 236
Earl of Liverpool 232
Education Act of 1944, 79–80, 123
Education Act of 1993, 234
Ellis, Havelock 66, 96
Ellison, Dr Stanley 172, 179
embarrassment 4, 7, 101, 130, 244, 246,
257, 260–261, 303

emergency contraception 3, 7, 26, 189, 315
   available over the counter 240
   in supermarkets 3
   teaching children about 7
Evangelical Revival 32, 34–39
Evangelicals 38, 40, 41, 47
'Every child a wanted child' campaign 113
Exeter Education Committee 129
explicit sexual images 120, 122, 169, 174,
   188, 233, 261
exposing the genitalia 247–248

F

facts about contraception 246
facts about sex 81, 126, 178, 302
fallacy of 'safer sex' 304–306
fallacy of sexual ignorance 301–303
fallacy of sexual promiscuity 300–301
false presuppositions of sex education 300
family
   breeding ground of traditional morality 265
   cause of misery 52
   different forms have equal moral validity 276
   family created by marriage 268
   FPA position statement 275
Family and Youth Concern 5, 204, 233
Family Planning Association. *See also* FPA
   literature
   book list 124, 126, 136, 164
   campaign to undermine the family 187
   changed name to Family Planning Association
   78
   contraceptive clinics 152
   develops role in sex education 148, 152
   educating the educators 145, 162, 168, 171
   extension of contraception services 117
   fiftieth anniversary 182
   five targets 168, 217
   Manifesto for Sexual Health 227
   moral framework for sex education 13
   saturation family planning 135
   sex before marriage 271
   sex education in school curriculum 217
   should be abolished 164
   threatened legal action 153
   training courses 113, 190
   unmitigated evil 153
   view of marriage 270
   view of parents 149
   view of traditional morality 24, 139
   welcomes contraceptives in schools 1
Family Planning Information Service 170,
   172, 188, 191, 216
Fit for the Future (1976) 173
Fletcher, Joseph 102
Forster, EM 70

Fowler, Norman (MP) 198
FPA literature. *See also* Family Planning
   Association
   4 Boys 20, 25, 238
   4 Girls 238
   Answering your child's questions 236
   Danny's Big Night 216
   Getting it on 159
   Is everybody doing it? 25, 238
   Learning to Live with Sex 23, 24, 157,
      164, 171, 172, 179, 271
   Straight facts about sex and birth control
      136, 144
   Talking to your children about sex 244
   *The weird and wonderful world of Billy
      Ballgreedy* 246
free advice on family planning 105
free contraceptives 110, 137, 138, 140,
   149, 239
free family planning for under-16s 142, 143
free love 51, 53, 54, 64, 266
Freud, Sigmund
   Bloomsbury Set 59
   Darwin's theories of evolution 58
   deep hostility to Christian faith 61
   female sexuality 60
   homosexual love for Fliess 60
   human nature fundamentally bisexual 61
   Oedipus complex 59–60
   separated sex from morality 62
   sympathetic to ideas of Nietzsche 58
Fruits of Philosophy 55

G

Garden of Eden 250, 266
Gardiner, George (MP) 177
Geffen, John 154
General Medical Council 127, 184
   advice on confidentiality 194, 199
   contraceptives for under-age girls 211
   controversy within medical profession 194
   row with BMA 211
George III, King of England 34
Gibbens, Judge Brian 196
Gillick, Gordon 195
Gillick, Victoria 9, 192–212
   A Mother's Tale 192
   appeal to Law Lords 206
   comments of agony aunts 201
   Court of Appeal 200, 202
   High Court Case 194
   judgement of Law Lords 207–210
   persecution 205
Grant, Linda
   Sexing the Millennium 103
Grapevine experiment 136
Greater London Council 219

Greene, Sir Hugh, Director General BBC 103
Groothuis, Douglas
    Unmasking the New Age 18

H

Half our Future 104
Havard, Dr John, secretary of BMA 197, 198,
    199, 207
Hayhoe, Barney (MP) 207
Health Education Authority
    AIDS video - *Your choice of Life* 233
    does not encourage marriage 273
    involved with sex education 139
    mission to change sexual culture of country 234
    produces sex education materials 12
    promotion of sexual health 233
    responsible for HIV prevention 218, 232
    surrounded by controversy 236
Health Education Authority literature
    AIDS and You 218
    AIDS: What Everyone Needs to Know 218
    Lovelife 22, 24, 27, 28, 272
    One Love 20
    Safer Sex and the Condom 218
    Sexual health for men 273
    Sexual health matters for young women 18
    Your Pocket Guide to Sex 236
Health Education Council 148, 152, 157,
    173, 183
    'Ave you got a male assistant, Miss? 170
    Casanova advertisement 113
    extra funds to expand education 138
    information on contraception 216
    national campaign against ignorance 151
    pornographic nature of literature 190
    promotes *Make it Happy* 174–175
    promotion of homosexuality 223
    sex outside marriage 141
    urged to spend more on sex education 169
Health of the Nation 233
'healthy' choice 16, 17, 233, 285, 291, 296
heterosexism 220, 222
Himmelfarb, Gertrude 17, 42, 47, 57, 70,
    72, 259
    The De-moralization of Society 57
HIV – Facts for Life 19
HIV and AIDS: guide for Education Service 232
Holbrook, David 152
Holroyd, Michael
    Lytton Strachey 68
homosexual sex 68, 82, 109, 126
homosexuality 24–25, 65, 66, 70, 88,
    130, 223
House of Lords
    1973 debate on sex education 139–144
    1976 debate on sex education 157–166

Howard, Michael (MP) 223

I

ignorance 105, 110, 148, 159, 243,
    247, 274. *See also* sexual ignorance
illegitimate births 43, 113, 138, 176, 218, 319
information about sex 107, 109, 174, 286
informed choice 6, 16, 22, 97, 106, 108,
    228, 240, 245, 286, 295, 296. *See
    also* informed decision, 'healthy' choice,
    positive sexual choices
informed decision 217, 296, 297, 304
Inner London Education Authority 220, 221
International Planned Parenthood Federation.
    See IPPF
IPPF 94–97, 110, 145, 241, 296
    abortion a human right 95, 97
    compulsory sex education 95, 97
    emergency contraception 189
    family planning pioneers 95
    mistake to enter moral debates 97
    Youth Manifesto 97, 241
Isaac and Rebekah 252

J

Jackson, Dr Peter 174
Jakobovits, Immanuel, Chief Rabbi 202
Jenkin, Patrick (MP) 182, 188
Jenny Lives with Eric and Martin 223
Johnston, Raymond 169
Joseph, Sir Keith (MP) 135, 137, 153, 312
Just 17   228, 236, 281

K

Kennedy, David
    Birth Control in America 95
Kenny, Mary 176
Keynes, Maynard 68
King, Dr Ambrose 172
Kinsey, Alfred 80–92, 136, 241
    amoral approach 91
    atheist as college student 80
    extramarital sexual intercourse 87
    heterosexual-homosexual rating scale 89
    homosexuality common 87
    hostility to Christian morality 84
    no sexual behaviour abnormal 84
    premarital sexual intercourse 86
    Sexual Behavior in the Human Female 80
    Sexual Behavior in the Human Male 80
    sexual contacts with animals 89
    sexual experimentation on children 81
    sexual nature of children 82–83
    sexual outlet 83
    sexual repression and frustration 84
    unscientific nature of methodology 81
    Victorian sexual morality 85

Kinsey's grand scheme 90
Kinsey, Sex and Fraud by Judith Reisman 81
Knapman, Colin 129–131
Knight, Dame Jill 154, 194, 223
Knowing me, knowing you
    Pete Sanders and Liz Swinden 16, 226,
    288–289

L

Labour Government 13, 105
Labour Party 78, 111, 138, 148, 157,
    175, 223
Labour-controlled councils 222
Lady. *See also* Baroness
Lady Alma Birk 112, 117, 137
Lady Helen Brook 105, 177, 186, 273
Lady Ruthen of Freeland 161
Lady Saltoun 220
Lady Young, junior Education Minister 188
Lamb, Kenneth 121
Lambeth Conference
    1920, 77
    1930, 79
Learning to Live with Sex. See FPA literature
Livingstone, Ken 219
local authorities promote homosexuality 220
London Lesbian and Gay Switchboard 25
London Rubber Industries 157, 163
Longford Report (1972) 124, 131–133
Lord. *See also* Duke, Earl, Marquess, Viscount
Lord Aberdare 143
Lord Alexander of Potterhill 160
Lord Avebury 142, 304
Lord Brandon 9, 206, 208
Lord Bridge of Harwich 206
Lord Buckmaster 215, 216
Lord Campbell 220
Lord Clifford of Chudleigh 163
Lord Crowther-Hunt 164, 165, 166
Lord Denning 221
Lord Devlin 195
Lord Elton 233
Lord Ennals 233
Lord Fraser of Tullybelton 206
Lord Fraser's competencies 207, 211–212
Lord Justice Eveleigh 202
Lord Justice Parker 202
Lord Longford 122, 160
Lord Molson 143
Lord Scarman 206, 208
Lord Skelmersdale 222
Lord Somers 163
Lord Stallard 236
Lord Stamp 141
Lord Sudeley 162
Lord Templeman 10, 206, 209

Lord Wells-Pestell 157, 164, 168
Lord Winstanley 215
love bus 239
Love for Life 16, 17, 297
Lovelife. See Health Education Authority
    literature
Luff, Peter (MP) 237

M

Macara, Dr Alexander 194
Mace, David 106, 108
Mackie, Alastair 154, 169
Make it Happy by Jane Cousins 174, 177,
    179, 190, 241, 247
Malthus, Thomas 52
Malthusian League 78
Maranatha Community 281
Marie Stopes International 79
Marquess of Lothian 161
marriage 46–47, 267–268, 270–273
    and other 'stable' relationships 270
    attacked on moral grounds 265
    ideological attack 51–52, 269
    lifelong, secure, relationship 269
    mandate to be fruitful 268
    obstacle to sexually free society 266
    one lifestyle choice 270
marriage ordinance 267
Maslow, Abraham 17
Massey, Doreen 236, 243, 287
maternal role 268
Mawhinney, Brian (MP) 237
Mellor, David (MP) 225
'Men Too' campaign 216
Mercury, Freddie 231
Merry-go-round series. *See* BBC
Methodism 36, 39–41
Miles, Dame Margaret 175
Mill, John Stuart 54
Mills, Peter (MP) 184
Ministry of Health
    birth control advice to married people 78
Mitchell, Elizabeth 129
Modern Churchmen's Union 123
modesty 38, 45, 46, 250–258
    New Testament teaching 255
moral development 6
moral evil 280, 309–310
moral framework 13, 14, 129, 218, 258
moral instruction 303
moral law 267, 279, 298, 301, 306, 307
moral relativism 14, 15, 296
moralisers and moralising 5, 10, 28, 124,
    130, 186, 205, 239, 296, 300
morality 66, 71, 72, 76, 80, 84, 91, 99,
    107, 130, 209
morality of desire 18–19, 21, 282

Morgan, Patricia 95, 300
morning-after pill. *See* emergency contraception
Mortimer, Dr Robert, Bishop of Exeter 131
motherhood 256
Mothers' Union 185, 206
Muggeridge, Malcolm 131
Mullinar, Gill
  Developing sex education in schools 14, 273
Murley, Sir Reginald 200

N

nakedness 254
  approval of 101, 130, 253
  covering 254
national condom week 226
national curriculum
  weapon to indoctrinate children 277
National Health Service Reorganisation Bill 138
National Marriage Guidance Council 119
National Secular Society 55, 124
National Strategy for Sexual Health 240
Nationwide Festival of Light 169
Neo-Malthusian cause 54
new morality 101, 102, 103, 106, 173, 266
new women 47, 64, 66, 67
Newsom, Sir John 104, 110, 131
NHS Family Planning Act – 1967, 109
Nietzsche, Friedrich
  first immoralist 56
  influence of 57–58
  unmasking Christian morality 56
  virtues became values 57
Noah 251
non-judgemental 19, 276, 283, 288

O

Oddie, William 273
  the real child abusers 235
Order of Christian Unity 161, 171
Orr, Edwin
  Second Evangelical Awakening in Britain 43
other stable relationships 6, 270
Owen, Robert 51, 265
own decisions 126, 296
own set of values 14, 22, 58
Oxford History of England 47

P

paedophiles 84, 90, 174, 190
pagan creed 28
parental responsibility 307–308
parents
  despised by Brook and FPA 178
  inadequately prepared for sex education 153
  not talking about sex. *See* talking about sex
  views of sex education 236
Parents Project

encouraging parents to talk about sex 236
Peel, Sir John 137, 171, 172, 200
persecution of the Gillicks 205
pharmacists pilot family planning literature 190
Phillips, Melanie 294
Phillips, Roderick
  Untying the Knot 46
Place, Francis 52, 55
Pomeroy, Wardell 24, 91, 104, 106, 241
  Boys and Sex 136, 241
  Girls and Sex 24, 136, 241
Population Countdown Campaign 152
pornographic 132, 188, 190
positive images of homosexuality 220, 222
positive moral framework 295
positive morality 178
positive sexual choices 16, 233, 282, 286,
    291, 295
positive values 7, 28, 244, 245
postmodernism 21–22, 55
Pregnant at School (1979) 175
prepared for sex 23, 26, 27
pro-choice 21, 22, 108, 126
pro-choice dogma 297–298
  Making a Decision 297
promiscuous sex 22–24, 125
Proom, Jack 123
propaganda 77, 96, 113, 122, 140, 153,
    163, 189, 235
propaganda of sex education 299–300
purity of speech 249

R

Ramsey, Arthur, Archbishop 122
Reich, Wilhelm 59, 98–101, 241, 265
  approval of nakedness 100
  family 101
  marriage 99
  natural morality 99
  premarital chastity 100
  sex education 100
Reisman, Judith
  Kinsey, Sex and Fraud 81
Responsible Society 144, 171, 172, 179,
    185, 190
Return to Modesty by Wendy Shalit 257–258
Ribeiro, Aileen
  Dress and Morality 103
Riches, Valerie 132, 152, 185, 190, 197,
    204, 210, 233, 236
Robertson, Dr David 238
Robinson, Bishop John
  Honest to God 102
Robinson, Kenneth (MP) 105, 111
Rogers, Dr Adrian 183–185
  advice to parents 193

opposes BMA 197
Ronald Butt
  activities of family planning missionaries
    153
  BBC promotes condom campaign 219
  BBC's *Newsnight* programme 205
  children proselytised in sex education 204
  offensive sex education teaching aids 188
  real issue in Gillick case 204
  unofficial agents of the state 173
  'What every parent should know' 176
Royal College of Nursing 206, 237
Royal College of Obstetricians
  and Gynaecologists 226
  Unplanned Pregnancy report (1972); 137, 140
  Unplanned Pregnancy report (1991); 226

S

Sackville, Tom (MP) 234, 237
  Brook's national conference 235
'safe sex' condom campaign 218
safer sex 7, 25–26, 27, 187, 306
Salvation Army 196, 199
Sanger, Margaret 94, 95–97, 241
Schofield, Michael 113, 119, 174
Schools Broadcasting Council 118, 122, 132
Scott, Drusilla 178
Section 28, 223
self-control 250, 307
self-esteem 6, 16–18, 107, 295
Service, Alastair 111
  chairman Birth Control Campaign 138
  chairman FPA 168
Sex and Relationship Education Guidance 6–7
sex education
  A Pause sex education programme 3
  abstinence 20
  approval of nakedness 263
  books in the 1960s 104
  'Christian' version 280
  debate on sex education. *See* House of Lords
  devil's cunning scheme 310
  educating children about families 276
  evolved out of the sexual revolution 241
  explicitness of films 120
  FPA develops its role 151–153, 158
  hostile to Christian morality 295
  identifies a set of values 14
  ignores marriage 270
  in schools 154
  mantra 151, 241
  moral evil 280
  moral framework 13
  opposition to marriage 273
  plea for more 117
  pornographic in nature 133, 190
  positive values 14

prevents unwanted pregnancies 170
pro-choice 21
'pro-choice' dogma an essential element 298
programme for teachers 183
propaganda devices 299
real objective 240–241, 320
replaces moral authority of family 277
should not emphasise marriage 270
tacit encouragement of sexual activity 132
Sex Education: The Erroneous Zone
    124–126, 164, 165
Sex Education Forum 224
Sex education guidance for schools 13–14
sex education school TV programmes 110
sex educators wrong in predictions 212
Sex Lessons for Kids. See Christian Institute
sex word games 246
sexual abstinence 20–21, 99, 108, 290, 292
sexual choices 107, 136
sexual explicitness 132, 263
sexual facts 301–302
sexual ignorance 1, 4, 6, 10, 75, 102, 125,
    168, 188, 301–304
sexual immorality 254, 256, 269, 301,
    302, 306
sexual language 74, 109, 246
sexual nature of children 82
sexual nature of mankind 266–267
Sexual Offences Act 1956, 9, 208
sexual orientation 25, 90
sexual purity 38, 248–250, 255, 262, 307
sexual revolution 71–72, 72, 76, 79, 96, 108
  Nietzsche's contribution 58
  pioneers of 65
sexual temptation 262
Sexuality Information and Education Council
    of USA. *See* SIECUS
sexually explicit materials 247
sexually transmitted diseases. *See* STDs
Short, Dr David 150
Short, Renee 189
SIECUS 106–109
  link with Kinsey ideology 241
  sexual abstinence 20, 290
  sexual orientation 108
SIECUS literature
  *Guidelines for Comprehensive Sexuality
    Education* 106
  Premarital Sexual Standards 106, 246
  Sex, Science and Values 107
  Talk about Sex (1992) 247
  The Sex Educator and Moral Values 107
single parent homes 309
situation ethics 101–102
Social Exclusion Unit 1, 5. *See also* Teenage
    Pregnancy report
SRE & Parents (2001) 244

Stallworthy, Sir John 149
STDs 25, 26, 195, 199, 234, 302,
    incidence 27, 317-18
    increase at the end of the 1960s 114
    reduce the risk of infection 225
Steel, David (MP) 111, 135
Stephen, Virginia 70
Stokes, John, (MP) 189
    denounces FPA and Brook in Parliament
        186–187
Stopes, Marie 67
    contribution to sexual revolution 79
    explicit language 75
    first birth control clinic 77
    free love 76
    Marie Stopes and the Sexual Revolution by
        Rose June 76
    Married Love 74
    met Margaret Sanger 76
    plotting overthrow of Catholic dogma 76
    prophetess bearing God's message 77
Strachey, Lytton
    Eminent Victorians 69
    infiltrated his libertine beliefs 69
    Lytton Strachey by Michael Holroyd 68
    revolution in sexual behaviour 69
    Victorian hypocrisy 68
Straight Facts about Sex and Birth Control 172
Suffolk Area Health Authority 192
survey of teenage sexual behaviour 258
sword of the Spirit 310

T

Tackling Heterosexism
    A handbook of lesbian rights 219, 221
talking about sex 7, 243–245, 245, 303
    British reluctance 235
    contrary to biblical teaching 308
    national campaign 5
    parents not talking to children about sex 5
Taylor, Elizabeth 231
Teenage Living & Loving by James Hemming 19
Teenage Magazine Arbitration Panel 238
teenage pregnancy 1, 10
    reducing the rates 3
teenage pregnancy co-ordinator 2, 5
Teenage Pregnancy report 1, 4–6, 243, 296, 301
teenage pregnancy strategy 5
Tewson, Florence 144, 148
Thatcher, Margaret (MP) 119, 200
The Milkman's on his Way 221
The Playbook for Kids about Sex 221
The Scheme of Education in Personal Relationships
    booklet of Exeter Education Committee 129
The Sexual Revolution by Wilhelm Reich 98–101
Trollope, Anthony 45–46

V

values continuum 14, 284, 288
values clarification 14–16, 295
Vaughan, Dr Gerald (MP) 179, 197
Veith, Gene Edward
    Guide to Contemporary Culture 21
Victorian guilt and ignorance 29
Victorian literature 41
Victorian modesty 44–45
Victorian morality 47
Victorian prudery 31
Victorian values 17, 42
Victorians 31, 68, 71, 75, 85, 102,
    159, 248, 262
Viscount Barrington 143
Viscount Ingleby 140, 164

W

Walton, Sir John 211
Wells, HG
    affair with Rebecca West 67
    Ann Veronica 67
Wenham, Gordon 251
Wenham, John
    The Enigma of Evil 253
Wesley, Charles 35, 37
Wesley, John 32, 33, 35, 39, 310
West Norfolk Health Authority 193
Weyman, Anne 1
White, Dr Margaret 150, 186, 201
Whitefield, George 33, 35, 36, 310
Whitehouse, Mary 103, 118, 120, 122,
    171, 176
    Whatever happened to Sex? 171
Wilshire, David (MP) 223
Windeyer, Sir Brian 172
Woodroffe, Caroline 112, 197
Woolf, Leonard 70
Woolf, Mr Justice 194, 195
World AIDS Day 224, 232
World Health Organisation 97, 178, 275
Wright, Gerald, QC 194, 200

Y

Yeazell, Ruth
    Fictions of Modesty 45
Young, Sir George (MP) 187
Your Choice for Life
    24-minute advert for condoms 233
Your Passport to Sexual Health (Marie Stopes)
    26